INTRODUCTION TO THE
SURVEY OF ENGLISH PLACE-NAMES

PART I

ENGLISH PLACE-NAME SOCIETY

The English Place-Name Society was founded in 1924 to carry out the survey of English place-names and to issue annual volumes to members who subscribe to the work of the Society. The Society has issued the following volumes:

The volumes for the following counties are in an advanced state of preparation: *Berkshire, Cheshire, the City of London.*

All communications with regard to the Society and membership should be addressed to:

THE HON. SECRETARY, English Place-Name Society, University College, Gower Street, London, W.C.1.

INTRODUCTION TO THE
SURVEY OF ENGLISH PLACE-NAMES

PART I

Edited by

A. MAWER *and* F. M. STENTON

CAMBRIDGE
AT THE UNIVERSITY PRESS
1969

Published by the Syndics of the Cambridge University Press
Bentley House, 200 Euston Road, London, N.W.1
American Branch: 32 East 57th Street, New York, N.Y. 10022

Standard Book Number: 521 07498 3

First published 1924
Reprinted 1925, 1929, 1933
Reissued 1969

First printed in Great Britain
at the University Press, Cambridge
Reprinted in Great Britain
by William Lewis (Printers) Ltd, Cardiff

TO THE MEMORY OF
HENRY BRADLEY
GREATEST OF ENGLISH
PLACE-NAME SCHOLARS

PREFACE

THE general purpose of the present book—the first part of the *Introduction to the Survey of English Place-names* —cannot be better stated than in the words in which it was first announced. 'The first part of this volume will consist of a series of chapters by scholars expert in the various fields of place-name study. The purpose of these chapters will be to state the present state of our knowledge and indicate the lines along which the possibilities of future progress lie.' It is the pleasant duty of the editors to record their grateful appreciation of the generous way in which distinguished scholars, both English and foreign, have responded to their invitation and written a series of chapters which will, it is hoped, not only fulfil their immediate purpose as a record of work done and a stimulus to future endeavour, but will also lay firmly the foundation of that co-operative effort by which alone the Survey can be carried to a successful conclusion.

The list of contributors differs in two cases from that originally announced. When the book was first planned Dr J. H. Round very kindly undertook to write a chapter on the 'Feudal Element in English Place-names,' but early in the present year he was obliged, owing to persistent ill-health, with great regret finally to abandon the idea. Especial gratitude is therefore due to Professor Tait, the President of the Society, for the chapter on this subject which he has written at extremely short notice.

The second change is the loss of the General Introduction promised by the late Dr Bradley. The loss of that introduction is to be regretted, not only for itself, but for all that it would have represented, for Dr Bradley's interest in place-name study was life-long. There is, perhaps, some danger that the value of his contribution to it may come in time to be underestimated. His name is associated with no large constructive work upon this subject. For the most part, the illuminating suggestions which scholars owe to him have to be sought in reviews, and in scattered communications to periodical literature. Bradley is not the only scholar who has chosen to allow work of the highest permanent value to appear in an ephemeral form. His criticism was never merely destructive, and the suggestions which he threw out by the way were founded on knowledge of a range which few scholars have ever equalled. In his work on place-names, as in other fields, he showed the true genius of the scholar in his power of arriving through a kind of intuition at conclusions which brought immediate conviction to pedestrian students, and more than once during Bradley's long life of scholarship he enjoyed the student's happiest fortune, the discovery of new evidence to confirm conjectures which he had made while the material before him was still incomplete.

Dr Bradley had another strong claim upon our attention. A great part of his life's work was given to the *New English Dictionary*, the greatest example of co-operative scholarship in our generation. He was as keenly alive to the difficulties and dangers of co-operation as to its value and necessity, and it was therefore a peculiar source of encouragement to the founders of this co-operative society that from the time when it was first proposed, he gave it the benefit of his careful thought and considered judgment. Dr Bradley was not a man of rash enthusiasms, but when once the natural caution of the scholar had been given full play, and he was convinced that a thing was good, no one could be more loyally helpful in trying to carry it through. It is difficult to overestimate the loss which his death means to the Survey and its work. We dedicate this book to his memory in grateful appreciation, and in the hope that his scholarship will be an ideal and an inspiration for all who take part in the Survey of English Place-names.

The book owes much to the proof-reading of Professors Tait and Ekwall. Exigencies of time unfortunately prevented Professor Ekwall from seeing the final proofs of his own chapters.

A. M.
F. M. S.

June, 1924

CONTENTS

CORRIGENDA

p. 18, l. 10 from bottom. On *Birkby* and *Bretby*-names see further PN NRY 211.

p. 29, l. 1. On the name *Pensax* see further PN Wo 67.

p. 101, l. 16. Delete '*Sister*'

p. 109, n. 2. For 'Cotteridge' read 'Cotheridge'

p. 119, l. 12 from bottom. For 'Poynetts' read 'Poynatts'

p. 119, ll. 21–4. Delete 'and in this connection...Old English times'

p. 122, ll. 4–6, 15–17. Delete the references to Peperharow and Blo' Norton.

p. 122, l. 17. Mr P. H. Reaney (*Englische Studien*, LXI, 80) points out that Warley Semeles is now Little Warley and appears as *Warle Setmoles* (1252–8 AD). *Septem molarum* is a Latinisation of the surname (cf. William de *Septem molis* or *Setmoles* 1242–59 AD) of a family owning land in Warley in 1212.

p. 125, l. 9. Mr P. H. Reaney (*u.s.* LXI, 80) writes: '*Beauchamp Albrich* is not identical with Belchamp (*not* Beauchamp) Walter but survives as Allbrights formerly (*in*) *Bello Campo Sancti Ethelberti* (1294 FF), a small chapelry in Belchamp Otten.'

p. 131, l. 12. Insert 'Hugh de Gunville, 1233'

p. 131, l. 20 from bottom. Read 'Shillyngeston John Eskelling, 1226 FF' and for footnote 5 read '1444 (Ancient Indictments).'

p. 132, l. 22. Add 'Tuz Seinzton Lucas de Tuz Seinz, 1242 Towsington (in Exminster)'

p. 146, l. 12 from bottom. For 'the only example' read 'almost the only certain example'

p. 148. Dr Ritter (ES 62, 109) has an interesting note on the element *cistel, ce(a)stel, cæstel* in OE charters. *stan cestil* in BCS 282 is given as the name of *uno acerbo lapidum* and he suggests that this should be connected with ON *kǫstr*, 'heap,' rather than with Lat. *castellum*, such an etymology agreeing closely with its actual usage in the one passage which is in any way helpful as to its meaning.

p. 149, l. 20 from bottom. Read 'Oxenhoath'

ABBREVIATIONS

AFr	Anglo-French	NFr.	Norman-French
ASC	*Saxon Chronicle*	Nt	Nottinghamshire
BCS	Birch, *Cartularium Saxonicum*	Nth	Northamptonshire
		O	Oxfordshire
Beds	Bedfordshire	OBret.	Old Breton
Berks	Berkshire	OCorn.	Old Cornish
Bk	Buckinghamshire	ODan.	Old Danish
Brit.	British	OE	Old English
C	Cambridgeshire	OFr.	Old French
Ch	Cheshire	OGer.	Old German
Co	Cornwall	OHG	Old High German
Corn.	Cornish	ON	Old Norse
Cu	Cumberland	ONhb	Old Northumbrian
D	Devonshire	OScand.	Old Scandinavian
Dan.	Danish	OSwed.	Old Swedish
Db	Derbyshire	OW	Old Welsh
DB	Domesday Book	par.	parish
dial.	dialect(al)	pers. name	personal name
Do	Dorset	pl.	plural
Du	Durham	p.n. (PN)	place-name
EHR	*English Historical Review*	R	Rutland
		r.	river
Ess	Essex	RBE	*Red Book of the Exchequer*
FA	*Feudal Aids*		
Gael.	Gaelic	Sa	Shropshire
Gl	Gloucestershire	Sanskr.	Sanskrit
Ha	Hampshire	Sc.	Scotland, Scottish
He	Herefordshire	Scand.	Scandinavian
Herts	Hertfordshire	Sf	Suffolk
Hu	Huntingdonshire	So	Somerset
IPM	*Inq. post mortem*	Sr	Surrey
Ir.	Irish	St	Staffordshire
K	Kent	Sx	Sussex
KCD	Kemble, *Codex Diplomaticus*	Thorpe	Thorpe, *Diplomatarium Anglicum*
L	Lincolnshire	TN	*Testa de Nevill*
La	Lancashire	TRE	Temp. Reg. Edw. Conf.
Lat.	Latin	TRW	Temp. Reg. Willelmi
Lei	Leicestershire	VCH	*Victoria County Histories*
ME	Middle English		
MHB	*Monumenta Historica Britanniae*	W	Wiltshire
		Wa	Warwickshire
MHG	*Monumenta Historica Germaniae*	We	Westmorland
		Wo	Worcestershire
Mon	Monmouthshire	WS	West Saxon
MWelsh	Middle Welsh	Wt	Isle of Wight
Mx	Middlesex	Y	Yorkshire
Nb	Northumberland	YC	*Yorkshire Charters* (ed. Farrer)
NED	*New English Dictionary*		
Nf	Norfolk		

PHONETIC SYMBOLS USED IN TRANSCRIPTION
OF PRONUNCIATION OF PLACE-NAMES

p	*p*ay	z	*z*one	r	*r*un	e	*r*ed
b	*b*ay	ʃ	*sh*one	l	*l*and	ei	fl*ay*
t	*t*ea	ʒ	a*z*ure	tʃ	*ch*urch	ɛː	*the*re
d	*d*ay	θ	*th*in	dʒ	*j*udge	i	p*i*t
k	*k*ey	ð	*th*en	ɑː	f*a*ther	iː	f*ee*l
g	*g*o	j	*y*ou	ɑu	c*ow*	ou	l*ow*
ʍ	*wh*en	χ	lo*ch*	ai	fl*y*	u	g*oo*d
w	*w*in	h	*h*is	æ	c*a*b	uː	r*u*le
f	*f*oe	m	*m*an	ɔ	p*o*t	ʌ	m*u*ch
v	*v*ote	n	*n*o	ɔː	s*aw*	ə	*o*ver
s	*s*ay	ŋ	si*ng*	oi	*oi*l	əː	b*i*rd
		yˑ	Fr. t*u* (long)				

Examples:

Harwich (**hæridʒ**), Shrewsbury (**ʃrouzbəri, ʃruːzbəri**),
Beaulieu (**bjuːli**).

CHAPTER I

METHODS OF PLACE-NAME STUDY

by *W. J. Sedgefield*

I N most countries, probably in all, the place-names are now
of two kinds. They are either (1) Descriptive, consisting of
one or more words used in the ordinary speech of the people
and recognisable as such by their users, or (2) 'Proper' names,
not used as words in ordinary speech, and with no present
meaning or connotation in themselves. To the former class
belong such names as Broadfield, Beechwood, Grandville,
Beaumont, Neumünster, Mülhausen, etc., where the constituent
elements are the common words broad, field, beech, wood, etc.
In the latter class are such names as Carlisle, Trent, Paris,
Beaune, Aachen, Trier, which have to-day no meaning except
as names or labels of the place they respectively denote. In
addition to the above two classes we may distinguish an
intermediate class, including place-names evidently composed
of two or more elements of which one, usually the suffix, is a
word still in common use, while the other is meaningless. This
class is represented by such names as Brentwood, Banfield,
Gréville, Montmeyran, Limburg, Wiesbaden, where the elements *-wood, -field, -ville, mont-, -burg, -baden* are to-day in use,
whereas *Brent-, Ban-, Gré-, -meyran, Lim-, Wies-*, convey no
meaning to the people who use these names. A very large
proportion of the place-names in modern Europe are totally
or in part without meaning in themselves, and this is especially
the case in England. Many educated persons of course, thanks
to the writings of the late Canon Isaac Taylor and others, are
aware that originally such suffixes as *-thorpe, -by, -ham, -ton*,
etc., had specific meanings, but it seldom occurs to them that
the first part of a place-name may also have had a meaning.
Yet a glance at the earliest recorded forms of place-names
which now have no meaning will show that they are often
spelled quite differently and are revealed as words once used
in ordinary speech of the people, as well as names of persons,
some of which have long ceased to be used. Some forty or
fifty years ago it occurred to scholars that a careful examination
of the early forms of place-names would yield valuable information as to their original meaning, that is, the meaning at
the time when they were conferred on the places. Such investigations were, however, at first a mere skimming of the

*Place-
names and
their
meaning*

rich stores of material available. The foundations of scientific place-name study in this country were laid by the late Professor W. W. Skeat, a pioneer in many departments of English studies, who declared that the methods of investigation were identical with those of the etymologist.

Of late years surveys of place-names in the Scandinavian countries have been carried out by competent scholars, thanks to State support, and the results obtained have proved of the greatest value to the investigators of such names in our own country.

Sources and collection of material The first step to be taken by the investigator is to collect all the early forms of the place-name; the next is to arrange and examine the evidence. It is, however, not sufficient to limit our enquiry to the name under immediate consideration. We must bring to bear upon it the evidence of all names containing the same or similar elements. Indeed, the farther afield the investigator pushes his researches the better will he be equipped for dealing with any given name.

For early spellings, or 'forms' as we shall call them, a mass of material is available, both published and unpublished. No country is richer than ours in documents illustrative of its early history. First and foremost come the Saxon Charters, then the many volumes published by the Record Commission, such as Charter Rolls, Close Rolls, etc., also Pipe Rolls, Account Rolls, Assize Rolls, etc.[1], Inquisitions, Feudal Aids, Chartularies, Surveys, Registers, Ancient Deeds and Charters, documents published by record and archaeological societies, old maps, and last, but far from least, Domesday Book. The indexes to the volumes published by the early nineteenth century Record Commission and later by the Public Record Office, as well as to other publications, are valuable to the student; in every case where possible the modern names of the early forms are given in the P.R.O. editions. It is true that identifications of the early forms are not always to be relied on, but it is generally possible for the investigator to check any error in this direction. Working through the MSS. of early documents is often an arduous task, as the writing has faded, but this must be undertaken when the MSS. have not yet been copied. The most difficult part of MS. work is the transcription of place-names, especially where the copyist is unfamiliar with the nomenclature of the district. In particular, in thirteenth century

[1] Rich stores of early material, even of the twelfth and thirteenth centuries, still await publication, e.g. the unpublished Pipe Rolls, especially those of Richard I and John, together with a mass of Assize Rolls between 1200 and 1300.

MSS. it is often difficult to distinguish between the letters *c* and *t*, and between *u* and *n*.

When we have completed our collection of early forms of the place-names of a district, of *all* names, that is, including names of fields and farms, we must proceed to arrange them provisionally under each name in chronological order. To each form we append the date of the document in which it appears, as exactly as can be ascertained from internal or external evidence. Here it may be noted that a spelling which occurs in a later document is sometimes older than one taken from an earlier source, having been copied from a still earlier document, now perhaps no longer in existence. For this reason spellings of fifteenth century and even much later documents must not be disregarded. Moreover, it frequently happens that no quite early form of a place-name is extant. Another point to bear in mind is that it is often useful to know the relative frequency of occurrence of particular forms at certain periods or in individual documents. *Arrangement of material*

The names of the district or region should further be grouped topographically, preferably by parishes, so that the part played by local configuration (rivers, hills, etc.) in the formation of the names may be readily grasped.

We are now in a position to inspect the record of the names of the district. The first thing that will strike even the untrained eye is that in a very considerable number of cases the earliest recorded form of the name is very different from the modern form and reveals at once its original meaning. For example, the original form of the name in many cases will be found to be a man's, more rarely a woman's, name in the possessive case followed by a word in common use at the time, indicating some form of land division or human habitation or topographical feature. Thus Thulston (Db) meant 'Thorulf's farm'; Wyaston (Db), 'Wighard's farm'; Eglingham (Nb), 'the homestead of Ecgwulf's people'; Kimberley (Nt), 'Cynemaer's *ley* or clearing,' Brighton (Sx), 'Brihthelm's farm'; Arnside (We), 'Arnulf's or Arnwulf's head or hill'; Oughterby (Cu), 'Ughtred's farm'; Ulverston (La), 'the farm of Wulfhere' (*v.* p. 65); the Domesday form *Chenulueslei* shows that Knowsley (La), was 'Cenwulf's *ley* or clearing,' and the early spelling *Rothelueswurth* is clear proof that Roddlesworth (La), meant 'Hrothwulf's farm.' In other cases, also numerous, the first part of the name in its earliest form will be found to be, not a personal name, but an ordinary word, like the word which forms the suffix. Thus Calverley (Y), meant 'the calves' *ley*'; Preston (La) was 'the priests' farm'; Ritherhope (La) *Names simple of interpretation*

B

meant 'cattle valley'; Pyrton (O) was 'peartree farm or orchard'; Stratford (Wa) was 'the ford by or on the made road'; Mapledurham (O) was 'mapletree farmstead'; Ratcliffe-on-Soar and Radcliffe-on-Trent (Nt) meant 'the red cliff.'

Obscure *names*   In only too many cases, however, the earliest discoverable form remains just as meaningless as it is to-day, and was often without meaning for our Anglo-Saxon forefathers. Such names often show no trace of a suffix and the spelling is usually identical with or closely resembles the modern form of the name. To this class belong such names as Dethick (Db), Frenze (Nf), Chatteris (C), Noctorum (Ch), Seagry (W), Dyance (Nb), Pentrich (Db), Heene (Sx), etc. There can be little doubt that in many instances names of this character were originally of Celtic or even pre-Celtic provenance, adopted by the Anglo-Saxons, yet meaningless to them and therefore frequently mispronounced and misspelt.

Doubtful *names*   Lastly there is a very numerous class of place-names of which the early forms are not capable of immediate, certain, and complete explanation. The doubtful part of these names is generally the first element, the suffix often being of the usual type. It is these names that provide the most difficult problems for the investigator; for their resolution he must call to his aid every particle of evidence available and must observe certain principles and methods which we shall briefly set forth. But before doing so we may note that as the discussion of such names occupies a great proportion of any book dealing seriously with place-names and the results of the investigation are so often indecisive or unsatisfactory, there not unnaturally arises in the mind of the reader, untrained in the methods and unacquainted with the difficulties of the enquiry, a feeling of impatience and disappointment. We hope to show that such an attitude is not justified; when he has sifted and scrutinised the whole of the available evidence and employed a strictly scientific method, when he has carefully weighed and discussed the possible alternatives, the investigator has done all that can be expected of him. He is at least as candid as the historian; he certainly does not suppress, belittle or distort any evidence in the interests of a theory. He gives all the evidence, tests each suggested explanation, and gives his reasons for accepting or rejecting any of them. In many cases he can only offer two or more alternative solutions of varying degrees of plausibility. His caution and reluctance to dogmatise are in striking contrast to the cocksureness of the amateur solver of place-name meanings, who may be met with in all parts of the country.

Professor Skeat's assertion that the methods of place-name study are identical with those employed by the etymologist requires some modification. The etymologist deals with words which have retained a definite meaning for their users right up to the present day or up to the time when they ceased to be used; the place-name investigator deals with words which are in common use centuries after they became meaningless for their users. Further, the etymologist is concerned with the development of the meaning of words quite as much as with changes in their pronunciation, whereas the meaning that chiefly concerns the place-name student is the *original* meaning, that which was in the minds of the people who first gave and used the name. To arrive at this meaning it is necessary to establish the original form of the name. In many cases, as we have seen, that form is recorded in an early document, and the meaning is at once obvious. In other cases, also numerous, the earliest discoverable forms, i.e. the pronunciations, are so little changed that the originals can be restored with certainty. But in the majority of cases the earliest recorded forms have already undergone such change that the recovery of their originals is no longer easy or certain. *[margin: Etymology of p.n. as distinct from ordinary words]*

It is to be noted that while the place-name student is mainly concerned with the original meaning of a name, he may in some cases be concerned with the meaning, whether true or false, which a later generation may have attached to the name, leading thereby to a change of form which may not be in accord with strict phonological law.

Early place-name spellings are found to be of two kinds: they may be (*a*) traditional, or (*b*) phonetic. In the great majority of cases a scribe uses the spelling he has been taught for ordinary words, and in the case of place-names that which he finds in the document he is copying, making no change; this is the traditional spelling, which often has persisted from Anglo-Saxon or early Middle English times to the present day. After the Norman Conquest many English place-names had to be written down for the first time by Norman scribes or English clerks educated in Normanised schools. There being no recognised system of spelling English place-names, these scribes or clerks either wrote down what they heard from local speakers in court or on the spot, or else wrote out a document from the dictation of others who were not necessarily local people. Phonetic spelling is found especially in Domesday Book and elsewhere during the eleventh and twelfth centuries, and was often retained in later times, except in cases where a scribe had access to an Anglo-Saxon charter containing the name. *[margin: Early p.n. spellings]*

Spelling and pronunciation   Thus we see that a purely chronological arrangement of the early forms of a place-name is by no means always an accurate register of the successive changes of pronunciation of the name. The investigator, bearing this in mind, proceeds to apply the rules of phonology, that is, the science of gradual and unconscious sound-change, in order to establish what may be called the 'sound-pedigree' of the name from the evidence of the early spellings. The history of the sound-changes that have taken place in the English language has been very carefully studied, and it is found that they follow rules which admit of precise formulation. The investigator finds in the rules or so-called 'laws' of phonology[1] one of his most potent instruments for arriving at the earliest form and consequently the earliest meaning of place-names. This is the explanation of the large space which in recent studies of place-names is devoted to discussions of changes of pronunciation and hence of spelling which have taken place in most names. These discussions are intended primarily for persons with phonological training who are in a position to accept or reject the explanations suggested by the investigator.

Place-name study and phonological law   In quite a number of cases we are unable to establish the sound-pedigree of a name in conformity with strict phonological law; at some point we are able to show that there is an interruption in the normal sound-development and that the modern form of a name cannot be derived phonologically from the earliest recorded form. Here we must assume that some principle of analogy, e.g. 'popular etymology,' has intervened. Occasionally also the current written form has influenced the pronunciation, and this has led to the preservation of spellings, such as *Daventry* for *Daintry*, which record these artificial pronunciations. But unless such influence can be demonstrated, we must insist on satisfying phonological requirements. We need hardly say, however, that no phonological explanation of a place-name can be admitted which does not fit the known topographical or historical facts.

When we compare the modern pronunciation of many place-names with the pronunciation to which the spelling of the earliest forms bears witness, we may find it hard to believe that so great a change was possible. But our doubts will vanish when we can adduce and account for the different stages of the change from the earliest period right down to the present day. The earliest form of the name Abram [eibrəm]

---

[1] The reader may be reminded that in science a law is a compendious statement of what is observed to occur under certain conditions.

(La) is *Adburgham*. The difference is remarkable, but the following sequence of early forms arranged in chronological order reveals to the trained eye, or rather the ear, of the phonologist the gradual change which has taken place in the pronunciation: *Adburgham* 1199, *Abburgham* 1246, *Abraham* 1372, *Abram* 1461.

We must now attempt to give an idea of the manner in which the pronunciation of place-names has changed. If we compare the modern pronunciation of the names (not their spelling) with that of their earliest forms we notice that in the great majority of cases the former is the shorter of the two, often much the shorter. This is a result of the dropping out of both vowels and consonants. Further, the surviving vowels and consonants are often themselves different from their originals. All these changes have also occurred in the words of ordinary speech, but here the loss of vowels and consonants has been far less extensive than in the case of place-names. The reason for this is twofold. For one thing, most place-names are compounded of two or even three words, whereas the proportion of such early compounds still used in ordinary speech is very small. In the second place, place-names, or the majority of them, lost their meaning centuries ago, so that there was not the usual check on change that operates in words that are in everyday use with a meaning known to all. *[margin: Changes of form and pronunciation and their causes]*

By far the most important factor in sound-change in the English language is, and has been for many centuries, the 'accent,' as it is usually called, or as we prefer to term it, the stress-accent, or, simply, the stress. As everyone knows, certain syllables of English words of more than one syllable are pronounced with greater energy or emphasis than others, as in the words *fáther, remáin, bítterly*. In these words we notice that while one syllable has a strong stress the others have hardly any stress at all. In many words, however, there is an intermediate degree of stress as in the words: *òvertúre, àddréss-bòok, àftèrglòw, oùtlándìsh*, where the syllables marked with the figure 2 are not so strongly stressed as the syllables marked 1, but are more strongly emphasised than those marked 3. These degrees of stress in diminishing order we shall refer to henceforth as 'chief' or 'strong,' 'secondary' and 'weak.' Now it is found that in English words a vowel under the chief stress always tends to remain clear and recognisable, even though it may in course of time change its quality; for example Chaucer's pronunciation of *devise* [deví·z] has now become [diváiz]. The same rule applies to a vowel under the secondary stress, as in *lòdestàr, gàràge, waìstcòat, grìndstòne*. But in Chaucer's time, *[margin: (a) Stress-accent]* no less than to-day, there was a tendency in words that are constantly being used to weaken the secondary stress. As soon as this happens the vowel that was distinctly pronounced loses under the secondary stress its clear character and becomes either the obscure sound called by phoneticians the 'murmur-vowel' [ə] or an indistinct [i]. A good example of this is the word *garage*, which on its introduction to our country was pronounced as a French word [gará·ʒ], then with the chief stress shifted to the first syllable, the second syllable acquiring a secondary stress [gǽrà·ʒ], and finally it is often treated as a purely English word [gǽrɪdʒ], with the second syllable weakly stressed and pronounced like the final syllables of such words as *marriage, carriage, courage*, etc. Another example is *waistcoat*, which is pronounced by some people [wèiskoùt] and by others [wèskɔ̀t] or [wèskɪ̀t]. Turning to Chaucer again, we find precisely analogous changes taking place. Sometimes he pronounces the word *nature* [nà·tý·r] and at others [nà·tý·r], so that the strong and the secondary stresses interchange. In later times this word, now [neitʃɔ̀], has come to have a weak stress on the second syllable and its vowel is now [ə]. A secondary stress usually occurs in the second part of a word compounded of two simple words. In this respect place-names differ in no respect from the words of ordinary speech; thus the Anglo-Saxon word *tūn*, which has given our word 'town,' when it is used as the second element of a place-name is now pronounced [tən] or even [tn], as in *Sutton* [sʌtn], originally *sūþtūn*. Now the vowel of an unstressed or weak-stressed syllable has a tendency to disappear; thus *halfpenny* is commonly pronounced [héipni], *laboratory* [lǽbrətri] or [ləbɔ́rətri]. In the same way place-names of two or more syllables have in a very great number of cases lost their weak-stressed vowels and thus become shorter.

(b) *Loss and addition of consonants*   Another cause of shortening is the dropping of consonants. In familiar, rapid, speech there is a strong tendency to modify or do away with any consonant which checks the flow of the speech-current, on condition that the word remains recognisable by the hearer. An example of a consonant being modified occurs in what students of language term 'assimilation.' Thus Sandford becomes Sam(p)ford, Beanfurlong gives Bamfurlong, etc. Very frequently a consonant is dropped in combination with other consonants; thus in ordinary speech *nestling* is pronounced [néslɪŋ], *asked* is [ɑ·st], etc. Among place-names Alciston (Sx) was originally *Ælfsiges tūn*, Hincksey (O) was *Hengestesīeg*, Aislaby (Du) meant 'the *by* or village named after Aslakr,' etc. Conversely, in some cases the insertion of a new consonant seems to facilitate the pronunciation of others, as in *thimble* from OE *þymel*; *thunder*, OE *þunor*; *empty*, OE *æmetig*, etc., and in the names Embleton (Nb) for *Emelesdun*; Kimberley (Nt) for *Cynemæres leah*, etc.

In addition to the change produced in a vowel by the shift of stress already noticed there are other cases where a vowel undergoes change independently of stress. In the first place, an OE long vowel followed by two or more consonants is shortened in Old or Middle English; compare *child* with *children*, *keep* with *kept*, etc. The shortening also takes place before one consonant when the following syllable contains an *r*, as in *south* and *southern*, *heath* and *heather*, etc. Secondly, short vowels have been far less subject to change than long vowels; thus *nest* is identical in pronunciation with the OE *nest*, *sit* was *sittan* in OE, etc. Among place-names we may again instance *Sutton* as an example of shortening of a long vowel before a consonantal combination, while as an example of the resistance to change of a short vowel we note that the *y* [i] of *Lytham* was short in its OE original *hliþ-um*, '(on) the dunes.' But it must be noted that an OE short vowel was generally lengthened in Middle English in an *open* syllable, i.e. a syllable ending in a vowel, as in Chaucer's [na·me], from OE *năma*, modern English *name* [neim], or in our word *over* [ouvə], OE *ŏfer* [ŏver], as in the name Overton, OE *ŏfertŭn*, 'the upper farm.'

(c) *Lengthening and shortening of vowels*

The foregoing is a very summary statement of some of the phonological principles that guide the investigator in his efforts to establish the original form of a place-name and the exact sequence of sound-changes that have occurred in the subsequent pronunciation of the name. It will have served its purpose if it makes clear to the untrained reader that the phonologist's methods and the tests that he applies are of a strictly scientific nature. Moreover it should also show that the phonological discussions in place-name books, which may seem uninteresting and of doubtful value, are on the contrary absolutely essential if the confidence of experts is to be won, and must claim priority over the other lines of attack.

We will now return to our list of early forms, which, it will be remembered, have been arranged in chronological order.

It very often happens that among these forms we can distinguish two, sometimes even three, varieties or 'types,' as we may call them. A very frequent case is where the suffix or 'terminal' is not the same in all instances. This arises from the early weakening of the stress on the terminal and the resulting obscuration of its vowel, as explained above, as well as from

Variant types of the same name

the loss of its first consonant, especially if this is *w* or *h*,· so that the endings *-hill*, *-well*, *-wall*, *-hale* are very often confused, and *-ton*, and *-den* or *-don* interchange. Occasionally we infer that more than one ending may have been in use at the same time, as in cases where *-hurst* and *-wood*, or *-shaw* and *-scough*, were used indifferently. The cases where the *first* element of a name varies among the early forms are much less common, but have to be reckoned with, as they are of greater importance, since they affect the original meaning of the name. For example, the earliest forms of Leverton (Nt) vary between *Legretune* or *Leirton*, and *Leverton*; Hathersage (Db) has two early form-types, *Hathersegg* and *Haversegg*; Oakerthorpe (Db) has no fewer than four early types, *Ulkelthorp*, *Ulkerthorp*, *Ulgarthorp* and *Okethorp*. In dealing with these various types of first elements, which are often most puzzling to the student, we must make it quite clear that the modern form of the name can come from only one of the early types, the remaining types having died out. Occasionally more than one type of a name persists till comparatively recent times, as in the case of Liverpool, which sometimes appears as *Leverpole* in documents at the end of the seventeenth century and *Litherpole* at the beginning of the same century. In not a few cases two early types may have come from a still earlier one that has disappeared, as the sound-development varies somewhat according to dialect; thus it is possible that two early types of the name Liverpool, viz. *Liver-* and *Lever-*, may come from the man's name *Lēofhere*, as the Anglo-Saxon stressed diphthong *ēo*, which generally became *e* in Middle English, in some dialects changes to a short *i*. But in certain cases the presence in early forms of two types of first element cannot be explained by the principles of sound-change. We have therefore to cast about for some other explanation, and we usually have grounds for concluding that one of the types is due either to the influence of another name in the neighbourhood or to the working of what is known as 'popular etymology.' The last-named phenomenon is due, in the words of Professor Wyld, to 'a persistent tendency to explain what we do not understand in language by identifying it with something else, the meaning of which is clear.' Familiar examples are *crayfish* for the French *écrevisse*, and *sparrowgrass* for *asparagus*, etc. Among place-names we may instance Filbert Haugh (Nb), spelt in the thirteenth century *Hilburhalgh*, 'Hildeburh's haugh'; Strangeways (La), *Strangwas*, *Strangways* 1326, *Strangwyshe* 1551; Bearpark (Du) for the French *beau repaire*, 'beautiful retreat,' etc. We thus see that the gradual change of pronunciation of a place-name according to certain 'laws' is occasionally interrupted by the working of analogy, a factor of the greatest importance in the history of language. But these laws do not cease to hold good, their incidence is merely changed; thus they no longer apply to the word *écrevisse* as used by English people, but to the substituted word *crayfish*.

As we have already seen, in many cases a knowledge of local configuration will be of great help. It may enable us to decide, for example, between confused suffixes. Thus when early forms leave us in doubt whether the original suffix was *-hale* or *-hill*, a knowledge of the actual local conditions may resolve our hesitation at once. In the past, failure to remember this precaution has led to some mistakes on the part of place-name students. We have previously remarked that a satisfactory investigation and explanation of any individual place-name involves the study of all the other names of the district. In practice this is not always sufficient, for there are many cases where light is thrown on the origin of a name by the early forms of places in distant parts of the country. The necessity of studying all the names of a district is well seen in those regions where there was a mixture of English and Scandinavian inhabitants, especially in Cumberland, Westmorland, the West Riding and parts of Lancashire. *Importance of (a) topography*

Local history and archaeology often supply important evidence of former conditions. Thus quite a number of places were called after Norman families who held them, the royal grant which established the family being often extant. Again, place-names sometimes record a church or other building which has long ceased to exist. In other cases evidence of a different condition of the surface of the country-side is furnished; for example, of a forest which is now agricultural land or of a fen or moor which no longer exists. It is for these reasons that the publications of local societies are of such value to the student of place-names, who indeed must make a point of himself visiting and travelling over the region he is dealing with, or at least of consulting local residents, if he is to obtain the most satisfactory results. *(b) history and archaeology*

In the preceding exposition we have had to notice that the elements of English place-names have their sources in four languages, viz. first, English, including Anglo-Saxon, or as it is frequently called by scholars, Old English, and transitional or early Middle English; secondly, Scandinavian; thirdly, Norman and Anglo-Norman French, and lastly, Celtic. Without anticipating the fuller treatment which the elements from *The special problems of* each of these sources will receive in subsequent chapters of this volume, it may be as well to make a few observations on these sources of place-names in connection with what we have already said about the methods employed by the investigator.

(a) *Anglo-Saxon*   First, with regard to Anglo-Saxon, the reader of a book on English place-names may notice that the original form of a name is in many cases given in Anglo-Saxon words as they would occur in a literary text of, say, King Alfred's time. But this is done merely for the sake of uniformity and convenience. As a matter of fact, many place-names do not go back to before the Norman Conquest, so that, strictly speaking, the original form of the name should be given as it actually was at the time when it was conferred on the place, i.e. in the early Middle English period, which, roughly speaking, extends from about 1150 to 1300. Further, it is possible that the pronunciation of the simple countryfolk that gave the names or used them may have been different occasionally from that of the higher classes of the population. Again, when dealing with Anglo-Saxon, and especially with Middle English, forms of names, it is essential for the student to determine so far as possible the dialect of the forms.

A very large proportion of the Anglo-Saxon personal names which we find in the earliest forms of place-names occur repeatedly in numerous records; in not a few cases we are justified in assuming the existence of a personal name for which we have no direct evidence. A notable peculiarity of the Anglo-Saxon charters is the occurrence of place-names consisting of two words of which the second is usually an ordinary word common in such names, while the first may be either a person's name, otherwise unrecorded, or an ordinary word whose meaning is uncertain or quite unknown. It has generally been assumed that the first element in such cases is a personal name, but this is not at all certain. In fact there is reason to believe that these elements may be in some cases of Celtic origin. A book that has been of great service to investigators is Searle's *Onomasticon Anglosaxonicum*, which purports to contain all the Anglo-Saxon personal names occurring in early sources. But its value is greatly impaired by the fact that a large number of the names included are not Anglo-Saxon at all, but continental Germanic names or even Celtic ones; moreover, many of the words entered are precisely those elements of place-names which we have just mentioned as possibly not being personal names at all. A fresh study of Anglo-Saxon personal names is therefore needed.

The Scandinavian element of our place-names is of great interest, as we have here abundant confirmation of what we learn from the historical record of the successive waves of immigration and settlement carried on by adventurers from parts of Scandinavia and from the Scandinavian colonies during more than a century and a half. The fact that in the case of the Scandinavian place-names we have a chronological *terminus a quo* makes the explanation of their first elements a much more simple matter than in the case of the OE names, which, as we have already shown, frequently leave us in doubt as to whether we are in presence of a personal name, of an ordinary word, or of an anglicised form of a Celtic word. It is found that a very large proportion of the names of Scandinavian origin have a personal name as their first element. The investigator has to be on his guard against taking it for granted that a Scandinavian word used in the composition of English place-names had exactly the same meaning as it had, or as it has at the present day, in Scandinavia. This applies especially to words denoting land-division or features of the country-side. A modern parallel is found in the differing application of such words as *paddock*, *field*, *creek*, etc., in the United States or the British overseas dominions. *(b) Scandinavian*

The chief difficulty in connection with the Norman-French influence on place-names in England is due not so much to the words used in their formation as to the spelling of the English names by Norman scribes, who, though on the whole they tried to represent the pronunciation of what they doubtless regarded as outlandish words, were not acting on any uniform principle. The question of Norman spelling of English names in Domesday Book and other documents has of late been carefully investigated by Professor Zachrisson and other scholars, and it is now possible for the place-name student to understand the exact significance of spellings which at one time were regarded as hopelessly confused and lawless. *(c) Norman-French*

A much larger proportion of English place-names have Celtic elements than was at one time suspected, and, from evidence that is accumulating, scholars are coming to the conclusion that in many parts of the country the Britons were not so thoroughly driven out or slaughtered as we have been taught to believe. The investigation of the Celtic element in English place-names is a peculiarly delicate and difficult task, and hitherto investigators have not pushed their enquiries very far in this direction, with the exception of Professor E. Ekwall in his *Place-Names of Lancashire* and in a minor degree one or two other scholars. The fact is that there are very few experts *(d) Celtic influence on our p.n.*

indeed engaged in the study of English place-names who are equally competent in all the languages involved in their special application to that study.

There are, in conclusion, two classes of place-names of which it is necessary to speak, which differ in some ways from the names which we have been considering hitherto and which in a very large number of cases do not admit of interpretation in our present state of knowledge. These are the names of rivers and mountains, but especially of rivers. There can, however, be no doubt that in the great majority of such names we have to deal with Celtic or pre-Celtic words. Some names of English rivers and occasionally of mountains are clearly identical or of common origin with names of the same class in Europe, so that a thorough investigation of the continental forms will be a necessary prerequisite of the study of English names of rivers and mountains.

CHAPTER II

THE CELTIC ELEMENT

by *Eilert Ekwall*

THE Celtic place-names in England fall naturally into two
groups, which must be kept carefully apart, British and
Irish-Gaelic (Goidelic) names. The former group is easily the
more important, but the Irish-Gaelic names, though not very
numerous, offer points of no small interest.

The British[1] element offers extremely difficult etymological *The
problems. The British place-names, which must have been British
taken over at an early date, have been transmitted to us element*
through the medium of English, and may be supposed to have
undergone radical changes due to sound-substitution, sound-
changes, and popular etymology. Comparatively few have
been found in very early sources. The changes exhibited by
names recorded in early sources tell us how cautious we must
be in dealing with names only found in later ones. The names
Kinver and Morfe, as it happens, are found in an original eighth
century charter[2], where they appear as *Cynibre* and *Moerheb*
(*Moreb*). But for the form *Cynibre* we could not have been sure
that the second element of Kinver is Welsh *bre*, 'hill.' In the
case of Morfe, we could hardly have formed a guess as to the
original form without the OE reference. The etymology still
remains obscure. A further difficulty, in dealing with British
place-names, is the fact that little has been done hitherto
towards dealing systematically and on modern philological
lines with the place-names of Wales and Cornwall, etc. Holder's
Altceltischer Sprachschatz is invaluable, but only contains names
found in the earliest sources. McClure's *British Place-Names
in their Historical Setting* contains very valuable material and
important contributions to the etymological explanation of
names, but it must be used with some caution. The place-names
of Wales are on the whole *terra incognita*. The copious notes,
by Dr Henry Owen and Mr Egerton Phillimore, to the edition
of Owen's *Pembrokeshire* are a mine of useful information and
undoubtedly the most important contribution to the problem,

---

[1] By British names are here understood names that may be supposed
to have been adopted from a British source, whatever their ultimate
origin (British in a stricter sense, Latin, pre-Celtic).

[2] BCS 154.

but do not amount to a systematic study of Welsh place-names. The important material found in the early chartularies, the *Liber Landavensis*, the *Book of St Chad*, the *Survey of Denbigh*, etc., has been very little used hitherto. Of course many etymologies of individual names have been published, but most of the work remains to be done. Cornish place-names have not been systematically dealt with. The British place-names that have been most carefully investigated are those of Brittany, on which Loth's *Chrestomathie Bretonne* gives valuable information.

Even names found in very early sources, as in Ptolemy, offer difficult problems. Under the circumstances it can hardly be expected that we shall ever be able to explain definitely all the names that may be considered or suspected to be pre-English and are found only in later sources. In many cases we must be content if we can point out analogous names in Wales or Brittany. The British origin of such names may be assumed, even if the ultimate etymology must be left open.

A comparison between the earliest forms of names found in pre-English sources and their English forms shows that British place-names must have been largely adopted at a time when the British language had passed or was passing into Welsh. In some ways the tendencies of early Welsh and Old English coincided, as in regard to *i*-mutation and syncope or apocope, and the strong reductions and changes exhibited by British place-names may be due either to British or to English tendencies. But many changes must be due to British sound-development. Thus Brit. *Corinium* must first have become something like *Cerin*[1], before it was adopted. Otherwise the palatalisation of the initial sound of *Cirencester* would be inexplicable. OE *Searo(burg)* for Brit. *Sorbio(dunum)* pre-supposes a Brit. change of the *o*, possibly due to *i*-mutation. *Wrekin* (OE *Wrocen-*) from *Viroconium*, goes back to a Brit. form with loss of *i* between the *v* and the *r*. Intervocalic *s* seems to be regularly absent in Brit. loanwords, except *Thames*, which was very likely adopted before the time of the Saxon settlements in Britain. The *s* has been lost in *Trent* (Bede, *Treenta, Treanta*) from *Trisanton*. Also the Welsh change of *j* to *ð* is evidenced in place-names. Brit. *Novios* appears as *Nith*. Welsh *mynydd*, 'mountain' (from *monijo-*), is the source of *Mynd* (Sa). It is evident therefore that in explaining British place-names we cannot start simply from the forms in Holder or the bases in Stokes, *Urceltischer Sprachschatz*. We must

---

[1] W. H. Stevenson, *Archaeologia*, LXIX, 200 ff.

always reckon with the possibility of later British sound-changes having taken place[1].

It has been already hinted that sound-substitution and popular etymology must have played an important part when the British place-names were assimilated to the English nomenclature. Popular etymology must be responsible for the change of *Eburacum* to *Eoforwic*. The shortening of *Durnovaria* to *Dorn-* in OE *Dornsæte* cannot be due to simple sound-development. The importance of sound-substitution and the like, however, should not be overestimated. Many radical changes can be easily explained as due to the joint operation of British and Old English sound-developments. The change from *Rutupiæ* to OE *Repta-* (in *Reptacæstir*) may seem violent, but offers nothing very remarkable. The vowel of the stressed syllable is no doubt due to a British sound-change. The loss of the medial vowel would take place in Old English, and metathesis of *tp* to *pt* would naturally follow, as *tp* was an unknown combination. The frequent combination of British names with OE *ceaster* would lead to strong reductions, as in Manchester, from OE *Mamecestre* (Brit. *Mamucium*), or Mancetter (Brit. *Manduessedum*).

A study of British place-names will have among its chief *Surviva* aims the establishment of the extent to which a British popu- *of a* lation survived after the Anglo-Saxon conquest, the relation *British population* between Britons and Anglo-Saxons after that event, and similar problems. The view often held that the British population was exterminated or swept away, seems to have lost ground of late years. The numerous British place-names in England tell strongly against it.

Written evidence of the survival of a British element in England is slight, except for the western counties. All such evidence, found in chronicles, laws, etc., should, of course, be carefully examined and weighed. More information can be

---

[1] Place-names thus give valuable information on the British dialects of Britain. It is interesting to find that certain Welsh sound-changes can be traced in various parts of England. The lengthening of short vowels found in modern Welsh before certain consonants in monosyllables is proved by names such as *Preese*, *Roose*, to have taken place in Shropshire and Lancashire. The lengthening must be early. The change of unstressed *u* to a mixed vowel, [ə], written *y* in Welsh, seems to have taken place over a wide area. *Cremple* (Y) (now Crimple Beck) apparently represents a Brit. *Crumpull*, 'crooked stream,' in which the first *u* was modified so that Engl. *e* could be substituted for it. The Welsh change of initial *l-* to voiceless *l* (*ll*) seems to belong also to the dialect of Cumberland, as indicated by spellings such as *Polthledick* (by the side of *Polhedick*) in the Lanercost Cartulary (MS.).

gained from a study of place-names containing some word denoting 'Britons.' It is highly desirable that a systematic investigation of such names should be undertaken.

Here belong first of all the numerous names containing OE *Wealas*, 'Welsh,' as Walcot, Walton, etc., and *Brettas*, 'Britons,' as Bretton. It is not certain that all the Walcots and Waltons have as first element the gen. pl. of *Wealas*. Some may go back to OE *weald-* or *wealltun (-cot)*. The majority no doubt go back to OE *Wealacot, Wealatun*. However, the OE word *wealh* also meant 'a serf, a slave' in general, and a *Wealatun* might conceivably have been named from some non-British serfs. The probability is, of course, that the majority of serfs were Britons. A careful investigation will have to reckon with these circumstances. Here only a few further remarks can be offered. There are places called Walcot (Walcote, Walcott or Wawcott) in Berks, Np, Lei, Nf, L, Wa, Wo, Sa. Waltons are found in numerous counties. There are, for example, five in Lancashire, two in Surrey, two in Derbyshire. Wallasey in Cheshire is *Walea* in DB; the meaning is evidently 'the island of the Welsh.' The parish was formerly an island. The modern form of the name seems to be due to the addition of a second *ey*, 'island,' to the genitive of the original name. There are Brettons in Db and Y. In an examination of the name-type it will be of importance to establish the situation of the places. Such an examination may give a hint as to the status of the British population.

Names such as Walton do not necessarily prove the survival of a British language. Nor do they point to a large percentage of Britons; they indicate rather that British villages must have been an exception, as such a name as 'the village of the Britons' was significant enough. Nor do they necessarily indicate the long survival of a British element. In this respect place-names of Scandinavian origin containing a word for 'Britons' are of more value. Such names are few; Bretby, Db (*Bretebi*, DB) is evidently OScand. *Bretaby*. The same is the source of one Birkby in Y (*Bretebi*, DB), two Birkbys in Cu, and one Birkby in La. There used to be a *Brettegate* in York[1]. Names of this kind tell us that so late as the time of the Scandinavian immigration there were Britons in England, recognised as such by language or other characteristics. Names such as Walton, Bretby, also indicate that the Britons in England did not in all cases live as serfs on the estates of their conquerors, but to some extent in separate villages or homesteads. It is known, of course, that such was the case in the part of Wessex conquered at a comparatively late period.

[1] On *Birkby* and *Bretby*-names see further PN NRY 211.

The number of British words adopted by the Anglo-Saxons *British* was admittedly small, and only a few British words are among *words as* the topographical terms that enter into English place-names. *elements*
Widely spread in England is *coomb*, *combe*[1], 'a deep valley,' *place-* from Brit. *kumbā*, Welsh *cwm*. Names containing this element *names* are found in greatest numbers in the south-west, occur occasionally in most other districts, but are rare or absent in the eastern counties (Förster, *Keltisches Wortgut im Englischen*, 14 f.). The absence of the element in some parts may of course be due to topographical circumstances.

torr, 'a high rock, a peak, a hill,' is found as a common noun in Old English and in modern dialects, especially in the south-west, but also in Db, St, Nb, Sc. It is frequent in the place-names of Devon, as Bagtor, Loughtor, Sheepstor, Torbryan, Torpeak, is fairly common in So, as Torr, Dunster, while it seems to be rare in other districts. The source is an OW *torr*, as in *Torr-y-mynydd*, OW *Tormeneth*, identical with Welsh *tor*, 'belly, boss.'

The element *funta*, found in several place-names, as Bedfont (Mx), Havant, Mottisfont (Ha), Fovant, Teffont, Urchfont (W), is apparently identical with OCorn. *funten*, MWelsh *fynhawn*, 'spring, well,' frequent in Cornish and Welsh place-names, and ultimately Lat. *fontana*. OE *funta* can hardly be a loan direct from Latin.

Here probably belongs the word *pill*, 'a tidal creek,' used on both sides of the Bristol Channel. The word is found in Old English (*pyll*) and is identical with OW *pill*. It occurs in names such as Walpole (*Wallepille*, DB), Huntspill, Pylle (So).

A common element in place-names is *brocc*, 'badger' (from Brit. *brocco-*, Welsh *broch*), found in Brockholes (Y, La), Brockhall (La), etc. It is not always possible to decide whether names contain OE *brocc* or *brōc*, 'brook.' Some other elements occur only occasionally. Thus ONhb *carr*, 'rock,' found in Carham (Nb) and one or two other names, seems to represent a British word cognate with Welsh *craig*, 'rock.' ONhb *luh*, 'lake,' in the lost Lowes (Nb), apparently goes back to OW *luch*[2].

Incidentally it may be mentioned here that some words of Latin origin found in place-names may have been introduced into English by the medium of a British language. Such are

---

[1] The fact that the Brit. word coincided in form with OE *cumb*, 'basin, bowl,' as suggested in NED, may help to explain its acceptance and common use. See also Part II.
[2] On the last-mentioned three elements Förster, *Keltisches Wortgut*, may be compared.

c

chester, foss, not found as a common noun, but occurring in place-names such as Foss Dyke (L), Fosse Way, perhaps Catfoss, Foston (Y), *port, wich, wick* (Lat. *castra, fossa, portus, vicus*). *Fossa, portus, vicus* are evidenced in British languages (OW *fos, porth, gwic*), but there is no trace in them of Lat. *castra*. The problem will have to be carefully gone into. Also the curious name Dovercourt (Ess) (*æt Douorcortæ*, tenth century, BCS 1289, *Druurecurt*, DB) may belong here. The first element is a well-known Brit. word for 'water.' The second looks like Anglo-Lat. *cortis, curtis*, 'court.' Also place-names of Latin origin, as Aust (Gl), Speen (Berks) (from Lat. *Augusta, Spinæ*) belong to this category.

A further source of information is to be found in the British personal names occurring in English place-names. Valuable material for this question has been collected by Förster[1]. A full list of place-names containing British names in *Cad-*, as OE *Ceadda, Ceadwalla*, is given pp. 66 ff. Several additions might no doubt be made to Förster's list. Thus Chertsey seems to contain Brit. *Cerotus*, found in a Brit. inscription from London (Holder, p. 994). Branxton (Nb), Branscombe (D) (*æt Branecescumbe*, BCS 553) and Branksome (Do) probably have as first element OW *Branuc*. In drawing conclusions from personal names it should be remembered, however, that British names may have been introduced as a result of ecclesiastical relations or the like, and that a name may have become popular in a district because it was borne by some person of note. Thus the fame of Bishop Ceadda (Chad) partly accounts for the popularity of his name in the West Midlands, the diocese of Lichfield. The name Ceadwalla (Welsh *Cadwallon*) was borne by an early West Saxon king. King Ceadwalla no doubt got his name because of connections between the West Saxon and Welsh royal houses, not because it was already in common use among the Saxons.

Territorial names of British origin Territorial names of British origin are of exceptional interest and importance because they indicate that the Anglo-Saxon invasion did not mean the total destruction of the old territorial division. They tell strongly against the theory of a wholesale extermination or displacement of the Britons.

A name such as *Kent*, OBrit. *Cantion*, is of little value for the present question, for the name would be known to the Anglo-Saxons before the invasion. The same may have been the case with the names *Thanet* and *Wight*. More important is the name *Lindsey*, the name of northern Lincolnshire, called *provincia Lindissi, Lindissæ provincia* by Bede, *Lindesse* in

[1] *Op. cit.* 60 ff.

ASC 838, 873, *Lindissa* by Alcuin. The name is no doubt derived from *Lindon*, the old name of Lincoln, with a Brit. suffix; we may compare *Loidis*, the old form of Leeds. *Lindon* itself means 'the pool' or 'the lake,' and refers to the pool formed by the Witham in Lincoln; no doubt the pool was formerly much more extensive than now. *Kesteven* (*Chetsteven*[1] DB), the name of another district in Lincolnshire, may very well have as first element the Brit. word for 'wood' found in Welsh *coed*.

Most remarkable are the names *Deira* and *Bernicia* for the two old Northumbrian kingdoms. The English names (*De(i)ri*, *Bernicii* in Bede) are really tribal names derived from old British names of the districts. Deira appears in old Welsh sources as *Deiv(y)r*, *Deur*; Bernicia as *Breennych*, *Brennych*, *Birneich*, etc. *Deivr* is usually identified with Welsh *deifr*, 'waters,' while *Bernicia* is held to go back to a Brit. *Briganticia*, derived from the tribal name *Brigantes*. There seems to be no reason to doubt the substantial correctness of these derivations. The two old Northumbrian kingdoms thus have British names, presumably the old British names of the districts.

It is less surprising to find British territorial names preserved in districts that were conquered by the Anglo-Saxons at a later period. The western part of Yorkshire, the Celtic kingdom of Elmet which included Leeds (*Elmete*, *Loidis*, Bede) apparently remained independent till at least the second decade of the seventh century[2]. The name Elmet is still used as an addition to two names, *Barwick* and *Sherburn in Elmet*. The name *Loidis* is preserved in *Leeds*[3] and perhaps some other names in the West Riding. There is good reason to believe that *Craven*, the name of a district in north-west Yorkshire, is also British. The name, which appears as *Crave* in DB, as *Crafna* in Richard of Hexham, may be derived from Welsh *craf*, 'garlic,' and be related to *Cremona*.

Names of districts conquered still later are of no importance as evidence, but are otherwise interesting. Such are *Devonshire*, OE *Defnascir*, which contains the old tribal name *Dumnonii*, *Cornwall*, OE *Cornwealas*, 'the Welsh of Cornwall' (cf. Brit. *Cornovii*, *Cornavii*, Welsh *Cernyw*, 'Cornwall,' Latinised *Cornubia*), and *Cumberland*, 'the land of the Britons' (cf. Welsh

---

[1] The form *Ceoftefne* in Ethelwerd depends on Savile's sixteenth cent. transcript of an early eleventh cent. MS. now charred into illegibility.

[2] For Elmet v. *Hist. Brittonum*, ed. Mommsen (MHG), 206. The name is identical with *Elfet*, a district in Carmarthenshire.

[3] An attempt at explaining the name is made by Förster, *Englische Studien*, LVI, 220 ff.

Cymry, 'Britons'). *Archenfield* (*Ircingafeld*, ASC 918) in Herefordshire is OW *Ercing*.

It has often been suggested that *Berkshire* contains the British tribal name *Bibroci*; early forms render this impossible. The statement that the British *Parisii* are commemorated by *Paris*, said to be an old name of the district of Horncastle (Rhys, *Celtic Britain*, 309 f.), is founded on unsatisfactory evidence[1]. It is also doubtful how far OE tribal names, such as *Gifle*, *Hicce* in the Tribal Hidage, represent old British names. *Gifle* is more probably derived from the river name *Ivel* (Beds), and the *Hicce*, whose name is preserved in the present *Hitchin*, may have got their name from the river *Hiz*. Both the river names are very likely British.

British names of towns, rivers, etc. British names of towns, villages, rivers, etc., are found all over England, but a closer study reveals the fact that the various districts differ as regards the British names in use. Some types of name are found all over the country. Others are restricted to tne parts that may be supposed to have remained British comparatively long. The types of names found all over England are (1) names of old important centres, Roman stations and the like, (2) names of rivers, hills, forests, etc.

Names of important centres Even if old British cities or Roman stations were destroyed by the invading Anglo-Saxons, the old names would frequently adhere to the sites. Old names of this kind are common in Kent, where we find Dover, Lympne, Reculver, Richborough (the old *Rutupiæ*); and the old names of Canterbury (*Daruernon*, *Durovernum*) and Rochester (*Durobrivis*) are still found in OE times (*Doruuernis*, *Dorubreui(s)*, Bede). Also in other parts of England names of this kind are often found preserved. We may note London, Winchester, Salisbury, Dorchester (Do, O), Exeter, Cirencester, Gloucester, Worcester, Wroxeter, Mancetter, Penkridge, Lichfield, Dunwich (*Domnoc*, Bede), Brancaster, Lincoln, Doncaster, York, Catterick, Ilkley (if identical with Ptolemy's Ὀλικανα), Manchester, Carlisle, Corbridge (if identical with the old *Corstopitum*). A few others might be added, but the identification is not always certain, as in the case of Binchester (identified with *Vinovia*), Branton (He) (identified with *Bravinium*, *Brannogenion*). Some names were in use in OE times, as *Andred*, *Uerlamacæstir* (Bede).

Here may be mentioned some names not recorded in British sources, which may be supposed to have denoted places of some importance, or structures of a more lasting kind than

---

[1] *v.* Stevenson, EHR xx, 474–6.

ordinary British villages. There is an element *Eccles* which occurs, alone or in composition, in various parts of England, and which has been derived from a Brit. form of Lat. *ecclesia*, OW *eccluys*, Welsh *eglwys*, Brit. *eclēs*. Eccles is found in K, Nf (twice), La, and we find Ecclesfield (Y), Eccleshall (St), Eccleshill (Ch, La), Eccleston (Ch, 2 La), Eccleswall (He), Exhall (OE *Eccleshale*) in Wa. It may be that some of these should be explained differently[1], but the majority at least no doubt belong here. Another name of this type is very likely Liss (Ha) (*Lis* DB), which it is difficult to separate from Welsh *llys*, 'a palace.' Chatteris (C) may belong here. It may be identical in origin with Catterick (Y), or it may be derived from early Welsh *cader* (cf. Ir. *cathair*), 'a fort,' an element possibly found in some other names. No doubt other Brit. names in various parts belong to this category, though proof is impossible at present.

It is so generally held that names of English rivers and streams are nearly all of British or pre-English origin that it is more important in this place to put in a warning against overestimating the British element than to draw attention to it. Some scholars seem to prefer to assume pre-English origin for river-names even though they look as Germanic as possible, are easily and naturally explained from native roots, while a connection with British word-material has not been made out and is difficult to find. There are many names of rivers or streams that are obviously English, as Wantsom (K), Wensum (Nf) (OE *wendsum*, 'winding,' according to Dr Bradley's ingenious suggestion), Browney (Du), Bourne, Ea, Rea, Fleet, innumerable compounds, such as Blackwater, Holbrook, etc. A good many are Scandinavian, as Brathay (La), Greta (Cu, Y), Rothay (We), Artlebeck (La), Skell (Y). Back-formations are very numerous. The oldest known case is *Wærlame* (Saints of England) from *Wærlamacæstir*. Later, such formations become very numerous. Examples are Eamont (We) (really OE *ēa-gemōtu*, the name of the junction of the river with some other river; *Amoth* occurs in very early sources as the name of the river), Chelmer (from Chelmsford), Thet (from Thetford, OE *þēodford*), Pang (from Pangbourne), Mole (from Molesey), Yeo (from Yeovil, itself an old name of the river). Back-formations seem to be particularly common in the east of England, where comparatively few old names of rivers are preserved.

Rivers and streams

---

[1] Some names in *Eccles*- might contain an unrecorded pers. n. *Eccel*, derived from OE *Ecca*. *Ecclesforte* (sic), BCS 1264 (apparently the present Ashford, Mx), contains such a name (with palatal *c*), as shown by forms like *Echele-*, *Echelesford*, thirteenth cent. (Gover, *PN Mx*).

On the whole it may be said that the majority of old names of rivers are pre-English, that is, in most cases at least, British, while names of small streams or brooks are to a great extent English or Scandinavian, but in the western counties even names of unimportant streams are frequently pre-English.

The British river-names offer extremely interesting problems, but they have never been systematically dealt with, and only a few scattered remarks can be offered here.

A noteworthy fact is that very often the same name, frequently in a slightly varying form, is found attached to more than one river or stream. Many such common names are old words for 'river' or 'water.' Here belong: Avon (cf. Welsh *afon*, 'water, stream'), found only in the south-west and in Scotland; Axe, Exe, Esk, Usk, Wiske, all forms of Brit. *Isca*, which meant 'water'; Dover (K), Dover Beck (Nt), Doverdale (Wo), Dore (He) (from *Dobrā* < *Dubrā*; cf. Welsh *dwfr*, 'water'), also found in several compound names, as Calder (L, Y), Conder (La), etc., and Deverill (W), Deerness (Du), etc.; Ouse, three different examples (identical with Ir. *os*, 'water,' Sanskr. *útsa*, 'well'); Stour (which has been derived from a root *steu*, *stou*, 'to drip'); Wey, Wye (from a root *ueiso-*, 'fluid'; cf. Welsh *gwyar*, 'gore, blood'). A word corresponding to Welsh *glais*, 'stream,' is frequent as the second element of names, as Douglas (La), Devil's Water (Nb), Dowles (Sa) (first element Brit. *dubo-*, 'black,' in Welsh *du*), Gaunless (Du). Welsh *frwd*, 'a stream, a torrent,' is the second element of Winfrith, Wynford (Do), both named from brooks.

Some names of rivers are derived from adjectives, as Dove (Db, Sf, Y) (from *dubo-*, 'black'), Leadon (Gl), Ledden, Lidden (Do) (cf. Welsh *llydan*, 'broad'), Brue (So) (Welsh *bryw*, 'brisk'), Cam (Gl) (cf. Welsh *cam*, 'crooked'), Dee, early *Deva*, 'the holy one,' Taw (D) (literally 'the silent one'), Worm (He) (Welsh *gwrm*, OBret. *uuorm-*, *uurm-*, 'dun'). Several are derived from names of trees or plants, as Derwent, Darwen (La) (from *deruā-*, 'oak'), Leam (OE *Limene*[1], Wa), Lymn (L), etc., perhaps Leven (La, Y) (from a word meaning 'elm'; cf. Welsh *llwyf*, Ir. *leamh*), Corse (Gl) (cf. MBret. *cors*, 'rushes,' Welsh *cors*, 'bog,' *corsen*, 'reed').

Some common names, obviously of British origin, are etymologically more or less obscure, as Alne, Allen (Brit. *Alaunos*, *Alauna*), Frome, Kennet, Kent (OBrit. *Cunētio*), Tame, Thame.

Rivers and streams have often given names to villages or homesteads. In many cases the river-name has been forgotten

---

[1] BCS 978 (A.D 956). The charter is wrongly referred by Birch to Staffordshire.

and is preserved only as or in that of a place on the river. It is therefore frequently very plausible to derive names of villages or homesteads from an unrecorded river-name. Thus Great and Little Glen (Lei) are both on the same stream, but at a considerable distance from each other. We may confidently assume that the river was once called *Glen*, a well-evidenced river-name. Terling (Ess) is on a stream called the Ter. The latter name is no doubt a back-formation, but it seems very probable that the name Terling is derived from a lost stream-name identical with Tyrl (Wo). Wendover (Bk) is no doubt an old name of the stream that rises near the place.

Many English names of hills are British or contain British *Hills* elements. Several are well-known British names for 'a hill' or 'ridge.' Brit. *barro-* (Welsh *bar*, 'top, summit') is the source of Barr (St) (OE *æt Bearre*, BCS 987, apparently referring to this place). Barr is near a hill. Brit. *brig* (Welsh *bre*, Corn. *bry*, Ir. *bri*), 'hill,' is found in several compound names, as Bredon (Wo), Breedon on the Hill (Lei) (*Briudun*, Bede)[1], Brill (Bk) (olim *Brehull*), Mellor (La, Db) (identical with Welsh *moelfre*, 'bare hill'), perhaps Clumber (Nt) (*Clunbre* DB; near a lost place, *Clun*, called *Clune* in DB), Kinver Forest (OE *Cynibre*). The last three names would seem to be altogether British, while Bre(e)don and Brill have apparently had an English element added to an earlier British name. All the places mentioned are on or near hills. Welsh *bryn* (OBret. *bren*), 'hill,' is the source of Bryn (Sa). Malvern may well have as second element a mutated form of the same word; the first might be Welsh *moel*, 'bare.' Welsh *cefn*, 'back,' is probably the source of Chevin (Y) and may be the base of Chevening (K). OW *carrecc*, 'rock,' may be the source of Cark (La), and Crayke (Y) may be identified with Welsh *craig*, 'a rock.' Brit. **croukā* (Welsh *crug*, 'mound, hill') is the base of Creech (Do), Crich (Db), Crutch (Wo), Crick (Nth) and others. Welsh *mynydd*, 'hill,' is found in Long Mynd (the name of a prominent ridge in Sa). Mindrum (Nb) seems to be a compound of this word and *drum*, 'a ridge.' Brit. *penno-* (Welsh *pen*), 'head, top,' explains Penn (St), Pendle (La) (from Penhull), Pennard (So) and others. Welsh *rhiw*, 'hill,' is found in Cumrew (Cu), Wardrew (Nb), but the names are very likely old Brit. names of villages.

[1] Mr Crawford (*v.* p. 155) looks upon the second element of these names as Brit. *dūnon*, 'camp,' in which case they would be altogether British; OE *dūn* would then have replaced Brit. *dīn*, the form to be expected at the time of the adoption.

Many more instances might be added. It is evident that we are justified in deriving any name from a British source, if there is reason to believe that it is an old hill-name.

Names of forests, etc. The obvious examples of British names of forests are not so numerous as those of names of rivers and hills. Old forests disappeared with the spread of cultivation, and their names were lost or preserved only as those of some village or district.

A common element in place-names is British *cēt* (Welsh *coed*), 'wood,' found, for instance, in Chetwode (Bk), Cheetwood (La), Chute Forest (W). The element enters into several place-names, as Culcheth, Penketh, Tulketh (La), Orchard (Do), but these are probably old British village names. The majority of presumably British names of forests are etymologically more or less obscure, as Blean (K), Chiltern (O), Morfe (Sa) (OE *Moerheb*), Lyme (St), etc. *Bearruc*, the name of the forest that gave its name to Berkshire, seems to be derived from Brit. *barr*, 'hill,' and may have been an old hill-name, as was apparently Kinver. The localisation of the forest of *Bearruc* in the vicinity of Letcombe Basset, suggested by Stevenson[1], goes well with such a theory. Andred, the old name of the Sussex and Surrey Weald, is derived from that of the old city of *Anderida*.

We may here add a few notes on some other names of natural features.

Welsh *rhos*, 'a moor, a wood,' etc., is found several times in place-names, but the original meaning is not clear. Roose (La) may mean 'moor, heath.' Ross (He), Roos (Y), Ross (Nb) are on low ground. A meaning 'wood' is possible. The last two are near promontories. Perhaps the original meaning of the names was 'headland'; Ir. *ross* has this sense.

Cambois (Nb) and Cams (Ha) (olim *Cameys, Cammes*) may well be identified with Ir. *camus*, 'a bay,' Welsh *Cemmaes, Kemeys*. Cambois is at the mouth of the Wansbeck, while Cams is on Portsmouth Harbour.

Names of villages, home-steads, etc. Other British names than those falling under the categories just dealt with are very rare in the greater part of England. Hampshire, for instance, makes the impression at first sight of having a fair number of British names, but on closer inspection the majority turn out to be original names of rivers or hills or the like. Avon, Candover, Itchen, Meon are on rivers of the same name. Testwood is on the Test. Mitcheldever is on a stream formerly called *Myceldefer*; the name is a hybrid formation with OE *micel*, 'great.' Andover is on the Anton and is no doubt an old name of the stream. The villages called Ann (*at Annæ*, BCS 597) are on a stream that falls into the

---

[1] Asser's *Life of Alfred*, 156.

Anton; no doubt the stream was once called *Ann*. Ringwood (OE *Rimecuda*) might have a British first element, but it would then seem to be an old name of a wood.

In the circumstances students would do well to try as far as possible to explain place-names belonging to other categories with the help of Germanic material. The fact that a name is difficult to explain or has an unusual appearance should not be taken to point to pre-English origin, unless there is some special circumstance to render it plausible. It would be easy to adduce a good many instances of names that have been declared by scholars to be pre-English, but turn out on closer study to be good English ones. One example must suffice. Dr Ekblom[1] declares that Preshute (W) cannot possibly be a Germanic name. The name, however, is simply a compound of OE *prēost*, 'priest,' and the word found in Sheat (Wt), Sheet (Ha), which is a derivative of or cognate with OE *scēat*, 'a corner, projection.'

It is also to be noticed that the British names found in the eastern, in fact the greater part of England are mostly un-compounded names, as Brent, Cray, Kennet, Thames, Dover, London, York, etc. The few compound names are of the old type, i.e. they have the defining element first, as *Lētocētum*, 'grey wood' (preserved as the first element of Lichfield), Wendover, 'white water' (cf. Welsh *gwyn*, 'white'), Penkridge (Brit. *Pennocrucium*), Crimple Beck (Y) (cf. *supra*, 17 *n.* 1). This type of compound has in the later Celtic languages been largely replaced by one in which the defining element is placed last. Examples are Bryn-mawr (*bryn*, 'hill,' and *mawr*, 'great'), Carmarthen (Welsh *caer*, 'town,' and the old name of the place), Llandudno, 'the church of St Tudno,' Tre Gwalchmai, 'Gwalchmai's homestead,' etc. This type of compound hardly ever occurs except in the western counties of England. A possible exception is the curious *Beneficean*, 'the Beane,' ASC 913, if it is correctly explained by Dr Bradley as 'the little Beane' (Welsh *bychan*, 'small'). *[Late compounds]*

Some districts, including the western counties generally, show a larger percentage of British names than others. Villages and homesteads often have names that go back apparently to British names of villages or homesteads. Even small brooks frequently have British names. Compound names are common, and compounds of the later type occur. A considerable percentage of British names (among them names of villages), and the occurrence of compounds of the later type, and of numerous compound names generally, are circumstances

[1] *Place-names of Wiltshire.*

that point to a long survival of a British population and an intimate intercourse between Britons and English.

Dorset and Wilts   British names begin to be common in Dorset and the adjoining parts of Wiltshire. A good many places derive their names from British names of insignificant brooks. Examples are Dewlish (on Devil's Brook), Fontmell, Iwerne, Pimperne, Winfrith, Wynford; Toller also seems to belong to this category. Other British or apparently British names are: Orchard (OE *Archet*, from Welsh *argoed,* 'shelter of wood'), Lytchett (*Lichet,* DB), Mayne (Welsh *maen,* 'stone'), Worgret (*Were-, Wiregrote,* DB). From south-west Wiltshire may be mentioned the interesting old stream-names Deverill and Fonthill (OE *Defereal* and *Funtgeall*), which seem to have the same second element, Welsh *ial,* 'fertile or cultivated region[1],' the first being Welsh *dwfr,* 'water,' and the element *funta* mentioned *supra,* p. 19, respectively. These are apparently compounds of the later type. British names no doubt occur in other parts of Wiltshire, but the majority are original names of rivers or hills. We may here record the remarkable fact that Asser, the biographer of Alfred the Great, himself a Welshman, mentions Welsh forms of some Dorset and Wilts names, as *Durngueir* for Dorchester and *Guilou* for Wiley (r.), which may indicate that a British language was still spoken to some extent in these districts as late as about 875.

Devon and Somerset   In Devon and Somerset, of course, British place-names are common. In Devon the population retained its British language long. Here we find numerous late compounds, as Clovelly (first element Welsh *clawdd,* 'trench'), Dunchideock (*Dun-* perhaps Welsh *din,* 'fort'; cf. Corn. *dun, din,* 'a hill'). Somerset also has numerous British names, as Dundry, Watchet (OE *Wæcet*), Wearne (Welsh *gwern,* 'alders, marsh').

Glos and Worc   In Gloucestershire and Worcestershire British names are fairly common in the parts adjoining Wales and Herefordshire. From Gloucestershire may be mentioned Lancaut (OE *Land-cawet,* 'the church of St Cewydd'; *Podum Ceuid, Lann ceuid* in *Lib. Landavensis*), Netherwent, near the boundary of Monmouthshire[2]; Penpole (OE *Penpau;* cf. Welsh *pen,* 'end,' and *pau,* 'district'), Maisemore (Welsh *maes,* 'field'), Newent and others north-west of Gloucester. Llanthony, near Gloucester, took its name from the famous old monastery of Llanthony in Wales. In Worcester we find near the boundary of Hereford-

[1] The meaning 'upland cultivated ground,' quoted from the Bangor district (v. *The Bulletin,* I, 97), would suit the names admirably.
[2] Cf. Owen's *Pembrokeshire,* III, 188 *n.* 3. Cymmorodorion Record Series (London, 1906).

shire close together, Penhull, Pensax[1] (perhaps 'Englishman's
end or boundary'), also Carton (olim *Carkedon*; cf. Cark, p. 25),
and the curious Mamble, which may well be suspected to be
British. In other parts of the two counties the British element
does not seem to be very prominent.

Herefordshire and Shropshire hold a position of their own. *Hereford*
Welsh names are very common in the border districts. In
Herefordshire Welsh names are very frequent west of the Wye
in the district of Archenfield, which long enjoyed local
autonomy. Here we find such names as Cefn-coed, Clodock
(*ecclesia S. Clitauci* in *Lib. Landavensis*), Coedmoor, Daffaluke
(olim *Diffrinluke*; cf. Welsh *dyffryn*, 'valley'), Gillow (Welsh
Cil Luch), Moccas (Welsh *Mochros*), etc. There are interesting
cases of translation of Welsh names, as Bellimore from Welsh
Bolgros (Welsh *bolg*, 'belly,' and *rhos*, 'moor'), Bridstow, from
Welsh *Lann San Bregit*. West of the Dore are numerous purely
Welsh names, as Maes-coed, Rhedynog, Tre-wern, Ty Cradoc,
etc. These names do not necessarily point to a survival of a
Welsh element from early times to our days. There has been a
good deal of Welsh immigration into the border districts at a
late period. We may here refer to Canon Bannister's interesting
remarks in his *Place-Names of Herefordshire*, vii ff. Of particular
importance is the remarkable fact that the farm- and field-
names of Dorstone about the middle of the thirteenth century
were preponderantly English, whereas they are now mostly
Welsh. Canon Bannister enumerates from the thirteenth
century such names as *Benfelde, Dudintone, Huntehulle, Rede-
waldebrok, Stevenehus*, while the modern names are such as
Bedw, Brynspard, Mynyddbrith, Pwll Cam. East of the Wye
the Welsh element in the place-nomenclature is not particularly
strong. Certainly Welsh are Caradoc (olim *Cair cradoke*, etc.),
Penallt (on the Wye) and the old district name Maund (olim
Magene and the like, OE *Magesætan*); Pencombe may belong
here.

In Shropshire Welsh names are numerous in the Forest of *Salop*
Clun and the Oswestry district, where we find names such as
Argoed, Llan Howell, Llan Maddock, Pant-y-Lidan, Bron-y-
Garth, Hengoed, Morda (olim *Mordaf*, 'Great Taf'), Morlas,
Nant-y-gollen, Nant-mawr, Wern-ddu, etc. No doubt these
are to a great extent due to late Welsh immigration. In the
rest of Shropshire British names are less numerous, but by no
means rare. They seem to be found especially in the hilly
districts south of Shrewsbury. Prees (Welsh *pres*, 'meadow'),
Wenlock[2] (perhaps Welsh *gwyn*, 'white,' and *lloc*, 'monastery')

---

[1] *Op. cit.* III, 262. On the name *Pensax* see further PN Wo 67
[2] *Gueneloch* Giraldus Cambrensis (Rolls ed. VI. 146).

may be mentioned. Other names that may be reasonably suspected to be British are Haughmond (olim *Hagemon*), Hodnet, Kinlet. Condover and Cound (*Conedoure* and *Cuneet,* DB) are obviously British, but may be derived from a river-name; both are on Cound Beck.

Cheshire   It is somewhat surprising that the British element in Cheshire is comparatively slight. Safe examples seem to be: Crewe (two different examples; *Crev, Crevhalle*, DB; cf. Welsh *cryw*, 'ford'), Ince (on the Mersey; cf. Welsh *ynys*, 'island'), Landican (*Landechene*, DB; apparently Welsh *llan*, 'church,' and the name of a saint, e.g. OW *Tecan*), Liscard (olim *Lyscark*, 'the hall on the cliff'; the place is in Wallasey par.), Werneth (a derivative of Welsh *gwern*, 'alders'). Tarvin is an old stream-name. Some uncertain cases might be added.

Lanca-   In Lancashire the British element is a good deal more promi-
shire   nent. Here are some compounds of the late type, as Culcheth, Penketh, Tulketh (cf. Welsh *cil*, 'corner, retreat,' *pen*, 'end,' *twll*, 'hollow,' and *coed*, 'wood'), Treales (identical with Welsh *Treflys, Trellys*, apparently 'the village of the court'), besides a good many other names. It is particularly interesting to find that there are unmistakable, even if small, clusters of British names in certain districts, notably the old Newton hundred, round and south of Wigan, and in Amounderness hundred. In the former district we find Culcheth, Haydock, Kenyon, Ince, Wigan, the lost Rosket, and near it are Chaddock, Penketh, Eccleston. Makerfield, the old name of the hundred, seems to have a British first element. In Amounderness are Eccleston, Preese, Preesall, Treales, Tulketh. Both districts are flat and not separated by natural boundaries from the surrounding ones. In Lancashire at least, the British settlements were evidently not restricted to the hilly parts, though it has lately been suggested that the Britons were on the whole hill people and that the cultivation of the lowlands was carried out chiefly by the Anglo-Saxons.

Yorks,   In Yorkshire we might expect to find a good many British
Du,   names in the western parts where the Britons retained their
Nthb   independence till a fairly late time. This expectation is not fulfilled. British names, except those of rivers or hills, are very few. The reason may well be that in this district the British names had to compete not only with Anglian, but also with Scandinavian ones. The hilly tracts of Durham and Northumberland show a greater percentage of British names. This is the case particularly with the parts adjoining Cumberland, where there are such obvious examples as Glendue (*Due* perhaps a river-name), Plenmeller (*Plen* perhaps Welsh *blaen*, 'point,

end '), Wardrew (second element Welsh *rhiw*, 'hill'). Cases such as Lampart (*Lampard* 1291), Tecket (*Ty coed*, 'house in the wood'?), Troughend (*Trequenne* 1279; first element perhaps Welsh *tref*, 'hamlet'), Warcarr (olim *Wyrthkeryne*) are plausible instances.

In Cumberland British names, including compounds of the late type, are numerous, and there are a fair number also in Westmorland. They are particularly numerous in the north-east of Cumberland, along the Irthing and the Northumberland border. We may mention Blencarn, Blindcrake, Carlisle, Cardew, Castle Carrock, Cumdivock, Cumrew, Trierman, stream-names such as Poltross, Powmaughan (olim *Polmergham*, i.e. Brit. *poll*, 'stream,' and early Welsh *Merchiaun*[1], pers. n.), the lost *Sechenent* (= Welsh *Sychnant*, 'dry valley'), Temon (olim *Nenthemenon; nent* = Welsh *nant*, 'valley'); in Westmorland, Glencoyne, Penrith. Of particular interest are hybrids consisting of a British topographical term and an English place-name, as Cumwhitton (second element English *Whittington*), Carlatton (Welsh *caer*, 'fort,' and English *Latton*), Carhullan (Welsh *caer* and English *Holand*). A name such as Carhullan seems to be analogous to Carlisle, which consists of Welsh *caer* and the old name of the town, *Luel* from *Lugubalia*. The OE names seem to have been adopted by Britons, who formed new names by combining them with Brit. *caer, cwm*. Names like these indicate that an English population had been superseded by a later influx of Britons. *Cu and We*

The numerous British place-names found in England prove that the British population cannot have been exterminated or swept away even in the parts first occupied by the Anglo-Saxons. In some parts a British element must have survived for some considerable time after the conquest, and the Britons seem to some extent to have lived in villages of their own. *General conclusions*

One question remains to be briefly discussed. Why did so few names of villages and homesteads, but so many names of other descriptions survive? Several circumstances have to be taken into consideration. No doubt British villages were to a great extent destroyed in the course of the invasion. The British buildings, at least in some parts, seem to have been of a primitive character. Giraldus Cambrensis describes the Welsh houses of his time as mere huts made of boughs of trees. Houses, even churches, were frequently made of wicker work. Such houses were likely to be totally destroyed. The British names would often be difficult to pronounce and learn. But

---

[1] This identification has been made by Professor M Förster in a private communication to the present author.

these circumstances are hardly sufficient as explanation. The following should also be considered. British villages seem to have been small, and the homesteads in them to have been more scattered than in Germanic villages. It is easy to understand that the Anglo-Saxons would not simply take over the British villages. They would introduce a division of land that was in accordance with Germanic custom. This would lead to the disappearance of British villages. If it is true, as has been suggested, that the Britons preferred the uplands, while the Anglo-Saxons settled chiefly in the river valleys and the lowlands, the new settlements would to a great extent be made in districts not before inhabited. Lastly, we should reckon with the possibility that at the time of the invasion village names had not yet acquired the fixed character they have in later times. In those old days, when there were no charters, places often changed their names. It would be different with names of rivers or hills. It was of no particular importance for people of a more primitive age to have a generally recognised name for a village, but it was important to have a name for a river or hill. Streams were important boundary-marks, and hills would be important as land-marks, places of rendezvous, etc. Names of rivers or hills and names of cities would be known over a wider area than village names. Probably rivers and hills got fixed names earlier than villages. Anyhow the Anglo-Saxons found it necessary to give names at once to the chief topographical features, and they frequently ascertained and adopted the British names.

The Goidelic (Irish-Gaelic) element

The theory concerning the Celtic immigrations now most generally accepted is that the first Celtic population in England was Goidelic, but that later on the Goidels were conquered by Britons and partly driven westward to Ireland. This theory is not founded on very strong arguments. The chief reason for accepting it is really the fact that it is somewhat difficult to believe that the Irish should have come over to Ireland direct from the Continent. Yet some scholars hold that they actually did reach Ireland direct from France or Spain, not by way of England. The latter theory seems to the present writer to have considerable probability.

If the usual theory is correct, there is no reason why there might not be some Goidelic place-names in England, preserved from the time of the early settlements. As a matter of fact, however, no certain Goidelic names have so far been pointed out among the early place-names of England, and it seems we must assume that if the Goidels once inhabited what is now

England, their language and place-names must have been totally superseded by British. The Goidelic elements found in the English place-nomenclature are due to later influence.

The English (in England) have never come into such a close contact with Goidels as with Britons. The Irish-Gaelic element in the English place-nomenclature is therefore small. The Gaelic place-names in Scotland do not concern us here. In England Irish-Gaelic influence could only make itself felt slowly and occasionally. Irish monastic settlements might lead to the introduction of an occasional place- or personal name. Thus Beckery near Glastonbury (*Bekeria*[1], BCS 1277), which is identical with Ir. *Bec-Eriu*, 'Little Ireland,' a well-known name of small islands, suggests an Irish colony of monks at Glastonbury. A similar case is the old name of Flatholme in the Bristol Channel, (*æt, into*) *Bradan Re(o)lice*, ASC 918 A, 1067 D. *Relic* seems to be Ir. *relic* (*reilic*), 'a churchyard.' Names of Irish saints would sometimes find their way into English. Malmesbury has as first element the Ir. *Maeldubh* (or *Maeldubhan*). Isolated Irish or Gaelic settlements may have given rise to some names, such as Shotton, Shotwick, Shottery[2]. Some Gaelic immigration into the northern counties is possibly to be reckoned with, and some place-names may have arisen owing to it, but it is difficult to find absolutely unequivocal examples.

Some place-name elements were introduced from Gaelic into the English dialects of Scotland and handed on to those of the north of England. Such are *bog, crag, glen, linn* (at least in the sense of 'a pool'). *Bog* is found early in Northumbrian place-names. *Crag* is well evidenced from an early time in the northern counties (*Blakrag* 1242, *Buckecrag* 1266). The element, according to Förster, is British, but its distribution would rather suggest introduction from the Gaelic language of Scotland. *Glen* is partly British; Gaelic origin is probably to be assumed only for late names.

The majority of Goidelic place-names or place-name elements found in England seem most probably to have been introduced by Scandinavians[3]. They might be more correctly dealt with in connection with the Scandinavian element, but as there

---

[1] 'Bekeria, que parva Ybernia dicitur.'

[2] Down to the reign of Alfred *Scottas* was the ordinary word for Irishmen. OE *Scot* by regular development should have given *Shot*. The form *Scot* seems due to Latin influence.

[3] A monograph on this problem has been published by the present writer under the title *Scandinavians and Celts in the North-West of England*, Lund, 1918.

may, at least in some cases, be various opinions regarding them, they are best discussed here.

The Scandinavian settlements in the north of England are to no small extent due to Norwegians who had come over from Celtic lands in the West, Ireland, the Isle of Man, etc., where Norwegian colonies were founded at an early date. Norwegian colonies are found especially in the north-west of England, but to some extent elsewhere. They seem to belong on the whole to the tenth century. The Norwegians in Ireland would be influenced by Celtic language and civilisation. They adopted many Celtic words and names. Some of the latter are well evidenced in Iceland, which was partly colonised by Norwegians from Ireland and the western islands. There is reason to assume that the Norwegians who settled in the north-west of England had been to some extent Celticised, and to them may be ascribed the introduction of many Goidelic names and place-name elements into England.

Of place-name elements introduced in this way the most obvious case is *ergh*, 'a shieling,' from Ir. *airghe*, Gael. *airidh*, 'a shieling.' The element is common in Cumberland, Westmorland and Lancashire—Birker, Mosser, Salter, Winder, etc. (Cu), Docker, Mansergh, Ninezergh, Skelsmergh, etc. (We), Arkholme, Anglezark, Docker, Goosnargh, Grimsargh, Torver, etc. (La), and occurs more rarely in Cheshire (Arrow in Wirral) and Yorkshire (as Battrix, Feizor, Golcar, West Riding; Argam, Arram, Arras, East Riding; Eryholme, North Riding). The distribution of this word and the fact that it is so frequently combined with Scandinavian elements point decisively to introduction through the medium of Scandinavians. Some of the *erghs* are among Domesday manors. This proves that the element must have been introduced early, no doubt by the original Scandinavian settlers.

Ir. *cro*, 'a sheepfold,' may be the source of Crew, near Bewcastle, and the first element of Crewgarth (Cu). *Cross* is also a very probable example. It is found in place-names most frequently in the parts of England where Scandinavians are known to have settled, and it is combined chiefly with Scandinavian words. But introduction into Anglo-Saxon direct from Ireland is possible. Ir. *cnoc*, 'a hillock,' seems to be the source of Knock (We) and to occur in some other names.

Finghall (Y) (*Finegala* DB), if it is correctly identified by A. Bugge[1] with *Fine na n-Gall*, 'the district of the Northmen,' the name of a district in Ireland, is very interesting, for it must then have been transplanted from Ireland into Yorkshire,

[1] *Vikingerne*, II, 278.

very likely by Scandinavians. A somewhat similar example is the name *Diuelin-*, *Dyuelynstanes*, which denoted some locality in York (Fountains Cartulary). *Diuelin-* is apparently the Scandinavian form of Dublin (*Dyflinn*), or else the OE form of the name (*Dyflin*).

Numerous Goidelic personal names are evidenced in place-names, many obviously of Scandinavian origin. Examples are: *Corc* in Corby (Cu), *Duban* in Dovenby (Cu), *Glassan* in Glassonby (Cu), *Mael Maire* in Melmerby (Cu, 2 Y), *Maelchon* in Melkinthorpe (We), *Beccan* in Becconsall, Bekansgill (La), *Dubgall* in Duggleby (Y), *Colman* in Commondale (Y), *Crossan* in Corsenside (Nb)[1].

That the Norwegian settlers were to no small extent Celticised is seen from other remarkable facts. The Norwegians in Cumberland to some extent used the Goidelic way of forming patronymics, as is seen by the expression *Thorfynn Mac Thore*, 'Thorfinn son of Thore,' found in an eleventh century charter (Gospatric's charter). They also adopted the Celtic way of forming compounds with the defining element last (cf. p. 27), as shown by certain compound place-names in Cumberland and Westmorland, also, though more rarely, in Lancashire. Examples are: *Bek Troyte*, later Troutbeck, 'the beck of Troite'; *Briggethorfin*, 'Thorfinn's bridge'; *Brigsteer*, 'Styr's bridge'; *Setforn*, 'Forni's shieling.' Some formations of this kind have a Scandinavian first and a Goidelic second element, as Gillcamban, Setmurthy, *Becmelbrid*.

It is possible that with the Norwegian immigrants were a number of Irish people, presumably as serfs or servants. But it seems improbable on general grounds that such an element could have been very strong. If there had been a very strong Goidelic admixture in the Scandinavian population we should also expect a considerable number of purely Goidelic names in the north-west. But this is not so. The Goidelic element in the place-nomenclature is bound up in a very marked way with a Scandinavian one. Names such as Ireby, Ireton no doubt point to a certain amount of Irish immigration, but it is by no means certain that these names always mean 'the village of the Irish.' *Iri* was used as a personal name in Iceland. Also *Iri* might have been used as a sort of nickname of a Scandinavian who had come from Ireland.

[1] On names found in early sources reference may be made to Bugge, *Vikingerne*, II, 278 f.

D

CHAPTER III

THE ENGLISH ELEMENT

by *F. M. Stenton*

I

THERE is an embarrassing volume of material for the study of the English element in English place-names. Apart from the Danelaw, the south-west of England, and the shires of the Welsh border, the overwhelming majority of these names are of purely English origin. Even in the regions where Scandinavian settlement was most thorough, much of the older English nomenclature has persisted to the present day. Any discussion of the different elements of which this nomenclature is composed would be out of place in a short essay. All that can be attempted here is an indication of the way in which the evidence supplied by place-names can be brought to bear upon the study of Early English society. Even this limited attempt must of necessity be tentative. The outlines of this society are indeed tolerably clear, but its detail is obscure, and it so happen that the obscurity hangs most thickly over just the agrarian field in which the student of place-names is especially interested. Pre-Conquest laws and charters have little to say about the forms of settlement adopted by free men of humble rank, and the facts which they occasionally give will sometimes bear contradictory interpretations. Nevertheless, an opinion must be formed upon subjects such as these if the information derived from the study of place-names is to be used for the purposes of general history. It is easy, and correct, to translate the place-name Ednaston by 'Eadnoth's farm,' but the translation means little until some impression has been formed of the social conditions under which the name arose.

Descriptive names   It may at once be admitted that the greater number of English place-names tell nothing of importance for social history. The innumerable names like Radford, Tilehurst, Hindlip, Langdon, 'red ford,' 'brick wood,' 'hind leap,' 'long hill,' may be interesting for purposes of topography, but are not, regarded singly, of much use as historical material. They are simple descriptive phrases, and the information which can sometimes be extracted from them relates rather to the nature of the ground than to the life of the people settled upon it. There is more to be learned from the place-names in which the name of a person is applied to some natural feature, such as Pendeford, 'Penda's ford,' Ordsall, 'Ord's nook,' Lewknor, 'Leofeca's bank.' Names of this kind make an important contribution to the history of English personal nomenclature. They illustrate the individualistic element in Old English rural society. They even offer an occasional hint which may be of service for the history of law. It can at least be said that such place-names as Anslow in St and Kimberley in Nf, derived respectively from the feminine names *Ēanswið* and *Cyneburh*, show that women were capable of holding land before the Conquest. The value of such names would be greater if more were known of the circumstances under which they arose. It is, for example, impossible to say why Ardley in O was called after Eardwulf's *leah* rather than after the farm, the *tūn*, in which he lived. The truth would seem to be that place-names arose spontaneously, that the choice of a name was often determined by some local feature prominent enough to men who were preoccupied with the soil, but having no especial significance in the countryside. And although the origin of many place-names may now be inexplicable, there can be no question that the Anglo-Saxons were remarkably sensitive to diversities of ground.

If many place-names of this kind are intrinsically trivial, they sometimes suggest interesting conclusions when they are studied in groups, when, in particular, it can be shown that certain types of name are characteristic of a particular region. In the south-east of Berkshire, for example, within an area rather more than twenty miles long and rather less than ten miles wide, there occur the names Bradfield, Englefield, Burghfield, Wokefield, Stratfield, Swallowfield, Shinfield, Arborfield, Binfield, Warfield, Winkfield. All these names but two, Binfield and Arborfield, occur in Domesday Book[1]. Bradfield is mentioned in a charter of the seventh century[2]; Englefield, which occurs in the Anglo-Saxon Chronicle under the year 871, obviously goes back to a time when Anglian settlers in Wessex were rare; Shinfield is a name of archaic type[3]. These names when taken together undoubtedly suggest that the Saxon settlement of this region was only made possible by the clearance of woodland[4], and that therefore compact villages sur-

---

[1] Both Binfield and Arborfield are mentioned in early thirteenth century documents. A place named *Weonfeld*, adjacent to Burghfield, existed in the tenth century (BCS 888). The name survived, in the form *Wenfeld*, as late as the reign of Edward I, but has now disappeared.

[2] BCS 74.   [3] Representing an OE *Scȳningafeld*.

[4] *feld* in OE denotes 'open' country. See Part II.

rounded by arable fields of the type usual in more open country are likely to be rare in this quarter. It is probable that when the distribution of the various suffixes employed in ancient village names has been studied in sufficient detail in other shires it will offer useful suggestions as to the kind of country which most attracted early settlers. It may thus confirm or qualify the conclusions suggested by the distribution of the earliest Anglo-Saxon archaeological remains. A series of ancient place-names, in themselves of little interest, may sometimes make a definite contribution to the earliest English history.

Among the great mass of descriptive place-names, the most interesting are those which relate to the beliefs of the heathen time. Names of Germanic gods enter, though rarely, into English local nomenclature. Woden is the chief of them. Wednesbury (St), and Woodnesborough (K) each mean 'Woden's hill,' Wensley (Db) means 'Woden's *leah*[1].' If the great earthwork called Wansdyke was not regarded as his work, it was at least sacred to him. Other gods have left slighter traces, but the Surrey place-name Tuesley probably contains the name of Tiw, and Thunderley and Thundersley (Ess) the name of Thunor. The memory of the dragons and goblins of Germanic mythology is preserved in such names as Drakelow (Db), 'dragon's mound,' and Shuckburgh (Wa), 'spectre's barrow.' The OE word *hearh*, 'temple or sacred place,' forms the modern place-name Harrow, is the second element in Pepper Harrow (Sr), and the first in the name Harrowden, borne by villages in Nth and Beds. Names like these, of a specifically heathen cast, had little chance of survival. Many place-names carrying heathen associations must have been abandoned as a result of the conversion. Names of this kind can only have survived through the mental inertia of those who used them, and their rarity is by no means remarkable.

Early records and village-names

The evidence of Domesday Book is enough to prove that, south at least of Mersey and Humber, most of the villages which appear in later medieval records had already come into being by the death of Edward the Confessor. Some of them may have arisen but a short time previously. According to a good tradition, the origin of Waltham Holy Cross in Essex was a 'pauper tugurium,' by which apparently a mean hunting lodge is meant, built by its lord, Tofig the proud, in the reign of Cnut[2]. External evidence of this kind is rare, and the

[1] See Part II.
[2] *De Inventione Sanctæ Crucis*, ed. Stubbs, 9.

history of most villages begins with their description in the
Domesday Survey. Here and there, new market towns, like
Newbury in Berkshire, arose in the twelfth or thirteenth
century. A monastery, such as Kirkstead (L), or the hunting
box of a Norman lord, like Belper (Db), might attract settlers
to a spot which had not been occupied before. Late settlements
of this kind generally reveal something of their history in their
names, and in any case are too few seriously to affect the
general antiquity of English village geography. If, as often
happens, a village bearing an Old English name is omitted
from the Domesday Survey, there is generally reason to believe
that it is included in the description of some larger estate. In
the part of Berkshire which lies between the Thames at Sonning
and the Hampshire border at Sandhurst there are at least
eight places, each bearing an Old English name, of which Domesday Book makes no mention[1]. Each of them appears in later
records as a tything of the bishop of Salisbury's great manor
of Sonning, and it is safe to conclude that they are all covered
in Domesday by the name of the manor to which they belonged.
The student of village origins is justified in relying upon the
competence of the Domesday clerks, but an exhaustive
enumeration of English villages was no part of their duties.

It is not to be denied that often in the course of the early
Middle Ages, the men of a village with a wide territory separated
into two or more distinct communities. Colonisation of this
kind doubtless lies behind many names like Peatling Magna
and Peatling Parva (Lei), Church Lawford and Long Lawford
(Wa). Nevertheless, even when Domesday gives only one name
to a territory afterwards divided between two villages, it does
not follow that the colonisation had not already occurred. In
the same way, the hamlets and isolated farms revealed by
medieval records may already have existed in 1086, although
they are included in Domesday under a general description of
the village within whose boundaries they lay. What is more
important to the student of local nomenclature, the names
may often have existed at that time, although no one then
lived at the places which they denoted. Many names of farms

---

[1] Wokingham, Ruscombe, Winnersh, Woodcray, Woodley, Sandford,
Sandhurst, Sindlesham. Of these names, Ruscombe occurs in a document of 1091; Wokingham, which from its form must be very ancient,
occurs in 1176; Winnersh, Sindlesham, Woodley and Sandhurst are all
mentioned between 1220 and 1230. Sandford and Woodcray are both
recorded during the reign of Henry III.

and hamlets can be identified with boundary marks in Old English charters, near which men came to settle in course of time. The boundaries of Little Haseley (O) begin 'at *Roppan-ford*' and later in their course pass 'over against *Stangedelf.*' The first of these boundary marks gave name to the Domesday manor of Rofford, near Haseley, and the name of the second is borne by the two adjacent hamlets of Upper and Lower Standhill. The antiquity of other names of this kind can be proved indirectly. Some of them are derived from personal names obsolete long before the Conquest, others are identical with, though obviously independent of, the names of ancient villages, and may reasonably be considered of equal antiquity. For the student of the English element in place-names, the private charters of the twelfth, and the assize rolls of the thirteenth, century are hardly less important than Domesday Book itself.

There is every reason to think that the village colonisation which can be traced in the Middle Ages was only the last phase of a process which had begun before the oldest English records were written. Innumerable Domesday villages, as well as innumerable farms and hamlets, bear names which resemble or are identical with the names of boundary-marks recorded in old English charters. The name Harston, which occurs in C and Lei, means literally 'boundary stone.' There are many parallels among old English boundary names to the Derbyshire village name Allestree, 'Æthelheard's tree,' and the Warwick-shire village name Austrey, 'Ealdwulf's tree.' Names like these suggest movement outwards from the core of some earlier settlement to some point on the border of its territory. They are rare in the earliest records, but already in 778, Offa could speak of the *viculus qui nuncupatur æt Segcgesbearuue*, 'Secg's wood,' with reference to Sedgeberrow (Wo). It is significant that Offa thought fit to define the position of this 'viculus' more precisely by stating that the land which he was granting lay *in australi occidentalique parte torrentis qui vocatur Esigburna*. Names of this type, which are very numerous, suggest that the villages which they denote were not formed until sufficient time had passed for personal names to become attached to natural features. They also suggest that the English settlement of conquered regions was a slow business, that new villages were being formed throughout a long period, in which there was time for many changes in social order and agrarian organisation.

The conditions under which the settlement must have taken place point to a similar conclusion. It seems certain that upon the occupation of new territory the kings, chiefs, and free men who had taken part in the expansion received allotments proportionate to their several ranks. It is at least possible that some of the great estates of the early Middle Ages, estates for which an ancient origin may in any case be assumed, descend, in fact, from the time of the migration and the movements which followed it. The great manor of Bensington (O), for example, which stretched continuously for thirteen miles from Henley across the Chilterns to the river Thame, is best understood as representing an allotment made to some king or other military leader when the Saxons occupied the country east of Thames. Within so wide an area there was room for a gradual settlement, which might extend over centuries, and for the development of very different forms of rural community. This means, in turn, that within such an area very different types of place-name are certain to arise. The manor as a whole will probably bear a name of archaic character. Bensington itself is derived from a personal name Banisa, never found in independent use, but resembling other personal names employed in the migration period[1]. But the other place-names within the manor, such as Warborough, Henley, and Nettlebed, are far from suggesting antiquity. Warborough means the fort where watch was kept, Henley means 'the high *leah*,' Nettlebed means what it says. These names might have arisen at any time in the OE period, Nettlebed might be still later. Moreover, within such an estate, there was land enough for the endowment of king's followers, whose names might have become attached to the property which they held of the king's gift. It so happens that no existing place-names within the precincts of the manor seem to have arisen in this way. But the absence of such names does not affect the conclusion that within a single, compact, royal estate, place-names may be found of any date from the migration period to the eleventh century.

Throughout this period the basis of society was the *ceorl* of the laws, the free, but not noble, landholder, the man to whom *ceorla-tun* in Mercia and Wessex the wergild of 200 shillings belonged. It is to him that the laws refer when they are expressed in general terms, and it was on him that the chief fiscal burdens of early English society fell. Even in the seventh century he can be seen living with his fellows in agricultural communities which have no obvious lord. 'If ceorls have common meadow or other share-land to enclose, and some have enclosed their share, others not, and beasts eat their common crops or grass, let him go whose is the opening and make amends for the

[1] See *infra*, 172.

damage done to those who have enclosed their shares, and let them claim from those who own the beasts such amends as are proper[1].' This famous passage invites many questions to which no precise answer can be given, but it shows at least that an agrarian system which accounts for the principal features of medieval rural economy already existed in Wessex in Ine's time. It certainly does not prove that the normal West Saxon village was composed of free peasants owning no lord, but it shows that such villages were numerous enough to call forth an express enactment in a highly laconic body of law. Traces of such communities undoubtedly exist in the numerous and widely distributed places bearing the name Charlton from OE *ceorla tun*, or Carlton[2]. In these names, the suffix *tun*, which is best translated by 'farm,' must have the wider sense of 'village,' and denote a settlement of free peasants. The fact that such names were sufficiently distinctive to pass into permanent use would prove, if proof were needed, that Old English society was not entirely composed of villages of independent *ceorls*. Nevertheless, in view of the many place-names which superficially at least suggest that the villages to which they refer were under a lord when the names arose, it is well to remember that local nomenclature also bears its testimony to the existence of the free village community.

The Eadnoth-estun-type   It is, in particular, necessary to remember the existence of this fundamental class of free peasants when considering the many place-names in which a terminal denoting a place of settlement is preceded by a personal name in the genitive case. There can be no doubt that, as a whole, these names are later than the ancient compounds which contain the element *-ing(a)*, of which more will be said hereafter. It is significant that many of them, especially those which end in the terminal *tun*, are derived from compound personal names, such as Wulfstan, Eadnoth, Ealhmund, characteristic of the personal nomenclature of the higher social ranks of the tenth and eleventh centuries[3]. Names like *Wulfstanestun* and *Eadnothestun* occur in every shire, but are most apparent in Devon and Somerset, the northern Midlands and the counties along the Welsh border, all of them districts which have yielded little evidence of heathen Germanic settlement. Moreover, with the Danelaw, many place-names ending in *tun* are derived from

[1] Laws of Ine, § 42.
[2] The name *Carlton* is only relevant to this argument to the extent that it may represent a Scandinavianising of an earlier *ceorla-tun*. See *karl*, Part II.
[3] *v. infra*, 177.

Scandinavian personal names which cannot have been used in England until late in the ninth century. Thurgarton and Rolleston (Nt), Thurmaston and Thrussington (Lei), Thurvaston and Keddleston (Db), contain respectively the Scandinavian personal names *Þorgeirr, Hróaldr, Þormóðr, Þorsteinn, Þorrøðr*, and *Ketill*. Such compounds show that in the Mercia of Alfred's time it was customary to form place-names by prefixing a personal name to the element *tun*. It is probable that the place-names of this type in which the first element is an OE personal name belong to the same stratum of nomenclature as these Anglo-Scandinavian formations. It should also be noted that many place-names of similar character are derived from feminine personal names. Wollaton (D) and Kinoulton (Nt), for example, contain respectively the feminine names *Wulfgifu* and *Cynehild*. Despite the classic case of the sixth century queen *Bebbe*, who gave her name to Bamburgh (Nb), the female names which enter into local nomenclature suggest a more settled condition of society than is likely to have prevailed for many generations after the settlement. On all grounds it is probable that place-names of the *Eadnothestun*-type belong to a late phase of Early English history.

On the surface, the place-name *Eadnothestun* means that the *tun* in question belonged to Eadnoth. In many cases this superficial interpretation is doubtless correct. It is more than probable that many names of this type originally denoted the farm belonging to the man whose name stands as the prefix. Many medieval villages must have arisen by the gradual accretion of dwellings around some original homestead. Regions of ancient woodland or of light soil were throughout the Middle Ages distinguished by settlement in hamlets or isolated farms. The name of the first settler may often have remained permanently attached to such communities. It does not follow that he was always a man of rank. The *ceorl* of early times might be an important person. He might have free dependents under him, and the buildings of his farm might cover a considerable space of ground. A settlement founded by a wealthy *ceorl* could soon become the nucleus of a group of dwellings, and ultimately pass into a Domesday hamlet, or even village. His sons might keep together after his death, each in his own farmstead, with his own dependents around him. Whether, in such circumstances, the arable land of the settlement would be divided into strips, and distributed in intermingled shares, would depend partly upon the wishes of the settlers and partly upon the nature of the ground. Early medieval documents reveal many instances of compact tenements, obviously of high antiquity, and individualistic cultivation must have played an important part in Old English rural economy.

On the other hand, many villages in regions of early open field cultivation bear names of the type *Eadnothestun*. It would be very unsafe to conclude, on the mere evidence of the names, that these villages had all developed from individual settlements of the kind which has been described. In many cases, the geographical position of a village and its whole recorded history all point to its foundation as a village community[1]. When this is so, the position of the man who gave his name to the village becomes an important, but a most difficult, question. It is natural to assume that he was in some way superior to the other men of the community, that, for example, he was a man of rank, a *gesith*, or king's companion, at the head of a community of *ceorls*. Even so, it is necessary to remember that the *ceorls* formed the basis of the community and that their independence was not affected by the relationship in which they stood to the great man of their village. In other words, the familiar features of later manorial society must not be carried back to the remote age in which village communities arose. Moreover, the application of names of the *Eadnothestun*-type to archaic village settlements may be explained in other ways. These names, after all, arose naturally in the speech of unreflecting neighbours, who called a place after some feature which attracted their attention. If, for example, a community of *ceorls* included some man notably distinguished from his fellows by wealth or influence, the group to which he belonged might easily be called after his name—his *tun*, or farm, would be the salient feature of the village as it appeared to persons outside. The spontaneous origin of place-names is the fundamental fact which governs their interpretation.

Personal names repeated in neighbouring p.n.   Sometimes, though less often than could be wished, local nomenclature itself offers a hint as to the position of the men who have left their names attached to places. When two place-names in the same neighbourhood are derived from the same personal name, it is natural to infer that each place was called after the same person. When the personal name is rare, or otherwise unknown, the inference is undoubtedly justified. The name Tewkesbury, for example, is certainly derived from a personal name *Teodec*, which is never found in independent use. It occurs again in the name of Tidsley Copse, seven miles

---

[1] In 1086 Woolstone (Berks), OE *Wulfricestun*, situated in the open country at the foot of White Horse Hill, contained a population of twelve villeins and twenty-four bordars.

from Tewkesbury across the Worcestershire border. Unless
the Teodec of Tewkesbury and the Teodec of Tidsley were the
same man, a singular coincidence has taken place. It would
seem, therefore, that the man who gave name to Tewkesbury
had property in a place at least seven miles distant . If
so, it at once becomes probable that he was a man of local
importance, who might well have possessed the *burh*, 'the
fortified dwelling,' to which the termination of the name
Tewkesbury to all appearance refers. Similar cases occur in
other parts of England. In Berkshire the name *Tubban ford*
occurs near to *Tubban ieg*, 'Tubba's island,' which has given
name to the modern Tubney. In Buckinghamshire, a stream
coming down from the neighbourhood of Waddesdon, *Wottes
dun*, 'Wott's hill,' was called in the eleventh century *Wottes broc*,
'Wott's brook.' In north Oxfordshire, two adjoining parishes
are called Horley and Hornton. Neither place is mentioned
before the Conquest, but the name Horley represents an OE
Hornan-leah, and the name Hornton, an OE *Horning-* or
Horninga-tun. Cases like these, which could easily be multi-
plied, go some way to support the opinion that the men from
whose names the names of places were formed were generally
more than peasants, even if they tell nothing definite about
their status or their position in relation to their neighbours.

More interesting than the examples which have been quoted
are two remarkable pairs of names which probably arose
within a few generations of the migration. In the extreme north
of Lincolnshire, a place named Wintringham stands near the
bank of the Humber, and a place named Winterton stands
rather more than a mile inland. Each name is derived from a
rare, but adequately recorded personal name, *Wintra*. It is
obvious that these names must be connected, but it is hard to
define the connection, and, in particular, to distinguish
between the meanings borne respectively by the *ham* and the
tun of 'Wintra's people.' Whatever the distinction may be, it
must also apply to the equally remarkable pair of names
Sneinton and Nottingham. Sneinton, now part of Nottingham,
is not mentioned before the Conquest, but medieval spellings
show that the original form of the name was *Snotingatun*. The
name Nottingham represents an OE *Snotingaham*, which lost
its initial *s* under French influence in the early twelfth century.
The personal name *Snot*, 'the wise,' from which each name is
derived, has not yet been recorded in England, but its existence
is proved by the appearance of a patronymic derivative,

Snotyng, at a later time[1]. That the names *Snotingaham* and *Snotingatun* stand to each other in the same relation as the names *Wintringaham* and *Wintringatun* is certain. It is possible to assume that in each case the name ending in -*ham* is the older, that, for example, Winterton was founded as a colony by the men of Wintringham. It is perhaps more probable that the *Wintringas* of Wintringham were Wintra's immediate followers, and that the *Wintringas* of Winterton were less closely associated with him—were men who owned him as lord or leader rather than men of his household or his personal dependents. In either case these remarkable names cannot be ignored in any attempt to understand the actual nature of the settlement.

II

Locative forms of place-names   In late OE documents a place-name normally appears in the locative case, governed by a preposition such as *æt, on* or *bi*. The usage can be traced back to the ancient time before Bede. The curious form *on Tiddanufri* occurs in Eddi's *Vita Wilfridi*. Place-names of this type often appear in early charters. An original text of 758 speaks of the land of ten *cassati æt Onnan-forda* and the *viculus qui nominatur æt Segcgesbearuue* has already been quoted. But in the eighth century the form in which a place-name should be expressed was a matter for the discretion of the individual clerk, and the nominative case was frequently employed. Ecgberht of Kent, for example, grants ten sulungs to the bishop of Rochester *in loco ubi nominatur Hallingas*. In the tenth and eleventh centuries the use of the locative, with a precedent *æt*, became almost a matter of rule among the clerks who wrote charters for Athelstan and his successors. That they should have adopted so inelegant a usage is remarkable. It clashed violently with the elaborate Latin in which they delighted, and it is often introduced in phrases which have a distinct note of apology. King Eadgar, for instance, when granting land at Welford (Berks) to Wulfric his thegn, is made to say that the land lay *in illo loco ubi iamdudum solicole illius regionis nomen imposuerunt æt Welig-forda*. In a Kentish charter of 946 King Eadmund speaks of land *ubi ruricoli appellatiuo usu ludibundisque uocabulis nomen indiderunt æt gamelanwyrðe*. Phrases like these cast the responsibility for the uncouth name on the cultivators of the soil. Their meaning should not be pressed too far. Tenth century clerks were more concerned with the manner than with

---

[1] In a list of burgesses of Dunwich, relating to the twelfth century and preserved in a thirteenth century copy.

the matter of what they wrote. But they can safely be followed in their implication that for a long time the men of the countryside had been employing the oblique case of place-names in common use.

The place-names which occur in the earliest English texts have as a whole a different character. They include a number of descriptive names, like *Sandtun, ad Barue, ad Tuifyrdi*. They also include names of which the first element is a personal name in the possessive case, such as Rendlesham (Sf) and *Dæccanham* (Dagenham, Ess). But the names which are characteristic of this earliest period are names of peoples rather than of places. Bede, for example, referring to the foundation of Ripon, describes it as *monasterium triginta familiarum in loco qui uocatur in Hrypum*. He states that his own monastery of Jarrow was situated *iuxta amnem Tinam in loco qui uocatur in Gyruum*, and that the monastery of Barking, which bishop Earconwald founded for his sister stood *in loco qui nuncupatur in Berecingum*. These are all plural names, and they must originally have denoted the people who settled at the places to which the names referred. The name Jarrow, for example, means grammatically 'among the Gyrwe.' Nothing more is known about the Northumbrian *folc* which bore this name, but it appears again in the midlands, where the North and South Gyrwe occupied a considerable territory in the neighbourhood of the fens[1]. In the name Barking, the element *-ingas* denoted men who were perhaps descended from, and certainly stood in some recognised relation to, a man bearing the name *Beric(a)*. Names like these may once have covered a wide area, and only gradually have become restricted to the place where habitation was thickest, or where the original settlement had been made.

Place-definitions in the earliest texts

Late in the seventh century begins the series of Old English charters, which form the basis of the study of pre-Conquest local nomenclature. The later documents in this series, those in particular which come from the tenth and eleventh centuries, are distinguished by remarkable topographical precision. In each case, the land which forms the subject of the grant is called by a definite name, and its limits are defined by a set of boundaries written in Old English. In the earlier documents the topographical indications are much vaguer. In the seventh and eighth centuries, it was sometimes considered enough to define the position of an estate by naming the river near which it lay. Cœnred, father of Ine, king of Wessex, states that he

---

[1] On the derivation of this name see Ekwall, 'OE "Gyrwe,"' *Beiblatt zur Anglia*, 1922, 116–18.

has given to a certain abbot thirty *manentes de aquilone rivus nomine Funtamel.* Later evidence shows that the land which he gave comprised the medieval village of Fontmell (Do), but the terminology of his grant suggests very strongly that the division of the country into villages, each permanently known by its own name, had not gone far by his time. In a charter of 739, king Æthelheard of Wessex grants to Forthhere, bishop of Sherborne, twenty *cassati in loco ubi dicitur Cridie*—twenty hides, that is, by the river Creedy[1]. An indefinite reference of this kind was evidently sufficient in his time, but in the tenth century, the need of a more accurate description of the land led to the writing of a detailed set of boundaries, which shows that the estate comprised at least ten medieval parishes. Each parish bears a name of early English character, and many of the names may have arisen already by the date of Æthelheard's charter, but it would be highly unwise to assume that they denoted places of permanent habitation in the first half of the eighth century.

Regiones, provinciae   In other early texts, the position of an estate is fixed not merely by the name of a river, but also by that of some *provincia* or *regio* within which the land lay. These *provinciae* are often mentioned by early writers, and their names are sometimes, though rarely, preserved in modern nomenclature. Bede, for instance, records that bishop Wilfrid died *in provincia quae uocatur In Undalum.* The meaning of this name is unknown, but it still survives as the place-name Oundle (Nth), and it is plainly a plural formation of the same type as Bede's *in Gyruum,* of which something has already been said[2]. Each of these *provinciae* is best understood as a *folc,* containing some round number of households contributing to the king's food-rents and to the provision of fighting men. They belong to a phase of local organisation earlier than the division of the land into shires, and therefore little is known of their boundaries. It can at least be seen that they varied greatly in extent. Some of them, the South Gyrwe for example, had a *princeps,* or ealdorman, of their own. Others must have been insignificant divisions of some larger people. Their origin is obscure, but it is suggestive that in Old English translations of Latin texts the word *provincia* could be represented by the word *mægþ,* of which the original meaning was 'kindred.' The tenth century translator of the eighth century *Life of St Guthlac* renders *in provincia Wissa* by the phrase *on þaere maegða Wissa.* It is

[1] *Crawford Charters,* ed. Napier and Stevenson, no. 1.
[2] *Supra,* 47. The difficult place-name Groton (DB *Grotene*) in Suffolk probably belongs to the same class.

therefore possible that the name was first applied to groups of settlers so small that they might really claim descent from some common ancestor, and was afterwards extended to larger peoples, such as the Hwicce of the lower Severn, or the Gyrwe of the fens.

The importance of the *provincia* in the earliest English topography is brought out clearly by charters of the eighth century. In 736 Æthelbald, king of the Mercians, gave to his *comes* Cyneberht the land of ten *cassati in provincia cui ab antiquis nomen inditum est Husmeræ juxta fluvium vocabulo Stur*[1]. The river is the Worcestershire Stour, and the name of the *provincia* still survives in that of Ismere House, near Kidderminster. The significant fact is that no place-name, in the strict sense of the expression, is mentioned in the charter. From other evidence it would seem that the incidence of royal service fell in the first place on the *provincia*, and was distributed by its free householders among themselves. They would soon become acquainted with the terms of a royal grant relating to their country and with the way in which it affected the apportionment of rent or service to the king. They would know the estate to which the grant referred, and the question of its exact boundaries would hardly arise in a thickly wooded and sparsely populated region like West Worcestershire. Under such conditions it was unnecessary for a royal charter to contain a precise indication of the place which was the inhabited centre of the property, even if, which should not be too easily assumed, any centre of habitation had as yet arisen there. Names were still loosely attached to places. They were gradually arising in common speech as the settlement of the country became more intensive, but no pressure of any government as yet compelled the permanent employment of a name from one generation to another.

This fluidity of nomenclature could not last long. Before the end of the eighth century the normal charter defines the land to which it refers by some place-name which is obviously regarded as permanent. Nevertheless, in early texts an established place-name is often accompanied by the name of a neighbouring river, or, more rarely, by that of a *provincia*. The transition from the archaic to the modern system of nomenclature is well marked in the elaborate phrases in which Æthelbald, king of the Mercians, the grantor of the Ismere charter, defined the position of twenty hides which he gave to his *reverendissimus comes* Æthelric. *Est autem idem ager qui traditur in regione quae antiquitus nominatur Stoppingas, in*

[1] BCS 154, a contemporary text.

loco qui vetusto vocabulo dicitur Uuidutuun, juxta fluvium quem priores nostri appellare solebant et adhuc nominantur Aeluuinnae. Although the place-name *Widutun* was admitted to be ancient, it was clearly felt wise to define the land more fully by the names of the neighbouring river and the surrounding *regio*. A generation later the name of the *regio* or *provincia* has almost disappeared from the charters. The disappearance roughly coincides with the development of the practice by which a king, when granting an estate by charter, set out a description of its boundaries. The earliest boundaries attempt no precise definition. *Ab australi plaga Uuisleag, ab occidente Rindburna, a septentrionale Meosgelegeo, ab oriente vero Onnanduun,* is a typical example of these early outlines, which remain the normal method of definition well into the ninth century. But already in the third quarter of the eighth century, the attempt could be made to indicate all the prominent features on the border of an estate, and when the granting of royal charters was resumed in the tenth century after the dislocation caused by the Danish wars, the detailed list of boundary points became a permanent feature of such documents. The change was not merely a matter of formal accuracy. As the settlement of the country proceeded the need for a precise delimitation of properties became urgent. By the tenth century the principal features of village geography had already become fixed in the counties from which adequate records of this date have been preserved.

Folk-names, i.e. names in -ingas   Among the names of ancient *provinciae* to which reference has incidentally been made, two, the *in Berecingum* of Bede, and the *Stoppingas* of Æthelbald's charter to Æthelric, end in the plural form of the element *-ing*. These names are important as a link between the *folk*-names and place-names restricted to some particular spot. The established cases in which a folk-name ending in *-ingas* has passed into, and survived as a place-name are rare. Barking is one, and Yeading (Mx) must be another, for king Æthelbald of the Mercians refers to the *regio* called *Geddinges*[1] in the *provincia* of the Middle Saxons. In view of this example it becomes probable that a considerable number of place-names ending in the plural *-ingas* were originally folk-names. Reading, for example, is never described as a *provincia* or *regio*—perhaps because it is not mentioned before the year 871—but the Domesday place-name *Redinges* covers an area at least seven miles wide, a territory quite large enough for an early *folc*. It is altogether improbable that the men of the seventh and eighth centuries were thinking of area

[1] BCS 182, a late copy.

when they used the words *provincia, regio* or *mægð*. For them the number of free households in a district was the important question, for on it turned the apportionment of public burdens. In the dark age which followed the migration, no folk could have long retained the whole of a territory much greater than was required for the support of its population. In the generations following the original settlement, and long before the beginning of written record, there must have been competition for land between one *folc* and another, even if the *folc* itself was competent to settle disputes between the individual households of which it was composed. A *folc* which declined in numbers would soon feel the encroachment of an increasing community in its neighbourhood. It is not strange therefore that already in the eleventh century many small places bear names which in structure cannot be distinguished from the undoubted ancient folk-names.

It is, indeed, highly probable that some among the many names ending in *-ingas* which distinguish such a county as Sussex were originally folk-names rather than place-names. The *Hæstingas*, for instance, who have left their name to Hastings are called *gens Hestingorum* in an annal relating to the year 771[1], and in the early eleventh century they are mentioned beside the South Saxons in a list of districts ravaged by the Danes[2]. Definite evidence of this kind is rarely to be found, but it can at least be said that most names of this type are sufficiently ancient to have arisen as names of *regiones* or *provinciae*. Two distinct lines of inquiry unite to prove their antiquity. Many of them are derived from personal names which are never recorded in use in England, but are equivalent to Germanic names found in early continental documents. The personal name *Hæst(a)*, which has produced the form *Hæstingas*, is not otherwise found in England, but corresponds exactly to the Germanic stem *haist*, 'violence,' which enters into a number of continental compound names[3]. As a whole, place-names ending in *-ingas* belong to the time when the Angles, Saxons, and Jutes in Britain had lost few of the stems once common to them and other Germanic peoples. Unless very inaccurate conclusions have been drawn from the earliest English records, many of the stems which occur in names like *Hæstingas* had fallen out of employment before, at latest, the end of the seventh century. Even if it were unsupported by other evidence, the linguistic argument would be sufficient to prove

[1] Simeon of Durham, *s.a.*
[2] ASC *s.a.* 1011 E.
[3] Ekwall, *PN in -ing*, 59.

the great age of the large body of place-names belonging to this type.

But the geographical argument is equally strong. It has long been recognised that place-names ending in -*ingas* occur in greatest number in the regions exposed to the first attacks of the English invaders. They are characteristic of the sea-board shires from York to Sussex. They are still common in many eastern inland shires, they become rare in the true midlands, and are no longer found in the west. It cannot be by chance that, as a whole, they are commonest in just the regions which have yielded the best archaeological evidence of heathen Germanic occupation. In Kent, East Anglia and Sussex, for instance, where many burial grounds of the heathen time prove early and thorough settlement, place-names of this type are common, and most of them are derived from very archaic personal names. On the other hand, the western shires of Wessex and the counties along the Welsh border, where such place-names hardly occur, have produced little or no archaeological evidence of heathen settlement. A coincidence of this kind should never be regarded as absolutely settled. The discovery of early burial grounds depends on chance and timely observation. The completest map of such sites can only approximate to their real distribution. It is therefore not strange that sometimes, as in Essex, few early burial places have been discovered in a county distinguished by many names in -*ingas*. It is much more remarkable that in Berkshire, where few names of this kind occur, archaeological evidence carries the beginning of Saxon settlement back to at least the early part of the sixth century. Nevertheless, if England is regarded as a whole, the coincidence is far too close to be accidental, close enough, indeed, to show that the great body of these names must have arisen in the heathen time.

It is natural to expect that a long series of place-names of so great an age would throw some light on the problems of the earliest English society. If the suffix -*ingas* had borne a constant meaning, it would permit far-reaching inferences. There is no doubt that the suffix could be used to form a patronymic from a personal name, that the name *Readingas* might have meant 'Reada's sons' in the literal sense. It is highly probable that some among the many place-names ending in this terminal denoted the settlement of a group of persons, each of whom claimed descent from a common ancestor. But more than this cannot safely be said, for the suffix could certainly cover a man's dependents, free and unfree, as well as his children. It is also possible that in some cases a personal name followed by this suffix denoted the military leader of a group of settlers rather than the founder of a family. It is not a rash assumption that for some time after the settlement many such groups held together under a common name derived from that of the man who had led them in the migration. Moreover, the use of the suffix in the names of *provinciae* shows that it could also cover a body of persons too large to have stood in any close relation to the man from whom the group took its name. The *Hæstingas* cannot all have been the sons of *Hæsta*, and it is very unlikely that they were all his immediate dependents or followers. The original *Hæsta* may have been an early chief, and the *Hæstingas*, his men. He may equally well have been the eponymous ancestor of some early tribe. The distribution of names ending in *-ingas*, and the other evidence which proves their early origin, show that the terminal must reflect the conditions of the time following the migration. But the high antiquity of these names, which gives them their unique interest, prevents their precise interpretation.

Later in ultimate origin than the names which have been discussed, but still belonging to a very ancient stratum of nomenclature, are those in which a terminal denoting some definite place of settlement follows a compound containing the element *-ingas*. Names of the type *Woccingaham*, which has become Wokingham, exist in great numbers beside names like *Woccingas*, which has become Woking. The former are true place-names, *Woccingaham* means 'home of Wocc's people.' In names like this, which denoted some particular settlement, the 'people' covered by the element *-ingas* must have stood in some close relation to the man after whom the settlement was called, though it would be rash to define that relationship more closely. In England as a whole, names in *-ingaham* are more widely distributed than names in *-ingas*. Each type of name is characteristic of the regions of early Germanic settlement, but it is probable that names like *Woccingaham* continued to be formed for some generations after the type *Woccingas* had become obsolete. In any case, it seems certain that similar names with a different terminal continued to appear for a long time after the first migrations. Names like *Wulflafingatun, Peartingawyrth, *Geatingadenu, Waldringafeld* all refer to the occupation of a particular spot by a group of persons rather than by an individual. Many of them occur in districts where an early settlement is made improbable by the nature of the ground. *Geatingadenu*, for example, the modern Yattendon in Berks, stands on the Reading Beds, a formation unattractive to early settlers, in a district which even to-day

-inga-names

is thickly wooded. It is improbable that any new names of this kind arose after the end of the eighth century. Most of them are, no doubt, far earlier. But it would clearly be unsafe to assume that names suggesting group-settlement are confined to the time of the actual migration or to the period immediately following[1].

Conclusion   The earliest English place-names are difficult material to handle for historical purposes. They lead to much inconclusive discussion, and they yield few assured results. Nevertheless, they are far older than the earliest written information as to the nature of English society, and they offer suggestions which cannot be ignored. In particular, they suggest that the original settlement of at least the eastern third of England was the work of communities rather than of individuals. The rarity in the oldest texts of names which imply settlement by individuals —names like *Wulflafestun* or *Winecanfeld*—cannot be accidental. The vagueness of early terminology does not alter the fact that the oldest English local names are group-names. The nature of the groups may be indefinite, but they cannot have been temporary associations of fortuitous individuals. The community which is implied in such a name as *Readingas* must have held together for some time for its name to have passed into permanent use. It is easy to forget that early place-names must have meant something to the neighbours who created them. If in the sixth century the names generally current were group-names, it becomes impossible to maintain that the settlement was the work of individual settlers. From this standpoint it is immaterial whether these archaic bodies were family groups, settlements of a military leader with his men, or even folk-settlements forming an appreciable part of some early kingdom. In any case, these earliest English place-names were created by men who as yet thought less of the land itself than of the groups of people settled on it. And this indication of mens' habits of thought deserves to be considered in any attempt to understand the social conditions of the centuries which followed the migration.

[1] On names of the type Avening (Gl), i.e. 'settlers on the Avon,' see Part II, s.v. *ing*.

CHAPTER IV

THE SCANDINAVIAN ELEMENT

by *Eilert Ekwall*

I

THE Danish attacks on the coasts of England commenced *The Scan-* in earnest about 820. About the middle of the century *dinavians* the Danes began to winter in England. After some years of *in England* raiding, during which the enemy wintered now in Kent (851), now in East Anglia (866), now in Mercia (868), now in Northumbria (869), systematic settlements began to be made. In 876 Healfdene (Halfdan), the leader of the Danish army, 'dealt out the lands of Northumbria, and they began to plough and till them.' Next year a settlement was effected in Mercia, doubtless in the district later dependent on the Five Boroughs. In 880 the army settled in East Anglia and divided the land among themselves. The extent of the original settlements is not known. Some of the territory occupied seems to have reverted shortly to English authority. The boundary between the Danes of East Anglia and the English, fixed by Alfred and Guthrum's Peace, which was concluded in 886, was to follow the Thames, the Lea to its source, a straight line from that point to Bedford, and then the Ouse as far as Watling Street.

The reconquest of the Danelaw really began with the Peace of 886. A large part of Essex was retaken in 913. The East Anglians followed three or four years later[1]. The whole of Mercia was in English possession in 919. After that date it is hardly to be supposed that any fresh Scandinavian settlements were made south of the Humber. The bulk of the Scandinavian place-names in these districts must have been given by the Danes who settled between 877 and 919, and their descendants.

The kingdom of York, which may be supposed to have embraced Yorkshire, and parts of the adjoining districts, remained independent much longer. The men of York submitted to Æthelfled in 919, but on her death in the same year they may have regained their independence. In 924 the men of Northumbria, English, Danish and Norwegians alike, made submission to Edward. In the following years the Scandinavians of Northumbria were now independent, now under the English

[1] The exact dates of the reconquest of the various districts are, of course, somewhat uncertain.

crown, till at last in 954 they finally drove out their Norse king and submitted to Eadred. During its spells of independence York was in close connection with the Viking kingdom of Dublin.

Probably somewhat later, from about 900 onwards, a Scandinavian immigration took place on the west coast, in Cumberland, Westmorland, Lancashire, and Che shire. The information to be obtained from early sources with reference to this immigration is scanty, but there is good reason to suppose that the settlers in these parts were chiefly Norwegians, who came over from older colonies in Ireland, the Isle of Man, and the Hebrides. It is known that there was an intimate connection between the kingdom of York and the Norse kingdom of Dublin before and after the year 900. It is possible that the Norwegian immigration on the west coast was to some extent due to it.

The later Scandinavian raids and conquests were hardly of much importance from our point of view, and may be disregarded.

The information to be gleaned from early sources on the Scandinavian settlements in Britain is insufficient to enable us to form an opinion on the nature of the settlements, their geographical extent, the approximate proportion of Scandinavians to the English in the various districts, and the like. Scholars have endeavoured to throw light on these questions by various means. Archaeology and anthropology have been called to their assistance. It has been shown that in certain districts a Scandinavian territorial division has replaced the old English; that a fresh system of land measurement was introduced; that early records tell us about a new social system; that Scandinavian judicial customs have taken the place of the earlier English; that a Scandinavian coinage (*mark, ore*) was introduced. The remarkable number of small freeholders and free peasants in Danelaw districts, in contrast to the rest of England, has justly been attributed to the Scandinavian conquest. Last, not least, the evidence of place-names has been adduced.

The importance of place-names for the question under discussion was apparently first recognised or at least demonstrated by the Danish scholar, Worsaae, in his book *Minder om de danske og nordmændene i England, Skotland og Wales*, Copenhagen, 1851 (English translation, 1852). Later works that make use of this kind of evidence are Taylor, *Words and Places*, 1864, and *Names and their Histories*, 1896; Steenstrup, *Normannerne*, Copenhagen, 1876–82; Alexander Bugge, *Viking-*

erne, 1904-6; Collingwood, *Scandinavian Britain*, 1908; Mawer, *The Vikings*, 1913. Of works dealing with separate districts may be mentioned especially Robert Ferguson, *The Northmen in Cumberland and Westmorland*, 1856, and Streatfeild, *Lincolnshire and the Danes*, 1884.

A special work devoted to Scandinavian place-names in England is being published by Dr Harald Lindkvist, of whose *Middle English Place-Names of Scandinavian origin* the first part was published at Uppsala in 1912. This is an important and scholarly work, but the point of view from which the place-names are dealt with is mainly linguistic. The bulk of the volume treats of Scandinavian place-names containing a Scandinavian inflexional form, the diphthongs *ei, au, ey*, and the vowels *ā, ȳ, ǒ*. The introduction, on the other hand, deals fully with questions of a general character, such as the distribution of names. It need hardly be said that Dr Lindkvist's book has been of great help in the writing of the present chapter.

As Professor Mawer, in the second part of the present volume, is going to deal fully with the chief elements in English place-names, including those of Scandinavian origin, only a very brief survey is given here, except in the case of the two most important elements, and a general reference is given to the second part. It has seemed desirable, however, that at least a brief survey of the Scandinavian elements should introduce the present chapter, if for no other reason than to bring home to the reader the very rich and varied character of that element. *Elements found in Scandinavian place-names*

The most important Scandinavian word for 'a village' or 'a homestead' found in place-names is *by* (ODan. *by*, ON *bœr, býr*). Names in *-by* are found in all the counties where a considerable Scandinavian settlement took place. *By* is extremely rare as a common noun in English, and there is reason to believe that all or practically all English place-names in *-by* are Scandinavian in the strictest sense. Apparent exceptions will be discussed *infra*. *By* alone is never used as a place-name. The first element is often a personal name; the same is often the case with Swedish names in *-by*. The theory that the form *-by* proves Danish origin cannot be upheld. Names in *-by* are common in the Wirral district, where a Norwegian settlement must be assumed. The DB form *-be* (*-bei*), which has been held to reflect the usual Norwegian *bœr*, is found also in the eastern districts, and it should be noticed that English *y* occasionally appears as DB *e, ei*.

Next in importance is *thorp*. There was also an OE *þorp* (*þrop*), and some names in *-thorp* are no doubt English, but the great frequency of names in *-thorp* in the Danelaw as compared with other English counties shows that there the majority of *thorpes* must be Scandinavian. Dan. *thorp* means 'a hamlet, a daughter settlement from an older village.' This is no doubt the meaning also of the element in Scandinavian place-names in England. That many of the places with names ending in *-thorp* are of comparatively late origin is suggested by their situation on very low-lying land. The first element is not rarely a Norman name. Particularly significant is the circumstance that in many cases *thorpes* were named from an adjacent village, evidently the earlier settlement. In Nf we find Burnham and Burnham Thorpe, Saxlingham and Saxlingham Thorpe, Shouldham and Shouldham Thorpe. Similarly, in Sf there are Ixworth and Ixworth Thorpe; in Lei, Barkby and Barkby Thorpe; in Nt, Mattersey and Mattersey Thorpe. The circumstance adduced also explains why Thorp is so common as a place-name without any distinctive addition, and why combinations such as *Osmundistone cum Parva Thorpe, Colton cum Thorpe* (1316 FA) are frequently met with. *Colton cum Thorpe* is 'the village of Colton with its hamlet (thorpe).'

Other important Scandinavian elements usual in names of villages or homesteads are rare. OScand. *staþir* (pl.) is common in Icelandic names, while Danish names with this element would seem to belong to an early stratum. Some names found in Norwegian districts in England, as Croxteth, Toxteth (La), may contain this element. Scandinavian names in *-heimr* probably belong to the time before the Scandinavian settlements, and it is doubtful if the element occurs in England except as a result of Scandinavianisation of English names in *-ham*. The elements *hūs* and *tūn* are common to English and Scandinavian. The distribution of names such as News(h)am (*-husum*) rather suggests that they are to no small extent Scandinavian. ODan. *tūn* is rare in place-names, and names in *-tūn* in Danelaw districts should probably be looked upon as English, even if they have a Scandinavian first element. But in Iceland names in *-tūn* are common, and there is no reason to doubt that the Norwegian settlers in England might have used the element.

Scandinavian elements denoting 'a hut, a shieling' are:— *booth*; *lathe*, 'a barn'; *scale*, 'a hut, a shed.' Dial. *seat*, 'a dwelling, a pasturage,' common in names of old shielings, as Swainshead (La), seems to be ON *sǣtr*, 'a shieling.' Elements denoting 'a piece of land,' 'a pasture,' or the like, are:—*eng*, 'meadow'; *flat*, 'a shot or furlong'; *garth*, 'an enclosure'; *sleet*, 'a flat meadow'; *thwaite*, 'a clearing, a meadow,' etc., common especially in the north-west, but by no means rare in Danelaw districts.

Scandinavian elements are particularly common among so-called nature-names, a great many of which, however, have developed into names of villages or homesteads. Words for 'hill, hillock, mountain' are:—*bank* (also 'bank of a river'); *breck*, 'slope, hill'; *fell*; *how*, 'mound, hill, mountain'; *hoveth* (ON *hǫfuð*, ODan. *hoved*), lit. 'head,' but also 'hill' and 'promontory'; *nab*, 'a peak'; *lythe*, 'a slope'; *meol*, 'a sand-hill'; *rig*, 'a ridge.' Of occasional occurrence are ON *gnípa*, 'a steep hill,' as in Knype (We), Knipton (Lei), ON *kleif*, 'a steep hill,' as in Claife (La). Words for 'a promontory':—*ness*, at least partly Scandinavian; *odd*, as in Greenodd (La). Words for 'island':—*holme*; *scar*, *skerry*; ON *eyrr*, 'a sand-bank,' as in Ayre (La). Many names in *-ey* no doubt contain Scand. *ey*.

Words for 'a valley':—*gill* and its cognate ON *geil*, 'a narrow ravine'; *grain*, 'branch of a valley'; *scarth*, 'a pass'; *slack*, 'a shallow valley'; *wray*, 'a corner.' Words denoting 'a forest, wood, grove'; *with* (as in Tockwith (Y)); *skew*, *scough* (ON *skógr*); *lund* (often changed to *-land*); *storth*, 'brushwood'; *hagg*, 'wood marked out for felling.' Words for 'moor, heath, marsh':—*car*, 'wet ground'; *mire*; ON *saurr*, Dan. *sør*, *sor*, 'mud, wet ground' (as in Sowerby); ON *heiðr*, 'heath' (as in *Heith*, *Heid*, early forms of Lincoln Heath).

Words denoting 'a stream, a lake' or the like:—ON *á*, 'river,' as in Greta, Ayton (Y); *beck*; ON *lœkr*, 'a brook' (perhaps in Leck (La), Leake (Nt)); *force*; *tarn*; *keld*, 'a spring'; *wick*, 'a bay'; *crook*, 'a bend'; *-min*, *-myn*, as in Airmyn (OScand. *mynni*, 'mouth of a river').

Words for 'a road, a passage':—*gate* (common in the street-names of many towns); *wath*, 'a ford'; ON *eið*, 'unnavigable part of a river' (as in Knaith (L)). Words for landmarks:—OScand. *hreysi*, 'a cairn' (as in Raisbeck (We)); OScand. *varði*, *varða*, 'a cairn'; OScand. *rá*, 'a landmark, a boundary line' (as in Raby); *stang*, 'a pole.'

Names of animals:—OScand. *geit*, 'goat'; *gríss*, 'pig'; *hestr*, 'horse'; *ikorni*, 'a squirrel'; *maurr*, 'ant'; *trani*, 'a crane'; *refr*, 'a fox' (as in Reagill (We)); *ulfr*, 'wolf.'

Names of trees and plants:—OScand. *askr*, 'ash-tree'; *eik*, 'oak'; *ling*; *seave*, 'rush'; *star*, 'sedge.'

Various:—OScand. *leir*, 'clay'; *steinn*, 'stone.'

Adjectives:—OScand. *blár*, 'dark, blue'; *breiðr*, 'broad'; *forn*, 'old'; *grár*, 'grey'; *hár*, *hór*, 'high' (as in Hognipp, Hugnype, old forms of High Knipe (We)); *lágr*, 'low'; *skammr*, 'short'; *rauðr*, 'red'; *vátr*, 'wet.'[1]

---

[1] For illustrations of all or most of these see further, Part II.

Scandinavian personal names are of course common in place-names. A valuable special work dealing with Scandinavian personal names in England is Björkman's *Nordische Personennamen in England*, Halle, 1910, to which the same author's *Zur englischen Namenkunde*, Halle, 1912, is in reality a supplement.

Danish and Norse test-words The majority of the elements enumerated and also of the personal names found in place-names are common to Danish and Norwegian. But some may be looked upon as fairly safe indications of either a Danish or Norwegian provenance as the case may be. *thorp* is very rare in Norway and Iceland, and a frequent occurrence of names in *thorp* is a sign of Danish colonisation. *bōth* is a Danish form. So is *hulm*, a rarer side-form of *holm*, which is both Danish and Norwegian. *toft* is rather Danish than Norwegian. Norwegian test-words are *breck, buth* (ON *búð*), *gill, scale, slack*, also *ergh* (cf. *supra*, 34). But *by*, as has already been pointed out, is not a safe criterion. Also *thwaite* has been held to be a Norwegian test-word. No doubt the element is most common in districts that were probably colonised by Norwegians, but the element was also used in Denmark. The personal names had better be used with some caution, especially as the early Danish personal names have not been collected sufficiently fully.

Various types of Scandinavian influence In trying to draw conclusions from place-names it is of importance to realise clearly that the Scandinavian influence on the English place-nomenclature took various forms, and that the same conclusions should not be drawn from all names revealing such influence. Many place-names can be proved definitely to have been coined by Scandinavians, that is by people speaking a Scandinavian tongue. We may call these Scandinavian names in the strictest sense. They prove a Scandinavian immigration into the district where they occur. Others contain a combination of a Scandinavian and an English element. Most of these may be looked upon as English formations, having been made by English people out of an English and a Scandinavian word. Such names reveal Scandinavian influence, and they often prove a Scandinavian immigration into the district where they are found, but their value as evidence is not nearly as great as that of Scandinavian names in the strictest sense. Thirdly, English names often appear in a Scandinavianised form. This type offers particular interest, and will be fully discussed.

It is not always possible to distinguish neatly between these types. The Scandinavians and English, who lived side by side, spoke languages nearly akin, and many elements are common to both languages. But a close examination shows that in practice the difficulty alluded to is not so frequently met with as might be supposed.

To Scandinavian names in the strictest sense belong first of all names containing a Scandinavian inflexional form.

The most obvious examples are names containing a Scandinavian genitive in -*ar* or a plural in -*ar*, -*er*. Of the latter type is Sawrey (La) (olim *Sourer*, from ON *Saurar*). The former type is particularly important. A fairly full list of such names is given here[1]. Cumberland: Beckermet, Bowderdale, Harter Fell, while Borrowdale was formerly *Borcherdale*. From old sources come: *Butherhals, Butherthwait, Stangerhouet.* Westmorland: Stangerthwaite, Winderwath, with Borrowdale, formerly *Borgherdal*. Lancashire: Amounderness, Byerwath, Elter Holme, Fouldrey, Furness, Harterbeck, Litherland (two), the lost *Stangerhou*. Yorkshire, West Riding: Aismunderby, Beckermonds, while Thurlby is in DB *Toredderebi*. North Riding: Airsholme, Amotherby, Marderby, Shunner Howe, perhaps Helperby, Hinderskelf (olim *Hilder-*). East Riding: Holderness, Scorbrough (*Scogerbud* DB), perhaps Helperthorpe. Lincolnshire: Dalderby, Londonthorpe (olim *Lunder-*) and *Lunderberge* from an old source.

As will be seen, the names with the very common Scandinavian genitive ending -*ar* are not very numerous, and the impression may well be created that Scandinavian place-names in England are not to a very great extent formed in accordance with the ordinary Scandinavian principles, or at least that a wholesale refashioning of them has taken place. But on closer inspection we find that names with a genitive in -*ar* are mostly found in districts known to have been at least partly colonised by Norwegians, while they are rare in preponderantly Danish districts. Even in the east of England a Norwegian element is to be reckoned with. It is significant that one of the examples from the East Riding, Scorbrough, contains the typically West Scand. form *búð*. This gives us the clue to the matter. The *r* of the genitive ending -*ar* was a special sort of *r*, developed out of a voiced *s* (*z*). It was very liable in Danish and Swedish to be lost, particularly before a consonant. In West Scandinavian it was normally preserved. A typical instance is OSwed. *hæstanir*, 'the horses,' as against ON *hestarnir*. So we expect the *r* to have been dropped in Old Danish and Old Swedish in compound names with a second element beginning

Scandinavian names in the strictest sense

---

[1] Most of the examples are in Lindkvist, *op. cit.* 1 ff., who also gives some other (mostly doubtful) examples. On formations like Allerdale cf. *infra*, 69.

in a consonant. This is actually the case. The forms normally found in early East Scandinavian sources are such as ODan. *Gutmundatorp, Sigbiornatorp, Sigrithæköpinge, Asvardebode,* OSwed. *Arnbiornaþorp, Hagbardaclef, Hagbarðæthorp, Haldanathorp, Halwardhaby, Romundabodha,* etc. (from *Gudmundar-,* etc.). The normal ODan. genitive in names of this kind was *-a,* later *-æ, -e.* This accounts for the rare occurrence of *-ar* in Danish names in England. As the *-r* was retained to begin with at the end of words, it might be introduced occasionally also into compound names; this to some extent accounts for the isolated instances with *-er-* in the Danelaw. The normal forms would be those without *r.* Incidentally we may remark that *bylaw* is the Danish, *bierlaw* the Norwegian form.

An examination of the forms in early Middle English documents proves this theory to be correct. The Lindsey Survey from the early twelfth century, which is characterised by very archaic language, has numerous spellings, such as *Aluoldabi, Aslocahou, Hawardabi, Osgotabi, Osoluabi*[1], *Ounabi,* which form obvious counterparts of the early Scandinavian forms enumerated. Also *Ounebi* and the like occur. Domesday spellings such as *Esbernebi, Hauuardebi, Osbernebi, Offerdebi, Osgotebi, Salmundebi* obviously represent ODan. forms with a genitive in *-a.* Similar spellings occur in other early documents. Names like these contain Scandinavian inflexional forms and are Scandinavian in the strictest sense.

To the OE genitive in *-es* corresponded the Scand. genitive in *-s,* without a vowel before the *s.* The *s* was voiceless. It made a preceding voiced consonant voiceless, e.g. *v* becomes *f, d* or *ð* becomes *t.* A consonant was apt to be lost before the *s; ts* often became *s.* The OE ending *-es* later lost its vowel, but not until after the beginning of the ME period. In Domesday Scandinavian names frequently appear with the genitive in *-s* (without a vowel before it); sometimes an inorganic vowel is introduced after the *s.* Examples are *Branzbi, Branzeuuelle, Staxebi, Tormozbi, Turalzbi, Winzebi*[2]. Clixby (L) is *Clisbi* in DB, *Clifsebi* in the Lindsey Survey; the first element appears to be OScand. *Klyppr.* The *s* of the Scand. genitive was and remained voiceless. In not a few cases, therefore, even the modern form of names gives clear evidence of the genuine Scand. form having been adopted and perpetuated. Braceby

---

[1] Scand. *Asgautr, Asulfr* had the genitive in *-s. Osgotabi, Osoluabi* would seem to contain genitives in *-a(r)* due to analogy. *Osgota-* might also belong to a weak *Asgauti* (gen. *Asgauta*); cf. ON *Algauti* by the side of *Algautr.*

[2] Cf. also Lindkvist, *op. cit.* 29.

(L) (*Breizbi* DB), Rauceby (L) (*Rosbi* DB), Winceby (L) (*Winzebi* DB) contain ODan. *Breth*, *Rǫth* (from *Breiðr*, *Rauðr*), *Vindær*, and represent ODan. forms such as *Breiþsby*, *Rauþsby*, *Wintsby*. Sometimes the modern pronunciation retains the old Scand. form even better than Domesday. Laceby, Ulceby go back to ODan. *Leifsby*, *Ulfsby*, while Domesday has the Anglicised forms *Levesbi*, *Ulvesbi*. If names of this kind had been Anglicised, they would have developed a voiced *s* and appeared in a different form.

One more Scand. inflexional form may be mentioned. Weak nouns had the genitive in *-a* (masc.) or *-u* (fem.). The corresponding OE form was *-an*. This *-n* was lost early in Northumbrian, while it was retained south of the Humber. But in compounds such as OE *Addantūn* the *n* was often dropped even south of the Humber by the time of Domesday, and the absence of the *n* in names of this kind in the Midlands does not prove Scandinavian origin. But it is noteworthy that Scandinavian place-names seem never to show any trace of this *n*, while it occurs frequently in English names. This indicates that names containing Scand. weak genitives in *-a* or *-u* were not generally Anglicised by the addition of the OE ending *-an*. It is significant that Carleton sometimes appears in early sources as *Carlenton*. This is a hybrid, formed by English people from Scand. *Karli* or *karl* and OE *tūn*. In forming the name the English made use of an English genitive *Carlan* or, if the name means 'the village of the churls,' *carlena* (from the borrowed *Carla* or *carl* < OScand. *Karli*, *karl*).

It will be seen that names containing Scandinavian inflexional forms are far more common than has been hitherto realised. The genuine Scandinavian forms have been preserved with a faithfulness that is really remarkable. This circumstance also gives us the clue to the explanation of many names that have hitherto baffled investigators. Wasdale (Cu) (*Wascedale*, thirteenth century) and (We) may be easily explained from ON *Vatzdal* (from *Vatnsdal·*), with loss of *n* between the *t* and *s* and subsequent assimilation of *ts* to *ss*. Wastwater (*Wassewater*, thirteenth century) is a later formation. The curious name Goxhill (L and Y) (in early documents *Golsa*, *Gousla*, *Goussa*, etc.) may be a compound of ODan. *Gauks* or *Gauts*, genitive of *Gaukr* or *Gautr*, and ODan. *lā*, 'water along the sea, a creek.'

Among Scandinavian names in a stricter sense may also be counted the majority of names containing two Scandinavian elements, even if they contain no unequivocal Scand. inflexional form. Also a good many hybrids, which will be noticed further on, may be reckoned among strictly Scandinavian names in so far as they must have been formed by Scandinavians.

Refashion-ing of English names by Scan-dinavians When Scandinavians settled in an English district, they would to a large extent adopt names already in use, but in many cases these names contained unfamiliar sounds or combinations of sounds. Sound-substitution would then take place. Sometimes a Scandinavian word would replace an English synonym. Both phenomena are of very frequent occurrence, and a great many apparently hybrid names on closer inspection turn out to be purely English in origin, though more or less Scandinavianised. In a great number of cases such Scandinavian adaptations have ousted the old form. It is obvious that these phenomena testify to a very strong Scandinavian influence.

Substitution of Scandinavian sounds for English ones has often been assumed by previous students. Especially it has frequently been pointed out that *sk* has often replaced OE *sc*. The OE *sc* in most cases passed into *sh*, a sound unknown to early Scandinavian languages. The *sk-* found frequently in English place-names must be due to foreign influence, and no doubt we have chiefly to reckon with Scandinavian influence. In some cases *sk* has no doubt replaced OE *sc* owing to the inability of Scandinavians to pronounce the sound. A certain case is Skyrack (Y), the name of a wapentake, which represents OE *scīr-āc*, 'oak where the shire moot was held.' Shireoaks occurs elsewhere in England as a place-name, while the word corresponding to OE *scīr* is not found in Scand. languages. Moreover, the DB spelling *Siraches* points distinctly to a form with *Sh-*, which was thus still in use in the eleventh century.

Another safe case is Scalford (Lei) (*Scaldeford* DB), clearly 'the shallow ford.' There is no Scand. word corresponding to OE *sceald*. Plausible examples are also the following. Skillington (L) (*Scillintune* in a charter of *c.* 1066, *Schillintune* DB). Some names in *Skip-* seem to contain OE *scīp*, a side form of *scēap*, 'sheep,' as Skipton (Y) (*Sciptone* DB, *Scipeton* Simeon of Durham), still famous for its sheep-markets, Skipwith (Y) (*Schipewic* DB, but *Schipuith* in the twelfth century). In neither case is derivation from *skip*, 'ship,' plausible. Skipwith has also had OE *wīc* replaced by Scand. *viðr*, 'forest.' Scopwick (L) is probably a Scandinavianised form of OE *scēapwic*, 'sheep farm.' Here also the stressed vowel (originally *ā*; cf. *Scapeuic* DB) seems due to Scand. influence. Skiplam (Y) is *Skipnum, Scipnum* in early sources; it appears to be the dat. pl. of OE *scipen*, 'byre.' Skirlaugh (Y) (*Scherle, Schires-*,

Scirelai DB) is no doubt identical with the well-known name Shirley (OE *scīr*, 'bright,' and *lēah*, 'clearing'). The form of the second element may be due to the same influence; cf. *Braithlagh*, an early form of Bradley (We). Matlask (Nf) (*Matelasc, -esc* DB) may be OE *mæðel-æsc*, 'ash where the moot was held'; cf. OE *mæðelstede*, 'council-place.'

Germanic *g, c* were sometimes palatalised in Old English, as in *child, yellow.* The change was unknown to the old Scandinavian languages. There is some diversity of opinion as to whether palatalisation took place in Northumbrian, but it seems to be getting more and more widely recognised that in most positions palatalisation is a universal English sound-change. At least before *e* a *g* was no doubt palatalised all over England. The *G-* in Gilling (Y) (*In Getlingum* Bede) is therefore probably due to Scandinavian influence. Keswick (Cu, Nf, Y) is probably identical with Cheswick, Chiswick, from OE *cēsewic*, 'cheese farm.' Kildwick (Y) seems identical with Childwick (Herts). In both cases the *k* is probably due to Scandinavian adaptation. The names cannot be Scandinavian, and the normal English development ought to have been Cheswick, Childwick.

In Scandinavian languages there was no medial or final *d* in words except when long (i.e. doubled) or after certain consonants, as *l, n.* An English *d* in such a position would be apt to be replaced by a *ð* or possibly *dd* or *t*. A *ð* has taken the place of OE *d* in Mythop (La), Meathop (We), from OE *midhop*, while Midhope, Middop (Y) retain the OE *d*. Goathland (Y) (*Godeland, Gotheland*, early twelfth century) is probably an OE *Godan land*. Goodmanham (Y) (*Godmundingaham* Bede) appears occasionally in early sources as *Guthmunde(s)ham*. The form *-forth* for *-ford* may at least partly be due to Scandinavian influence. Louth (L), perhaps *Hludensis monasterii* in Simeon of Durham, is on the river Lud, from which it no doubt took its name. Probably the old name of the stream was identical with Loud (La), and Louth is due to Scandinavianisation, but a definite decision is impossible in the absence of certain OE forms.

In Scandinavian languages *w* never occurred before *u*, having been lost early in that position. In the pronunciation of Scandinavians an OE *Wulfherestūn* would therefore necessarily become *Ulfer(e)stūn*[1]. Ulverston (La) probably got its form in such a way.

Substitution of a Scandinavian synonym for an English place-name element is extremely common. The few OE docu-

---

[1] *Ulnoþ*, in a Danish runic inscription dating from *c.* 1140, is an adaptation of OE *Wulfnōð*.

ments preserved from Danelaw districts allow us to prove such substitution in a surprisingly large number of cases.

Scand. *konungr* (*kunungr*) has replaced OE *cyning* in Coniscliffe (Du), found as *Ciningesclif* in ASC, as *Cincgesclif, c.* 1050. Very likely the same phenomenon has taken place in other names, as in Conishead (La). OE *ēa*, 'river,' corresponds to ON *á*. Eamont (Cu) is *æt Eagemotum* in ASC. The usual medieval form which has replaced the English name is *Amot*, and this is ON *ámót*, 'junction of streams.' Modern Eamont probably goes back to *Amot*. OE *hēafod* corresponds to ON *hǫfuð*, ODan. *hoved*, 'head.' Howden (Y) is found in a document of 959 as *Heafuddæne* and the like, but in DB as *Houeden, Hovedene*. It is difficult to see how the change from *hēafod-* to *hoved-* can be explained unless we assume that the Scandinavian form has replaced the English one.

OE *circe* has been supplanted by Scand. *kirk* in Peakirk (Nth) (*æt Pegecyrcan*, KCD 726).

OE *stān* corresponds to Scand. *steinn*. A great number of names have as first element *Stain-*, as Stainburn, Stainland, Stainley, Stainton (cf. Lindkvist, *op. cit.* 82 ff.). Stainburn in Otley appears as *Stanburne* (printed by Birch as *-burhe*) in a charter of 972 (BCS 1278) and in DB. Stainley near Ripon is *Stanleh* in the same OE charter, *Stanlege* in one of *c.* 1030 (YC 7), *Stanlei* in DB. We may further note that Stainland is *Stanland* in DB, Stainton by Tickhill is *Stantone* and *Staintone, ib.* Obviously the names are English, and *Stain-* is due to Scandinavian influence. It can hardly be doubted that, in general, names in *Stain-* that have as second element an English word (as Stainfield (L), also Staining (La)) are in reality OE names in *stān-*. So also Rudston (Y) (*Rodestan, -stein* DB), in which the English form has eventually been victorious, is clearly OE *rōd-stān*, 'rood stone.' The place was named from a monolith near the church.

OE *wēt*, 'wet,' seems to have been replaced by OScand. *vátr* in Watton (Y), which appears in Bede as *Ueta dun*, but in DB as *Wattune*. At least an English change of *ē* to *a* is difficult to account for.

Not quite so clear is the case with Beckwith (Y), which appears in an OE charter of 972 (BCS 1278) as *Becwudu*. If *Bec-* is OScand. *bekkr*, 'brook,' the original name was probably *Bekkviðr*, and OE *-wudu* shows substitution of the OE word for the Scandinavian one. But *Bec-* may have some other etymology.

Occasionally an OE word has been supplanted by a synonymous but not etymologically corresponding word. Holbeck

(Nt) appears as *holan broc* in a charter of 956 (YC 2). Badby (Nth) is *Baddan byr(i)g* five times, *Baddan by* twice in an original charter of 944 (BCS 792). The original form was evidently *Baddanburg.* Similar cases are no doubt Naseby (Nth), Quenby (Lei) (*Navesberie, Queneberie* DB).

Substitution of the same kind has doubtless taken place in many other cases, though it cannot be proved in the absence of OE forms. Thus Eagle (L) (*Aclei, Akeley, Aycle* DB) may be taken to represent OE *Āclēah,* whose first element was replaced by Scand. *eik,* 'oak.' Braithwell (Y) (*Bradeuuelle* DB) and Brayton (Y) (*Breiðetun, c.* 1030) very likely go back to forms with OE *brād,* 'broad,' later replaced by Scand. *breiðr.* OE *circe* has no doubt sometimes been supplanted by Scand. *kirk* in other names than Peakirk, as in Bradkirk, Kirkham (La). OE *ēast* may well have been replaced by Scand. *aust* in some names, such as Owston, Owstwick. Gateforth, though appearing as *Gæiteford, c.* 1030, is probably an OE *gātaford,* 'goats' ford.' The common *-heim* for *-ham* in early sources is no doubt due to Scandinavianisation. OScand. *meðal,* 'middle,' has probably replaced OE *middel* in some names, as Methley (Y) (*Medelai* DB), Melton (Y) (*Middeltun, Midel-, Medeltone* DB), perhaps Methwold (Nf) (*Methelwade, Mateluualde* DB). Melton (Sf) is actually *Middelton, Meðeltone* in a charter of 1060 (Thorpe, 590 f.). Scand. *rauðr,* 'red,' frequently appears combined with *clif.* As Scand. *klif* is a rare word, it seems plausible that at least in some instances Rawcliffe (Rockliffe, etc.) is a Scandinavianised form of the common *Red-, Radcliffe* (OE *rēadaclif*). Both elements have been Scandinavianised in the thirteenth century form *Askebek*[1] for the stream on which Ashbourne (Db) stands.

We may add here a few remarks on the reverse phenomenon, which accounts for a good many apparent hybrids. Sound-substitution no doubt took place to a great extent when the Scandinavian place-nomenclature was assimilated to the English. But this process of assimilation extended over a long period of time, and it is not always easy to distinguish sound-substitution from English sound-development. Moreover these cases offer comparatively small interest, as apparent hybrids have rarely arisen in this way. By way of example we may here mention *Ash-* for Scand. *Ask-* (in *Ashby*, from earlier *Askeby*, etc.), which was later associated with Engl. *ash.* *Anglicising of Scandinavian names*

Substitution of an English for a synonymous Scandinavian element, on the other hand, has often taken place. Late changes due to popular etymology are not here considered.

[1] Communicated by Professor Stenton.

F

Scand. *aust*, 'east,' has been replaced by *east* in East Riding, in DB *Oustredinc, Estreding*. The Kirkstead Cartulary has *Oustbec* and *Estbec* as the name of the same brook. No doubt the original name was *Austbek*. Scand. *fagr*, 'fair,' was the original first element of Fairthwaite (La), as shown by forms such as *Fauerwayt, Fagherthwayt* in early sources. A sound-change of *Fagr-* to *Fair-* is not absolutely impossible, but at least it is evident that the name is no hybrid. Very likely the Scand. word is the original element of other names in *Fair-*. An old Scand. word for 'four' (ON *fiurir*, ODan. *fyuræ* or *fyræ*) was originally the first element of Forehoe Wapentake (Nf), as indicated by the regular spelling *Feorhou* in DB, later replaced by *Fourhow*. OE *fēower* does not account well for the old form. The second element of the name is Scand. *haugr*, 'mound.' The name means 'the four mounds.' To OE *nēowe*, 'new,' corresponds OScand. *nýr*. It cannot be doubted that many names such as Newby originally had as first element the Scand. word, later refashioned to *New-*. Newball (L) is identical with the well-known Scand. name *Nýbøle*, later *Nibble, Nöbble*, etc. The word *bøle*, 'homestead,' is otherwise unknown in England, and a hybrid formed with it and the Engl. *new* is highly improbable. The earliest known example of the name, *Neobole* in the Lindsey Survey, which would seem to represent a Scand. *Nÿubøle* (pl.), corroborates this. It is possible that early spellings such as *Niehusum, Nietona* DB, *Nehusum* 1182–5 (YC 199) for Newsham, Newton (Y), or *Nehus, Neus* (twelfth century) for Newhouse (L) go back to Scand. forms such as *Nÿuhūs*, 'the new houses.' Newbigging (Cu), pronounced 'Nibbican,' and Nibthwaite (La), apparently from *Nýbý-* or *Nýbúð-þveit*, are perhaps cases in point, but the early spellings have the English form *New-*.

There are many other cases where similar transformation is plausible, though there are no early forms that can be adduced in corroboration. Thus some names in *-burgh, -borough*, with a Scand. first element, very likely originally contained the Scand. *borg*. A very plausible case is Flamborough (*Flaneburg* DB). Also Flookborough (La) may be mentioned. Denby (Db, Y), 'the village of the Danes,' may well be an adaptation of a Scand. *Danabýr*. But a form *Dænir*, with *i*-mutation by the side of *Danir*, occasionally occurs also in Scandinavian. It is extremely probable that Scand. *vatn* has been replaced in some names of lakes by *water*. This is particularly plausible in the case of Elterwater (La), which has as first element a Scand. genitive form and is a counterpart of Scand. *Elptarvatn*, 'lake of the swan.' Also Windermere, earlier *Winandermere*, 'the lake of Winand,' may well represent a Scand. *Vinandarvatn*.

Sometimes, when we find an English and a Scandinavian element used side by side in a place-name, it is impossible to decide which is the original one. Examples are East Keal, called *Estrecale* in DB, *Oustcal* in the Lindsey Survey, East-burn (Y), called *Austburne* in DB, later *Estbrunne*, East Marsh (Y), *Austmersk, Oustmersc* DB. Hawkshead and Ramshead in Bolton-le-Sands (La) appear equally early as *Houkeshout, Ramshouth* and *Haukesheued, Ramesheued*; we do not know if OE *hēafod* or ON *hǫfuð* is original. OE *geard*, 'yard,' and Scand. *garth* are sometimes found in the same name. In some cases we have to reckon with the possibility that different names were used from the first by the English and Scandinavians in a district. An extremely interesting case is Bleasby (Nt). The modern name, of course, goes back to an Old Scand. *Blesaby*. But in the earliest known reference to the place the name appears as *Blisetun, Blisemere* (charter of 956 in BCS 1029 and 1348). The latter must represent the English forms of the name, used side by side with *Blesa-* or *Blisaby*. Birkland (Nt) appears in early sources as *Birkelund* and *Birecwde*[1].

The preceding sections will have shown that hybrids in a real sense are not by any means so common as might have been expected or as, at first glance, they seem to be. But of course hybrids there were and in large numbers. But it should be borne in mind that hybrid names were formed not only by English, but also by Scandinavian speakers. Many hybrids are demonstrably Scandinavian, being formed by Scandinavians from an English (or pre-Scandinavian) and a Scandinavian element. *Hybrids*

Here belong first of all names containing a pre-Scandinavian place-name, especially a river-name, inflected in the Scandinavian way. Examples are: Allerdale (Cu), in the earliest form *Alnerdall*, 'the valley of the Ellen' (in early sources *Alne, Alen*), Ennerdale (Cu), 'the valley of the Ehen' (in old sources *Eghen*), Nidderdale, 'the valley of the Nidd,' Miterdale (Cu), a place in the valley of the Mite, lit. 'the valley of the Mite.' Dunnerdale (La) is probably 'the valley of the Duddon.' In old sources are further found: *Alwennerdale* (Nb), 'the valley of the Allen,' *Hwerverdale*[2] (Y), 'Wharfedale' (Simeon of Durham), *Nidderminne* (Y), 'the mouth of the Nidd.'

Unequivocal analogous cases with an English personal name inflected in the Scandinavian way are not on record, but in all probability forms such as *Aldulvebi, Adredebi, Bernedebi* (for

[1] Communicated by Professor Stenton.
[2] But Wharfe may be a Scandinavian name.

Audleby, Atterby, Barnetby (L)), which contain OE *Aldwulf*, *Eadred, Beornnoð*, are perfectly on a par with the above-mentioned *Salmundebi*, etc., and are examples of the ODan. genitive in *-a* from *-ar*. No doubt other names in *-by* with an English personal name as first element may be looked upon as really Scandinavian. Also other names with a pre-Scandinavian place-name as first element may be judged of in the same way, as Airedale, Airmyn (Y), Burscough (La), 'the forest at *Burh*,' etc.

Certain examples of Scandinavian hybrids containing English loan-words of other kinds are the two remarkable Osmotherleys (La, Y). Both have as first element the genitive *Asmundar* (from *Asmundr*), the second element being OE *hlāw* and *lēah* respectively. These words must have been adopted early by Scandinavians. Windermere may belong to this category. Stixwould (L) is probably a further example. The first element is Scand. *Stīgr*. The form *Stix-*, in spite of *Stigesuuald* DB, seems to be due to the Scand. genitive *Stīgs*. The second element is OE *wald*. Other examples of this type are doubtful. It has been suggested that Hinderwell (*Hildrewelle* DB) and Ilderton (Nb) (*Hildertona*, twelfth century) contain *Hildar*, the genitive of ON *Hildr* (fem. pers. n.), but the etymology is not certain. Some names not containing Scandinavian inflexional forms no doubt belong here. Thus the common name Willoughby in some instances probably contains OE *welig*, 'willow,' which would consequently seem to have been adopted early by Scandinavians. But all Willoughbys do not contain the word *willow*. Some may have as first element a personal name *Viglaugr* or *Vigleikr*. There is a Willoughby, possibly one of the Lincs ones, which appears as *Willabyg*, c. 1066 (Thorpe, 595). Cf. also *infra*, 81.

English hybrids

Hybrids formed by English people from one English and one Scandinavian element are of course extremely frequent. We may here distinguish, at least theoretically, two categories. Among names of villages and names found in early sources the most common type of hybrid is that containing a Scandinavian personal name combined with an English element, for instance, Grimston, Helhoughton, Kettlestone, Thurgarton (Nf), Claxton, Thurlaston, Thurmaston (Lei), Thurstonfield (Cu), Thursfield (St), from Scand. *Grímr, Helgi, Ketill*, etc., and Engl. *tūn, feld*. Names of this kind do not occur with the same frequency in the various parts of Scandinavian England. They offer a good deal of interest, as will appear presently. They are analogous to Scandinavian hybrids such as Audleby. They need not indicate that the said Scandinavian personal names had been adopted by English people. As a rule they probably imply that Scandinavians had settled in districts chiefly inhabited by English people. The Scandinavian villages or homesteads were named by English neighbours from Scandinavian owners.

The other type, though a good deal more common, is much less interesting, because it is rare among names of villages, which we may look upon as on the whole the earliest placenames. This type embraces names consisting of a Scandinavian common noun and an English word. Most names of this kind denote minor places, fields, brooks and the like, and they probably arose to a great extent after the Scandinavian languages had ceased to be spoken in England. The words found in such hybrids are mostly such terms as *beck, car, booth, thwaite, toft*, which were introduced at a comparatively early date into English and became part and parcel of the English vocabulary. Hybrids of this kind, as has been already hinted, have small value as evidence of a Scandinavian settlement. Words such as *beck, booth* may be supposed to have spread at an early date to districts where Scandinavian settlements were never made. The conclusions as regards the Scandinavian immigration found in the later sections of this article are founded mainly on Scandinavian names in the strictest sense, Scandinavianised English names and hybrids of the type Thurgarton.

The fact that real hybrids, that is such hybrids as are not due to later modification, are rare among names of villages and in general among old names, is important, because it shows that at the time when the village names arose the Scandinavian and the English elements were on the whole kept well apart. There is reason to believe that if a place-name contains an element that may be either English or Scandinavian, as *bergh, hus, land*, this element is probably English if the other element is English, Scandinavian, if the other element is Scandinavian. We should not take it for granted that such elements (*bergh, hus*, etc.) are necessarily English when they occur in names of English places.

II

The following sections will deal chiefly with the distribution of Scandinavian place-names in England. In drawing conclusions from the material, certain broad principles should be borne in mind.

In the period of the Scandinavian invasions place-names were not generally, as now, given deliberately by the inhabitants of the places themselves. They arose spontaneously, unconsciously. They came to be attached to places, so to speak. The name that presented itself most naturally, whether derived from some local characteristic, the owner's name, or some other circumstance, came to be used in referring to the place. At first alternative names might be used[1], but one would soon oust the others. The names would be given rather by neighbours than by the inhabitants of places. Place-names thus indicate the predominant nationality of the population of a district. A Scandinavian place-name need not indicate that the place had Scandinavian inhabitants. If a few Scandinavians or Scandinavian families settled in an English district, the probability is that they would leave at most very slight traces on the place-nomenclature. The names of some of them would perhaps be attached to some place-names of English formation. In this way would arise names such as Thurgarton, Kettlestone, mentioned in a preceding paragraph. On the other hand, the occurrence of Scandinavian place-names in the strictest sense, or Scandinavianised names in a district, proves it to have been strongly Scandinavian. We may draw this conclusion even if the majority of place-names are English, for the Scandinavians evidently to a very great extent adopted names already in use. Whether Scandinavian names of the type in question indicate a numerical superiority of Scandinavians may be open to doubt. At least at the time of the earliest settlements the political supremacy might well outweigh a numerical inferiority. But a strong Scandinavian element must have existed where Scandinavian place-names occur. A single Scandinavian place-name indicates a Scandinavian district, not the settlement of an isolated Scandinavian or Scandinavian household. A district in this sense would not of course be tantamount to a large unit, a hundred or the like. A small cluster of homesteads might suffice to give rise to Scandinavian place-names.

Because place-names were in the old days not given deliberately, transference of actual place-names from Scandinavian countries has probably not taken place to any great extent. Of course, similarity of situation might occasionally remind settlers of their old home and cause a place to be named from a Scandinavian homestead or village, but certain cases of such transplantation of Scandinavian names have not yet been pointed out in England.

There is a remarkable Old English document which tells us that what has been said in the preceding paragraphs is not mere

Thus Whitby is said to have been once also *Prestebi*.

theoretical speculation, and which shows that a considerable
Scandinavian immigration may leave quite slight traces on
the place-nomenclature. It is the document printed as No.
1130 in Birch's *Cartularium Saxonicum*, which dates from
about 972–992, and deals with lands acquired by Bishop
Æthelwold at the refoundation of Medeshamstede (Peterborough) abbey. It gives considerable numbers of names of
men selling parcels of land to the bishop, witnesses to the sales
and sureties for a good title. The district of the transaction is
north-western Northamptonshire, the neighbourhood of Stamford and Oundle. The persons mentioned are local landowners.
Altogether some seventy names are mentioned. Of these
twenty-eight are certainly Scandinavian, the rest being English
or possibly English. But it is possible that the English personal
nomenclature was more varied than the Scandinavian, and
what we want really to know is the proportion of persons with
English and with Scandinavian names. It is impossible to find
this out definitely, because the various persons are only occasionally distinguished by the addition of a title or by-name.
We must therefore be content to take each name to represent
only one person, unless there is a distinctive addition to show
that different persons are meant, as *Ulf Eorles sune*, *Ulf
Clacces sune*, *Grim on Castre*, etc. We then get sixty-nine (or,
if Bishop Æthelwold, Abbot Ealdulf and Alderman Æthelwine
are counted, seventy-two) persons with English, thirty-seven
with Scandinavian names. This way of calculation is slightly
more to the advantage of the Scandinavian element than the
other. People with English and with Scandinavian names are
living in the same village. As a rule father and son both have
English or Scandinavian names. But there are some exceptions,
as *Leofsie Þurlaces sune*, *Æthestan Catlan sune*. It is worthy of
notice that the Scandinavian way of forming the patronymic,
Catlan sune, is used, not the English in *-ing*.

We may confidently assume that the people with Scandinavian names were on the whole descendants of Scandinavians
who had settled in the district about a century earlier. The
considerable percentage of Scandinavian names must indicate
a Scandinavian immigration of some importance. We might
therefore expect to find numerous Scandinavian place-names
in this district. That expectation is not fulfilled. The old document mentions a good many villages. All have purely English
names, except *Anlafestun*, which has a Scandinavian first
element, and Maxey, whose first element, *Maccus*, may be an
Irish-Scandinavian personal name; *Finnesthorpe* may, but need
not be, Scandinavian. At present very few place-names in the

district are Scandinavian. Two or three of the few names in
-*thorpe*, especially Gunthorpe and Apethorpe, seem to be
strictly Scandinavian names. Peakirk has been Scandinavianised. Maxey has just been accounted for. In this district, then,
the Scandinavian element, though evidently considerable, was
not strong enough to affect the place-nomenclature very much.

A comparison may be made with a document of about 1050
(YC), in which the festermen of bishop Ælfric are given. The
number of persons enumerated is about seventy-five. Only
some eighteen of these seem to have undoubtedly English
names. Some nine of the names are corrupt or of doubtful
provenance. At least forty-five of the festermen seem to have
undoubtedly Scandinavian names. Eight place-names are
mentioned. Four of these are English (Cawood[1], Hambleton,
Burton, Hillam), two are Scandinavian (Barmby, Kirkby),
while Brotherton is a hybrid and Brayton is very likely a
Scandinavian adaptation of an OE *brādatūn*. The district is
that of Snaith and Sherburn-in-Elmet, where Scandinavian
and Scandinavianised place-names are numerous, while English
names are no doubt in the majority. Here the Scandinavian
immigration was strong enough considerably to modify the
place-nomenclature.

The remarks made will have shown that the interpretation
of the place-name material is a very intricate task. They will
also have shown that the absence of Scandinavian place-names
in a district need not prove that no Scandinavian immigration
took place. It can only tell us that no very great immigration
took place.

If Scandinavian settlements were made in a district not at
all or only sparsely inhabited before, we may assume that the
Scandinavian element in the place-nomenclature would be
much stronger than if they were made in districts with a
numerous English population. There would be no or few
English place-names for the settlers to adopt.

Scandinavian place-names have no doubt to a great extent
replaced earlier English ones. But there are very few cases
actually recorded. The only really safe instance is Derby,
which has taken the place of an earlier *Norðworðig*. Whitby
is said to have been formerly *Streoneshalh*, but the latter is
possibly to be identified with Strensall. Yet there can be no
doubt that Whitby had a name before the Scandinavian time,

---

[1] The English origin of *Ca-* in Cawood is disputed by Dr Lindkvist,
who thinks the element is Scandinavian. If so, Cawood is a hybrid.
But the fact that *Ca-* is never combined with certainty with a Scandinavian word tells in favour of English origin. v. *ka*, Part II.

though we do not know what it was. Probable cases of a change of the kind in question are many names such as Crosby, Kirkby, for it is improbable that all places with such names date from the Viking Age.

There is *a priori* the probability that Scandinavian place-names in the Danelaw are, on the whole, of Danish extraction. This is corroborated by the large number of *thorpes* found in most Danelaw counties. Other test-words are of little importance. *booth* plays an insignificant part in the eastern districts, and *hulm* is rare. *Distribution of Scandinavian names. Danish names*[1].

Danish names form a marked characteristic of the place-nomenclature of Yorkshire, where the first Scandinavian settlements on a large scale were made. These names are found in all parts of the county, and in great numbers in the level districts of the East Riding, which we may suppose the Danes first 'dealt out.' A careful investigation of the Scandinavian element, in comparison with the English element, will give extremely interesting results. But in Yorkshire we have also to reckon with Norwegian names. The Yorkshire names include numbers of strictly Scandinavian names, especially names in -*by*, many Scandinavianised names, and other names interesting from our point of view. *Yorkshire*

From Yorkshire the Danes passed into Durham and Northumberland, but a considerable number of Scandinavian names is found only in the southern part of Durham. Near the Tees are found several names in -*by* (Aislaby, Killerby, Raby, Selaby, Ulnaby). There are some also in the Wear district (as Ornsby, Raceby, Rumby). The Scandinavian settlements in Durham were not nearly so considerable as those in Yorkshire, but by no means insignificant. But in Northumberland Scandinavian names are relatively few. The majority consist of or contain words adopted early into northern dialects, as Crookham, Kirkhaugh, Toft House, Walker, Haining, Newbiggin. Even Copeland probably represents a common noun, *kaupland*, 'bought land,' used in the dialect. Some contain a Scandinavian personal name, as Dotland, Gunnerton, Ouston. Under the circumstances the probability is that doubtful names should rather be explained as English than as Scandinavian. *Durham and Northumberland*

It is extremely doubtful to what extent Danes settled in Cumberland, Westmorland and Lancashire. Here a Norwegian

---

[1] With the account here given should be compared that of Dr Lindkvist, *op. cit.* xxxix ff. The survey given in the present chapter is based on independent examination of the early material except in the case of certain counties whose place-nomenclature has been fully dealt with in monographs.

colonisation took place, and the Danish settlements that may
have been made in the districts would be merged in Norwegian
ones. There is the possibility that the fairly numerous names
in *-thorpe* in the Kendal district of Westmorland owe their
origin to Danish settlements, and the same may be true of
Hornby and Thirnby in north Lancashire, whose first elements
point to Danish rather than Norwegian origin. A small Danish
colony must have existed near Manchester, on the northern
bank of the Mersey, as indicated by the names Flixton and
Urmston (*Flik, Urm* are Danish, not Norwegian), Hulme,
Oldham (formerly *Aldehulm*) in Withington, Levenshulme and
one or two others. The colony also embraced the adjoining
part of Cheshire, where several Hulmes are to be found. In
other parts of Cheshire Danish names are very rare.

Midlands The Danes settled in large numbers in parts of the Midlands, the
counties of Lincoln, Nottingham, Leicester, Derby, Northampton, Rutland, which include the district of the Five Boroughs.
In all these Scandinavian names are plentiful. On some of these
counties more detailed information will be given in the sequel.
In Northamptonshire Scandinavian names are somewhat
scattered, but the majority are found in the north-western
part, on both sides of Watling Street, where there are several
names in *-by*. Stafford may also be included with this group,
though Scandinavian names are few. Hulme, near Stoke-upon-
Trent, and Swinscoe may be mentioned. There are also a few
names with a Scandinavian word or personal name as first
element, as Croxton, Drointon (from *Drengetun*), Gunston.
Warwickshire is also comparatively free from Scandinavian
names, but the parts along the border of Leicestershire and
Northamptonshire form an exception. Just west of Watling
Street are found several typically Scandinavian names, such
as Monks Kirby, Rugby, Willoughby, Toft, Wibtoft.

East Anglia It is usual to group with East Anglia, Cambridge, Essex,
Huntingdon, Bedford, Buckingham. On Norfolk and Suffolk
some remarks will be given later. A few notes must suffice for
the others. In Essex there are very few Scandinavian names.
There is a small group on the sea, close to Walton-on-the-Naze:—
Kirby-le-Soken, Clacton and perhaps Thorpe-le-Soken, which
are memorials of a small Scandinavian colony in the district.
In other parts there are at most some names with a Scandinavian first element. It is therefore improbable that Layer
represents Scand. *leir*, 'clay.' It is probably OE *leger* in some
sense, as 'camp' or 'grave-yard.' In Cambridgeshire there
are only slight traces of Scandinavian influence. Toft, Carlton,
Croxton may be mentioned. Bedfordshire shows the same

state of things. Holme, Carlton, Clipstone are about all the certain examples among names of villages. Thurleigh is Leigh in early sources and Tingrith is probably native. Buckinghamshire has an almost purely English place-nomenclature. Ravenstone appears to have a Scandinavian first element, Skirmett to be a Scandinavianised form of *scīr-mōt*. Huntingdonshire has a few more· examples. Toseland (*Toleslund* DB) is a Scandinavian name in the strictest sense. The hundred name Normancross is remarkable. There is a Holme, near Denton Fen, and a Port Holme near Huntingdon. Connington, 'the king's village,' seems to be a Scandinavianised name. Keston and Copmanford have Scandinavian first elements. In all these counties it would no doubt be easy to collect a good many names of minor places with at least partly Scandinavian names, and a Scandinavian immigration is proved to have taken place by the occurrence of Scandinavian personal names in early sources.

It may be added here that place-names with a Scandinavian personal name as first element are found occasionally also in other counties than those enumerated. But all the names that have been so explained are not safe cases. Tusmore (O), for instance, is probably OE *þyrsmere*. Some other names that seem to contain personal names in *Thur-*, are in reality to be explained differently. Thurleston (D), for instance, contains OE *þyrel*, 'hollow,' and *stān*, 'stone,' and the same is probably the etymology of some other Thurl(e)stones.

It has already been suggested (p. 56) that the Scandinavians *Norwegian* in Cumberland, Westmorland, and Lancashire were chiefly *names* Norwegians, who had migrated from colonies in Ireland, the Isle of Man, and the Hebrides. This theory is corroborated by the testimony of place-names. Norse test-words are frequently found in the place-names of these districts, as ON *búð* (in Bowderdale (Cu), Bouth (La)), *gil* (common), *skáli* (as Sosgill (Cu), from *Saurescale*, Scales (La)), *brekka* (as Larbrick, Warbreck (La)), *slakki*, etc. Names in -*ergh* (cf. *supra*, 34) are common.

In Cumberland and Westmorland the Scandinavian element *Cumber-* in the place-nomenclature is very considerable. The distribution *land and* of the Scandinavian element has never been investigated in *land* detail. Norwegian names are to be found all over the districts. The hilly tracts of the Lake District seem to have been first colonised by Scandinavians. Very few old names of English origin are to be found there. Characteristic elements of the district are *fell, thwaite, tarn, wray*.

In Lancashire Norwegian place-names abound all along the *Lanca-* coast. In the narrower northern parts they are frequent all *shire*

over the district; in the hilly tracts old names are mostly
Scandinavian, while in the more low-lying parts village names
are on the whole preponderantly English. In the more southern
parts Norwegian names are common only along the sea. They
are frequent in the Hundreds of Leyland and (the western
part of) West Derby, but comparatively rare in those of Black-
burn and Salford and the rest of West Derby. They are most
common in very low-lying districts, which may be supposed to
have been uninhabited before the Viking Age. But they are by
no means restricted to such parts. In Amounderness Hundred
we notice the interesting fact that several townships have com-
posite names consisting of one Scandinavian and one English
name, as Westby with Plumpton, Little Eccleston with Larbrick, Bispham with Norbreck, etc.

Cheshire   A Scandinavian immigration into the Wirral peninsula of
Cheshire can be exactly dated. An Irish source tells us that
King Ingemund had been expelled from Ireland and eventually
had land given to him and his followers by Æthelfled, the Lady
of the Mercians, near *Castra*, i.e. Chester. The event must have
taken place immediately after the year 900 or 901. The colony
then founded has left its mark in the numerous Scandinavian
names in Wirral. There are several *bys*: Frankby, Greasby,
Helsby, Irby, Kirby, Pensby, Raby, Whitby. Thingwall is in
the centre of the district, and other Scandinavian names occur,
as Meols, Tranmere (olim *Tranemel*), Ness, Neston, Storeton,
Thurstaston.

Yorkshire   From Cumberland, Westmorland, and Lancashire the Norwegians penetrated into the adjoining counties, especially
Yorkshire, where they must have been very numerous in the
West Riding and the western part of the North Riding.
Names in *-gill, -scale, -breck* are common. There are some
erghs, as Battrix, Feizor, Golcar. The extent of the Norwegian
colonisation and its relation to the Danish settlements cannot
be determined without a special investigation. Also the western
parts of Durham and perhaps Northumberland were reached
by Norwegian settlers. There are names in *-gill* at least in
Durham, as Snaisgill (olim *Snelesgile*) near the Tees.

The   Some Norwegian immigration is to be assumed also in the
Danelaw Danelaw proper. This is indicated by names such as Normanby,
Normanton, 'the village of the Norwegians,' found in Yorkshire, Lincolnshire, Derby, Leicester, Nottingham, and Rutland. Such immigration is particularly to be reckoned with in
East Yorkshire, where it is easily accounted for by the intimate
relations between York and Dublin in the tenth century. Names
in *-ergh* occur here. The elements *breck, būð, scale, slack* occur

occasionally. In Cleveland, near Whitby, was formerly a
place The Breck (*Brecca* DB). On Scorbrough, see *supra*, 61.
Burnolfscales in Guisborough and *Raufscales* in Kildale are
mentioned in the Guisborough Cartulary. *Grenesdaleslack* in
Willerby, *Halle-*, *Refholeslac* in Huggate, are in twelfth century
documents in YC 1230, 1264. Other examples could be added.

It has been suggested that the Norwegian immigration was
on the whole of a peaceful nature, not implying a previous
conquest. The fact that Scandinavian names in the western
counties are most common in hilly or very low-lying districts,
which we may suppose to have been waste land before the
Viking Age, may seem to point in this direction. But the
general remarks in the earlier paragraphs of this section should
render us cautious in drawing such a conclusion. The Scandinavians did not settle exclusively on land before unoccupied,
and they formed colonies of their own in old English districts.
The name Thingwall (near West Derby) tells us of a Scandinavian colony in the Liverpool district with a thing-place of
its own. Amounderness Hundred was named from a Scandinavian chieftain. The statement of the Irish chronicle about
the Scandinavian settlement in the Wirral district, according
to which Ingemund had land given to him by Æthelfled, is not
sufficient proof of a peaceful settlement, for the chronicle goes
on to say that Ingemund shortly turned his weapons against
his benefactress and began to besiege Chester.

A few notes may be added on the Scandinavian names in *Wales,*
Wales and on the islands off the south coast of England. It is *etc.*
impossible to determine to what extent such names may be
due to Danes or to Norwegians. Scandinavian names of
islands, skerries, and headlands are particularly common.
Anglesea and Priestholm in North Wales seem to be Scandinavian, and the same may be true of Orme's Head in north
and Worms Head in South Wales. Several islands off the
Pembroke coast have Scandinavian names:—Gateholm, Grass-
holm (olim *Gresholm*), Ramsey, Skokholm (*Stokholm, Scokholm,*
thirteenth century, very likely originally *Stokkholmr*), Skomer
(olim *Skalmey*). Midland Isle was formerly *Middleholm*. Two
skerries in St Bride's bay are called Black and Green Scar.
An island *Trellesholme* is mentioned in 1327. A headland on
the mainland is called Nab Head (cf. ON *nabbr, nabbi,* 'point'),
and a bay at Milford Haven is Angle (perhaps ON *ǫngull,*
'hook'). In Glamorgan we find Sker Point (olim *Sker*) and
Tusker Rock (apparently *Thurse scar*). *Blakescerre* and the like
in old sources may refer to one of these. Finally two islands
in the Bristol Channel, now reckoned with Somerset, Flat-

holme and Steepholme, are to be mentioned. The Anglo-Saxon Chronicle under the date 918 tells us that Danish vikings occupied Steepholme for a time.

Names like these do not, on the whole, owe their origin to Scandinavian settlements. They show us a Scandinavian influence of a new kind. They are to be looked upon as sailors' names. Islands, headlands and the like were important landmarks and would often be used as temporary shelter. It is no wonder that the Scandinavian vikings gave names early to such. But what is very interesting is that such names were so frequently adopted and have been preserved to the present day. It is quite possible that Alexander Bugge is right in his conjecture (*Vikingerne*, II, 334 f.) that the Scandinavians who gave these names were rather traders than vikings.

But Scandinavian settlements were to some extent founded also in Wales. It is very difficult, however, to distinguish Scandinavian from English names. In Pembroke Fishguard (Scand. *fiskigarðr*) and Freysthrop look Scandinavian. In Glamorgan[1] Scandinavian names are well evidenced. Swansea (*Sweynesse* 1153–83, *Sweinesei* 1210) seems to be *Sveins ey.* Laleston, formerly *Lageleston*, contains the nickname *Lageles*, which is ultimately Scand. *lǫglauss*, 'lawless.' *Crokeston* was formerly near Laleston. But Scandinavian names are best evidenced in the Cardiff district. A street in Cardiff is called Womanby, formerly *Hundemanby*. Near the town are Homri, formerly *Hornby*, and Lamby, formerly *Langby*; the latter, it is true, is in Monmouthshire, just over the border. There must have been a Scandinavian colony of some importance in the Cardiff district. From this Scandinavians seem to have penetrated some way inland, as indicated by three place-names in Herefordshire:—Arkstone, Swanston, Thruxton.

It is interesting to find at least two place-names in the Isle of Wight with Scandinavian personal names as first elements:— Brenson (*Brandestone* DB) and Swainston.

The preceding survey has necessarily been of the briefest. In a careful and detailed study of the Scandinavian place-names of the various districts it will be necessary to establish the distribution of names in detail. Such an investigation will indicate to what extent Scandinavians settled in various parts, the nature of the settlement, the relations between Scandinavian and English names and so on. It has been thought advisable in this survey to examine a little more in detail the

---

[1] Cf. the interesting papers by Dr Paterson in *Archaeologia Cambrensis*, 1920 ff. Dr Paterson is apt to overrate the Scandinavian influence.

Scandinavian place-nomenclature in two or three districts. This will give us an opportunity of touching upon various questions bound up with the main problem and of showing how different Scandinavian influence can be in various districts. It will also give us an opportunity of testing some of the suggestions made in the preceding sections.

In Suffolk the Scandinavian element is not very prominent. *Special* Scandinavian names in the strictest sense are few. They are to *survey of* be found mostly in the low-lying districts at the mouth of the *(a) Nor-* Waveney, where there are two names in -*by* (Ashby, Barnby), *Suffolk* *folk and* Lowestoft, Lound, also some names in -*tūn* with a Scand. first element, as Carlton, Flixton, Gunton, Somerleyton. Some examples are found farther inland, along or not far from the Waveney and the Little Ouse: Wilby (somewhat doubtful[1]), Coney Weston (*Cunegestuna* DB), Thrandeston, Thwaite, Wickham Skeith. Near Bury St Edmunds is Thingoe Hundred, in which is Risby. In the rest of the county there are hardly any Scandinavian names in the strictest sense. Colneis (Hundred) on the coast (in which is a village named Eyke) is perhaps an exception. Some names, such as Flowton, Gosbeck, Kirton, Thurlston, Thurston, which are at least partly Scandinavian, are found here and there, mostly in the coast districts.

In Norfolk the Scandinavian element is much more pronounced, but we can draw a distinction between the hundreds in the east, on the lower Waveney and the Broads, especially Flegg, Loddon, Clavering, Henstead, North and South Erpingham Hundreds, and the rest of the district. In the east names in -*by* are frequent. There are Filby, Herringby, Mautby, Ormesby, Scratby, Stokesby, Thrigby, Ashby, Billockby, Clippesby, Hemsby, Oby, Rollesby in Flegg; Ashby in Loddon; Aldeby, Kirby in Clavering; Kirby in Henstead; Alby, Colby in South Erpingham. Also other typically Scandinavian names occur, as Crostwick, Crostwight, Felbrigg, Haddiscoe, Repps, Rockland. Hybrids with a Scand. personal name as first element are found, but are not characteristic of the place-nomenclature. We may mention: Carleton, Hillington (*Helgatūn*), Skeyton, Thurgarton, Thurlton, Thurton. Scandinavianised names are Keswick, Matlask. In the remaining hundreds names in -*by* are remarkably scarce. There are Tyby (Eynesford Hundred, and Wilby[2] in Shropham (not a safe instance). Other Scandinavian names in the stricter sense are:—Guestwick (from -*thwaite*), perhaps Colkirk, some names of hundreds (on which

---

[1] Early spellings, such as *Wīlebegh, Wīlbeghe, Wīlebeigh,* may point to OE *bēag,* 'ring,' as second element.
[2] The DB forms are *Wīlebey, Wīlgeby, Willebeith.*

see *infra*), and several names in *-thorpe*, as Alethorpe, Algars-
thorpe, Bagthorpe, Besthorpe, Bowthorpe, Flockthorpe, Gas-
thorpe, Gunthorpe, Ingoldisthorpe, Rainthorpe, Sculthorpe,
Swainsthorpe. We may add Boyland (olim *-lund*), Holme,
Rockland, Keswick, Scarning. Hybrids with a Scandinavian
personal name as first element are very common, as Aslacton,
Carleton, Croxton, Garveston, Grimston, Helhoughton, Kettlestone, Kilverstone, Reymerston, Scoulton, Thuxton.

The lists given are not quite complete, but they embrace
the majority of Scandinavian or partly Scandinavian names of
villages. They bring out clearly the difference in character
between the Scandinavian elements in the east and the rest
of the district. The former is characterised by *bys*, the latter
by *thorpes* and hybrids of the type Thurston. The obvious
inference would seem to be that the Scandinavian colonies
were founded in the first instance in the tracts on the lower
Waveney and that from there settlers found their way up
along the rivers. But what we know of the Scandinavian
colonisation tells us that this must be a wrong conclusion. The
victorious army would not march right through Norfolk and
settle on the lower Waveney. More probably the centre of the
settlements would be Thetford, where the army had wintered
in 870. The explanation of the curious distribution of Scandinavian place-names is probably simply this. The Scandinavians settled about equally thickly all over (or over most
of) the district. But in most parts there was a considerable
English population, and the Scandinavians were not numerically
strong enough to affect the place-nomenclature very seriously
except in the very low-lying district on the lower Waveney,
which was probably not much inhabited before the Scandinavian time. In most of the districts the Scandinavians to
a great extent adopted names already in use, but when new
settlements were founded, probably at a somewhat later period,
these often got names with suffixed *Thorpe*. It is possible that
the large number of Scandinavian names in the lower Waveney
district may to some extent be due to a later influx of Scandinavian settlers, who might have been induced to come over
after the conquest had been made by the army. In point of
fact it is somewhat difficult to believe that the army can have
been numerous enough to account for the very extensive Scandinavian colonisation in England, and a reinforcement by later
settlers from Denmark is plausible, but there is no necessity
to adduce this explanation in order to account for the place-
nomenclature of the Waveney district.

In Suffolk the Scandinavian settlements on a large scale

must have been restricted to certain parts, especially the
southern bank of the Waveney. Smaller settlements were
probably made in various parts. The hundred name Thingoe
(with Risby) points to a colony with its separate *thing* in the
district of Bury St Edmunds.

Scandinavian place-names are not very common in the fen
districts (Holland), but extremely numerous in the other parts,
Kesteven and Lindsey. In some of these parts the Scandinavian element predominates over the English. Most strongly
Scandinavian are the Wolds district (inclusive of the adjoining
lower land to the east, on the sea, and to the west) from south
of Horncastle to the Humber, and south Kesteven; as a third
district we may add that on the lower Trent. In other parts
the Scandinavian element is less dominant. *(b) Lincolnshire*

The Scandinavian place-nomenclature of Lincolnshire is
characterised by the remarkable number of names in -*by* and
the rare occurrence of hybrids. There are a good many names
in -*thorpe*, mostly with a Scandinavian first element, but not
nearly as many as names in -*by*. It is noticeable that they are
particularly common in the very low-lying coast districts,
which indicates that they are on the whole later settlements.
The *bys* are rarely on very low land. Streatfeild's theory that
the *thorpes* were the earlier and more important settlements is
not well founded. Some of the *thorpes* are on very low ground
indeed. Scandinavianised names are numerous in Lincolnshire.

In trying to account for the distribution of the Scandinavian
names, it will first of all have to be borne in mind that the
first settlements would be made by the army in the central
parts, for instance Lincoln, from which Roman roads branched
out in all directions, and Stamford. The settlements were not
founded, as Streatfeild held, by Scandinavians landing on the
coast and penetrating inland. The different frequency of
Scandinavian names in the various districts is no doubt due
to more circumstances than one. Considerations of a military
nature would play an important rôle in the earliest colonisation.
It would be desirable that the host could be easily collected
and quickly moved from one spot to another. The chief means
of communication were the Roman roads, and it is evidently
not due to chance that there seems to be a certain connection
between Scandinavian place-names and the Roman roads.
From Lincoln two roads ran south, Ermine Street to Stamford
and Castor, and King Street over Digby and Sleaford to Bourne
and Castor. Names in -*by* are thick on the map, as even a
cursory glance will show, along both roads and in the country
between them. This is the strongly Scandinavian Kesteven

G

district. North of Lincoln Ermine Street continues to Winter-
ingham, following the eastern side of the Edge, the long narrow
ridge east of the Trent. Here names in -by skirt the eastern
side of the road, being rarer on the western side, except near
the mouth of the Trent. Another road ran from near Lincoln
north-east till it joined the road from Horncastle to Caistor
and the Humber. This last road followed a ridge of the Wolds.
Along these roads the Wolds and the coast districts were easily
reached. It should further be borne in mind that large tracts
are very low-lying and would be uninhabitable or unattractive.
This is the case with the broad Witham valley, which has been
completely drained only in recent times, parts of the Ancholme
and Trent valleys, and some of the coast districts. The highest
parts of the Wolds (above 450 ft.) were for obvious reasons
avoided. If we consider these circumstances, the distribution
of the Scandinavian names does not offer much that is at all
remarkable. Of course, it cannot be expected that settlements
would be made with exactly the same thickness everywhere.

It is true the comparatively rare occurrence of Scandinavian
names in the Trent valley (except its northernmost part) and
the prominence of the Scandinavian element in the Wolds, 'the
bleak hills,' as Streatfeild terms them, is striking, at least at a
first glance. Her it should be remembered that it is by no
means self-evident that the Trent valley would be particularly
attractive even where it was not liable to floods. The soil
seems to be poor in parts of the district. On the other hand,
the soil in the Wolds is said to be quite good, and the district
might have special attractions, such as large forests with plenty
of timber and opportunities for hunting. The relative thickness
of the English population would also be of importance. In
districts where there was a strong English population, the
Scandinavian element would not assert itself in the place-
nomenclature so easily as it would in parts sparsely inhabited.
Very likely the Wolds were not much inhabited in the pre-
Scandinavian time. The extent of the Scandinavian colonisation in the various districts may not have varied quite so
much as the place-names seem to indicate.

In Lincolnshire we see the Scandinavian influence at its
highest. No doubt Scandinavian names have to a considerable
extent displaced Old English ones. The strength of the Scandinavian element is particularly brought out by the proportions
between strictly Scandinavian names and hybrids such as
Carlton. The latter type is extremely rare. Only a few examples
have been met with, as Branston, Carlton, Normanton, Bark-
ston in Kesteven, Carlton in the South Riding, Carlton,

Scampton in the West Riding, Croxton in the North Riding. This indicates a strong ascendancy, perhaps even a numerical superiority of the Scandinavian over the English population, at least in parts of the district.

The Scandinavian element is very strong in some parts of Leicestershire, being less prominent in others. Leicester was one of the Danish strongholds, and we might expect to find Scandinavian place-names in greatest frequency in the surrounding district. There are certainly *bys* and *thorpes* all round Leicester, but not in very large numbers. The most strongly Scandinavian district is that east and north-east of Leicester, the Wreak valley and the uplands north and especially south of the said river. This is the rich Melton Mowbray district, roughly Framland and East Goscote Wapentakes. The centre of the district would seem to have been Melton Mowbray, in the time of Domesday the head of a large soke. The name Melton itself is a Scandinavianised form of OE *Middeltūn*. The *thing*-place of Framland is no doubt indicated by the name Great Framlands near Melton Mowbray. In this district the Scandinavian place-nomenclature is of exactly the same nature as in the most Scandinavianised parts of Lincolnshire. Names in *-by* abound, while *thorpes* and hybrids of the type Normanton are relatively few. The great number of Scandinavian names is particularly striking because it is obvious that the district, even that of the uplands, must have been thickly populated before the arrival of the Scandinavians, as shown by the numerous English place-names.

In the remaining districts Scandinavian names are more scattered. Evidently the Scandinavian settlements were not so important in them. But a number of names in *-by* are found clustered in various parts, and there is reason to believe that the Scandinavian colonisation was fairly considerable all over Leicestershire.

In Nottinghamshire and Derbyshire the Scandinavian place-nomenclature is quite different in character from that of Lincoln or Leicester. The characteristic feature of the Scandinavian element is the prevalence of names in *-thorpe* and hybrids of the type Thurgarton over names in *-by*. As regards Nottingham, it is first noteworthy that there are few names in *-by* and strictly Scandinavian names generally in the hundreds east of the Trent on the Lincoln border. Names in *-by* are most common in Bassetlaw Wapentake, north Notts, but the district is large, and the nine *bys* are scattered in small clusters: Bilby, Barnby and Ranby; Scrooby and Serlby; Budby, Thoresby and Walesby. The Scandinavian settlements would seem to

(c) Leicestershire

(d) Nottinghamshire and Derbyshire

have been made chiefly west of and not very far from the Trent. Inland the number of Scandinavian names decreases.

In Derbyshire the Scandinavian element in the place-nomenclature is still less prominent. A notable exception from the general rule, however, is Repton Hundred, south of the Trent. Here are in a small area three *bys* (Bretby, Ingleby, Smisby) and the interesting Foremark (earlier *Fornwerk*, 'the old fort'). The district adjoins Leicestershire; just over the border, in that county, are Appleby, Ashby de la Zouch, Blackfordby, the lost Kilwardby. These *bys* clearly form a cluster indicating a compact Scandinavian colony. In the rest of Derby hybrids of the type Thurvaston preponderate. In the south-western part, this type seems to be the only one represented in the Scandinavian place-nomenclature.

Evidently the Scandinavian colonisation of Nottingham and Derby cannot have been as considerable as that of Lincolnshire. But, on the other hand, it should not be underrated. Taken together, the names in *-by* or *-thorpe*, and other strictly Scandinavian names and Scandinavianised names are not so very few, and they are found with greater or less frequency over these counties. All that can be said with certainty is that the Scandinavian element, in most of the districts, was outnumbered by the English element.

III

Wapen-takes. Ridings *Scandinavian institutions, etc.* The Scandinavians introduced new divisions of land. The old division into hundreds was largely replaced by that into wapentakes, found in Lincoln, Rutland, Leicester, Derby, Nottingham, [Northampton[1],] Yorkshire, Lancashire, Durham[2], apparently also in Cheshire and Cumberland[3]. The division into Ridings, still in use in Yorkshire, and formerly also in regard to Lindsey, is Scandinavian, as indicated by the name, OScand. *þriðjungr*. The division has counterparts in Scandinavia, the most striking analogy being that of the Island of Gotland, which was formerly divided into three *thrithings*, each with its *thing*, a division still in force for ecclesiastical purposes. A division into bierlows or byrlaws instead of townships was used in some parts of the north (Lancashire and Yorkshire); the addition Bierlow found

Bierlows

[1] The double hundred of Nassaburg, Nth, between the Nene at Peterborough and the Welland at Stamford is described as a wapentake at an early date.
[2] Sadberge wapentake in south Durham, often mentioned in early sources.
[3] NED, s.v. *wapentake*.

in some names, as Brampton, Ecclesall, Brightside Bierlow, is
a memorial of the old division. The source seems most probably
to be an old Scandinavian *byjarlǫg*, corresponding to Swedish
byalag, 'village community.' Also the division of land into
carucates instead of into hides may be mentioned here. It is
found in Derby, Nottingham, Lincoln, Leicester, Rutland,
Lancashire, Yorkshire, also in Norfolk and Suffolk, and may
once have existed elsewhere.

Hundreds and wapentakes frequently have Scandinavian or
Scandinavianised names. This is a clear indication of the
Scandinavian ascendancy. It is of especial importance that
Scandinavian names of hundreds are frequent in Norfolk,
where the Scandinavian element in the place-nomenclature is
not quite so strong. In Yorkshire several names of wapentakes
have names in *cross*, often with an obvious Scand. first element,
as Buckrose, Ewcross, Osgoldcross, Staincross, and the lost
Sneculfcros (DB). Other Scand. names are Hallikeld, Holderness, and Agbrigg. Gilling, Skyrack, Staincliff are at least
Scandinavianised. In Lincolnshire, as might have been expected, cases are numerous:—Aslacoe, Aswardhurn (*Aswarde-
tierne* DB, 'the thornbush of Asvarðr'), Aveland (*Avelunt* DB),
Calceworth (*Calsvad* DB, i.e. *Kalf's vað*), Candleshoe (*Calnodes-
hou* DB), Gartree, Haverstoe (*Hawardeshou* DB), Langoe,
Lawress (*Lagulris* DB, *Lagolfris* Lindsey Survey), Louthesk
(at least Scandinavianised, *esk* seems to be OScand. *eski*,
'ashtrees'), Ness, Skirbeck, Walshcroft (*Walescros* DB), Wraggoe (*Waragehou* DB). In Leicestershire we find Framland
(*Franelund* DB). From Northamptonshire may be mentioned
Neueslund DB; from Nottinghamshire, Lith, *Oswardebec* (DB).
Norfolk examples are:—Forehoe, Gallow, Greenhoe, Grimshoe,
Brothercross, Guiltcross, Wayland (*Wanelund* DB), perhaps
Flegg (*Flec* DB). A certain Suffolk instance is Thingoe (*Thinge-
hou* DB), and Colneis may be another. From Lancashire may
be adduced West Derby, Amounderness, and the old district
names Cartmel and Furness.

It is an interesting fact that in many cases the name of a
hundred has as first element a personal name found also as
part of the name of a place in the hundred. Examples are
particularly numerous in Lincoln: Aswardby in Aswardhurn,
Calceby in Calceworth, Candlesby in Candleshoe, Hawerby in
Haverstoe, Walesby in Walshcroft, Wragby in Wraggoe, perhaps Hawthorpe in Aveland. A possible Yorkshire example is
Bugthorpe in Buckrose. In cases like these the same person
must have given his name to the village and hundred. The
explanation may be, as suggested by Alexander Bugge (*Viking-*

*Names o[f]
hundreds
and
wapen-
takes*

erne, II, 326 ff.), that the *thing*-place was on the land of the chief of the district. This seems very probable in the case of Calceworth, which was no doubt named from the ford close to Calceby, where we must suppose the *thing*-place to have been. But the names in -*how* may well refer to grave-mounds. In Scandinavia it is usual for names of hundreds to have names in -*haugr* with a personal name as first element, and it is supposed that the mounds were grave-mounds, on which *things* were held. If this explanation may be applied to the English hundred names in -*how*, the names are very interesting, because they must go back to a time when the Scandinavians were heathens, that is, to a very early time indeed. Professor Stenton[1] draws this conclusion from two extremely interesting cases found by him, viz. *Leggeshou*, a place in Legsby, and *Katehou* in S. Cadeby. The places were evidently mounds in the territories of the said villages. These mounds did not give name to wapentakes. Another interesting name is Lawress, formerly *Lagolfris*. The second element is *hrīs*, 'brushwood, grove.' The first is evidently a personal name. It is tempting to derive it from an old Scandinavian *Lag-Ulfr*, analogous to Icelandic names such as *Laga-Ulfliótr*, *Lǫg-Skapti*, etc. Well known lawmen, called *Ulfliótr*, *Skapti*, were distinguished by the addition of *Laga-* or *Lǫg-* to their names.

Old Scandinavian *thing*-places are often commemorated by place-names. Thingwall (Ch and La) are well-known counterparts of *Þingvellir* in Iceland and *Tingvalla* in Sweden. A third Thingwall, near Whitby, is mentioned in old sources (*Tingwal, Thingwala*, twelfth century). A Scandinavian *þinghaugr* is the source of Thingoe (Sf) (already mentioned), and of Finney Hill, near Northallerton (*Thyngowe, Thynghou* in old documents). A *Thingou* in Frisby (Lei) and *Thinghou* in L are mentioned in old sources.

Drengs, holds, etc. The Scandinavian social system differed in many respects from the Old English one, and many changes were introduced by the Scandinavian settlers. We find the Scandinavian *drengs* commemorated in place-names such as Drinkstone (Sf), Dringhoe (Y), Drointon (St). A *hold* was in rank beneath a *jarl*. Very likely Holderness was named from a *hold*. The free landholder was a *bóndi*; this word enters into names such as Bonby (L), Bonbusk (Nt), Bongate (We). A freed man was a *leysingr*, but as the word was often used as a personal name, we cannot say whether names such as Lazonby mean 'the homestead of the *leysingr*' or 'Leysing's homestead.' A serf

---

[1] *Charters relating to the Gilbertine Houses of Sixle etc.*, Lincoln Record Soc. XVIII, XXXV.

was called *þræll*. Many names contain this word, as Threlfall, Trailholme (La), Threlkeld (Cu).

Old manorial records and the like tell us that the Scandinavians introduced new customs of husbandry or at least many new names of old customs[1]. In Lincolnshire, for instance, the nomenclature of the village institutions is largely Scandinavian. The homestead was a *toft*. The enclosed arable was the *wang*. A share in the common field is often called a *deil* (OScand. *deill*). *Stang* is often used as a measure of land instead of *rood*. The meadow is, of course, often *eng*. An enclosure from the waste is an *intake* (cf. OScand. *inntaka*) or in some places an *avenam* (OScand. *afnám*). A shot or furlong is sometimes called a *flat* (ON *flǫtr*, etc.) and this element is common in place-names. A full investigation of field-names and the like, especially in those parts of Scandinavian England where names of villages are mostly English, will probably often tell of a strong Scandinavian influence also where there are few Scandinavian names of other kinds. In some parts of the north place-names tell us that the Scandinavians introduced the old Celtic and Scandinavian custom of sending cattle away to shielings in the summer. Names in *-ergh*, *-booth* and (some in) *-set* originally denoted shielings, many of which, however, at an early date developed into separate settlements. *Agricultural terms*

The Scandinavians in England were no doubt converted early to Christianity, and it is no wonder that there are very slight traces in place-names of the ancient Scandinavian religion. Names in *Thor-*, *Thur-* have sometimes been held to contain the name of the heathen god *Thor*, but they have undoubtedly the personal name *Thor*, *Thur* as first element. Ullock in We, according to Lindkvist, contains the name of the god *Ullr*. It has been shown, however, that the original form is *Ulvelaik*, from ON *ulfaleikr*, 'wolves' play,' i.e. 'place where wolves play.' The only plausible examples of place-names containing the names of Scandinavian deities that have so far been adduced are *Othenesberg*, an earlier name of Roseberry Topping (Y), and Wayland (Nf). The former very likely means 'Othin's hill,' but early spellings with *Ou-* may possibly point to ON *Auðunn* as first element. Wayland (olim *Wanelund*) is supposed by Alexander Bugge to have as first element the gen. of ON *vanir*, the name of a kind of deities. But *Wane-* may also represent an unrecorded personal name. *Religious beliefs*

[1] Cf. Lindkvist, *op. cit.* lvii f., Alexander Bugge, 'The Norse Settlements in the British Islands,' *Trans. Royal Hist. Soc.* 4th Series, IV, especially 14 ff.

But there are possibly other traces of Scandinavian heathendom. On names in -*how* some remarks have already been offered. Names of wapentakes ending in -*lund*, as Aveland (L), Framland (Lei), show that *things* were often held in groves. The reason may very well be that the groves were originally heathen sanctuaries. In old Scandinavia groves were places of divine worship. Also other names in -*lund* and the names *Lound, Lund* themselves may in some cases refer to sacred places. The situation of such places may possibly sometimes give a hint as to whether such may be the case. The usual name for a heathen temple in Iceland was *hof*. It is possible that Hoff (We) took its name from an old *hof* in this sense.

Here may be mentioned a custom which recent research has shown to have a cultural origin or at any rate to have been connected with a heathen cult, viz. horse-racing. Many places in Sweden have names referring to old horse-races[1], as Hästeskede, Skee, etc., which contain the old Scand. *skeið*, 'race-course.' It has long been seen that there are similar names in England, viz. Hesketh (La and Y), Hesket (Cu, on the Petterill), Hesket in the Forest (Cu), Hesket Newmarket (Cu), all from Scand. *hestaskeiði*, 'race-course.' Here no doubt also belong Wickham Skeith (Sf) (south-west of Eye), Brunstock (olim *Bruneskayth*) near Carlisle, and the lost name *Skeyth*, which designated a place outside Leicester. Whether the races held at these places had anything to do with a heathen cult or not, they are of Scandinavian origin and testify to the popularity of horse-racing among the Scandinavians in England.

Popular beliefs survived the introduction of Christianity much longer than the heathen gods and their worship. Names containing such words as *elf, thurse* may date from quite a late period. Names with the word *thurse* (ON *þurs*, 'giant') are quite common; the second element is usually a word for ravine or fen. Thrushgill (La) is a case in point. Professor Mawer is inclined to believe that Troughburn (Nb) (*Trollop* 1352) contains ON *troll*, 'goblin.' Another example may be Trow Gill near Ingleborough Cave, a remarkable opening in the limestone.

Survival of Scandinavian speech   How long did a Scandinavian language continue to be spoken in England? Any evidence that may throw light on this important question should be carefully collected and sifted. The Scandinavians in England have left very few monuments and inscriptions behind. This is very remarkable in view of the fact that the custom of erecting runic monuments was very prevalent in Scandinavia about the time of the Scandinavian

[1] Cf. especially Wessén, *Namn och Bygd*, IX, 103 ff.

settlements in England. In Man, Scandinavian runic monuments dating from the eleventh century are numerous. One inscription in curious deteriorated Norse, however, is preserved in Lancashire, the well-known Pennington tympanon. It seems to date from the twelfth century. It proves that a Scandinavian language was spoken in Furness at least as late as 1100. The inscriptions on a dial-stone found at Skelton in Cleveland (date eleventh century) and on a stone in Thornaby-on-Tees church (from about 1100) are badly mutilated and do not tell us much about the Scandinavian dialect in north Yorkshire, but they seem at least to point to a late survival of the Scandinavian language in these districts. Also a Scandinavian inscription on the wall of Carlisle cathedral, dating, it is said, from the twelfth century, is preserved.

Place-names may tell us something of value when the material has been fully collected. Here only a few scattered notes can be given.

It is a remarkable fact that in Cumberland, especially in the Carlisle district, there are a number of names in -by with a Flemish or Norman personal name as first element, as Allonby, Aglionby, Lamonby, Rickerby, 'the by of Alein, Aguillon, Lambin, Richard.' These names arose as a consequence of the Flemish settlements in the time of William Rufus, after the conquest in 1092. These names cannot have been coined by Flemings or Normans, as Lindkvist thinks. Even if there are some names in -by in Normandy, the word by had doubtless gone out of use among the Normans long before the Norman Conquest. The names were not given by the Flemish or Norman settlers, but by the earlier inhabitants of the district. They show that by was still a living place-name element, and this seems tantamount to saying that Scandinavian was still spoken round Carlisle about 1100. The Scandinavian runic inscription at Carlisle tells us that there is no improbability in this theory. The same is the explanation of the names Halnaby and Jolby in north Yorkshire, if they are really so late as has been recently suggested by Col. Parker[1]. Jolby, of course, has as first element the Norman name *Johel*, and cannot be earlier than about 1100. There is no reason to believe that the names arose much later than about 1100. Jolby must have been in existence about 1170 at the latest. Halnaby was certainly not named from the Halnath de Halnaby, who flourished about 1200. Acharius de Halnaby, who is often mentioned in early sources, must have belonged to an earlier generation, and have flourished about 1175. In the early part of the twelfth century a

[1] *Yorkshire Archaeol. Soc.* Record Series, LXII (Introduction).

Scandinavian language may well have been spoken in some outlying parts of Yorkshire.

Certain sound-developments found in place-names point to a somewhat advanced stage of the Scandinavian language in England. The changes of *eo* to *yo* and *ea* to *ya* to be seen in *York* (from *Eoforwic*) and *Yatstainswad* from *Eadstan-*, found in a twelfth century text, seem to be comparatively late. The curious sound-substitutions to be observed in Shunner Howe, Shawm Rigg (Cleveland district) presuppose a late Scandinavian change. Shunner Howe (from OScand. *Siónarhaugr*) is *Senerhou* in early documents, later *Shunnerhow*. The latter form cannot have developed from *Senerhou*; the only possibility seems to be that it represents a later loan, after Scand. *Sio-* had become *Sjō-*, for which English *Sho-* was substituted. Shawm Rigg is in an early source *Halmerig*. It seems to be an OScand. *Hjalm-hryggr*. Here *Sh-* was substituted for *Hj-* just as it was in *Shetland* for earlier *Hjaltland*. We cannot date these Scandinavian sound-changes, but they presuppose a development of the Scandinavian language in England.

The curious phenomenon found in Norwegian dialects, which consists in the assimilation of a stressed vowel to the unstressed vowel of the next syllable (as *vuku* from *viku*), seems to occur in English place-names. Tarlscough, Tarleton (La), Tharlesthorpe (Y) contain the form *Tharaldr* from earlier *Thoraldr*. In Norway the form *Tharald* has not been evidenced earlier than about 1400. Of course it must be earlier, as it is found in England from about 1188, but it cannot be of very old date.

Alexander Bugge, *Norse Settlements*, p. 14, has pointed out the remarkable phrase *oust in wra* found in a Lincolnshire charter of the time of Henry II. The phrase is slightly Anglicised from Scand. *aust i vrá*. Two very similar cases are found in the Bridlington Chartulary, viz. *Bartholomew Suth in by* (Speeton (Y)) and *Robert de Suthiby* (Edenham (L)). *Suth in by* is an Anglicised form of Scand. *suðr i bý*, 'south in the village,' and *de Suthiby* preserves the original form still better, except that the prep. *de* has been added[1]. Such survivals suggest that a living Scandinavian language had been in use at a not very remote period.

[1] Professor Stenton supplies the further example of *Ralph Smith, Westiby de Saxeby* from the Barlings Chartulary.

CHAPTER V

THE FRENCH ELEMENT[1]

by *R. E. Zachrisson*

I

THE Norman invasion of England marks a new epoch in the history of the English language. The West-Saxon dialect, which had been used for literary purposes ever since the time of King Alfred, lost its importance and was to a great extent superseded by Norman-French, which for nearly three hundred years was the chief vehicle for literary enterprise and also—by the side of English—the conversational language of the higher and middle classes. Among the great body of clerks Latin also was undoubtedly used for these purposes. No discussion is attempted here of the various phases of the struggle between the English and the French languages from which the native idiom emerged victorious, though with such a strong admixture of French words that it could no longer be classified as a pure Teutonic language.

Words of French origin do not constitute, however, a very considerable element in English p.n. When Norman strongholds were erected they were often given French names, as Richmond (Y), the name of which was afterwards transferred to Richmond (Sr) (formerly called Sheen), Pontefract or Pomfret (Y) (*pont freit*, 'broken bridge') for earlier *Tateshale*. The Normans reveal their taste for places with beautiful surroundings in the numerous names beginning with *Beau-*, *Bel-* (in English *Beau-*, *Bew-*, and before certain consonants *Bea-*), such as Bewley (Du), Beaufort (So), Beaudesert (St), Beaumont (*passim*), Beauchief (Db), Belvoir (Lei), Beamish (Du). Many monasteries have French names, e.g. Meaux or Melsa (Y), cf. Meaux in France < Lat. *Meldis*; Rievaulx (Y), 'valley of the Rye'; Grosmont (Mon), 'great hill.' We also find a few other Norman names in most counties, e.g. Devizes (W) (*divisas*, 'boundary lands'); Butterby (Du) (OFr. *beau* and *trouve*, sb. 'find'); Haltemprice (Y), a castle so named from Fr. *haute emprise*, 'great undertaking'; The Isle (Du), Capel (K, Sf), Caple (He), Moat (W).

Norman place-names

---

[1] All early forms are printed in italics. The figure 1 after a form indicates that it is of pre-Conquest date, 2 = twelfth cent., 3 = thirteenth cent., etc.

Hybrid place-names

Hybrids made up of French and English elements are occasionally met with, e.g. Castle Combe (W), Haltwhistle (Nb) from *haut*, 'high,' and OE *twisla*, 'fork of a river,' DB *Durandestorp* (Lei). More often a French name is added denoting ownership, as in Stoke Mandeville (Bk), Hurstmonceaux (Sx), containing the family name *de Moncels*, Bridgwater (So), *Brugeswalteri* 3[1], 'Walter's bridge,' Amport (Ha) < *Anne Port*.

Norman substitutions

It sometimes happens that an English element is replaced by a French word related in either sense or sound, e.g. Belleau (L), for earlier *Helgelo* DB; -*mond* (OFr. *mont, mond*, 'hill') for -*mouth* or -*mot*, 'meeting of rivers,' as in Jesmond (Nb), *Jessemuth* 3, Beckermonds (Y) < *Bekermote* 2; -*ville* for -*well*, -*feld* (-*veld* in the south of England), as in Wyville (L) < *Wydewell* 4, Enville (St) < *Efnefeld* 2. Sometimes such modifications are confined to the early spellings, as when -*tot* is written for -*toft*, -*mareis* for -*merse*, 'marsh,' -*tuit, -tuoit* for -*thwaite*, -*hoi* for -*how, -hoo*.

The chief result, however, of the Norman influence consisted in the alteration of the phonology of already existing place-names. Before proceeding to a discussion of such changes, attention may be drawn to certain features in accidence and word-formation tending to prove to what a great extent the forms of English place-names had been assimilated to the rest of the AFr. vocabulary.

Norman suffixes

In Hampnett (Gl), Westhampnett (Sx) and in early forms such as *Wicmaret* DB = Wickmere (Nf), *Wivelescomet* DB = Wiveliscombe (So), *Bihamel* 2 for Little Bytham (L), and probably also in *Aswicktoftine* (L), now lost, a French diminutive suffix has been added after the pattern of similar formations in Normandy, such as Dannet, La Houlette, Flamanvillette, Tourplin. Here may also belong ME *Cernel*, etc., for Cerne (Do), cf. *Londel* in Normandy. The Norman suffix -*(i)ere* appears in Miserden (Gl), *Musardere* 3, so named from its Domesday lord, Hascoit Musard, a parallel to such usual formations as *Quettier*, *Quetterie* and *Torouddiere* in Normandy. The French preposition *de*, usual in early entries, such as *Richard de Croxtone, William del South*, seems to have been kept in Urton or Durton (La) < OE *ofertun* or *uferatun*.

The French nominative ending -*s* is added in *Portesmues* 3 = Portsmouth (Ha), *Bedefons* 2 = Bedfont (Mx), *Windesores* 2 = Windsor (Berks), etc. The interchange of nom. and acc. forms seen in OFr. *tes, tel*, from Lat. *talis, talem*, seems to be reflected in such variants as *Cerne* DB, *Cernel* 2 = Cerne Abbas (Do), *Pevense* 3 and *Pevensel* DB = Pevensey (Sx), *Pefenesæ* 1,

---

[1] See further, Chapter VI.

and *Sweinesel* 3 for Swansea (Glam). Cf. also OFr. *Bristout* and *Bristouz* = Bristol (So), on the analogy of *tous, tout*. The Latinised forms *Cornualliæ* 2 = Cornwall, *Tottonesium* 2 = Totnes (D), etc., give rise to French formations such as *Cornwaille* 2, *Toteneis* 3, found frequently both in English and French chronicles[1].

The French definite article *le, la* could be prefixed to any place-name containing words in appellative use, as in *La Fairok*, 'the beautiful oak' = Farock (So), *La Blakebrok* = Blackbrook (Db), *La Doune* = Down (K), Lappal (Wo) from earlier *Lappole*, i.e. 'the pool.' *Le* or *la* in this function merely translates the English article, which still lingers on in many p.n. consisting of words in common use, e.g. The Down (Ha), *Ladone* DB, The Low (Wo), The Heugh (Nb), etc. Somewhat more restricted was the use of *le* in descriptive additions to p.n., such as Chester-le-Street (Du), 'the chester on the Roman Road,' Mareham-le-Fen (L), Hamble-le-Rice (Ha), i.e. 'in the brushwood.' The origin of these forms is clearly seen in such early entries as *Thornton in the More* and *Thornton on the More*, by the side of *Thornton in Mora*, *Thornton the More*, and *Thornton le More*, and in such modern variants as Chapel-en-le-Frith and Chapel-le-Frith (Db), Hutton-le-Hole and Hutton-in-the-Hole (Y). Thornton-le-Moor is due to ellipsis or shortening of the fuller form *Thornton en* (or *in*) *le More*, where *in* and *le* are mere translations of the corresponding English words 'in,' 'on' and 'the.' This AFr. formula has survived to the present day in three or four score of names. By some popular notion *le*, later on, came to be looked upon as a preposition with the sense of 'on,' 'with,' or 'by,' and appears in this function in Preston-le-Skerne (Du) on the r. Skerne, St Peter-le-Poor, 'the church of the poor friars,' St Mary-le-Bow, built on arches or 'bows' of stone. In Marylebone *le* was added as a mere ornament, long after the original name Tyburn had been altered to *Maryborn* in commemoration of the church dedicated to St Mary, and in order to avoid unpleasant associations with the dreaded place of execution which once stood near the present Marble Arch.

Far greater is the influence which French has exercised on the forms of English names and p.n. Fully to appreciate the nature and extent of this influence we should try to picture

Use of le *in place-names*

Use of French

---

[1] These are to be kept apart from official Latin forms, such as *Bristollum* 2, *Bristolia* 4 = Bristol < *Brycgstow* 1, 'the place near the bridge,' which occur almost exclusively in early Latin records. The pronunciation of *l* in Bristol is due to the spelling, and did not become general until the eighteenth century.

ourselves in the England of the Norman and Angevin kings, when French was the language of fashion, learning and officialdom, known and spoken by every one who held or coveted a social position. Let us try and imagine the part played by French in a town of importance, such as Oxford in the late thirteenth century. All instruction in schools was given in French and as a rule by French teachers. The French element among the clergy was strong. Nearly all the highest dignitaries of Church and State—earls, bishops, abbots, judges and sheriffs, as well as a great many minor officials—were Frenchmen by birth or origin. In the town there resided many influential French burghers. There were also Frenchmen in humbler walks of life—soldiers, tradesmen and artisans. The surrounding country could glory in monasteries and abbeys which lay as thick as 'leaves in Vallombrosa.' Norman landowners lived in castles or manor-houses, but many of the farmers or small landowners were likewise of French descent[1]. For nearly three centuries after the Conquest French was spoken, by the side of English, not only by men and women of a high social position, but also by the middle classes and even considerably after that time it was looked upon as the more fashionable and refined of the two languages[1].

Influence on pronunciation   Naturally the Normans were bound to try and pronounce the names of the places which they occupied, and their vain attempts to reproduce the English sounds have left permanent traces in the phonology of many of the present-day names.

To begin with, unfamiliar sounds, or combinations of such, were replaced by others which the Normans knew from their own language, as in *Canute* for *Knut*, or in Cannock (St) for *Knock*. Later on, when the p.n. had been introduced into French speech, they were subject to the same changes which operated in ordinary French words, such as the dropping of *s* before *t*, in *-ceter* from *-cestre*. Orthographically the *s* remains in *Gloucester*, but has been lost in *Exeter*, which was formerly spelt *Excestre*.

The use of a few forms, such as *Londres* for *London*, and *Nicole* for *Lincoln*, seems to have been as a rule confined to French documents, but many passed from French into English speech, evidently because of the prestige which the French language enjoyed. The fact that the majority of English p.n. were recorded for the first time in Latin documents written by Anglo-French clerks likewise helped to lend authority to

---

[1] For further details see Vising, *Anglo-Norman Language and Literature*, Oxford, 1923, and P. Shelley, *English and French in England*, 1066 *to* 1100, Philadelphia, 1921.

the French forms. Moreover large areas in medieval England were held in fee not only by individual Normans but also by churches, monasteries, and other ecclesiastical institutions, and it was not unnatural that the manner of pronunciation used by the Norman lords and ecclesiastics should be adopted by the villagers. Another circumstance which helped to establish and support the French forms was that a great number of p.n. were also used as family names—a custom introduced by the Normans.

The French forms have often been victorious in the names *Distribu-* of places which played an important political or ecclesiastical *tion* part and in the population of which the French element was well represented. Instances to the point are the p.n. in *-ce(s)ter* for *-chester*, including Worcester, Leicester, Gloucester, Exeter, Cirencester. On the analogy of these the *-cester* forms have also survived in the names of many insignificant places, such as Frocester (Gl), Rocester (St), Craster (Nb). Cf. also Nottingham for *Snotingeham*, Salop for Shropshire, Salisbury for *Saresberie* (cf. *Sarum*), Jarrow for *Yarrow*, Durham from earlier *Dure(s)me* for *Dunelm*, *Dunholm*, Cambridge for *Grantebrige*. When the French forms have carried the day in the names of smaller places there was often in the village or its immediate neighbourhood a Norman castle, monastery, or manor-house, whose inmates set the fashion to the humbler villagers. This will account for the present pronunciation of Tutbury (St) for *Stutesberia*, Cerne Abbas (Do) for *Cherne*, Chatteris (C) for *Chateric*, Cannock (St) for *Cnoc*, Jervaulx (Y) for *Yorevallis* etc.

The French fashion in surnames has certainly turned *Wyde-welle* into Wyville (L) and the suffix *-feld* (Southern English *-veld*) in many p.n., e.g. Turville (Bk) and Enville (St), into *-ville*[1]. It has also helped to establish such French forms as *-cester*, *-ceter* for *-chester*; *-eie*, *-ey* for *-hethe*, cf. Stepney (Mx), *Stebenheth* and Dumphrey, pers. name < OE *Dōmfrið*; *t* for *th* in *Thur-* and *Thor-* names, cf. Torrisholme (La) < *Thoroldes-*, *Turoldesholm* and Turrel, pers. name < *Thurold*; *ail-* for *æthel-*, cf. Aylmerton (Nf) < *Aethelmǣrtūn* and Aylmar, pers. name < *Aethelmǣr*.

It seems as if the French forms were specially likely to prevail in the names of hundreds and administrative divisions which would be in official use, such as Riding (Y), Tring (Herts), Hinckford (Ess), Diss (Nf).

Hiz, the name of a small river in Herts, *-aun* for *-an* in

----

[1] In the earliest records the suffix is almost invariably *-well, -feld* in the p.n. but *-ville* in the corresponding pers. names.

r. Maun (Nt), Staunton, etc., as well as a good many instances of *le* in modern names, such as Chester-le-Street, may be due to a comparatively recent revival of the OFr. forms.

No special reasons—apart from general considerations—can be adduced for the victory of the French forms in several p.n., such as Turnworth (Do) for *Thorneworth*, Wing (Bk) for *Wit(e)hunge*, or for their persistent early occurrence in others as in *Cedre* for Cheddar (So), *Flessing* for Fletching (Sx), but closer investigations may reveal that many of these places were situated near a Norman centre or held by prominent Norman tenants[1].

When all the available evidence as to French settlements in England has been collected and sifted it will be possible to give a definite opinion upon the geographical distribution of the French element and indicate the particular areas in which the French influence was centred, but even then it will undoubtedly appear that the frequency of the French forms is a chronological rather than a geographical question. To judge by the material at hand it seems as if this influence had been particularly strong in the counties near London, but also in some parts removed from the centre, such as Gl and certain northern counties.

It is sometimes extremely difficult to tell if the alterations in a name are due to French or dialectal English sound-change. It may be found helpful to make the following distinctions. If some sound-changes which may be AFr. are confined to the early records (eleventh to thirteenth century) and moreover occur in different parts of England they are likely to be due to French influence. It may be objected that the local pronunciation of p.n. is more faithfully represented in the earliest records and that attempts may have been made at a later time, say after 1250, to normalise the spelling, but I am not convinced that such an assumption is correct. The combined evidence of the earlier spellings speaks in favour of a slow decrease in the French forms, parallel with the decay of French as a spoken language in England.

The first traces of French influence on English nomenclature are found in the names on coins struck by French moneyers from the Continent. Names and p.n. in the E-MS. of the Anglo-Saxon Chronicle, written after the Conquest, likewise exhibit such forms. This influence culminates in DB, where English

---

[1] This was actually the case with the little village of Whissonsett (Nf), *Wychingsete*. At Staunton (Nt) there lived an important family of Norman origin taking its surname from the place and continuing in the male line from the twelfth to the eighteenth century.

p.n. are recorded by French clerks on the oral evidence of English and French jurors chosen from the inhabitants of the various hundreds. An examination of certain of the maps in the excellent *Victoria County Histories* almost gives the impression that we are not in England but in Normandy where, a hundred or a hundred and fifty years earlier, the Scandinavian names underwent very much the same changes as in England. Practically all records of the twelfth century, such as the Pipe Rolls, *Documents preserved in France,* the *Red Book of the Exchequer,* are likewise interlarded with French forms. In the next century, as in the *Testa de Nevill* (or *Book of Fees*) and the Hundred Rolls, the Patent and Close Rolls, the French forms became rare and after the fourteenth century they are on the whole confined to p.n. in which they have been kept to the present day.

Before proceeding to a detailed discussion of phonology one may lay down two principles which are indispensable for a correct appreciation of the AFr. influence on the early spellings of English p.n.

(i) The evidence of such forms as occur only in DB should *DB forms* not, unless supported by obvious analogies, be trusted against the combined evidence of later forms, especially such as are derived from twelfth century sources, the chief reasons being not only the fanciful and inconsistent spellings in this record, but also the fact that all the MSS. of Domesday Book are copies of original returns which no longer exist.

The following few examples selected from a very large number of available instances will serve to prove the correctness of this principle: *Augustburne* DB = Eastburn (Y), *Estbrunne* 3 (ON *austr*, OE *ēast*); *Ledecestre* DB = Leicester, OE *Legraceaster*; *Nigravre* DB = Nether Avon (W); *Elmundewic* DB = Chelmick (Sa), in all later records *Chelmundewyk*; *Sextone* DB = Sefton (La), otherwise *Sefftun, Sefton,* etc.; *Acrer* DB = Altcar (La), otherwise *Altekar,* etc.; *Sulverton* DB = Swinnerton (St), otherwise *Swinaferton, Swinforton,* 'the farm near the swine ford.' Such early thirteenth century spellings as *Silverton, Soulverton* show that the erroneous DB forms were occasionally employed in other records of a later date.

(ii) No changes should be put down to French influence unless they are evidenced from spellings in early records. Even then, as a rule, we expect to find an interchange of French and English forms[1].

---

[1] The Exchequer and Exon. MSS. of DB are, according to the unanimous opinion of English experts, contemporary transcripts, probably copied several times, of the original returns and consequently

H

II

We may now proceed to give a more detailed account of the various changes to which English p.n. were subjected in early times when they were really loan-words in Anglo-French. As has already been pointed out these changes were of two kinds:

(i) An unfamiliar English sound or sound-combination was altered to suit the Norman pronunciation. This we may call **French sound-substitution.** Such changes took place immediately after the Norman invasion.

(ii) In their use as loan-words, the English p.n. were subjected to the same linguistic changes as took place in the AFr. language itself during the period of more than two hundred years when it was spoken as an independent dialect in England. This is **French sound-development.**

For practical reasons it will be advisable not to make any clean-cut distinctions between these two kinds of sound-development, but to treat together changes which for phonological reasons ought to be treated together[1].

The first and most important section will be devoted mainly to such changes as have permanently affected the pronunciation of a considerable number of modern names.

1. **The Anglo-French pronunciation of the English sound-combinations che, chi in -chester, Chippenham, Matching, -ich** in *Norwich,* **ca-, cha-** (OE ca, cea, cæ) in *Canterbury, Chadwick,* etc.

With the possible exception of a few isolated words, such as *chief < caput, cheval < caballum,* the early Norman dialect in its standard form did not possess the sound-combination *che, chi* [ʧe, ʧi] in an *initial* position. In such words as 'city,'

belong to the end of the eleventh century—a fact of very great importance from a linguistic point of view.

It should also be pointed out that the DB spellings may at times exhibit southern forms of p.n. in the north of England. Thus *a* appears for ON *ei* in *Bradebroc* DB = Braybrook (Nth), otherwise *Bray-* from ON *breiðr; Bradeuuelle* DB = Braithwell (Y), *Braythewell(e); Gadintone* DB = Geddington (Nth), *Geytington* 2–4, from ON *Geiti,* pers. name. Further, *sc* or *s* is often written for Scand. *sk.* An alternative explanation of such forms is suggested in Chapter IV.

[1] For additional instances of AFr. influence on English p.n. and a more detailed discussion of the various aspects of it, the reader is referred to the brief bibliography given at the end of this summary survey. The bulk of the material discussed in the sequel is derived from my earlier writings on the subject, with such corrections and revisions as have been considered necessary.

'cellar,' *c* was pronounced as [ts][1]. For this reason *che* and *chi* in English p.n. were pronounced by the Normans as [tse], [tsi] which were soon simplified to [se], [si][2].

This French pronunciation still prevails in a number of names containing *-chester* < OE *ceaster*. About seventy modern English p.n. contain *-chester*, and of these some sixteen appear in a French garb. This fact, in conjunction with the existence of early alternative forms such as *Chirenchestre* and *Cyren-cestre*, *Glouchestre* and *Gloucestre*, and spellings such as *Mat-singes*, *Witcingaham*, *Linz* (*v. infra*), where *ts*, *tc*, *z* indicate the early Norman pronunciation [ts] for *ch*, prove that we are concerned not only with Norman spellings but also with a Norman pronunciation, distinct from the English one, as in Gloucester, Leicester, Worcester, Cirencester (Gl), Bicester (O), Alcester (Wa). The majority of these names are now pro-nounced, at least locally, with two syllables: *Gloster*, *Bister*, etc. From the middle of the twelfth century the names occur with such spellings as *Glouceter*, *Leyceter*, *Worceter*, *s* having been dropped before *t* owing to the same phonetic tendency that changed early French *estre* and *hospital* into *être* and *hôpital*.

In Robert of Gloucester's Chronicle *Wyrceterre* rhymes with *better*. The intermediate form is seen in such modern spellings as *Exeter*, *Wroxeter* and *Mancetter*. The subsequent shortening or syncopation of *Gloucester* to *Gloster*, etc. (cf. Craster (Nb) < *Craucestre*, and *Lester*, *Wurster* used as surnames), is in accordance with well-known phonetic laws. The present tri-syllabic pronunciation of Exeter, Mancetter, Wroxeter is in all probability due to the spelling[3].

The French forms have also been kept in Cippenham (Bk), *Cippenham* 3, *Chippenham* 3 (< OE *Cipa* p.n.) and Cerne Abbas, Nether and Upper Cerne (Do), Cerney Wick, North

---

[1] Words of the type *chisel*, *cherry* are of comparatively late occurrence in English, and seem to have been looked upon as vernacular or less polite forms in early Norman.

[2] In DB and the earliest records the spellings *ce*, *ci* are fairly regularly used to represent the combinations [tse], [tsi] (which were substituted for English *ch* in *-chester*, *Chippenham*, etc., whereas *che*, *chi* are written for the hard *k* in *kill*, *kettle*.

[3] To assume loss of *s* owing to dissimilation is unnecessary and im-probable. The only similar case is Osbaldeston (La) < OE *Ōsbeald* pers. name, pronounced locally as [ɔˑbistn], where the loss of *s* is due to the accumulated consonants. It is only natural that words like *Gloucester*, with such a wide circulation both as p.n. and pers. names should be subjected to later French influence. Moreover *s* is lost or added in several other cases where dissimilation is out of the question, as in *Horncatre* for Horncastle (L), *Glatinbergère* (Mousket) for Glastonbury.

and South Cerney (Gl). All these, as well as Cirencester (Gl), from British *Caer Ceri*, in OE *Cirenceaster*, have probably been named after the rivers Churne and Cerne on which they stand. The Churne appeared in OE as *Cirnea*. The French forms are very persistent in many other names, e.g. Churchill (O), *Cercelle* DB, 2–4; Chertsey (Sr), *Certes(e)y(e)* DB, 3–5, *Ceorotesig* 1; Chittern (W), *Cettre, Cettra* 2–5, *Chytterne* 3; Cheddar (So), *Ced(d)re* DB, 3–5, *Ceodre* 1.

In a medial position the early Norman dialect had both *ts* and *ch* [tʃ], at least before *e*, as in *lecher* < *leccare, sace* and *sache* < *sapiat, manche* < *manica, lance*. It is therefore probable that in English p.n. of the same phonetic structure [ts] was used before *i*, whereas both [ts] and *ch* [tʃ] may have occurred before *e*.

Before *i* the AFr. forms have been kept in Messing (Ess), 'the settlement of the *Mæccingas*' < OE *Mæcca*, pers. name, whereas the neighbouring Matching exhibits the true English form. The two names occur in early spellings as *Matcinge* or *Metcinges* DB, *Macinges* 3, *Macchinge* 3, etc.; Whissonsett (Nf), *Witcingkeseta* DB, *Wychingsete* 3 < OE *wīcing* (cf. Witchingham in the same county); Whissendine (R), *Wichingedene* DB, *Wyssenden* 4; Dissington (Nb), *Dichintuna* 2, *Discintune* 2, 'the farm of the Dicingas.'

Many p.n. exhibit numerous early French spellings, e.g. Latchingdon (Ess), *Lacin-, La(s)cendon* 3, 4, 'the hill of the Læcingas' < OE *Læce*, pers. name; Bletchingley (Sr), *Ble(s)-cingele(ye)* 3, 4, 'the *leah* of the Bleccingas' < OE *Blæcca*, pers. name; Fletching (Sx), *Flescinges* DB, *Flessing* 3, possibly a tribal-name allied to OHG *Flaco*.

Before *e* the French pronunciation seems to have been kept in Diss (Nf), also the name of a Hundred, *Dice* DB, 2, 3, *Disce* 3, 4 (if the basis is OE *dīc*), and in Lintz Ford (Du), *Lince* 2, *Linz* 3, *Lyncheclouhe* 4, 'lynch,' cf. such early spellings as *Circelenz* DB = Church Lench (Wo) < OE *hlenc*, a variant of *hlinc*; *Cerzhulle* 2 = Churchill (O), *Pincebec* = Pinchbeck (L), and *Burbetc(e)* DB = Burbage (W), *Burhbece* 1.

In a final position -*ich* [itʃ] did not exist in early Norman, and its place was therefore taken by [its], [is], spelt -*iz, -is*. The French forms survive in Chatteris (C) < *Chateric*, probably a Celtic name. In early spellings -*wich* often appears as -*wiz*, -*wice*, and -*ditch* as -*dis*.

Initial *ca* and *cha* [ka], [tʃæ] were rendered promiscuously by *ca, cha, ca, ce*, in accordance with the interchange in early Norman in such words as *camp* and *champ, chaval, caval, ceval* (cf. English *chase* and *catch, cattle* and *chattels*), e.g. *Chadeledona* and *Cadeledone* = Cheldon (D), 'the hill of Ceadela'; *Cetriz, Catriz, Chateriz* = Chatteris (C). This interchange has not affected the modern pronunciation of the p.n. in question.

The treatment of OE [ʧ] in the earliest AFr. records may be summed up in the following way:

In positions where early Norman only possessed [ts], this sound was substituted for OE [ʧ]. Where in early Norman [ts] and [ʧ] interchanged, the interchange was transferred to OE words of a similar phonetic type. That [ts] and [ʧ] could easily be substituted for one another is clear from the appearance in later English of [ʧ] as a substitute for [ts], both in loan-words (*etch* < Du. *etsen*, *sketch* < Du. *schets*), and in native words (*Porchmouth* for Portsmouth (Ha), Pytchley (Nth) for earlier *Pyghtesle*).

2. Difficult initial sound-combinations are altered so as to suit the AFr. pronunciation.

Combinations with s + a consonant are altered in three different ways: (i) s is dropped, cf. Fr. *tockfisch* and *stockfisch*, (ii) a so-called prosthetic *e* is prefixed to *s*, cf. Fr. *e(s)crire* < *scribere*, (iii) a vowel (svarabakhti) is inserted between *s* and the following consonant, cf: Fr. *semaque* < *smake*, *senau* < *snauw*. Such a vowel seems only to be used between *s* and a voiced consonant, the reason being that at the time of the Norman conquest *s* was still pronounced before a voiceless consonant (k, p, t), but was being lost before voiced consonants (l, m, n, r, etc.), cf. *beast* < OFr. *beste*, but *blame* from OFr. *blasmer*.

In the following p.n. s has been dropped in the AFr. pronunciation: Nottinghamshire, Nottingham, *Snotingaham, -scir* 1, *Notingeham* 2; Tutbury (St), *Stutesberia* 2, *Toteberie* DB, 'Stut's *burh*[1].'

Forms with a prosthetic e added: *Estretone* DB = Stretton (St); *Esc(h)ardeburg* 3 = Scarborough (Y).

Forms with a svarabahktic vowel inserted: *Senelestun* DB = Snelson (Ch); *Selungesbi* DB = Slingsby (Y); *Selegile* 3 = Sleagill (We); *Sinitretone* DB = Snitterton (Db).

---

[1] In many early forms s is sporadically lost or added:

(i) Loss. *Notintone* DB, Sneinton (Nt), *Snotinton* 2. The French form still appears in Notindon Place in Sneinton; *Lafford* 2–5 = Sleaford (L), *Sltowaford* 2; *Lingeby* 3 = Slingsby (Y), *Slengesby* 3; *Tochestone* DB = Staughton (Hu).

(ii) Addition. *Esledes* DB = Leeds (K); *Stabelei* DB = Tabley (Ch); *Sperston* 3 = Epperstone (Nt).

The same interchange also occurs in a medial position. *Chileborneford* 2 = Chesilborne (Do); *Gowberkirche* 3 = Gosberton (L) < OGer. *Gausbert*, pers. name; *Meslingues* 3 = Malling (K); *Cameslingeham* DB = Cammeringham (L).

The combination shr [ʃr] is replaced by ser, sir, etc. (cf. Fr. *saloupe*, *chaloupe* < *sloep*) *Siropesberie* DB, *Sciropescire* DB, *Salopisbur*, 3, *Sillop* 3, *Salopscire* 2 = Shropshire, Shrewsbury.

The French forms have been preserved in Salop < *Salopscire*, with *l* for *r*, likewise due to French sound-change (cf. *infra*, 106)[1].

AFr. **ken, kan** are substituted for English **kn** (cf. Fr. *canif* < *knif*, and Canute for *Knut*): Cannock (St), *Chenet* DB, *Chnoc* 2, *Canoc* 2, still appears in a French garb; cf. *Chenares-*, *Kenares-*, *Neresforde* DB, (lost place) in Skelden (Y) < ON *Knǫrr*, pers. name; *Notingeleia* DB, *Nottingleya*, *-laiam*, 2–3 = Knottingley (Y), *Knottingleye* 3, 'the *leah* of the Cnottingas'; *Chenistetone*, *Nistetun* DB = Knighton (D, Berks).

AFr. **war, wer, r, wal** are substituted for English **wr, wl** (cf. Norman *velingue* < *wringla*): *Waragebi* DB = Wrawby (L), 'Wraghi's farm or village' (ODan. *Wraghi*, pers. name); *Weranghe* DB = Wrangle (L), *Wrangel* 4; *Rochecestre* DB = Wrøxeter (Sa), *Wrocenceaster* 1, the Roman *Viroconium*; *Walanceslau* DB = Longslow (Sa), 'Wlanc's barrow' (OE *Wlanc*, pers. name).

3. AFr. **dg** is substituted for English initial [j].

Initial [j], as in Yealand (La), did not exist in AFr., where Lat. *g* had developed into *dg* [dʒ], as in *gentle*, which represents an earlier pronunciation of Fr. *gentil*.

For initial [j] in p.n. the Normans substituted either *dg* (written *j*, *g*[2]) or *i* (as in *Iago*, pron. [iá:go], written *hi*, *i*). Cf. the double treatment in French of *hia* in *hyacinthus* which became either *hyacinthe* or *jacinthe*. This accounts for such early spellings as *Hyolgrave* 3, *Jolgreve* 4 = Youlgrave (Db), i.e. 'Iola's grove' (OE *Iola*, pers. name of English or Scand. origin); *Jalant* DB, *Hieland* 3 = Yealand (La) (v. *ealand*, Part II).

The AFr. pronunciation with *dg* has been kept in the following p.n.: Jarrow (Du), *Gyruum* 1, *Girvum* 2, *Jarwe* 3, *Yarow* 6, *Yarrow* Monastery 8; Jesmond (Nb), *Jesemuth* 3, *Jesmewe* 3, 'mouth of the Ouseburn,' which was formerly called *Yese*; Jagdon (Sa), *Jagedon* 3, *Yakedon* 5, possibly from OE *gēacadūn*, 'cuckoos' down'; Jevington (Sx), *Jevyngton* 3, *Yever(in)ton* 3,

---

[1] The OE forms are *Scrobbesbyrig*, *-scīr*, which regularly developed into Shropshire and *Scrobesburia*, where the difficult combination *-obzb-* was changed into *-owz-*, whence ME *Shrouesbury*, of which Shrewsbury is a mere spelling variant (cf. *shrew* and *shrow*, *shew* and *show*). The local pron. with [ou] is etymologically correct, whereas [u:] is a comparatively recent spelling-pronunciation.

[2] *g* can also be a survival of the OE spellings with ȝ.

which contains some OE name in *Gef-*; Jervaulx (Y), *Jerevall(is)* 3, *Gerevallibus* 3, *Gervaus* 3, 'valley of the Ure[1].'

The majority of p.n. beginning with *y* exhibit spellings with *j*, etc., in the earliest records. In the course of the fourteenth century such spellings became rare, e.g. *Jacheslea* DB = Yaxley (Hu) < OE **Gēaces-lēah* = (possibly) 'cuckoo's *leah*'; *Jernemuth* 3 = Yarmouth (Nf), 'mouth of r. Yare,' a river-name which may be found in Romano-British *Garianno* (abl.) = Burgh Castle[2].

4. The combination an is changed into aun.

AFr. *an* appears as *aun* in the spelling of ME loan-words, but from the beginning of the thirteenth century *aun* is also used to render the French or Norman nasal (cf. *grant, aunt*). At about the same time the *aun* spellings in p.n. begin to crop up. They occur frequently in fourteenth and fifteenth century records and have survived to the present day in twenty odd instances, e.g. Staunton, from OE *stān* + *tūn* (*v.* Part II), spelt in this manner in nine out of fifty modern examples, Saunton (D), 'sand-farm,' Braunston (Nth), 'Brand's farm,' and Brauncewell (L), 'Brand's spring' < ON or OE *Brand*, pers. name. In many of these *aun* is however locally pronounced [æn] and not [aˑn] after the French manner.

On the other hand the long *ā* in Cambridge is best accounted for as due to early AFr. *au*, as in *chamber* < *chaumber*. The OE form was *Grantanbrycg*, 'bridge of the Granta,' which in the French pron. became *Cantebrigge* 2, 3, with loss of *r* (cf. *infra*, 108) and substitution of [k] for [g] (cf. *infra*, 114), and subsequently *Caumbrege* 5, which is the basis of the present form[3].

---

[1] The river appears in early spellings as *Ior* 2, *Eowere* 3, *Yore* 3, 4.

The extremely rare dialectal change of [j] to *dg* ('jicks,' 'jallow') cannot account for such forms as *Jarrow*, etc., where *dg* is the normal Fr. substitute for English [j].

[2] Owing to confusion of letters *L* is often written for *J* in DB and other early records, e.g. *Loletune* DB = Youlton (Y); *Lachesham* 2, *Jakesham* 2, *Iakesham* 2 = Yaxham (Nf).

[3] *Granta* was the original name of the river, the early forms of which faithfully reflect the changes we have traced in the name of the town. Thus it is called the *Cante* in 1370, and Camden, writing in 1586, calls it *Grantum* or *Camum*. The original name of the neighbouring village of Grantchester was *Grantesete*, i.e. 'the settlers on the Granta.' In the thirteenth century *-cete* is written for *-sete*, and a hundred years later *-cete* was turned into *-cester*, on the analogy of the numerous p.n. which end in *-ceter*, *-cester*. The corresponding English form *Grantchester* appears in 1701. Spellings due to false analogy are found in several other names, e.g. Uttoxeter (St), earlier *Uttockeshedre* 2 and Cruwys Morchard (D), 'the orchard' < OE *æt þām ortgearde*.

5. Interchange of liquids (l, n, r).

Interchange of l, n, r, owing to dissimilation or assimilation.

Interchange of *l, n, r*, in two syllables of the same word, which is characteristic of the French language in all periods[1], is reflected in the early spellings of English p.n., especially in DB and records of the twelfth and thirteenth centuries. No definite rules can be laid down for these changes; at the utmost certain general tendencies can be traced. Thus dissimilation (*r-r* > *l-r*) seems to be more usual than assimilation (*r-l* > *r-r*), and cases where one of two consecutive *r*'s or *n*'s is changed into *l* are particularly frequent. Mishearing has undoubtedly played an important part, the entries in DB being often taken down on oral evidence. Some changes may have been caused by association with words known to the Normans from their own country, as when Bolmer, 'Bula's pond' or 'bull pond' in Falmer (Sx) appears in DB as *Bergemere, Burgemere* (cf. OFr. *berg* and *bourc*), or Ingoldmells (L), 'Ingvald's sand-hills' (OSw. *Ingvald*, pers. name) as *Guldesmere* (cf. OFr. *mere* < *mare*). The appearance of *r* for *n* and vice versa, as in *Estarforda* DB = Stanford (Nf), or *Kenebroc* 2 = Carbrooke (Nf), *Kerbrok* 3, 4, may sometimes be accounted for as a scribal error (*n* and *r* being much alike in the MS. of DB), although such an interchange also occurs in French p.n. as in Marville < *Manulfivilla*.

The AFr. forms have prevailed only in a few cases: Salisbury (W), *Searoburg* 1 (an OE remodelling of Romano-British *Sorbiodunum*), *Saresbury, -buria* 2–8, *Salesberia* 2; Salopia or Salop from earlier *Scropsire*, in which the combination *shrop*, which did not exist in AFr., was altered to *sarop*, whereupon **Saropscire* was turned into *Salopscire* (cf. *supra*, 104). Similar early forms are *Bilichangram* and *Belissolt* DB = Birchanger (Ess) and Bircholt (K), the suffixes being respectively *hangra* and *holt* in these two names. Cf. also *Herelou* 3 = Belleau (L), *Helgelo* DB < ON *Helgi*, pers. name (*v. supra*, 94); *Nicol* 2, a usual early French name for Lincoln; *Clolle* DB = Church Knowle (Do).

A similar interchange of *l, n, r* is found in several English dialects, though it is mainly confined to foreign words in the vernacular. Cf. *calavan* for *caravan*, *paltridge* for *partridge*, *synable* for *syllable*. Consequently p.n. forms of this kind which occur only or mainly in late records may be due to dialectal

---

[1] Cf. the English word *colonel* pronounced as *kurnel* <OF *coronel* for *colonel*, and such forms as *Boulogne* <*Bononia*, *gonfalon* <*gonfanon* and the following spelling variants in DB, *Morel-Morinus, Columbels-Columbers, Helion-Herion*.

sound-change. Thus Lindsey (Sf) is *Lillesey, Lelleseye*, 'Lil's island' (OE *Lil*, pers. name) in all early spellings down to the fourteenth century (*Linsey* Valor Eccl.). According to Hope, Alderwasley (Db), *Alrewasleg* 3 and Needham (Sf) are pro nounced locally as 'Annerslee' and 'Leedum[1].'

Dissimilation of n to r or l by m in the following syllable.

ME *Dunelm* 2, a weakened form of OE *Dunholm* (1056), was changed by the Normans to *Durelme* 2, *Dureaume* 2 (cf. *infra*, 113), *Duresme* 4, which in an English spelling garb became *Durham* 3. An exact parallel is offered by the French pronunciation of Zaandam in Holland, as *Saardam*. Cf. also *Lerham* DB = Lenham (K), *Leanaham* 1, and *Winesamstede* DB = Wilshampstead (Beds) < OE *Will(a)*, pers. name.

Interchange of unstressed le, re, ne.

This interchange, which is very usual in Fr. (cf. *Londres* < *Londinium, havne, havele* and *havre* < *hafen, title* and *titre, idle* and *idre* < *idolum*), was transferred to many early forms of English p.n.:—*Witrehame* 2 = Wittenham (Berks), *Wittanhamme* 1 < OE *Witta*, pers. name; *Sidreham, Sidelham* DB = Sydenham (D) < OE *sīd*, 'broad' or **Sīda*, pers. name; *Avere* DB = Avon, *Afen* 1. Especially when confined to later records, this change may be due to dial. English sound development. Cf. dial. *crupper* < *cripple, channer* < *channel*. *Appinknoll* 5 = Apperknowle (Db), *Apelknoll* 4[2]. Sometimes the change may be caused by popular etymology as when *Lunde(r)torp* DB <

---

[1] Interchange of *-ling, -ring, -ning* is very usual. *Walintune* DB = Warrington (La), 'farm of the Wæringas' (OE *Wǣr-* in pers. names), *Silingeham* DB = Sheringham (Nf), 'home of the Sciringas' (OE *Scīra*, pers. name), *Rauelinc-, Raverincham* DB = Raveningham (Nf), 'home of the Hræfeningas' (OE *Hræfen*, pers. name), *Avelinges* 2 = Avening (Gl), 'settlers near the Avon.' The changed form has been retained in Shellingford (Berks), *Scaringaford* 1, *Sellingeford* 2, 'ford of the Scæringas' (OE **Scæra*, pers. name), which may be due to Fr. influence (cf. *Frasnines* 2 = Fralignes, Aube, and OFr. *garin-, galin-, ganigal*), although an interchange of this kind is not foreign to English dialects, cf. *eveling, everin, evening*, etc.

In early AFr. spellings *l, n, r* are sometimes confused, apart from the proximity of the liquids: *Devenis* DB = Dewlish (Do); *Sperehou* DB = Spelhoe Hundred (Nth); *Cerchede* DB = Chelsea, *Cælichyðe* 1. The change of *nm* to *lm* or *rm* is English, cf. ME *elmyes* for *enemies*. *Kinemersdon* 3 = Kilmersdon (So) < OE *Cynemǣr*, pers. name. Walham Green (Mx) was originally *Wendon* 3, *Wanden* 3, which was turned into *Wanam* 6, cf. *Lunnon* for *London*; *Wormleytone* 3 = Wormleighton (Wa), *Wilmanlehtune* 1.

[2] In Apperknowle and in many other late cases this interchange may also be due to uncertainty as to the proper graphic rendering of a liquid that had been lost in the local pronunciation of the name. Cf. Prittlewell (Ess), *Prituwella* 2, *Putenewel* 3, *Preterwell* 5.

ON *lundar*, gen. sg. of *lund*, was altered at a very late date to Londonthorpe (seventeenth century). Most instances of *n* for *r* (*l*) in an unstressed position are, however, likely to reflect a sound-change of the same kind as that found in *messenger* < *messager*. Cf. Ashmansworth (Ha) and Rickmansworth (Herts) from earlier *Aescmeresweorþ* 1 and *Rikemaresworth* 4.

Loss or addition of r.

Dissimilatory loss of *r* was usual in OFr., but it is not unknown even in English. It is difficult to decide if such forms as *Chelesworth* 3 = Chelsworth (Sf), *Ceorleswyrth* 1, are due to English or Fr. sound-development. A fairly certain Fr. instance is Cambridge < *Grantebrige* 2, which exhibits other AFr. features as well (*v. supra*, 105); likewise early loss of *r* in a stressed syllable apart from dissimilation, as in *Chicheham* DB = Kirkham (La), and addition or loss of *r* finally, especially after stops and dentals, as in *Dertre* DB = r. Dart (D); *Fredrebruge* DB = Freebridge (Nf); *Helnache* DB = Halnaker (Sx) < OE *healfan æcer*, 'half a strip of ploughland'; *Selva* DB = Monksilver (So), cf. OE *Sulfre* as a river-name. In all probability this AFr. feature has remained in Reculver (K), *Raculvre* 3, *Reculf* 1 (the Roman *Regulbium*), which is not likely to be a contraction of *Raculfesceaster*, as has been suggested, supported perhaps by the analogy of the numerous p.n. in Normandy, where the suffix *-iere* has been added to a pers. name (cf. *supra*, 94), and to which there is at least one English parallel, viz. Miserden (Gl), for earlier *le Musardere* 3, 4, formed from the Norman name *Musard* with this suffix.

6. OE [θ] [ð] in the AFr. pronunciation.

Voiceless initial th [θ], as in *thorn*, was not known to the Normans who replaced it by *t*. The AFr. pronunciation has survived in a score or so of p.n. in various parts of England, e.g. Turnworth (Do), *Torneworde* DB, *Thorneworthe* 4; Tormarton (Gl), *Thormerton* 3 < ODa, *Thormar*; Torrisholme (La), *Turoldesholm* 3 < ON *Þóraldr*, pers. name.

The change occurs chiefly in pers. names, which often had corresponding forms in Normandy, seldom in well-known English words. The spellings with *t* are usual in DB and the earliest records, less frequent in the thirteenth and scarce in the fourteenth centuries. The distribution of the forms, locally and in the records, does not support the theory that *t* is due to the Scand. change of [θ] to *t*, which moreover did not take place until *c.* 1375. In a few instances, especially when *r* follows *th*, we may have to reckon with a vernacular soundchange, which at present is characteristic of certain Midl. and N. dialects. Cf. Threo or Treo Wapentake (L), 'three mounds,'

Thrandeston (Sf), dialectally pronounced as *Transon* < ON *Þrandr*, pers. name)[1].

With regard to [θ] **in a final position**, there was in early Norman probably an interchange of voiced and voiceless [ð] and [θ], resulting in the ultimate loss of the consonant, cf. OFr. *cariteth, carited, carite* < *caritatem.* In English p.n. a final *th* is occasionally lost as in *Tockui* DB = Tockwith (Y), *Ba* 3 = Bath (So), *Snay* 3 = Snaith (Y). At a later date the Normans turned [θ] into *t*, as in *Tokwit* 4. When a *t* appears in the present form of a p.n., as in Kellet (La), *Kelleth* 3 < ON *kelda* and *hlið*, or Orsett (Ess), *Horseth* 4 < OE *hǣþ* or *hȳð*, it may also be due to dial. sound-change.

In an intervocalic position there was in early Norman an interchange of forms with voiced *th* [ð], written *d* or *t*[2], and forms in which [ð] had been dropped. Cf. *Scudet* and *Scuet* < Lat. *scutatus, Waard* and *Wadard* < OGer. *Wadard*, pers. name, in DB. In the early records the same interchange appears in English p.n. containing an intervocalic [ð], but at a later date the dental [d] was substituted for [ð]. Cf. OFr. *braon* < OGer. *bradon.*

An excellent illustration of this double treatment of [ð] is offered by the early spellings of names containing Late OE *þriðing* < Scand. *þriðjung*, 'a third part,' denoting divisions of land in L and Y, and in Herts. The Ridings in Y and L appear

---

[1] Especially in the thirteenth and fourteenth centuries *th* is often written for etymological *t*, either as a learned spelling, cf. *Thames, thyme*, or owing to graphic confusion, e.g. *Thoft* for *Toft* < ON *topt*.

[2] This *t*, which is also written for a medial [d] and for both [ð] and [d] in front of liquids, is probably due to graphic confusion, caused by the loss of [ð] < *t* and *d*. The interchange also occurs in French words in DB, e.g. *Matelger* and *Maelger*, OGer. *Madalger*, pers. name, *Scutet* and *Scudet* < Lat. *scutatus, Odburuile* and *Otburgivilla* < OGer. *Autburg*, pers. name. English examples of *t* for [ð]: *Sutinton* 3 = Sodington (Wo) < OE *sūð-*, *Sutrete* DB = Southrey (L) < OE *sūð(e)ra*; *Rute* DB = Routh (Y); *Witme* 4 = Witham (L) < OE *Wiðma*. The rare instances when such a *t* is found in modern names reflect, however, in all probability a hitherto unnoticed dial. sound-change of [ð] > [θ] > [t] before liquids (cf. N.Eng. *hatell* 6, for *athel*); Mattersea (Nt), *Mathersey* 3, 4, 5, *Matersey* 6 < OE *Mǣþere*, pers. name; Cotheridge (Wo), *Coderugge* 3 < OE *Codda*, pers. name. Examples of [t] for [d]: *Peteorde* DB = Padworth (Berks), *Peadanwurðe* 1 < OE *Peada*, pers. name; *Getinge* DB = Geddinge (K), *Geddinc* 1 < OE *Gydda*, pers. name; *Bratewell* 2 = Bradwell (Bk); *Pitretone* DB = Puddletown (Do) < *Pydele* 1, a river-name.

In a similar way *d* is often written for *t*, but such spellings often reflect an English sound-change: *Widintun* DB = Wittington (Wo), *Huitingtun* 1 < OE *Hwīta*, pers. name; *Snodington* 3 = Sneinton (Nt) < OE *Snotingatun*; *Gadintone* DB = Geddington (Nth), *Geytington* 2 < ON *Geiti*, pers. name; Boddington (Gl), *Botintune, -tone* DB, 3, *Bodynton* 4 < OE *Bot(t)a*, pers. name.

in early spellings as *Westthrithing, Westtrying, Westreinge, Suttring, Westriding,* etc. Whereas the modern forms here exhibit *d* (West Riding from *West triding,* with subtraction of *t* < *th* and long *ī,* either due to the spelling or to French vowel-lengthening), the early forms with loss of *th* have carried the day in Tring (Herts), formerly also the name of a Hundred, < *Tredunge* DB, *Treunge* DB, *Trehynge* 4 (*h* for *d* as a hiatus-filler is very usual in early spellings of this type), *Trenge* 3. A variant with initial *th* has been kept in the pers. name *Thring.*

The following modern forms likewise exhibit **loss of inter-vocalic** [ð]: Wing and Wingrave (Bk), *Withunga, Withungrave* DB, *Wiungua* 2, *Wing* 3, *Wengraue* 3 < OE *Weopungum* (MS. *sic*) for *Weoþungum.* Early forms with loss of *th* are very usual, e.g. *Soynthone* 3 = Southington in Selborne (Ha), OE *sūð-*; *Bliemue* 3 = Blyth (Nb), 'mouth of r. Blyth'; *Rue* 3 = Routh (Y) < ON *ruð*; *Cneye* 3 = Knaith (L).

In spite of what has been asserted by several scholars there are no English parallels for the loss of an intervocalic *th* owing to isolative sound-change[1].

Modern forms exhibiting d < [ð] may be due to AFr. influence or to the isolative sound-change of intervocalic [ð] to [d] seen in modern dialects, as in *widdi* < OE *wīðig,* and ME *smyddy, smede* < OE *smiððe, schede* < OE *scǣþ.* Hendred (Berks), *Henreda* 2, *Hennariþ* 1; Roothing or Roding (Ess), *Ro(d)inges* DB, 'the settlement of the Hrothingas'; Fulready (Wa), *Fulrei* DB, OE *fūl* + *rīðig*[2].

[1] A few late instances have come under my notice and should, if genuine, be explained differently; *cloyng* for *clothing* because of *close* < *clothes, tiyng* for *tithing* < 'tith'ns,' with loss of [ð] in front of *n.*

Loss of [ð] and [θ] in front of a consonant may, especially in late instances and when more than one consonant follows, also be due to assimilation, in accordance with English habits of speech: *Orretone* DB = Otherton (St); *Surreia* 2 = Surrey, *Suðregeona* 1; *Hallege* DB = Headley (Ha); Frilsham (Berks), *Frilesham* DB, *Fridelesham* 3 < OE *Friothulf,* pers. name; *Wime* DB, *Wieme* 2 = N. and S. Witham and r. Witham (L); *Robery* 2 = Rothbury (Nb) < ON *Rauðr,* pers. name; *Roumarets* 3 = Rawmarsh (Y), from the same name or *rauðr,* 'red.'

[2] When a consonant follows, the change of [ð] to [d] is in most instances best accounted for as due to English sound-development:—
(i) A general tendency towards turning [ð] and [θ] into *t, d,* especially before open and stopped consonants, e.g. Sudbury (Sf, Wo) and Sudbourne (Sf) containing OE *sūð* and Southwick (Nt), pron. [sudik], Headworth (Du), 'heath-farm.' (ii) Combinatory sound-change of [ð] to [d] before liquids (cf. *fiddle* < OE *fiðele, murder,* etc.): Headley (Wo), 'heath-*leah*'; Widley (Ha), 'withy-*leah*'; Edderacres (Du), *Etheredesacres* 2; Hedingham (Ess), *Hidingham* DB, *Hithingham* 5, *Hedningham* 6, *Henig-* 3; Edington (W), *Ethendune* 3, *Eðandun* 1; Sodington (Wo), *Sodinton* 3, OE *Sūð-.*

Loss of t or d in proximity to liquids, which is usual both in early and modern forms, reflects a tendency towards assimilation found both in English (at least before *l*) and in AFr.: Strelly (Nt)[1], *Straleia* DB, *Stretlee* 2, *Strelley* 3; *Wallinghe Stret* 2 = Watling Street; *Stollant* DB = Studland (Do) < OE *stōd*; Chillington (D), *Chedelington* 5 < OE *Ceadela*, pers. name; *Porrige* DB = Potheridge (D), *Poderigg* 4 < OE *Podda* or *Puda*, pers. name.

In names which from a Norman point of view were pronounced with a final *-ee* a hiatus-filling i often appears between the two vowels (cf. AFr. *espeie* < *espee* < Gk *spatha* and ME *contreie*: *faye*, Mod. Eng. *fay* < OFr. *fae*, *faie* < Lat. *fata*), and at least a dozen such forms have been kept to the present day, evidently because they were easily associated with a similar and very usual suffix, i.e. *-eie* < OE *ēg* and were perhaps also supported by the English pers. names in which Norman *-frei* had taken the place of OE *-friþ* (cf. *supra*, 97): Putney (Sr), *Pottenhethe* 4, OE **Puttan-hȳð*; Childrey (Berks), *Cillanriþe* 1, *Celrea* DB, *Chelrey* 3, *Chelrethe* 3; Chelsea (Mx), *Cealchyðe* 1, *Cerchede* DB, *Chelsehithe* 5, *Chelsaye* 6; Stepney (Mx), *Stibenhede* DB, *Stubhuda* 2, *Stibbehe* 3, '*Stybba's *hȳð*.' In some instances *-ey* may also be due to the analogy of names containing *-ey* < OE *-ēg*[2].

Note. The Norman substitution of *ægel, ail* for OE *æþel* in pers. names, which is common from the time immediately after the Conquest, is perhaps best explained as due to the reduction of *aël* < *æþel* to *ail*[3] (cf. Fr. *aimant* < *adamantem* and *Oilard* DB, *Oirant* DB < OGer. *Odelbert* and

---

[1] Loss of the dental stops *t, d* in compounded *-ing* names, may also be due, at least in part, to a Norman tendency to simplify an unfamiliar sequence of sounds. The unfamiliar *Badinton, Badenton,* etc. were attracted by and assimilated to such groups of words as *Odemar, Todeni* < *Todiniacum*, in which *d* was pronounced as [ð] and subsequently lost in early OFr. e.g. Doynton (Gl), *Didintona* DB, *Doynton* 4 < OE *Dudda*, pers. name; Toynton (L), *Totintune* DB, *Thoyntona* 4 < OE *Totta*, pers. name; Sneinton (Nt), *Notintone* DB, *Snotinton* 2, *Snointon* 4, *Sneynton* 3 < OE **Snotingatun*. The same development has taken place in Taynton (Gl), *Tetintun, Tatintun* DB, and Bainton (Nth, O) < OE **Badingatun*.

In some of these names the unfamiliar Fr. diphthong *oi* was probably replaced by *ei*, a substitution which is also found in the ME forms of many Fr. loan-words, especially in the eastern parts of England.

Loss of *t, d* does not seem to take place in simple *-ing* names, such as Knotting (Beds) or Beeding (Sx), or in a medial position apart from the proximity of liquids, as in Load (So) < OE *lād*, or Rhode (Ha) < OE *rod*.

[2] The interchange of *-ede, -eie* and of *ægel, ail, adel* has given rise to numerous false spellings with *d* for *i, g,* e.g. *Estrede, -rea, -rei* DB = Eastry (K), *Eastrege* 1; *Ledecestre* DB = Leicester (Lei), *Legraceaster* 1; *Nigravre* DB = Nether Avon (W).

[3] A hiatus-filling *i,* is, however, evidenced in AFr. words of the same phonetic type (*baier* < Lat. *badare, loyer* < Lat. *laudare*).

OGer. *Audaramnus). It is not likely that æþel was mechanically replaced by ægel- (from the common OGer. names in Agil-), for pers.
names containing this element were very rare in OE and were in many or
perhaps in all instances, introduced from the Continent, cf. Aylmerton
(Nf), Almartune DB, Aylmerton 3, OE Aeþelmǣr, pers. nameɟ Abbotsley
(Hu), Alboldesle 3, Aylboldelle 3, Addeboldesleye 3, OE Aeþelbeald, pers.
name; Elton (Hu), Adelintune DB, Ailingtona 3, OE *Aeþelingatūn.
When the OE form is missing, the etymology of such p.n. is more or
less uncertain, for in the early spellings there is a hopeless confusion of
the name-elements Aeþel-, Aelf-, Ealh-, and even Eald- and Ead-. Cf.
however the pers. names Aylin, Aylwin <OE Aeþelwine, Aylmer, OE
Aeþelmǣr, Aylward, Aylard <OE Aeþelweard and Aeþelheard.

The changes which OE [θ, ð] underwent in AFr. pronunciation may be summarised as follows.

Initial OE [θ] was rendered by [t], final OE [θ] was dropped
or at a later date rendered by [t]. Intervocalic [ð], or [d] before
liquids, was kept—written t, d, th—or dropped, but at a later
date replaced by [d]. The stops [t], [d]—which often interchange
—might be dropped in compounded names, especially -ing
names, and before liquids. A diphthong ai, ei appears in names
ending in -ee, -ethe and in ægel-, ail- < OE æþel.

III

In this section some AFr. spellings and sound-changes are
dealt with which, so far as our present knowledge goes, have
not as a whole influenced the modern forms of p.n. The bulk
of the material is derived from a collection of forms for a
second part of the writer's Anglo-Norman Influence, etc. At the
present stage one cannot venture to make a clear distinction
between forms which are due to AFr. influence and forms which
might reflect English sound-changes. All the spellings and
forms included here are of frequent occurrence in the early
records.

1. AFr. e, a are written for
(a) OE æ, ea: Catriz, Cetriz 2 = Chatteris (C); Celdefordam,
Scaldefort DB = Shalford (Ess) < OE scealde; Metcinga DB,
Matcinge DB = Matching (Ess), OE Mæcca, pers. n.
(b) OE eo, ē and e, especially before n, l and in an unstressed
position: Rapendune DB = Repton (Db), Hreopandune 1;
Estrecale DB = East Keal (L) < ON kjǫlr; Naton DB = Knee-
ton (Y); Cameshing 2 = Kemsing (K), Cymesinc 1; -dane for
OE denn (usual); cf., however, dial. ME dane.
(c) OE ǣ; Strat(e) for Street, wate for OE hwǣte, etc. may
sometimes also be due to shortening of ǣ to ǎ, to ME dial.
ā < ǣ, or to Latinising.

2. AFr. *e* is written for OE *i*: *Hechelinge* DB = Hickling (Nt) < OE **Hicel*, pers. name; *treding* for *thrithing*, *cherke* for *kirke* (usual).

3. AFr. *e* is written for Early ME *æi*, *ei*, and vice versa: *Medewell* DB = Maidwell (Nth); *Snellewelle* DB = Snailwell (C); *Bene(r)s* DB = Baynhurst (Berks); *cle* for *clæy*; *Aichintuna* DB = Eckington (Wo), *Eccyncgtune* 1.

4. An unstressed *e*, *a* is occasionally dropped or added: *Linehalle* DB = Ellenhall (St); *Stope* DB = Easthope (Sa); *Apedroc* DB = Parrock (Sx).

5. OE [χ] in *cniht*, *hoh*, etc., is often written *c*, *ch* (pronounced as *k*), *s* (especially before *t*) or dropped: *Wit* and *With* DB = Isle of Wight (OE *Wiht*); *Lech* 2 = Lea (Db) < OE *lēah*; *chenist* for 'knight'; *brist*, *birst*, *bret* for 'bright'; *(h)oc* for OE *hōh*.

6. *l* is sometimes dropped, especially before cons., or vocalised: *Weranghe* DB = Wrangle (L): *Stapeford* 2 = Stapleford (Lei); *Elleord* DB, *Audeworth* 3 = Aldworth (Berks); *Beautesford* 3 = Belchford (L), *Beltesford* DB; *feud*, *felle* for 'field'; *Esma(u)rige* DB = Smallridge (D); *Sca(l)dewell* DB = Scaldwell (Nth) < OE *scealde*. Spellings with an unetymological *l* are usual: *Ulpesse* DB = Up Exe (D); *Alsemuda* DB = Axmouth (D), *Axamuða* 1; *Horsteld* 2 = Horstead (Nf).

7. AFr. *s*, *sc*[1] (pronounced as *s*, at least at an early date) are written for OE *sc* (pronounced as in *sh*ine): *S(c)aldeburne* DB = Shalbourne (W); *Siptone* DB = Shipton (O), *Sceaptun* 1. As OE *c* [tʃ] in *ceaster*, etc., was also rendered by AFr. *s*, there is great confusion between OE *sc* [ʃ] and *c* [tʃ] in the early spellings. Thus *s*, *sc*, *c* are written in DB both for [tʃ] and [ʃ]: *Berisout*, *Beriscolt* = Bircholt (K); *Hancese* = Hanchurch (St); *Ece* = Ash (K)[2]. In later records *ch* is frequently written for [ʃ] and *sh* for [tʃ], which may, however, sometimes reflect a dial. sound-change. *Shedeworth* 3 = Chedworth (Gl); *Chelford* 3 = Shelford (C). The change of [tʃ] to [ʃ] before a consonant is certainly dialectal: Wishford (W), *Wich(e)ford* 3, 4; Lashbrook (D, O) and Lashley (Ess), all contain OE *læce*. (See Part II.)

8. OE *w* is sometimes rendered by *g*, *v*, *o* or is lost, especially before *u*: *Gullingham* DB = Willingham (L), *Oistreham* DB

---

[1] The combination *sk* is written *sch* in DB, especially before *e*, *i*, as also in other early documents, though not consistently (cf. *supra*, 100 *n*.): *Schelmeresdale* DB = Skelmersdale (La), but *Scelmertorp* DB = Skelmanthorpe (Y), *Scheltone* DB = Skelton (Y).

[2] The occasional confusion of *c* and *ch*, *sc* and *sch*, *c* and *s* leads to such remarkable spellings as *Cheneffeldam* DB = Shenfield (Ess), *Taschebrok* = Tachbrook (Wa), *Tæceles broc* 1.

= Westerham (K), *soan* for *swan*, *vic* for OE *wīc*, *ude*, *ode* for *wude*, etc.

꒰. A voiced final consonant is unvoiced: *Rincvede* DB = Ringwood (Ha); *Gamillenkeia* 2 = Gamlingay (C); *fort* for 'ford,' *lant* for 'land,' also inverted spellings *fled* for OE *flēot*.

10. Initial *g* and *c* are confused, especially before *r*, *l*, *n*, more seldom initial *t* and *d*: *Gresinga-*, *Cressingham* DB = Cressingham (Nf); Cambridge (C) < OE *Grantanbrycg*; *Glanefel* 3 = Clanfield (O); *Gnolla* 3 = Knolle (Wo); *Gannoc* 3 = Cannock (St); *Dodintun* DB = Totton (Ha).

11. Unstressed *m* is turned into *n* finally after a vowel: *Lidun* DB = Lytham (La) < OE, ON *hlíðum* dat. pl.; *-on*, *-un* for *-um*, *-(h)an* for *-hamm*, *-hām*. But in many Midl. and S. p.n. *-on* for earlier *-um* is due to English sound-change: Coton (C) < OE *cotum* dat. pl.

12. A great many changes reflect a general tendency to reduce heavy combinations of consonants. Thus [*ks*] > [*s*]: *Bessintone* DB = Bexington (Do), *Bousore* DB = Boxford (Berks), *Boxoran* 1; *d, t, n* are dropped or added: *-tof* for *-toft*; *san* for *sand*; *-thor* for *-thorn*; *-hant* for *-han*, *-ham*; *-hest* for *-henst*; *-hest*, *-hert*, *-er(se)* for *-hyrst*, *-herst*; *-gar* for *-ȝeard*, etc. A vowel is inserted; *toren-* for *thorn-*. The combination *ing* in compounds appears as *i*, *in* or is dropped: *Tediworde* DB = Theddingworth (Lei); *Totintune* DB = Toynton (L); *Chenitun*, *Cenetun* DB = Kennington (Berks), *Cenig-*, *Cenintune* 1. Note that DB spellings with *i*, *in*, *ing* in p.n. of this type almost invariably go back to original names in *-ing*, for the weak gen. ending *-an* does not appear as *-in* in DB. Double consonants are simplified in the spellings of the early feudal records, short vowels are sometimes lengthened. The Normans no doubt often pronounced the names with the stress on the last syllable.

13. A genitival or medial *s* is omitted or erroneously inserted: *Claislea* DB = Cleley Hund. (Nth), *Rincteda* DB, Ringstead (Nf).

Summary Bibliography. Many questions concerning the Fr. influence on English p.n. have been incidentally dealt with by Skeat (*Notes on English Etymology*, 471, PN *Hu* 355, etc.), W. H. Stevenson, L. Morsbach, E. Ekwall (*Germanisch-Romanische Monatschrift*, v) and in numerous monographs on p.n. The spellings in DB have been examined by W. Stolze in *Zur Lautlehre der Ortsnamen im DB* (Berlin, 1902). The subject has been dealt with in the following books and papers by the present writer: *A Contribution to the study of Anglo-Norman Influence on English PN* (Lunds Universitets Årsskrift, 1919), *Some Instances of Latin Influences on English PN*, ibid. 1910, in *Studier i modern sprakvetenskap utg. av Nyfilologiska Sällskapet i Stockholm*, vols. v, vi; in *Anglia Beiblatt*, 1917; in *Archiv für das Stud. der n. Spr.* cxxxv; in *Englische Studien*, L, LII; in *Mod. Lang. Rev.* xii.

CHAPTER VI

THE FEUDAL ELEMENT

by *James Tait*

THE feudal element in the place-names of England consists of the Norman or Anglo-Norman additions to our place-nomenclature which arose out of, or at least reflect, the manorial system and military arrangements based upon land that spread over the length and breadth of the country after the Conquest. A few French names that do not come strictly within this definition may be included for the sake of completeness.

The Normans did not impose many new place-names upon the conquered land nor did these always displace English predecessors. Their castles, however, were sometimes planted on unoccupied sites or seemed to demand prouder names than the obscure villages they dominated. Their reforming monks settled by preference in the wilderness. *French place-names in England*

Of four great fortresses along the Welsh border which received French names, two, Montgomery and Caus (Sa), were called respectively after a castle and a district (Caux) in Normandy with which their founders were closely connected. The others, Mold (*Mons Altus, Mohaut*) and Grosmont (Mon), were given names descriptive of their situation, and this is the common type. Greatest of these as a feudal and ecclesiastical centre was the Yorkshire Richmond (*Richemont*), of which its Surrey namesake (formerly West Sheen) is a godchild no older than the reign of Henry VII. Montacute (So), DB *Montagud*, is a Latin form and so is Pontefract (Y), 'broken bridge,' the NFr. form being *Pontfreit* (Shakespeare's *Pomfret*). Both replaced older English names, Bishopston (*Biscopestone*[1]) and *Tateshale*.

The name of another great castle, Belvoir (Lei), belongs to a variety of the descriptive type of which the Normans were very fond and which shows a feeling for natural beauty, rare indeed in English place-names. Appreciation even of wild scenery seems attested by the two Beaudeserts (St, Wa). The gazetteers also record three Belchamps (Ess), two Beaulieus (Ha, Wo), one corrupted to Bewdley, a Beaumanor (Lei), Beauchief (Db), Beauvale (Nt), three Beaurepaires (Ha, Du,

---

[1] DB I, 93 (*Biscobestona, ibid.* IV, 261). The place appears as *Lutgaresberi* in the strange story of the finding of the Holy Cross of Waltham (ed. Stubbs).

I

Db), the two last compressed to Bear Park and Belper, seven
or eight Bellasis (two Du, two Y, Mx, Nb, Nf, Nth), including
the corrupt forms Belsize and Bellasize, and four or five
Beaumonts. They are, of course, of various dates and several of
them were originally names of new monasteries. Rewley
Abbey, Oxford (*de Regali Loco*) and Battle Abbey (Sx), DB
Labatailge, present a rather different type of name, and a less
mundane one than either is illustrated by Vaudey (L), *Vallis
Dei*.

A more critical mood is seen in Malsis (Y), IPM *Malasis*
and Malpas (Ch, Berks, Mon), 'evil pass.' That in Cheshire,
which displaced English *Depenbech*, derived importance from
the castle of one of the barons of the palatinate.

Frauncheville, 'free town,' the original name of the little
borough of Newtown (Wt), is a very late instance of a NFr.
name (1256).

In most of these cases the original spelling has been fairly
well preserved, if the pronunciation has been Anglicised, but a
place name which looks quite English may sometimes be purely
French. A striking instance of this is Miserden (Gl). Entered
in DB as *Grenhamstede*, the township was held from the Conquest to the beginning of the fourteenth century by the Musard
family as half a knight's fee and was known as *Le Musardere*,
'the home (or manor) of the Musards.' Hence, by somewhat
violent Anglicising, Miserden.

The 'Musardery' leads us by a natural transition to those
far more numerous local names which contain the names of
manorial lords, either compounded with English suffixes to
form new place-names or used uncompounded to distinguish
Hybrid places of the same name. Of these two uses, the first, though
place- the rarer, is the more interesting because it shows the normal
names process of place-name formation in Old English times still
followed for long after the Conquest, but with a French instead
of an English first element. This continuity may serve as a
warning to the reader not to regard our delimitation of 'feudal'
as more than one of convenience. The name of owner, lord or
prominent inhabitant had always been the commonest means
of distinguishing the 'hams' and 'tons' of the gradual English
settlement, and such names were still being coined in some
numbers during the period of nascent feudalism which preceded the Norman Conquest. Domesday Book contains the
names of between twenty and thirty vills which were clearly
called after the holder who is recorded for King Edward's
time. Good instances are *Blachemanestone* (K), now Blackman-
stone, from *Blacheman*; *Brismartone*, now Brigmerston (W),

from *Beorhtmær* (DB *Brismar*); and *Siredestona* (So), now
Shearston, from *Sired*. East Garston (Berks) is a less certain
but altogether probable and very interesting case. It does not
appear in DB, but the thirteenth century form, *Esegarestone*,
coupled with the mention of Esegar the staller as a tenant at
Lambourne in 1066, seems to justify Professor Stenton in
placing the name (if not the vill) among Edwardian creations.

This mode of making place-names survived the Conquest,
though now it was nearly always a Norman personal name
which was used to form a new name in which it was compounded with 'ton' in the south and with 'by' in the north.
As the places in question were usually small and obscure, it is
difficult in most cases to trace them back beyond the feudal
inquisitions of the thirteenth century. Some of them may be
of quite late date. It has been claimed that Rowlestone and
Gilbertstone in the district of Ewyas Harold (He) took their
names from two of the knights of that castle who are mentioned
by name in DB, but it is not impossible that, like the neighbouring Walterston, they may not be so early. If Denton, the
Cumbrian antiquary, had good authority for deriving Harraby
(Cu) from *Henry* Engaine, this place-name is carried well back
into the twelfth century. Flimby (*Flemingeby*, 1200) may, as
has been asserted, be a Flemish settlement of the last decade
of the eleventh, but here again certainty is wanting. Of the
other names in Cumberland which have been assigned to this
type, Aglionby (*Aglunby*, from *Aguillon* probably), Allonby
(*Aleynby*), Botcherby (*Bochardeby*), Moresby (*Moriceby*) and
Ponsonby (*Punzanby*) are certainly of post-Conquest but uncertain date, while Oughterby and Rickerby cannot be regarded
as clear cases since *Uhtred* and *Richeard* are both names that
occur under the Confessor. The existence of some of these
places before the end of the twelfth century is well attested
and we may fairly trace the group, though not in every case
immediately, to Rufus's conquest (in 1092) of a district
which afforded unusual scope for new settlement. No such
group is found in the more settled counties lying east of
Cumberland. Westmorland does not afford a single case, and
though Jolby certainly, and perhaps Halnaby, took their
names from a post-Conquest Joel and Halnath, and show
that 'by' was still a living suffix in Yorkshire, they are
sporadic instances.

Turning to the region of 'tons,' a search through the inquisitions in *Feudal Aids* reveals little trace of these new
formations in the East and Midlands. One striking case, not
noticed there, is that of Royston (Herts). The official name of

the little town which had grown up round the priory of *Crux Roesiae* on the border of Cambridgeshire and Hertfordshire, was still that of the priory in 1316, but there is other evidence that Royston was also in use under Henry III. Royston (Y) had quite another origin.

In eastern Wessex there are Marlston (Berks), *Marteleston*, 1316; Balsdon (Berks), thirteenth century *Balatteston*; Flamston (W), *Flambardeston*, 1354 (cf. Ranulf *Flambard*, Rufus' minister); and possibly Mainstone in Romsey (Ha), *Mayneston*, 1346. Herefordshire has four clear cases, Chanston (*Cheyneston*, 1303), Gilbertstone, Rowlestone and Walterston. It is only, however, in Dorset and Devon that this type of place-name becomes at all abundant. Dorset can show eighteen or nineteen clear instances (not all surviving) and Devon eleven. A full list of these and of some doubtful cases is given in an appendix below. In nine instances the family whose name is incorporated was in possession in the thirteenth and fourteenth centuries. Pulston (*Polayneston*) can be safely identified with the unnamed knight's fee in the hundred of St George which in 1212 was held by John Poleyn 'de Conquestu domini Regis Willelmi Bastardi' (TN 164). It had passed from the Poleyns before 1303. Many of these late names have sustained as thorough a levelling down as the oldest pre-Conquest forms and their origin is most thoroughly disguised. Thus *Bonevileston* has become Bunson (D), *Cheyneston*, Chenson (D), *Forsardeston*, Forston (Do), *Corbineston*, Corstone (D) and *Randolveston*, Ranston (Do).

The most curious of these hybrids was *Antiocheston*, long obsolete, which was held by Nicholas de Antioch in 1316. It is now Tarrant Rawston. More than a third of the Dorset examples were in the valleys of the rivers Tarrant, Frome, Piddle and Winterbourn and they interchanged with forms in which the river name was associated uncompounded either with the family name or with the hybrid itself. Thus *Antiocheston* and *Tarrente Antioch* were two names for the same place. The present Tarrant Keynston was *Tarente de Kaynes* in 1285 (when it was held by Robert de Kaynes) but appears in 1346 as *Tarente Kayneston* and later sometimes as *Kayneston* alone. On the other hand, *Frome Bonevileston* has settled down to Frome Bonvile.

The use of a river-name with a simple personal name (or other attribute of distinction) uncompounded, a usage which really falls into a category which will be dealt with later, occurs in several neighbouring counties, but Brixton (*Brightrichestone*, 1290) Deverill (W) seems the nearest parallel to Tarrant Keyns-

Rivers and place-names

ton and its like in Dorset. In the Wiltshire case, however, there is no hybrid formation, for Brictric (*Beorhtric*) was tenant TRE.

These river hybrids need not imply new settlements; there are many Tarrants, etc., in DB, all without distinctive attributes. Brixton Deverill itself appears simply as *Devrel*. But most of the late formations of this type seem to belong to small manors or quasi-manors of Norman creation within the bounds of the old townships, each bearing its proportion, usually fractional, of military service. It may be objected that as the creation of such manors was certainly not confined to the two counties in question, the proposed explanation fails to account for the absence of these hybrid names over the greater part of the area in which they might be expected to appear. It is certainly remarkable that Somerset, near neighbour of Devon and Dorset, shows not a single case in FA, though the 'villa del Estre' in the barony of Richard del Estre in 1166 (RBE, 1, 232) may possibly translate one. The place is said to be the present Stoke Trister. It is possible that there was more waste land fit for cultivation in Devon and Dorset. But the infrequency or complete absence of such hybrid place-names in other counties may also be explained by the use of a different system of nomenclature. It was very common, especially in the eastern counties, for small manors to be known elliptically as Grey's, Mortimer's, Carbonel's and the like. Of 118 manors in the thirty-three parishes of the Suffolk hundred of Babergh, nearly forty bore this type of name. A western case is that of Blanquettes or Blankets (Wo), so named from the family of Blanket who held it in the thirteenth and fourteenth centuries. Another interesting example is the little estate of Poynetts, near Hambleden (Bk), which preserves the name of Thomas Poynaunt, who held a sixteenth part of a knight's fee there in 1303. The present owner possesses an original deed by which Poynaunt made a grant of part of his land.

A French first element other than a personal name is rare, but there seems no doubt that Castleton (La, Db, Mon) is a case in point.

The many Newtons of late origin show that purely English *The* as well as hybrid compounds with 'ton' as second element *Newton* were still being formed. When Newtowns begin to appear 'ton' is evidently ceasing to be a living suffix.

Far more abundant and obvious relics of the feudal age than the small and often much disguised group of hybrid compounds are preserved in the widespread class of place-names in which NFr. personal names were attached uncompounded to existing names of places of more or less common occurrence and to new words like 'castle,' for the sake of distinction. The most numerous section of this class consists of names such as Stoke and Sutton, which recur almost everywhere and others, such as Combe and Compton, which are confined to more restricted areas. Stoke D'Abernon (Sr), Sutton Valence (K), Stretton Grandison (He), Combe Martin (D) and Compton Verney (Wa) are typical examples.

'Place' and 'South' and 'Valley' and the like are not very distinctive, but a place-name that was at first rare or even unique might come to demand distinction when shared by subdivisions of the original area. Professor Maitland has remarked on the tendency of certain English vills to throw off daughter vills of the same name, and the later division of many vills into two or more manors had the same effect. Rotherfield Greys and Rotherfield Peppard (O) may serve as an illustration of the way in which the difficulty was surmounted. The multiplication of vills named after a single river, Tarrants, Winterbornes, etc., may have been due to fission of original vills and, as we have already seen, the resulting confusion was met in the same way. Whether the Ings and Roothings of Essex are to be explained as river groups or as household groups, they fall into the same category and were similarly distinguished.

The distinctive name, though usually following, sometimes precedes the main one, as in Birts Morton (Wo) and Scott Willoughby (L), and is occasionally used indifferently in either position. Very rarely, this volatile attribute has become fixed to its principal and the whole has been levelled down like the mass of the older place names.

Thus Stoke Courcy and Stoke Gomer (So) have been reduced to the ugly Stogursey and Stogumber, and Cliff or Clive Wancy (W) to Clevancy. Boscastle (Co) for *Botreaux' Castle*, Costhorpe (Nt) for *Cossardthorp*, Perlethorpe (Nt) for *Peverelthorp* and Randalinton (Cu) for *Randolf Levington* are even more striking cases. Bassingthorpe (L) represents *Basewinsthorp*. In Painswick (Gl), Wickwar[r] (Gl), Towersey (Bk)—from the family of Tours (de Turri)—Clungunford (Sa) and Stokesay (Sa) the union is more mechanical.

The attribute is either a Christian name as in Burton Agnes (Y), so called from an early lady of the manor, Stoke Edith (He), said to commemorate an Old English princess, Lostock

Gralam (Ch), from Grelein de Rundchamp (late twelfth century) and Winterbourne Gunner from Gunnora de la Mere, wife of Henry de la Mere (*t*. Hen. III), or, much more commonly, an actual or potential surname. The nicknames which the Normans, like the elder Northmen, bestowed with such *Nicknames* liberality are abundantly represented. They are almost as uniformly unflattering as their place-names were appreciative. So aristocratic a sounding name as Pauncefote in Bentley Pauncefoot (Wo) had originally no better meaning than 'paunchface' (*Pauncevolt*). The large number of names beginning with Mal (Mau) is significant. Mauduit, 'ill-conducted,' though the family preferred to Latinise it 'Male doctus,' occurs in Easton Mauduit (Nth) and elsewhere, Malherbe, 'bad herb,' in Cricket Malherbe (So), Malmaynes, 'ill hands,' in Wimborne Malmaynes (Do), Malvoisin, 'ill neighbour,' in Ridware Mavesyn (St) and Mauleverer, 'bad harrier,' in Allerton Mauleverer (Y). Similar nicknames, in some of which the sting has become obscure to us, are contained in Acaster Malbis (Y), Lichet Matravers (Do), Norton Maureward (So) and Clifton Maybank, formerly *Maubanc* (Do), a solitary and remote relic of the barons of Nantwich (*Wich Maubanc*) in Cheshire. Marston Bigott (So) represents another variety of this class of personal name. Some have dropped out of place-names; South Holne (D) was once *Holne Orgoyllous* and Chignall Smealy (Ess) *Chigenhale Trenchefoil*. Among these lost names is a rare instance of a complimentary nickname. Knowstone (D) was in the thirteenth century *Knouston Beaupel*, Beaupel signifying 'fine skin.'

Many of the personal names used are those of place-names *Territorial* in northern France. These are very liable to strange perversions *names* on English tongues. Anyone well acquainted with the topography of northern France may detect Pecquigny in Moreton Pinkney (Nth) and Pont de l'Arche in Stanley Pontlarge (Gl) with little difficulty, but without the early forms some of these foreign names are quite unrecognisable. Thus Orcas in Sandford Orcas (Do) represents an original Orescuiltz, *Stoke Verdon* (W) has become Stoke Farthing, and *Yedefen Loges* (Wo) Edvin Loach. Damarel in Stoke Damarel (D) is a curious perversion of D'Aumarle. The attributes in Compton Greenfield (Gl) and Norton Hawkfield (So) look perfectly English, but represent an original Grenville and Hauteville respectively. On the other hand, Mansell in Hope Mansell (He) has nothing to do with Le Mans (adj. *Mancel*), for it was formerly *Maloisel*, a nickname meaning 'ill bird.'

Family names which were not territorial in origin were only

less open to corruption. Skilling (DB *Schelin*) in Okeford Skilling (Do) or Skillingstone, inevitably became Shilling. Musgrave in Charlton Musgrave (So) is said to be corrupted from the nickname Mussegros. Another curious perversion of a personal name seems to be post-mediaeval. Down to 1487 at least Fisherton Anger (W) was correctly written Fisherton *Aucher*. Possibly an 'n' had already crept in in pronunciation. That the change was due to a scribal confusion seems less likely at so late a date.

Ambiguous attributes   It is not always easy to distinguish family names in place-names from the names of adjoining places which were also sometimes used for distinction. Other local descriptive attributes also occur. Warley Semeles (Ess) looks as if it contained a family name until it is found Latinised as W. *septem molarum*[1]. Essex also furnishes a case, probably unique, of the distinctive personal name displacing the old name. *Salcote Verli* is now Virley. Equally rare is the translation of a NFr. personal name in Wynford Eagle (Do), the reason in this instance being that the escheated estates of the old Norman house of Laigle or Aquila were known as the Honour of Eagle. Chilvers Coton (Wa) is a very interesting case of simulation. Chilvers would naturally be taken as a NFr. personal name distinguishing one Coton from others, but it is really the original English name, thirteenth century *Chilverdescote* (containing OE *Cēol-friþ*), which lost its second element apparently under the influence of the neighbouring hamlet of Coton, whose name was attached to it uncompounded.

While the hybrid feudal place-names compounded with 'ton' kept to the beaten track of English word building, the larger class which is now under consideration struck out a new line. The English were not addicted to the use of nicknames and territorial designations and, if they felt the inconvenience of identical place-names, did not see their way to put an end to the confusion that resulted. Some apparent exceptions to this rule are irrelevant or doubtful. Richard's Castle (He) and Ewyas Harold (He) received their distinctive names from Norman followers of Edward the Confessor. Madeley *Ulfac*, now Madeley Holme (St)—for which Duignan gives no reference—is indecisive, for Ulfac (OE *Wulfhēah*) was undertenant

---

[1] On the other hand, Radford Semele (Wa) contains a real family name. Mr P. H. Reaney (*Englische Studien*, LXI, 80) points out that Warley Semeles is now Little Warley, and appears as *Warle Setmoles* (1252–8 AD). *Septem molarum* is a Latinisation of the surname (cf. William de *Septem molis* or *Setmoles*, 1242–59 AD) of a family owning land in Warley in 1212.

in 1086 and it is not stated that he had held the manor TRE. Stoke Edith (He) would be a more satisfactory instance if its supporters could agree as to who was father of the lady, king Egbert or king Edgar. A clearer case seems to be that of Wootton Wawen in which Wawen apparently preserves the name of the pre-Conquest holder, called *Wagene* in a charter of 1043 and *Waga* in DB. Another well-attested instance seems to be that of Clungunford (Sa), where *Gunward* was tenant, TRE. A distinctive epithet of another kind appears in DB in the case of Winterbourne Stoke (W), but its pre-Conquest origin is not thereby proved.

In Scandinavian England anticipation of Norman practice would be *prima facie* more likely, and in the case of Kirkby Thore (We) there is evidence of the existence of an important person of that name in Cumbria in the early part of the eleventh century[1]. But, of course, there may have been others of his name at a later time.

The date at which these additions began to become common needs working out. If Croome d'Abitot (Wo) and Redmarley d'Abitot (Wo) took their attribute from Urse d'Abitot, the notorious sheriff who died[2] in the reign of Henry I, and not, as Dr Round has suggested, from later and far less prominent representatives of the name, there is high probability that they did not stand alone. If, again, Skeat is right in explaining Hinton Waldrist (Berks) as 'Waldric's Hinton,' an early date for this case seems likely. Okeford Shilling (Do), as already stated, probably contains the name of the Domesday tenant Schelin. In the north Kirkby *Stephen* appears *c.* 1100. Turner's Puddle (Do) can hardly, however, be called after the DB undertenant Walter, whom Eyton, on what authority does not appear, describes as Walter le Tonnerre (*Dorset Domesday*, 40) for as late as 1303 the place was held by Henry Toner of the heirs of William de Gouiz.

The profound silence of DB must be discounted, for these attributes are seldom given in records before the thirteenth century and not with any fulness until the latter part of that century. Many are first attested in the fourteenth and even the fifteenth. Yet there is sufficient evidence that they were common enough in the latter half of the twelfth.

More significant than the silence of DB with regard to their use in the first age of the Norman settlement is its not infrequent reference to an *alia villa* where a vill has thrown off an offshoot. This shows that English lack of system still pre-

---

[1] EHR, xx, 61–2.
[2] *Dict. Nat. Biogr.* s.v. *Urse.*

vailed, to some extent at any rate. Two hamlets, called naïvely Otherton (St, Wo), survive to prove that here at least the compilers (or the juries) were not suppressing names.

How the attribute was first attached
As one would naturally suppose, the personal name used as a distinctive attribute was not at first indeclinable. Fortunately there is some evidence which shows how that stage was reached. A clear light is thrown upon the normal process in the case of Ashby Folville (Lei), which appears as *Essebia Fulconis de Folville* in a charter of the early years of Henry II[1]. It might have become Ashby Fulks or Fulk (cf. Fulk Stapleford (Ch)), but failing that the Fulk would drop out under a successor of a different Christian name and the place would be known as Ashby de Folville and ultimately as Ashby Folville. A *Charlton de Wardrobe* (L) took its name from a family of de la Warderoba, but the attribute has been lost since 1242 (TN 312 *b*). In *Tarente de Kaynes* (Do) the 'de' survived as late as 1285 (FA, II, I). If the attribute in this phase were Latinised it would naturally appear in the plural number. Hampton Gay (O) was *Hampton Gaytorum* (the 't' has been lost) in 1152[2].

At Tidworth (W) two manors were distinguished under Henry II as *Thudwrda Johannis Marescalli* and *T. Hugonis de Lacy*. But these designations are not found later than 1199.

The *Stokke comitis W. de Mandeville* (Herts) of 1220 has also not retained that distinction (it is not to be confused with Stoke Mandeville (Bk)) and *Stiuecle comitis David* (de Huntingdon) is now Great Stukeley (Hu)[3].

Dating of attributes
Where, as in these cases, the personal attribute contains a Christian name and belonged to a well known person, it is possible to fix its local application with some accuracy. Similar cases are those of Halesowen (Wo) which derives its epithet from a nephew of Henry II, son of his sister Emma and David ap Owen (*m.* 1174) and Sutton Maddock (Sa), named after Madoc ap Gervase Goch, hereditary interpreter between the kings of England and the princes of Wales, who also lived under Henry. Much more often, however, a close study of local family history is needed even to fix a superior limit of date for the use of the attribute. That in Scott Willoughby (L), which is thus distinguished from Silk Willoughby (so called from the hamlet of Silkby) is, for instance, supplied by an obscure charter of about the middle of the twelfth century, in

[1] Stenton, *Danelaw Charters*, 238.
[2] Cf. the existing Ashby Puerorum (L).
[3] For these cases see *Trans. Lancs. and Ches. Record Soc.* XXVII, 137–8. Stewkley (Bk) was once *S. Aristotle* from 'Master Aristotle the Judge.'

which William Scot appears as husband of one of the co-heiresses of Ralph Bernard of Willoughby[1].

These uncompounded attributes were not always permanent. *Lost* They could readily be replaced by others or disappear altogether. *attributes* The substitution of one name for another, a process in some cases several times repeated, illustrates the vicissitudes of families. A simple instance is that of Norton Bavant (W), which was *Norton Scydemor* in 1335 but had settled down to its present name by 1428. Beauchamp Walter (Ess) was *Beauchamp Albrich* in 1346. Sometimes two of these attributes have come down as alternatives. Winterbourne Gunner, or Cherborough (W), derives its first appellative from Gunnora de la Mere and the second from the Cherborough family. If the indexer of *Feudal Aids* is to be trusted, Compton Valence (Do) was known both by that name and as *Compton Pundelarge* c. 1430, but here only one attribute has survived.

The curious shifting between this loose use of the personal name and a compound of it with 'ton,' which is found in the south-west, has already been noticed. Tarrant Antioch and *Antiocheston*, *Shillingstone* and Okeford Shilling are Dorset cases.

Besides Christian names and surnames, there is the very *Official* large class of attributes which may be grouped as official. Some *attributes* are secular: King's, Queen's (Charleton Queen's (So)), Prince's (Prince's Risborough (Bk), but not Prince Thorpe (Wa), where Prince is a corruption of Preon's), Earl's, Countess (Countess-Thorpe (Lei)), Sheriff's (Sheriff's Brampton (So), Sheriff Hutton (Y)), Knight's (Knights Enham (Ha)). Others are ecclesiastical: Bishop's, Archdeacon's (Archdeacon Newton (Du)), Priest's (Priest Hutton (La)), Abbot's, Prior's, Monks', 'Canons', Nuns' (Nuneaton (Wa)), Temple, Friars' (which always means the brethren of the Hospital, or Knights of St John, not the mendicant friars whose rule forbad the holding of land; Fryer Mayne (Do) was *Mayne Ospitalis* in 1285).

A monastic manor might be distinguished by the name of the house to which it had been granted, as in the case of Stower (or Stour) Provost (Do), formerly *Sture Prewes* or *Pratellis* from the nunnery of St Leger at Préaux in Normandy and Weedon Bec (Nth) and Tooting Bec (Sr) from the great Norman abbey of Bec Hellouin.

As lay titles often became surnames, a place-name like Compton Chamberlayne (We) or Upton Prodhome (D) may only have a superficial appearance of belonging to the official group. *Stoke Ostrizer* (So), now Stocklinch Ottersey, is, how-

[1] Stenton, *Danelaw Charters*, 282.

ever, a clear case. It was held in 1285 by the service of mewing a hawk (*austurcus*), the tenant being William le Ostrizer.

Distinctive names of both the types which have been considered occasionally alternate with or yield to one or other of the large class of attributes which indicate not the feudal proprietor but merely size (Great (Much), Little), relative position by the quarters of the compass (North, South, etc.) or by altitude (Upper, Nether, Upland, etc.), the possession of a market (Blandford Forum (Do)), or a church (Church, Chapel, Steeple) or, if not peculiar in this respect, its dedication. One or two examples will suffice: Norton Lindsey or Superior (Wa), Norton Canes or Under Cannock (St), East Stower (Do), formerly *Sture Cosin*, Gussage St Michaels (Do) or (in fifteenth century) *Gussych Boun* (Bohun).

Latin forms

Names of the official and general types sometimes established themselves in a Latin form, especially in Dorset, where examples are Melbury Abbas, Whitchurch Canonicorum, Blandford Monialium, now Blandford St Mary, and Fontmell Magna.

Number and distribution of place-names with attributes

The number of place-names containing these uncompounded attributes is surprisingly large, even if we leave out of account not only the general but also the official group and confine ourselves to the personal names. A census made from Carlisle's *Topographical Dictionary of England* (1808), which records some that have since fallen out of use, gives a total not far short of eight hundred. Nor is this complete, for Carlisle does not include all hamlets and the *Feudal Aids* reveal scores of such attributes that became obsolete long ago. The distribution of the names is interesting. Thinly represented in the north, save in Yorkshire, which has fifty, and in the east, with the striking exception of Essex (43), they tend, on the whole, to increase in numbers as we go westward and southward. In the eastern Midlands, a fairly high proportion in Bucks, Oxon, Leicestershire and Northants is exceptional and the total for twelve counties (162) is only just higher than that for seven counties of the western Midlands from Mersey to Severn, including Warwick and Monmouth. The figures for the south-west show a big rise. The seven counties of the old kingdom of Wessex contain no less than three hundred of which only fifty are in Berks and Hants. Wilts has fifty-three, Devon fifty-seven, Dorset sixty-six and Somerset seventy-eight. Making every allowance for accident and the exclusion from our census of large classes of similar attributes which might (but are not very likely to) alter these proportions, there does seem to be a definite culmination of this kind of place-name in the south-western counties and this may have a historical reason. The high proportion here may indeed in part be due to the frequency of certain common names requiring such distinction, as Charlton, Combe, Compton and Upton, but this cannot be all. Seeking for a fuller explanation, one naturally calls to mind Maitland's graphic contrast of the large centralised or, as he calls them, nucleated villages of the Midlands with the parishes composed of hamlets and scattered steads which border on the Celtic fringe. This multiplication of small settlements and the attraction of a pleasant land for the Norman intruder made it a region of little manors. In a township containing several of these, where the hamlets had no separate names, the need for distinction would be felt and would be naturally supplied by the use of the name of the manorial lord. Something too may be due to the taking up of fresh land here by Norman lords, to which a part of the group of new place-names compounded of their names and the suffix 'ton' seemed to us to point. It must be admitted that while Dorset and Devon show both features in a very marked degree, Somerset, which heads the list of place-names with uncompounded attributes, cannot, now at any rate, produce a single instance of the hybrid compound. For this difference we are hardly in a position to account without further research. It may be that Somerset was more completely settled than its neighbours, but this is merely conjecture. Local investigators may help to solve the problem by making their collection of the names of hamlets and ancient farms as complete as possible.

Less important than the distribution of this class of place-names, but not without its interest, is the result of an analysis of the comparative frequency with which the various NFr. personal names make their appearance in them. In those included by Carlisle it is rather ironical that the list should be topped (with fourteen cases) by the Bassets, those early twelfth century upstarts, whom Henry I 'raised from the dust, as I may say' (Orderic Vitalis), over the heads of the Conquest baronage. Two of these great houses, however, the Beauchamps and the Giffards or Giffords, run neck and neck in a close second to the Bassets. The Clintons, who were associated with the last named by Orderic in his derogatory remark, were not so widespread, but have left their name in Aston Clinton (Bk) and Baddesley Clinton (Wa). Some of the greatest baronial families are poorly represented or not at all. Courtenay, Ferrers, FitzPain, Grey, Hastings, Lacy, Mandeville, Marshall, Percy and Peverel among others make a fair show, but the great Nevill name is represented only by the small Dorset village of Fifehead Nevill, which did not belong to one of the greater Nevill families, though we may add Hallingbury Nevill (Ess) from the *Feudal Aids*. While the comparatively obscure family of Keynes (Cahaignes) occurs seven times, the famous names of Bigot, Bohun, Courcy, (De) Spenser, Mowbray and Scrope make only one appearance each. Even obsolete names would not make much difference here. The memory of the Mowbrays is still kept alive, however, not only by Melton Mowbray (Lei) but by the 'Vale of Mowbray,' the local name for the great plain of north Yorkshire of which Thirsk is the centre. Their heirs, the Howards, are commemorated only by Castle Howard, which is hardly a place-name and quite modern (1702). Balliol and Bruce do not appear at all. In Manningford Bruce (W), the attribute is merely a corruption of Braose or Brewose. There is nothing mysterious in this. Places which needed these distinctive additions were usually small and, if they formed part of a great barony, were normally in the hands of undertenants from whom they naturally took their distinctive name.

It must not be taken for granted that a village which bears a great name by way of distinction took it from the main line of the family or even from one of its recognised branches. The baronial houses had many ramifications, and a surname which was in origin a nickname or a local designation might appear independently in more than one quarter. Eyton, for instance, has told us that among the Count of Mortain's tenants at Montacute (So) in 1086 were three of his chief retainers, 'progenitors of as many Baronial houses, two at least of which were afterwards known by the name of De Montacute[1].' It may be doubted whether the Bigots who gave their name to Marston Bigott (So) could call cousins with the earls of Norfolk and hereditary marshals of England.

Only local research can satisfactorily settle such questions and in so doing perhaps fix incidentally the date at which the attribute was first attached. A Devonshire antiquary may be able, for instance, to settle just when the Peverells of Sampford Peverell, Weston Peverell and Aller Peverell in that county and (one supposes) of Bradford Peverell and Newton Peverell in Dorset branched off from the parent stock which held Hatfield Peverell in Essex in the latter half of the twelfth century.

The narrowly local character of many of the minor baronial and gentle families is indicated by the situation of places named after them. This feature is especially marked in the south-western counties which were off the main lines of communication and were rather isolated in consequence. Of six

[1] *Domesday of Somerset*, I, 166.

places bearing the name of Matravers (Maltravers) all but one are in Dorset and the sixth Henford Matravers is in the neighbouring county of Somerset. The FitzPains appear four times in Dorset, twice in Somerset and once in Devon. Tracy (3), Rawleigh (3), Damarell (3) and Pomeroy (2) are confined to Devon, Florey (4) to Somerset, Gunville (2) to Dorset and the list may not be exhaustive.

Three of the five Sollers cases are in Herefordshire and the others in Shropshire and Gloucestershire. But the feature is not of course confined to the south and west. The Le Pugeys of Stoke Poges (Bk) have also a memorial in the adjoining Oxfordshire, Broughton Pogges. Quite a considerable number are limited to the three counties of Leicester, Warwick and Northampton.

Of more widely-spread names, Basset is found in nine counties, Beauchamp in seven and Gifford in six. Ferrers ranges from Devon to Essex and Northamptonshire, Courtenay from Devon to Yorkshire.

Between one hundred and two hundred names occur more than once, but a much larger number make only a single appearance. Collected, they afford curious juxtapositions of vocables, some aristocratic in sound, others the reverse, partly French and partly English. Bagpuize, Bowells, Bubb, Coggles, Crubb, Goose, Gubbals, Puddock, Pudding and Wallop rub shoulders with Champflower, Courtenay, Curson, D'Evercy, Grandison, Lancelyn, Longueville, Monchensie, Montague, Morieux, St Quintin and Seymour, to take only a few instances. At first they must have been practically all French, but as the Normans settled down and sometimes took territorial designations from their manors and as the native element in the landed class grew in numbers, a considerable number of English names made their way in. For the addition of these attributes went on right through the Middle Ages and even beyond them. Hampton Lucy (Wa), whose owners are said, rightly or wrongly, to have furnished the original of Mr Justice Shallow, must have been one of the latest, for the Lucys did not acquire it until the reign of Queen Mary. Down to the Reformation it belonged to the monastic chapter of Worcester and was sometimes called Bishops Hampton.

But all that seems English is not of native origin. That *Anglicised forms* tendency of NFr. names to assume strange shapes on English tongues, which has already been noticed, is sometimes more subtle in its operation. A slight change is occasionally enough to give a name an English look. It has been suggested, for instance, that Murren in Newnham Murren (O) is OE *Morwine*,

but, apart from the rarity of OE personal names in this class
of names, there can be no doubt that it is merely an altered
form of the NFr. surname *Morin*. William Morin was a thir-
teenth-century holder of the manor. Again, the NFr. nickname Paganel or Paynel, 'little Pain,' which has survived
recognisably in Newport Pagnell (Bk) and several other cases
has been Anglicised in Littleton Pannell[1] (W). Passeleau or
Passelew has become Parslow in Drayton Parslow (Bk), Gouiz
Goose in Bradon Goose (So), Toner Turner in Turner's Puddle
(Do) and d'Iseni Disney in Norton Disney (L). Corfe Mullen
(Do) was Corfe Molyn in 1303 and Frome Billet in the same
county is found in its original form in 1285 as Frome Belet.
Milton Lilborne (W) looks English enough until confronted
with the 1281 form *Lillebon*. A curious and more extreme case
of Anglicisation is that of Stocklinch Ottersey (So) where the
attribute represents an original *Ostrizer* (*v. supra*, 125).

Such changes are, of course, mostly well known to the local
historian, but there is always a possibility that a scrutiny of
place-names of this type in other counties than his own may
give him new light in a dark place. The Cheshire historians,
for instance, would not have been so slow in identifying the
mysterious Maynes enumerated among the possessions of
Scirard or Sirard, a Cheshire tenant of the first earl of Chester,
had they known that of the two Maynes in Dorset, now known
as Little Mayne and Fryer Mayne, the first was in 1285 called
Mayne Sirard and was in fact still held by a family of Sirard
(later Sherard) clearly descended from the Cheshire Sirard.
There had been no suspicion up till this identification that
Sirard had not lived and died on his Cheshire estate.

Apart from such results, which may be rare, there is no
better way of realising the composition and distribution of the
Norman families in England than is afforded by a study of an
ordered collection of this interesting and rather neglected class
of place-names.

[1] This is the local pronunciation even in Newport Pagnell.

NOTE TO PAGE 125

Mr P. H. Reaney (*Englische Studien*, LXI, 80) writes: '*Beauchamp
Albrich* is not identical with Belchamp (*not* Beauchamp) Walter, but
survives as Allbrights formerly (*in*) *Bello Campo Sancti Ethelberti*
(1294 FF), a small chapelry in Belchamp Otten.'

APPENDIX

HYBRID PLACE-NAMES IN DORSET AND DEVON

DORSET

Antiocheston[1]	Nicholas de Antioch, 1316	Tarrant Rawston
Bardalveston		Burleston
(Bardolston)		
Bonvileston		Frome Bonvile
		(in Stinsford)
Brianeston		Bryanston
Forsardeston	William Forsard, 1285	Forston
		(in Charminster)
Gundevyleston	Hugh de Gunville, 1233	Tarrant Gunville
Harangeston	Adam Harang, 1285	Herringstone, Little
		(in Charminster)
Heryngston[2]		Winterbourne
		Herringstone
Kayneston	Robert de Keynes, 1285	Tarrant Keynston
Malgareston[3]		Mageston
		(in Gillingham)
Musterston	Richard de Musters, 1303	Muston
		(in Piddlehinton)
Phelipeston		Philipston
		(in Wimborne St Giles)
Polayneston[4]		Pulston
		(in Charminster)
Quareleston	William Quarel, 1303	Quarlston
		(in Winterbourne
		Stickland)
Randolveston		Ranston
		(in Iwerne Courtenay)
Shillyngeston[5]	John Eskelling, 1226 FF	Shillingstone or Okeford
		Shilling
Thomaston		Winterborne Thompson
Turbervileston[6]		
Walterreston		Waterston
		(in Puddletown)

Doubtful cases

Folardestone[7]		
Leweston		
Poerstone		Pierston[8]
(Powerestone)		(in Gillingham)

[1] The form (or forms) that seems nearest to the original is given in this column. From FA where not otherwise stated.

[2] This seems first to appear in 1431 and only as attribute. The place was Winterborne Harang in 1285.   [3] Cl R (1206).

[4] Members of the Poleyn or Polain family occur 1212 and 1242 in TN.

[5] 1444 (Ancient Indictments).

[6] Identified by the indexer of FA with Turberville's (now Bryant's) Puddle, but they were in different hundreds (FA, 42–3).

[7] TN 170 (1242).   [8] PN Do 8.

K

DEVON

Bonevileston		Bunson
		(in Chumleigh)
Bordevileston		? Burston
		(in Zeal Monachorum)
Champeleston	Ralph Champeaus, 1285	Champston
		(in Molland Botreaux)
Cheyneston	Thomas Cheygny, 1346	Chenson
		(in Chawleigh)
Corbineston	Peter Corbin, *c.* 1240	Corstone
		(in Broadwoodkelly)
Gerardeston[1]		
Lovelestone	William Lovel, 1303	Lovistone
		(in Huish)
Notteston	John Notte, 1428	Natson
		(in Nymet Tracy)
Steveneston		Stevenstone
		(in St Giles in the Wood)
Steveniston		Stevenston
		(in Upton Pyne)
Tuz Seinzton	Lucas de Tuz Seinz, 1242	Towsington
		(in Exminster)

Doubtful cases

Gerelleston	Grilleston
	(in Bishop's Nympton)
Hermaneston	Hampson
	(in Nymet Tracy)
Rollandiston	Rolastone
	(in Bramford Speke)

[1] *c.* 1242 (TN 189).

CHAPTER VII

PLACE-NAMES AND ENGLISH LINGUISTIC STUDIES

by *Henry Cecil Wyld*, with the assistance of
Mary S. Serjeantson

THE names of English places, and of physical features of the country, are for the most part composed of elements which exist also as independent words, and ordinary constituents of the English vocabulary, in OE and the subsequent stages of our language.

The outward and audible forms of these elements, generally fused into compounds, but sometimes uncompounded, undergo the same characteristic series of sound-changes, isolative and combinative, affecting both the quality and quantity of the vowel-sounds which they contain, and the character of the consonants, as from age to age have modified the sounds of all other words in the language. Apart from the occasional irregular changes introduced by analogy or popular etymology, it may be said that the forms of English p.n. have a normal, and regular phonetic development just as the other words have.

It is well known that in OE, and to a greater extent in ME, the same original vowels and diphthongs developed differently in the dialect of different areas, and this variety in vowel-sounds is reflected in ME, in the spelling both of p.n. and of independent words. These phonological variations, together with others in accidence and vocabulary, are recognised as being among the chief characteristics of the regional dialects of ME. It is highly desirable that there should be a detailed survey of the dialect characters of ME which should show the typical grouping of these, county by county, and an even minuter analysis of the linguistic features of smaller districts within the larger areas.

The difficulties in the way of such a survey have until recently appeared to be almost insuperable, owing to the fact that in spite of the large number of ME texts, and the dialectal variety which they exhibit, it is quite uncertain which precisely of the numerous local forms of speech most of these texts severally represent. We are very often reduced to contenting ourselves with such wide and vague descriptions as East Midland, West Midland, South-Western, and so on, as though there were no differences in the thirteenth and fourteenth centuries between the dialects of Nf, Sf, L and C; between those of Ess, K and Sx; those of He, Sa, Wo, St, Wa; or those of D, Do, Ha, Berks, and so on. While no doubt forms alien to the original dialect in which the ME text was written often do creep in through the scribes, we have to remember that there must have been many border dialects possessing features common to several of the main linguistic types and spoken in regions intermediate between several dialect areas. Thus, a combination of features in a text, which to our imperfect knowledge appears to be due to a jumble of forms from different dialects, may in reality represent a perfectly genuine type of English spoken in a particular area. The fact is that a detailed knowledge of the geographical distribution of the various characteristic dialect features has still to be slowly accumulated. Until this has been done, it would be rash to dogmatise as to which features may or may not have occurred, associated together, in one and the same dialect.

These questions can never be answered merely from an examination of the dialect features exhibited by the ME texts, no matter how thorough this may be, for the reasons indicated above. The object of these pages is to urge that information of an important kind may be derived from an investigation of the distinctive dialect features displayed by the forms of p.n. recorded during the ME period or earlier.

Reliability of p.n. forms   The question at once arises how far these can be trusted for the purpose. It would be very unfortunate to make exaggerated claims for the reliability of these forms as records of the actual pronunciation of the names severally, in the dialect of the area in which the places are situated, but it would also be foolish to dismiss this source of information as undeserving of serious attention without having enquired into the matter with some care. The following considerations may be urged. As has been said, the elements of which p.n. are composed appear, during the ME period, variously spelt, just as do independent words, and the former show precisely the same variations as the latter, and the variations are of a kind which is, by common consent of scholars, associated with dialect differences. It would be strange indeed then if, as a rule, the dialect type suggested by the spelling of a ME p.n. were not really that current in the place itself and the surrounding area. But the question is capable of test, by comparing the spellings found in the p.n. of a specific area with those of the corresponding words (that is words containing the same original vowel or diphthong, if not the identical word) in a text of approximately the same period, the dialect of which is definitely known. The results of such a test, applied to several texts representing various areas, by the present writer, and on a much more extensive scale, and more exhaustively, by Miss Mary Serjeantson, of Lady Margaret Hall, Oxford, have been to vindicate p.n. as a guide to the dialect features of an area. The forms agree, to a surprising extent, with those of texts from the same district. The early forms of p.n. are chiefly recorded in Chartularies of Abbeys, in Rolls, Inquisitions and other official documents. Names written down in the area itself by a local resident scribe are more likely to reflect in their spelling the type of pronunciation current locally than those recorded by a king's officer who, for all we know, may have had nothing to do with the neighbourhood, and who would therefore be likely to introduce forms different from those locally used, either by substituting, from time to time, a type more familiar to himself, or by incorporating forms found when copying the names from documents written by other scribes who were also strange to the district.

But, in most of the cases, a deviation from the true local type in the transcription of p.n. during the ME period is due to the tendency of official scribes to spell names according to the conventional London manner, and this naturally eliminates the specific regional characteristics. Such are the factors which tend to mar the clearness and reliability of the picture of dialect distribution afforded by the ME forms of English p.n. Yet in spite of everything, a systematic investigation of the names as recorded in documents of all kinds during the twelfth, thirteenth, fourteenth and early fifteenth centuries, reveals a perfectly distinctive and characteristic grouping of dialect features in each county; and further, if we regard the distribution of individual features over large tracts of the country, we obtain a consistent picture of great dialect areas, differentiated into sub-areas which shade off, and melt, one into the other without gaps or violent breaks in continuity. It should be said that the characteristic dialect features have often been eliminated from the modern forms of p.n. These are therefore frequently quite misleading for our purpose.

It will be well to enumerate some of the chief phonological *Chief* dialect features which occur alike in ME texts and p.n. forms, *phono-* mentioning the OE vowels and diphthongs, and the ME dialect *logical* *tests* variants, the geographical distribution of which, along with others, has been investigated by Miss Serjeantson, both from texts and p.n., representing the whole western part of England,

and in some cases, also the central areas, and eastwards until a definitely different type of dialect is reached. The questions which follow each mention of an OE vowel are those which we desire to see answered in respect of every area. (i) OE *æ*: does it appear as *e* (*æ*), or *a*? (ii) OE *ǣ*¹ (non-WS *ē*): has this the sound of [ɛ̄] sometimes written *ea*, and shortened to *ă*, or of [ē] sometimes written *ie*, and shortened to *ĕ*? (iii) OE *ǣ*² (*ā-i*); questions the same as for the preceding. (iv) OE *ȳ* (*ŭ-i*): does this appear predominantly as *u* (*ui*, *uy*), *i*, or as *e*? (v) OE *eŏ*: are these written *e*, or *eo*, *u*, *o*, *ue*, *oe*? (vi) OE *ēa-i* (WS *īe*, *ȳ*, *ī*, non-WS *ē*): does this appear as *u*, *i*, or *e*? (vii) OE *ĕa-i* (WS *ĭe*, *ў*, *ĭ*, non-WS *e*, *æ*): does this appear as *u*, *i*, *e*, or *ă*? (viii) OE -*ear*- + cons.: does this appear as -*er*- or -*ar*-? (ix) OE -*eald*-, -*ald*-: which type survives? the former, as -*eld*-, or the latter, as -*old*-? (x) OE -*an*-, -*am*-, or -*on*-, -*om*- (otherwise than before -*nd*): which type survives? (xi) OE -*ēah*-, -*ēag*- (-*ēh*-, -*ēg*-): do these appear as -*ēh*-, -*ēȝ*- (-*ēih*-, -*ēig*-), or as -*īh*-, -*īg*-? All the above vowels and diphthongs occur in words used as elements in p.n. but some appear only in a few words, and some of these words are not to be found as elements in the names of every area. Thus No. vi is hardly found except in OE *stīepel*, *stȳpel*, *stēpel*, 'steeple,' and OE *hlīepe*, etc., 'a leap'; No. vii occurs in p.n. apparently only in OE *wiell*, 'water-spring, well.' The latter element is fairly widespread, the two former by no means so. Nos. ii and iii, occurring respectively in OE *strǣt*, and in *hǣþ*, *hwǣte*, 'heath, wheat,' are most important points of dialect, but except by the help of rhymes, the quality of the vowels can only be determined, as a rule, in the shortened form, since the distinguishing spellings are nowhere consistently used. It is of the highest importance to settle this point if possible, because in some dialects both vowels were tense in ME, in others both slack, while a third dialect group distinguishes between them, having No. ii tense and No. iii slack. No. v is a valuable test for distinguishing between east and west, though there seems to be also a central area which has the western type (*u*, etc.) in No. v, whilst otherwise exhibiting on the whole eastern characteristics. Place-name elements with both short and long OE *eo* are sufficiently numerous and widespread. Of the former, *heorot*, 'hart,' and *neoþor*, 'nether,' and of the latter *dēoþ*, 'deep,' and *prēost*, 'priest,' and *dēor*, 'deer,' or OE *Dēora*, a pers. name, are fairly common.

It may be of interest to summarise briefly Miss Serjeantson's results up to date regarding the distribution of the ME type variously written *eo* (in early ME), *u*, *ue*, *o*, *oe*. These spellings certainly represented a rounded vowel, and most probably [y̆] quite early in the South-West and South-West Midlands. In confirmation of this Miss Serjeantson points to the rhymes *neode-hude*, 'to hide,' Layamon; and *duyre*, 'dear' (with inverted spelling), *huyre*, 'hire,' in the Southern Legendary. These rounded forms (spelt *u, o*, etc.) occur with varying frequency from the thirteenth century onwards, according to Miss Serjeantson, in the p.n. of the following counties: D, Do, Ha, Berks, W, So, Gl, O, Wo, He, Sa, St (Ch very slight and ambiguous traces), La; and further in those parts of the following counties which abutted upon others where the rounded type was normal: Sr, Bk, Wa, Db.

There appear to have been three distinct dialect tendencies in respect of the treatment of the OE *ĕo*, each extending over very large areas: (*a*) the diphthong was monophthongised direct to *ĕ* in late OE itself, see forms in tenth-century Sf charter (Sweet, *Second OE Reader*). (*b*) the diphthong was monophthongised to a rounded vowel, perhaps in late OE, survived as such well into the thirteenth century and was then unrounded to *ĕ*. When this happened the types (*a*) and (*b*) ceased to be distinguishable. (*c*) the diphthong becomes a rounded vowel, first [ø̆] then raised to [y̆] which remained henceforth, until gradually superseded almost everywhere by the [ĕ] type. In the (*a*) area so early was the change to *ĕ* that *eo* is sometimes used as a symbol for an original *ē*-sound, cp. *ceose*, 'cheese,' in the *Peterborough Chronicle*. Thus the phonetic value of the symbol *eo* in ME is different in different areas, and in any given text must be deduced from collateral evidence; it may be merely a traditional spelling, or, if the old *ĕo* words are also spelt *ue*, etc., in the same text, it may be safely held to express a rounded vowel. But even in areas where the evidence points to the existence of a rounded vowel, *e* is often written, both in texts and p.n., by the side of *u*, etc., probably because the *e*-type was already encroaching from other areas.

Miss Serjeantson has collected a large quantity of evidence regarding point (xi). The scribes of ME documents of all kinds seem to have been very shy of writing *hih*, etc., for OE *hēah*, *hēh*, 'high,' and *lyȝe*, etc., for OE *lēah*, *lēh*, 'clearing.' The usual types are *heie*, *hēh*, etc., *lei*, *lēȝ*, etc. (see Wild, *Chaucers Handschriften*, 1915, pp. 358 ff., on the general problem). But there is reason to think that in the dialect of many texts where the above spellings predominate, *ī* was nevertheless pronounced, and the MSS. of Chaucer illustrate this, for the rhymes show *y̆e*, 'eye,' to be Chaucer's regular form, though it is comparatively rarely written so except in rhymes. The fact is important because our present-day *eye*, *height* (pro-

Treatment of OE ĕo

OE ɛ(a)h, ɛ(a)g

nunciation, not spelling) and *high* are derived from the *i*-type,
though occasional rhymes, and the statements of grammarians
show that the other type of *high, height* still survives in the
seventeenth and early eighteenth centuries (cp. Wyld, *Studies
in English Rhymes*, 123). In attempting to discover the area
in ME over which the types were used which show a change
from *ē* to *i* before *h* and *ʒ*, the difficulty was to discover *i*- (or
y-) spellings in the p.n. At present the only thing that can be
said of Miss Serjeantson's results is that a most diligent search
has been rewarded by finding a certain number of *i*-forms in
some areas, but none at all in others. It is perhaps permissible
to assume that where the *i*-spellings do occur, although greatly
in the minority, they imply that that type was in use in the
local dialect. On the other hand one must be cautious in
drawing the contrary conclusion from a failure to discover them.
Miss Serjeantson's material derived from documents written
from about 1250 to about 1450, briefly summarised, yields the
following results, some of them rather inconclusive, in which
the total number of *i*-spellings to those of the other types is
given after the name of each county: from 1242 onwards, Ha,
14 *i*- to 150 others; Berks, 13 *i*- to 295 others; O, 12 *i*- to
330 others; Nth, 8 *i*- to 120 others; from the second half of the
thirteenth century, W, 58 *i*- to 250 others; Sr, 7 *i*- to 94 others;
Sx, 13 *i*- to 62 others; Db, 20 *i*- to 200 others. Other counties
which show very slight traces are Herts, 3 *i*- to 96 others;
Wa, 6 *i*- to 400 others; St, 4 *i*- to 350 others; Sa, 4 *i*- to 220
others; Nt, 3 *i*- to 120 others; from the fourteenth century,
Lei, 15 *i*- to 80 others. The following have either no *i*-forms,
or a negligible proportion: D, none in 500; So, none in 160;
Do, 1 in 60; Gl, 1 in 400; K, none in 80; Ess, 1 in 170; Sf, 1
in 130; Nf, 1 in over 100; Hu, 1 in 122; C, none in 150; L, one
in 73; Ch, 1 in over 200; La, none in over 900.

Applica-
tion of the
tests
    The results are not very conclusive, but they raise interesting
questions notably in regard to the dialect of two counties—
that of W in the p.n. of which the largest number of *i*-, or *y*-
spellings have been found, and that of La in which Miss
Serjeantson found none of those spellings at all, in a collection
of 900 forms of names in which they might have occurred.
We may briefly consider the bearing of the latter fact upon
the dialect of *Sir Gawayne* and of the alliterative poems (*Pearl*,
etc.). In these poems the spellings *yʒe*, 'eye,' and *hyʒe*, etc.,
'high,' are frequent, and *Sir Gawayne* rhymes them with others
ending in -*ie*, e.g. *ýe*, 'eye,' l. 228, with *studie*. Now it is frequently stated that the dialect both of *Gawayne* and *Pearl* is
that of La or Ch, though some authorities are inclined to fix

on La. But while *Sir Gawayne*, etc., are apparently written in a dialect in which -*ēh*- had become *ī* in the fourteenth century, there is no trace of -*ī*-forms in the old forms of La p.n., and those of Ch with one *y*-spelling out of 200 are not much better. Db, with about 1/10 *i*-, *y*-spellings of the total collected, is a more plausible suggestion but there are other reasons which make it difficult to place the poems there. In any case it will perhaps be wise to refrain, for the moment, from asserting positively that the dialect of *Sir Gawayne* is that of La, until some independent knowledge of this dialect in the fourteenth century is forthcoming.

In reference to the question of the general reliability of ME p.n. forms as a guide to the phonological features of an area, four tests may be cited as tending to show the value of these forms, even in the present imperfect state of our knowledge, at least as a general indication of, and fingerpost to, the facts. (i) It is generally admitted that *ĕ* for OE * y̆* is typical of Kentish, in fact the fourteenth-century *Ayenbite*, the purest Kentish text we have, has no other forms of words containing this OE sound except before -*ng*, *kyng*, etc. The Kentish names in FA, so far as I collected them, have 56 *e*-forms, but only 7 *u*-spellings, and 5 *i*-spellings. I eliminate -*cherch* as being of uncertain origin. (ii) In the *Ramsey Chartulary* (chiefly four-teenth century) I counted 132 *i*-s to 18 *u*-s, and 1 *e* in Hu. Here if anywhere we should expect *i* to be the prevailing type. (iii) From the *Feudal Aids, Hundred Rolls* and *Ramsey Chartulary* I collected 77 Sf names containing OE *y̆*, of which 36 were *i*, 32 *e* and 9 *u*. In Bokenham's poems (*c.* 1440), stated by the author to be in Sf speech, the *i*- and *e*-forms appear to be very equally divided, though the former pre-dominate. The *u*-spellings seem to be non-existent except in *sustyr*, where *u* may be explained as from ON *y*, or in another way. (iv) Finally, we may recur to the treatment of OE -*ēah*-, -*ēag*- in W, referred to above. The considerable number of -*y*- or -*i*-spellings found in the p.n. of this county suggests that if these are reliable as an indication of the phonological develop-ment in the Wilts dialect, the -*y*-, -*i*-spellings should occur also in texts written in that area. In the *Life of St Editha* (ed. Horstmann, Heilbronn, 1883) in MS. Cott. Faustina B iii, admittedly written in the Wilts dialect of about 1420, this expectation is very satisfactorily fulfilled. Miss Serjeantson's statistics of the spellings in this poem of the OE words *ēage*, *hēah* and *nēah* are as follows: *ēage* written *yȝe*, etc., eight times; *hēah* written *hyȝe*, etc., eight times; *nēah* written *nyȝe* four times. On the other hand *ēage* is written *eyȝe* seven times;

hēah is written *heyʒe* twenty-three times, and *heyliche* occurs once; *nēah* is written *neyʒe* four times, *ney* once, and *neʒe* once. But *heyʒe* (so spelt) rhymes six times with *ȳ*, *ladýʒe*, *signifý*, *seurlý*, *worthý*, *redý*, *alredý*, while *neyʒe* rhymes once with *enuyʒe*, and once with *by*. This seems to prove that *-ī-* was the common type of pronunciation for these words in W, and shows further that the *-ey-* was often written when the other type was actually pronounced, as in Chaucer's English. It also makes it probable that when a spelling, which is in any case rare, occurs at all, in a text or group of p.n., its appearance is significant of the fact that the type thereby suggested is a reality in the dialect of the particular area, and we may perhaps conclude that this type was more widespread there than we might gather from the infrequency of the spelling.

Con-clusions only tentative The facts which are here very briefly and incompletely stated do not at present justify dogmatic assertion in respect of the complex and difficult problems involved in the classification of ME dialects. They are, however, sufficient to warrant the statement that some fresh light on these problems has already been derived from the study of ME forms of p.n., and to inspire the hope that with patience and caution we may reach no small degree of certainty regarding many questions which are now obscure. This particular line of research is as yet in its infancy; we are still groping after the best method of approach, and at many points doubtless our method is weak. Such results as have so far been obtained are to a great extent tentative, and should be regarded rather as offering a general indication of what may one day be attained by a more exact and critical method, applied to a larger body of facts. We can dimly see a solution of several difficulties, but it would be both rash and dishonest to assert that one has been finally reached. It is better, for the moment, rather to underrate our claims.

General observa-tions In conclusion a few observations of a general character. (i) The general complexion of all dialects changes from age to age, both in respect of the actual phonological types which are current, and also, where more than one type of a given original sound is in use, in respect of the relative predominance of one or other. This is shown by the different degrees of frequency with which the variants are severally recorded in the documents. It follows therefore that the statistics collected to illustrate this point should show quite clearly how the facts stand century by century. (ii) In comparing the phonology of the p.n. of an area with a text, the comparison should be based on forms of names written at approximately the same period as that of the MS. with which they are compared. It is unsafe, without further evidence, to infer, from the presence or absence of a dialect feature in the documents of one period, that the conditions were precisely similar in the same dialect, at another period. This is the fallacy of those who deduce a certain distribution of dialect characters in OE from observations based upon ME documents, and of others who expect a contemplation of the confused and cloudy picture presented by the modern dialects, to afford sure guidance through the intricacies of dialect grouping in ME. (iii) Phonological inferences must be based only upon those elements of p.n. whose identity has been ascertained beyond all reasonable doubt. When possible, though the cases are few when it is so, the forms of the p.n. element should be compared with the same word occurring as an independent element of vocabulary in the text whose dialect is believed to belong to the same area as that in which the names are found. (iv) It generally happens that in a collection of p.n. forms of a given county, written down in a given century, two or even three types of the same original sound will appear. The same words are often recorded in more than one spelling; or of the words containing the same original vowel, some may occur more frequently with one spelling, others with another. In such cases it is important to note the relative frequency with which each type severally occurs. If one type is found in very slight proportions compared to another, it is probable that that which most frequently occurs is the predominant type in use in the dialect at that time. Again when the proportions are more equal, both types may be in use in areas within the county exposed respectively to dialectal influence which is different as the surrounding areas differ in character. It is desirable to locate as far as possible the areas in which this or that type is the more prevalent. The limits of dialect are not necessarily conterminous with county boundaries, but may cut clean across these. Again, there may exist within a large county considerable dialectal differentiations, and it is further important to bear in mind that border dialects, or types intermediate between two or more strongly marked and distinctive dialects, will probably arise. Dialect areas are not separated from one another by a ring fence, and we must not expect to obtain, from the early p.n. forms, a picture of a series of adjacent dialects, each perfectly clear-cut and consistent. No ME text presents us with such a consistent linguistic picture, except a few such as *Ayenbite*, from the very centre of dialect areas. The only way to construct a true picture of the dialect of an area in ME from the p.n. is to check our results by comparing the forms that the names from the same area take, in a number of documents, written at approximately the same period. When this has been done extensively we shall be able, with confidence and certainty, to eliminate the forms alien to the dialect and imported by scribes, and to recognise the really congruous features. The services which the Survey of English Place-names will render to students of English Philology, by providing them with a rich, well-authenticated material for such investigations as are here outlined, are incalculable.

CHAPTER VIII

PLACE-NAMES AND ARCHAEOLOGY

by O. G. S. Crawford

ARCHAEOLOGISTS can assist philologists to give a more *Archaeo-* precise meaning to words in several ways. By means of *logy and* field-work they can identify and explain the bound-marks of *place-names* OE land charters. Many of these bound-marks still exist in their original form; many, being natural objects, are indestructible. This method is slow because it is necessary to visit many sites difficult of access in order to determine their true character. But it is by far the surest way of discovering the meaning of topographic words, for it brings one face to face with the object described. Excavation and the record of apparently trivial finds may also point the way.

Two instances may be given to illustrate this method: *fāgan-flōre* (dat. sg.) means 'coloured or variegated floor,' *fagan* and in the instances given there can be little doubt that a *flore* Roman tesselated pavement is meant. One such is the village of Fawler (O). The early forms[1] prove that the name is derived from OE *fagan flore*. Now at the south end of the village a Roman villa with a tesselated pavement was actually discovered in 1865[2]. Archaeological proof could hardly be more complete.

Another instance occurs in the bounds of 'Eaton' on the Cherwell (BCS 607). The bounds begin as follows: *ærest from wifeles lace þæt swa up andlang riðiges þæt hit cymð to fagan floran, and þonne swa andlang slædes be þam twam lytlan beorgan þæt hit cymð to wulfunes treow stealle will.* Translation: 'First from Wifel's rivulet, thence up along stream till it comes to spotted floor, and then so along slade (flat valley-bottom) by the two little barrows till it comes to Wulfhun's tree stall well (?).'

The Eaton seems to be Water Eaton. *Wifeles lace* is probably the stream which passes on the north-west side of the

---

[1] *Fauflor* in 1205. See *PN O, s.n.*
[2] In the *Archaeological Survey of Oxfordshire* by the late Percy Manning, F.S.A., and E. Thurlow Leeds, F.S.A., the following references are given: *O.A.H.S.* New Series, II, 348, III, 39; *B.B.O.* IV, 17; Haverfield MSS. (Ashmolean Museum, December 24th, 1914. The *Survey* was published in *Archaeologia*, LXXI (1921). Mr Alexander apparently did not know of this pavement, since he makes no reference to the villa.

islet called Wilsey; the two little barrows were probably near Cutslow, and a reminiscence of the mysterious 'tree stall well' of Wulfhun is suggested by Pear Tree, a little further on. If so, the tesselated floor should be looked for between Cutslow and Wilsey, rather nearer the former place. Roman remains are common in the neighbourhood[1]. The old forms of Fawler, a hamlet in Kingston Lisle, Berks, prove that it has a similar origin, but no pavement has been recorded from there.

The fact that the Great Hall of Hrothgar in *Beowulf* is described as having a *fagne flor*[2] is significant, for it is another instance of familiarity with things Roman. No doubt the writer of the poem thought to enhance the magnificence of the hall by giving it a tesselated pavement. Such 'borrowings from the higher culture' still occur on the frontiers of civilisation.

seað   A rather peculiar application of the OE word *sēað* does not seem hitherto to have been noticed. Dr Grundy[3] has identified at least two *seað*'s.

   1. *igean seað*, BCS 705. (Bounds of Enford, W. O.S. 6-inch 48 N.W.)
   2. *ceolbrihtes seað*, BCS 748. (Bounds of Pewsey, W. O.S. 42 S.W.)

I have visited both sites. Each consists of a very deep embanked circular hollow, right at the bottom of a dry valley. *Igean seath*, at the foot of Coombe Down, Enford, is a very remarkable earthwork, and there is a gap in the surrounding embankment where a hollow way approached it from the large Romano-British settlement on Coombe Down. It was plainly the water supply of the Romano-British village; but it has never gone entirely out of use, nor has its true character been hidden from any but those responsible for the description 'old chalk pit,' which formerly appeared on the maps. It bears evidence at the bottom of recent digging; no doubt the water-level is still not far below its bottom. A labourer who has lived at Everleigh all his life told me that its present name is Sadler's Pit, because a man called Sadler was riding over the downs hawking and, not seeing the pit, he rode over into it and broke his neck (he was looking up at the hawk). His ride was connected with some service he was performing for Queen Elizabeth; he was returning from Sidbury Hill, where she sits on a

---

[1] Mr Alexander tries to make out (*loc. cit.*) that the 'flore' in these bounds is that at Fawler; but that is quite impossible. There is no Eaton on the boundaries of Fawler, nor indeed anywhere near it; and the Eaton in question must be on the Cherwell, which is mentioned by name in the bounds.

[2] *Beowulf*, l. 725.

[3] *Arch. Journ.* LXXVI, 230, 231, 249.

golden chair approached by an underground passage. The details are confused and irrelevant; it is the fact that folk-lore is attached to this pit that matters, corroborating its proved great antiquity. In wet years, I was further told, the pond is full to overflowing; my informant had seen it so. It was called Comesdeane Well in a Survey of 1591[1]. Such ponds are known as Spring Ponds in Wessex. Their age must be great. One on Rockbourne Down, described by Mr Heywood Sumner[2], may be as old as the Roman farm close by which he excavated; it is, at any rate, remarkable that these spring ponds are generally found in the vicinity of Celtic villages. They are not likely to be of later date, and some may well be of prehistoric origin.

The other spring pond, *Ceolbrihtes seath*, closely resembles the former. The entrance to it was from the south-west, where on the slopes of the hill are many Celtic lynchets, sure signs that a village (as yet undiscovered) cannot be far off. It was called Carrell Pit in the Survey of 1591[1].

It should be added that ponds filled by surface drainage or otherwise, on the tops of hills, are called *mere* in OE, instances of this word being very common in Wessex. I suspect that many of these upland ponds are as old as the spring ponds in the valleys, and, like them, are connected with Celtic upland settlements.

In addition to particular instances, such as the two discussed above, methods which are archaeological or topographical rather than purely philological often assist in defining the meaning of common words. For the sake of giving some sort of arrangement to scattered notes, these words may be grouped as follows:

I. Words describing enclosures.

(1) *ceaster*, (2) castle, (3) *stodfald* and other 'folds,' (4) *tun-steall*, (5) *burh*, (6) *briga*.

II. Words describing mounds, principally those which are artificial.

(1) heathen 'burials,' (2) *beorh*, (3) *hlaw*, (4) *haugr*, (5) tump, (6) *aad* (?) (7) ball, (8) butt, (9) moot.

III. Miscellaneous.

(1) The property of devils and giants, (2) 'harbours.'

I. Words describing enclosures.

The significance of OE *ceaster* in p.n. is not uniform. There is ceaster no instance within my knowledge in the south of England,

---

[1] *Wilts. Arch. Mag.* VI, 1860, 193–4.
[2] *Excavations on Rockbourne Down, Hampshire*, London (Chiswick Press), 1914, 1–12, with plan and view of pond.

where the suffix is applied to any site of later date than the Roman period; in Wessex it is usually applied to the site of the Roman towns and villas[1].

It will be necessary to examine the origin and meaning of *ceaster* rather closely, since it is one of the most important of 'archaeological' p.n. elements. It is the usual word in OE for a town or city; *ceaster-ware* means a citizen, *ceaster-weall* is a city wall. The word is a loan-word derived from the Latin *castra*. Presumably the Saxons learnt it on the Continent before they invaded Britain. It was not, as the older antiquaries believed, a direct inheritance from the Romano-British society[2]. Bede makes this quite clear. Thus he mentions a small abandoned city called in the language of the English *Grantacaestir*, a city by the English called *Kælcacaestir*[3]; the city of *Rutubi Portus*, which by the English is corrupted into *Reptacæstir*[4]; a city which the English call *Hrofæcæstræ*[5], from one Hrof, that was formerly the chief man of it; *Tiouulfingacæstir*, a city so called in the English tongue; the city of Verulam[6], now called by the English nation *Uerlamacæstir* or *Uaeclingacæstir*; *Ythancaestir*[7], in the language of the Saxons; *Tunnacaestir*, a city so called after Tunna, the abbot of a monastery there; the City of Legions, which by the English is called *Legacaestir*, but by the Britons more rightly *Carlegion*[8]. The word *castra* does not occur in any known Romano-British place-name except *Castra Exploratorum* (Netherby in Scotland)[9].

Ceaster, then, was the usual word for a (Roman) town. But it was also used in the north of England and in southern Scotland of earthworks of native construction.

Mr Hedley has made a complete list of place-names in Nb containing the word *chester*, and I am indebted to him for the following lists[10]:

---

[1] See further, Part II, s.v.

[2] Apart from Latin words known to have been used as loan-words in OE generally, almost the only certain example of a direct survival of a Latin place-name would seem to be that of *Spinae* in Speen (Berks).

[3] *Calcaria*, now Tadcaster (Y).

[4] Now Richborough (K).

[5] *Durobrivae*, now Rochester (K).

[6] *Verulamium*, now Verulam by St Albans (Herts).

[7] *Othona*, now Bradwell (Ess).

[8] *Deva*, now Chester.

[9] Quoted from *Early Fortifications in Scotland*, by David Christison, 1898, 105.

[10] A catalogue of Nb earthworks by Messrs Cecil and Percy Hedley was published in *Proc. Soc. Ant. Newcastle*, 4 S. I. 81–113.

A. 'Places where curvilinear earthworks ("British Camps") at present exist. They have no connection with Roman roads, and are frequently at high elevations; Ring Chesters is 1120 feet above the sea. Probably in most cases these were occupied in Roman times but *not* by Romans or Roman auxiliaries.' The figures refer as usual to the sheets of the O.S. 6-inch maps.

Blackchester, 10 S.E.; Nesbit Chesters, 14 N.E.; Chesters Hill, Belford, 16 N.W.; Chester Hill, Easington, 16 N.W.; Outchester, 16 S.E. (*Ulecestr*, 1242, see p. 149); Ring Chesters, 18 N.E.; Prendwick Chesters, 29 N.E.; Chester Cottage, Denwick, 31 N.E.; Hetchester, 43 S.E.; Chester Hill, Swarland, 45 N.E.; Greenchesters, 51 S.E.; Raechester, 61 S.E.; Hetchester, 69 S.E.; Ferneychesters, 70 S.E. (named after Shaftoe camps?); Bowchester, 19 N.E. (named after Gallow Law Camp?); Craster, 27 S.E. (*Craucestre*, 1244).

B. 'At the following places no remains of camps are now known to exist, but none of these instances are near Roman roads':

Blackchester Hill, Alnham, 37 N.W.; Chester House, Acklington, 46 N.E.; Whitchester, 67 N.E. (*Witcestre*, 1221); Ruchester, 76 N.E.; Hetchesterlaw, 79 N.W.; Haly Chesters, 9 N.E.; Gloster Hill (*Gloucestre*, 1178); Bellister (*Belecestre*, 1355).

C. 'Typical Roman Camps.'

Rudchester (*Vindobala*); Corchester (*Corstopitum*); Halton Chesters (*Hunnum*); Chesters (*Cilurnum*); Little Chesters (*Æsica*); Chesterholm (*Vindolana*); Chesterhope (*Habitancum*); High Rochester (*Bremenium*).

D. 'Names (unidentified) from a Survey of the Priory lands in the Black Book of Hexham (fifteenth century)':

Chestrez, Slaley; *The Chestres*, Little Bavington; *The Elichestrez, Chestrez* and *Goneld-chestres*, Heugh, Stamfordham.

Dr Christison[1] gives a list of Scottish p.n. ending in *chester*. There are fifty-one in all, *chester* uncompounded being the commonest. The majority, at any rate, of these Scottish *chester* earthworks, like those of Nb, are curvilinear and of 'native construction.' Dr Christison comments upon the obvious difference in status between the sites called *chester* in Scotland and those similarly called in the south of England. 'In England many important towns...still bear the name, while in Scotland with a single exception it is confined to insignificant forts, or to the country mansions and farmhouses.' But it was not confined to towns even in southern England. Professor Haverfield has given seven instances of the word in Somerset[2]: (1) Ilchester, a Romano-British village; (2) Stanchester in Curry Rivel parish, site of a villa or farm; (3) Stanchester in

---

[1] *Op. cit.* 106–9.   [2] VCH, So, I, 371.

Stoke-sub-Hamdon, where no remains definitely assignable to the Roman period have occurred; (4) Chesterblade (*Cestrebald*, 1225) in Evercreech, site of a farm...; (5) Newchester near Merriott, north of Crewkerne; (6) Stilchester in Barwick parish, a little south of Yeovil; and (7) Chestercroft, mentioned in the boundaries of North Petherton Forest, 1298[1]. Of these seven instances, however, we must rule out the two Stanchesters; for this word may contain not *ceaster* but *cestel*, a loan-word from *castellum*. No early forms are available for the Stoke-sub-Hamdon site, but that in Curry Rivel is given as *stankestlas* (= stone castle) in a charter of Aethelstan[2]. At the present stage, when a large number of early forms is not yet accessible, it would be dangerous to define too precisely the exact significance of modern p.n. containing *chester*. A special study of *stanceastla* has been made by Dr Grundy[3]. An undoubted instance of *ceaster* applied to a Roman villa is that of Woodchester, near Stroud (Gl) (716–743, BCS 164, *Uuduceastir*, v.l. *Uuducester*).

If the OE *ceaster* meant simply town, why was it applied to such sites as the Northumberland and south Scottish earth and stone forts? When attempting to explain this it should be remembered tl at the name may have been given inferentially, at a date when the forts were not actually in use. We know that at least one typical hill-top camp was inhabited in the middle of the fifth century[4]. On the other hand, it is certain that many *chester* sites in the south must have been uninhabited when they received the name. Two curvilinear earthworks in W were called *ceaster*; Casterley, in the parish of Upavon, excavated by Captain and Mrs Cunnington, and found to contain nothing later than the fourth century A.D.; and Chiselbury Camp, Fovant (*cester slaed burh*), tenth century[5]. Whether the occupation of these camps was such as to justify their being described as 'towns' after the fifth century at the latest is more than doubtful, and it is certain that villa sites like Woodchester (and other Stanchesters that could be cited) must have been deserted and in ruins when the Saxon names were first given to these sites.

castle   The modern word 'castle' is from a Norman-French word which in turn came from the Latin *castellum*. 'Castle' was

---

[1] Collinson, *Hist. of Somerset*, III, 60 *n*.
[2] *Cartulary of Muchelney*, So. Rec. Soc. 39.
[3] *Essays and Studies by members of the English Association*, 1922.
[4] Moel Fenlli, Denbighshire (*urbs*) *ex auct.* Nennius, *Hist. Brit.* cc. 32–5. See *Arch. Camb.* 7 S. I (Dec. 1921).
[5] See Dr Grundy's note on it in *Arch. Journ.* LXXVI, 194.

rarely used in England before the Norman. Conquest, but it became the usual word to describe a feudal stronghold. Its meaning, in fact, was the same then as now. There is therefore no connection between OE *ceaster* (from Latin *castra*) and ME *castell* (from Latin *castellum*), nor did they mean the same thing.

Many sites, particularly in Kent, bear 'mocking' names, which appear to have been given to places where the ruined vestiges of ancient buildings or defences were seen—courts which now the lion and the lizard keep—only that in this country, bats, rats, frogs, owls and sparrows have succeeded to the vacant seats of the mighty.

I have not the necessary local knowledge to say whether, in each instance, ancient remains are to be found, but they certainly occur in these few which I have examined personally. Similar names given in mockery are those compounded with 'beggar.' They are too numerous to name; the commonest is Beggar's Bush, but Beggar's Croft and Beggar's Haven or Heaven also occur. The same rustic wit is evident in such names as Lark's Lease (for poor soil), Starve Lark and Starveall, but here the intention is direct and obvious and has no archaeological significance. In addition to those given in the following list there are names like Frog's Hall, which is applied to deserted sites in marshy ground.

Rat's Castle.

At the foot of Old Winchester Hill (eight miles east of the camp), West Meon (Ha), 59 N.E.; between Cranbrook and Tenterden (K); near Oxenhoath, Hadlow (K); between Linton and Langley, south of Maidstone (K); in Frittenden, two miles south-west of Headcorn (K); Ratsbury Farm in Tenterden (K).

Spider's Castle.

Near Wye (K).

Sparrow's Castle, etc.

Birchington and Acol in Thanet, near Quex Park (K); Ash (K); Sparrow's Den, West Wickham (K).

Owl's Castle, etc.

Westfield (Sx); Owl's Wood, on Kent-Surrey boundary (which is a Roman road) (Sr), 21 S.W. (bronze celts found in 1900 in wood); Owl's Castle, on the Roman road from Old Sarum to Winchester, at the point where the road crosses the Hants and Wilts County boundary, east of Winterslow; Owlsbury between Uckfield and Isfield (Sx); Owl's Lodge, Sherfield English (Ha), 48 S.W.; Outchester, Bamburgh (Nb)—this was spelt *Ulecestr* in 1236 and is explained (*PN Nb, s.n.*) as being OE *uleceaster*, 'owl-(haunted) chester.' It is an ancient camp.

The word *ule* occurs in OE place-names in composition with *-beorh* (barrow), *-cumb*, *-del* (pit), *-hyrst* (wood), *-wylla* (well?), according to Bosworth-Toller's *A.S. Dictionary*.

Bat's Castle, etc.

An earthwork between Withycombe and Dunster (So); Bat's Wood, the name of the wood in which Oldbury Castle (K) is situated (oral information given me by an old inhabitant); Batsfold Wood, in Chiddingstone (K); Bat's Hogstye, an ancient earthwork near Aldershot (Ha); Bat's Corner, near Farnham (Sr); Bat's Grave, 'at the cross roads, near East Woodhay' (Ha)[1].

Mole's Chamber, on the east part of Shoulsbarrow Common, occurs at the source of the river Barle, six miles south of Linton (So, 44 N.E.), as the name of a cottage. It is ¾ mile east of Shoulsbarrow Castle, a square earthwork, but there may, of course, be no connection.

stodfald

A new and interesting problem arises from the use of 'studfold' (OE *stōd-fald*) as a place-name. Before discussing it fully it will be well to give a list of all the examples collected up to date.

I. Ancient.

1. *aldan stodfalde*, in the bounds of Grimley (Wo), BCS 462; another version of the same is in BCS 1139.
2. *alde stodfald*, in the bounds of land near *Blechenenwelle* (Blashenwell Farm, Corfe Castle, Purbeck), KCD, III, p. 433.
3. *stodfalde*, in the bounds of Overbury (Wo), BCS 541. This must have been somewhere on Bredon Hill.
4. *stodfald*, in the bounds of Norton (Herts), referring to the adjacent parish of Studfold; *Crawford Charters*, Napier and Stevenson, XI, 42. (This is the site given under 'Modern' 8.)
5. *stodfald*, in the bounds of *Baddanbyrig* (Badby, Nth); KCD 1356.
6. *ealdan stod faldæ*, in the bounds of Hayling (Ha); BCS 979.
7. *stodfaldun*, in the bounds of Bighton (Ha); BCS 1045.
8. *stodfaldan*, in the bounds of Farnborough (Berks); KCD 762.
9. *stodfalde*, in the bounds of Uffington (Berks); BCS 687. ('Near the N.E. end of the south boundary of Ashbury, Berks,' Dr Grundy, *Berkshire Charters*.)
10. *ealdan falde*, in the bounds of Chilcomb (Ha); BCS 620.

II. Modern.

1. Studfold, in the valley of Sally Beck, Ravenstonedale Common (We, 36 N.W.), parish of Ravenstonedale. This is situated on what appears from the map to be a Roman road. One mile to the south of Studfold, on the east side of the valley, is a farm called Streetside. Other significant names on the road are Cold Keld and Street (30 S.W.), a farm 300 yards south-east of the present road on Cole Moor. Entering Yorkshire the road passes Bluecaster Side and Gate, and continues on the same (east) side of the Rawthey Valley, past Straight Bridge to Milnthorpe, where a supposed (square) camp is shown (Yorks, 63 N.E.) on the north side of the river. East of Milnthorpe the Roman road joined the great north and south Roman road.
2. Stotfold, the name of a moor and three farms in the parish of Elwick (Du, 36 S.E., 44 N.E.). Spelt *Stotfeld* in the fourteenth century.

[1] Williams Freeman, *Field Archaeology*, 1915, 63-4.

3. Stotfield, Oxnam, Roxburghshire (27 S.E.). In the *New Statistical Account*, 1841, p. 261, it is said that a large 'pot or kettle' was found here.

4. Stutfall Castle, Lympne (K, 74 S.W.); the name of the remains of the walled Roman fort, spelt *Studfall* until quite recently.

5. Steadfolds, parish of Irthington (Cu, 17 S.W.), the site of a Roman fort. (See F. G. Simpson, *Cu. and We. Arch. Soc.* N.S. XIII, 387.)

6. Studfold (apparently the name of the site where the 'Greyhound' Inn stands), parish of Dean (Cu, 62 S.W.). A quarter of a mile to the N.E. stand the remains of a stone circle 'astride of a plantation fence; eight stones remaining of a circle 100 feet average diameter.' W. G. Collingwood, Inventory, referring to J. R. Mason, *Trans. Cu. and We. Arch. Soc.* N.S. XXIII, 34. VCH. I, 249.

7. Studfold in Ribblesdale (Y, 114 N.W.). Spelt *Stodfald* in DB. Stands on what appears to be a Roman road.

8. Stotfold (Beds, 27 S.E.). The VCH (General Editor and Miss Keate) says: 'Roman remains are said to have been found here, and Mr W. Ransom, F.S.A., has in his collection some plain pottery which came from this site' (VCH, Beds, II, 14, where reference is made to other publications). The site is on a Roman road.

9. Stetfold Rocks, Exmoor (So, 46 S.W.), one mile east-north-east of Exford. The name of a farm in the parish of Cutcombe spelt *Stedfold* on the 1-inch map of 1809.

10. Stotfield, name of a part of Grovely Wood (W, 59 S.E. and 65 N.E.), near Grovely Lodge, and on the Roman road. Spelt *Stotefold* in 1603 (Colt Hoare, *Modern Wilts*, IV, 186). The name seems to have had reference to the region between Grovely earthworks and the Roman road, since it appears twice on the O.S. map describing woods half a mile apart.

11. Studforth Hill, outside the Roman town of Isurium, now Aldborough, about 90 yards from the south-east corner Yorks, N.R., 138 N.W. The hill appears from the map to be an artificial mound.

12. Statfold, 2½ miles north-east of Tamworth, Staffordshire (59 N.E.); the name of a parish, country house, farm and cottages.

Stodfald meant 'an enclosure for a stud of horses,' and when we find the Saxons calling by this name the walled Roman enclosures of Aldborough, Lympne and Irthington, two (not mutually exclusive) explanations are possible. They may have actually used them as horse-folds, or they may merely have thought they looked like horse-folds. In early days there was need of an enclosure near the settlement in which the horses might be kept ready to be caught and saddled at a moment's notice. Such paddocks are found on every ranch to-day where horses are indispensable for getting about, and in the days before roads, or in rough country, where wheeled transport is out of the question, a horse-fold would be found near any farm. Other enclosures might or might not exist; the horse-fold however would be a primary necessity. Consequently it would be natural to give the name to any enclosure that resembled a horse-fold. In giving names to conspicuous objects their real purpose or character is often disregarded. This was clear during the war, when there were excellent opportunities for observing place-names in process of formation. A certain ruined farm on the Vimy Ridge was called the Glass House, because when seen against the sky-line it had somewhat the appearance of a greenhouse; yet no one imagined for a moment that it was really such. So the Saxons may have called the Roman forts 'stodfalds' without really believing them to be such, and with a full knowledge of their real nature.

Ancient stone and earthen enclosures seem often to have been called 'folds.' An *ealdan falde* is mentioned in the bounds of Chilcombe (Ha) (BCS 620). The Roman Camp near Forfar is called Harefaulds. 'Nightfold' is a not uncommon (and self-explanatory) name for the camps of Nb. The word 'pinfold' occurs immediately outside the ramparts of Over Burrow, the Roman fort in Tunstall (La), and 'pound' alone, e.g. Barley Pound (Ha), is often similarly used. All such names when occurring away from any known earthwork may conceal ancient remains, and should be noted for observation on the ground when opportunity occurs.

tunsteall   Another 'enclosure' word is Tunstall. The OE word *tūnsteall* is translated as 'a farmstead, farmyard (?)' in Bosworth-Toller, but it seems that the literal meaning should be 'enclosure place.' All farmyards are enclosures, but not all enclosures are farmyards, and the word, like 'studfold,' may sometimes refer to ancient Romano-British enclosures. Halliwell says that 'town-place' means a farmyard in Cornwall, but that does not prevent it from having, or from having formerly had, a wider connotation. The following instances have been collected recently, but are far from being exhaustive:

I. Ancient.

1. *tunsteal*, in the bounds of 'Clife,' KCD 636.
2. *ðane ealdan tunsteall*, in the bounds of *Haddun* (unidentified (K), BCS 562).
3. *þam ealdan tunstealle*, in the bounds of *Lohðeres leage* on Watling Street, between Edgware, the R. Brent and Hendon (Mx), BCS 1290. This is said by McClure to refer to the site of the Roman town of *Sulloniacae* on Brockley Hill (*British PN*, 107).

II. Modern.

1. Tunstall, parish in which the Roman fort of Over Burrow (La, 19 S.E.) is situated. The village of Tunstall is 1½ miles south of the fort and about the same distance west of the Roman road.
2. Tunstall, house and stream, north of the Wolsingham (Du, 25 N.W.). The parish boundary north of Wolsingham (where is a square earthwork called 'Chapel Walls') seems to indicate, by its straight adjustment, the course of a Roman road; but this is only conjectural.

3. The supposed Roman fort at Cleckheaton (Y, W.R., 232 N.W.) is in a field called Tunsteads, or Townsteads, a name which seems equivalent to Tunstall.

4. Dunstall Castle, three miles north of Upton-on-Severn (Wo).

5. Dunstall, ¼ mile south of Moreton-on-Marsh (Gl, 15 S.W.), near Coldicote Farm, and only one-third of a mile east of the Foss Way.

The termination -*steall*, which usually becomes -*stell*, seems to lose some of its specific meaning in composition: e.g. *ham-steall* means a homestead; *mylen-steall*, the site of a mill; *burg-steall*, the site of a *burh*; hence Burstall (Sf), Borstall (K), Boarstall (Bk). The use of the adj. *eald* with *tunsteall* (*u.s.*) points to the site of some ruined *tun*. The Northumberland *stells* refer to enclosures of stone, equivalent to the Wiltshire 'pennings,' but smaller; and the word is still in use there.

In most of the last instances there is apparent an occasional disregard for the true character of the objects named. Whether the Saxons used earthworks and Roman forts as studfolds, or whether they merely thought they had been built for that purpose we do not know. But in either case it is certain that this cannot have been their original purpose. The indiscriminate application of the word *ceaster* to towns, like Winchester, to earthworks, like Casterley and Chiselbury, and to Roman villas, like Woodchester, betrays an ignorance of the nature of, at any rate, the villas. This is the more certain because, when describing natural features (as in the boundaries of land) the rule of using one word with only one meaning, and that a curiously precise one, is strictly observed. The confusion of ideas in describing Roman and other remains may be due to two causes, to the break with the past which certainly resulted from the Saxon invasions, or to a lapse of time during which all memory of Roman civilisation and its works faded away. Folk-memory is curiously short and capable of surprising lapses. I was recently sent to see a reputed Roman road which proved to be a causeway not more than two centuries old at most. Conversely, prehistoric skeletons (and even burial-mounds) are sometimes regarded locally as relics of the Civil Wars. This apparent ignorance on the part of the Saxons about the nature of some existing 'Roman' sites can hardly be explained by the hiatus which undoubtedly occurred. Few minor local names are known which can be dated earlier than three, or at most two centuries after Romano-British culture was extinguished. During these centuries folk-memory had ample time to forget. The hiatus may have helped the process, but it can hardly have been the sole agent.

Real evidence for the hiatus is provided by the general character of the place-names, especially in the land-boundaries. Generally speaking, and apart from river names, they are purely Saxon. If we compare these names with the place-names of the Romano-British period on the one hand, and of the Middle Ages on the other, we see a marked difference. The Romano-British place-names are Celtic, slightly Latinised. There is hardly a single purely Latin word to be found in them, and that, in spite of the fact that Latin became a language spoken almost universally in Britain. The Romans imposed hardly any of their own personal names upon British towns. *Caesaromagus* and *Londinium Augusta* are the only known instances, if we exclude names with the termination -*iac* (*Sulloniacae*, *Vagniacae*), which seem to be evidence of personal nomenclature in place-names, and even in these instances the name may have been Celtic, not Latin. Compare this fact with the evidence of Bede, whose place-names show that Romano-British towns had in his time acquired names involving specific English personal names, ousting, in some instances, specific Celtic names (e.g. some of those cited on p. 146). So too we find comparatively few traces of Norman French in mediaeval place-names, in spite of the great abundance of contemporary place-names which have been recorded in writing. (The majority emanate from 'literary' sources, in monasteries, or from hunting, the privileged sport of the upper classes.) The older Saxon words survived, often down to the present day.

The reason, of course, is that neither the Romans nor the Normans exterminated the inhabitants they found here. The depopulation caused by the Saxon invasions may have been effected as much by migration as by slaughter on a large scale, but the result, in either case, would be a break in folk-memory. The common occurrence of the word *wealh* ('foreigner,' and in this case, Roman or Briton) proves however that some native communities did survive alongside the Saxons. For *wealh* meant anything belonging to the older culture—such as a bridge or a wharf on a Roman road[1].

burh   The ordinary OE word for a prehistoric hill-top camp was *burh*, which in the dat. case, *byrig*, has become *bury*[2]. The following list gives a few examples, selected at random:

Meresbyrig, the camp on Ladle Hill (Ha, 9 S.W.).
Welnabyrig, Woolbury Ring (Ha, 32 S.W.).
Mæðelgarsburh, Maugersbury (Gl, 22 S.W.); the camp, however, was at Stow-on-the-Wold as stated by Dr Grundy (*Times Lit. Suppl.* Feb. 1, 1923).

---

[1] E.g. *weala brucge*, where the Roman road from Silchester to Speen crossed the Kennet (BCS 802; Bounds of Brimpton, Berks). *wealas* (sic) *hupe*, a wharf at Staines (*Pontes*) where the Roman road from Silchester to London crossed the Thames (BCS 34; Bounds of Chertsey and Thorpe). The last example is doubtful as *wealh* may here be a pers. name.
[2] See further, Part II.

Maetelmesburg, the camp on Martinsell (W, 35 and 36), *magnum fossatum quod semper ducit circa summitatem montis de Matteleshore* (B.M. Stowe 925, fol. 190 *b*).

Sulmonnes burg, Salmonsbury, camp outside Bourton-on-the-Water (Gl, 29 S.W.) (BCS 230).

Searobyrig, Old Sarum (*Sorbiodunum*) (W, 66 N.E.).

The term was applied also to towns, e.g. *Rom-byrig, Lundenbyrig*, and seems therefore in both senses to have been almost, if not quite, synonymous with *ceaster*.

In the sense of a 'fortified manor house' *bury* survived in use down to post-Conquest times, for we find it compounded with the names of Norman holders. When used in this sense it refers naturally to the type of fortification most prevalent at the time, namely, the moated homestead. In this sense it is extremely common in Ess and Herts.

In Britain and other Celtic-speaking countries *briga* is an occasional element in place-names. The following examples occur:

1. *Brigomono*, given by the Ravenna geographer and probably in Scotland.

2. *Brige*, a station mentioned in the Antonine Itineraries, and to be located near Broughton in Hants, on the Roman road from Winchester to Old Sarum.

We may infer that *briga* entered into the composition of Bredon Hill, which in 780 was spelt *Breodun*[1]. Bredon Hill stands partly in Wo (48 S.E.) and partly in Gl (5 S.E.), and there are two hill-top camps on it. One, now nameless, was called *Baenintesburg* in 778–9[2]; the name survives in Banbury Stone, the name of an isolated rock on the north-west side of the camp.

McClure has the following remarks: 'There are several hills of this name in England. The first part seems to represent the Welsh *bre* (plural, *breon*) = hill, appearing in many compounds, such as *Penbre* (giving Pembrey, Pemberton, and possibly the Pepper in early place-names). *Moelfre* = bald hill[3]. The early form was *brig*. Holder (*Altcelt. Sprachschatz*) says that Brigden in Belgium represents an early *Brigodunon.…*'

In addition to the examples already cited, we may reasonably infer that the following name also represents an earlier unrecorded form *Brigodunon*: Breedon-on-the-hill (Lei, 9 S.E.), where is 'the strongest hill-fortress in the county,' standing on

---

[1] McClure, *British PN*, 193, *n.* 1, referring to B.M. Facs. I, 11.

[2] BCS 232: *Breodun, in cujus cacumine urbs est antiquo nomine Baenintesburg*.

[3] Carn Bre, near Camborne (Co), seems to contain the same word; and it probably enters into Brill (*Brehull*, 1331), an outlier of the oolite formation in Bk, corresponding exactly with Bredon Hill.

the summit of a lofty limestone rock (VCH, Lei, II, 246). It is *Briudun* in Bede.

Brigodunon would appear to be almost exactly equivalent to our phrase 'hill-top camp'; but it is a little difficult to apportion correctly the meaning of each of the two words composing it[1].

II. Words describing mounds, principally those which are artificial.

Archaeologists are necessarily concerned very closely with burial-mounds and grave-yards, which provide so much of their raw material. Place-names relating to these may be explained, and perhaps eventually classified, in the light of archaeological knowledge. The charters contain innumerable references to burial-sites, particularly barrows, and it will first be necessary to identify these bound-marks with precision. There are many cases where Dr Grundy's fine studies of the charters (now being published in the *Archaeological Journal*) may be supplemented by those who have intimate local knowledge, and Dr Grundy himself points out many such instances. (It may be added that air-photographs greatly assist in the work of identifying the bound-marks, for they reveal barrows, camps, trackways and cultivation-marks which would otherwise be overlooked.)

Heathen burials   One of the greatest puzzles in the charters is the precise reference of the phrase 'heathen burials.' Dr Grundy suggests that it refers to the grave-yards of pagan Saxons. It is difficult to see what else it can mean, for a round barrow is always called *beorh*. If it were possible to identify one such 'heathen burials' site with a known Saxon grave-yard, or to identify it so exactly that excavation would be practicable, the question might be solved. At present it must remain undecided.

beorg   The word *beorg* is, as has been said, the normal one in OE for what is now called a barrow[2]. In modern place-names *beorh* becomes *barrow, borough, burrow, berrow* or *bury*, through an intermediate ME *berg, berwe*[3]. Thus the tumuli now known (W, 42 S.W.) as Everley Barrows, were called *twig beorgas* in

---

[1] See further, for a slightly different view of these names, Dr Ekwall on p. 25.

[2] The word 'barrow' is the usual word current to-day, or until quite recent times, in Wessex. Since, however, precisely similar prehistoric burial-mounds are known in other parts of England by other names, they are all to be called 'tumulus' on the revised Ordnance Maps. This decision was arrived at reluctantly, since an old word is preferable to a new 'antiquarian' one like 'tumulus.' But it seemed desirable to use the same word for the same thing everywhere, and there would be considerable practical difficulties in adopting any other method.

[3] See further, Part II.

940 (BCS 748, original charter), and *the two burrowes nere adjoinyinge to Pewsey waie* in 1591[1]. Actually it is a group of four barrows; one is a disc-barrow, diameter forty-four paces, and another is low and inconspicuous; from a distance the other two, which are bell-barrows, stand up conspicuously, and account for their name[2].

beorg was the usual name for what we now call round barrows or tumuli, the burial-mounds of the Bronze and Early Iron Ages. Thus in Gnomic Verses (Cott. Tib. B 1, ll. 34–5) we read *beorh sceal on eorþan grene standan* ('the barrow must [or 'will ever'] stand green upon the land'). It was also applied to Long Barrows, the burial-mounds of the Neolithic or Late Stone Age. Thus the Long Barrow on Walker's Hill (Alton Priors, W, 35 S.W.) was called *Wodnes beorh* in 825[3]; now, by an interesting change, it has come to be called 'Adam's grave.'

The word 'barrow' in composition does not however always describe an artificial mound. Natural hills are sometimes so called, e.g. Black Barrow (several instances, one, Broomy Walk, New Forest, one in the Isle of Wight) and Creech Barrow in the Isle of Purbeck.

hlāw[4] was certainly applied sometimes to round barrows. hlaw *Cwichelmeshlaew* in the parish of East Hendred (Berks, 20 N.E.) is the most celebrated instance[5]. The modern name is Cuckhamsley Hill, but a still more corrupt form is preserved in the form of Scutchamer Knob Plantation[6], in which the barrow stands. In Derbyshire the word 'low' is now the usual one for prehistoric burial-mounds, corresponding with *beorh* (barrow) in the south. Thus amongst the barrows opened by Bateman[7] the following names occur:—Kenslow, Sharp Lowe, Booth Low, Round Low, End Low, Blake Low. These appear to be of the Bronze Age. But Mining Low and Ringham Low, which may be earlier, are given the same name[8]. I suspect

---

[1] 'Perambulation of Everley,' *Wilts. Arch. Mag.* VI, 1860, 193–4.

[2] All four were opened in the early nineteenth century by Thurnam; in one of the two bell-barrows he found a burnt burial with a bronze knife-dagger, proving the barrow to belong to the Early Bronze Age. The other, which was probably made at the same date, contained also a skeleton in the upper part, probably a secondary interment of Saxon age.

[3] See Dr Grundy's papers in *Arch. Journ.* LXXV, 177, and LXXVI, 160–1.

[4] See further, Part II.

[5] Another *Cwicelmes hlæw* occurs in the boundaries of Ardley (O), KCD 1289.

[6] Stenton, *PN Berks*, 31, refers to Asser (ed. Stevenson), 236.

[7] Described in his *Ten Years' Diggings*, 1848–58 (published in 1861).

[8] 'Archaeology of Derbyshire,' by J. Ward, *Journ. Brit. Arch. Assoc.* N.S. VI, 1900, 1–25.

that 'low' was used also to describe natural hills, for north-east of Calne (W, 27 N.W.) we find Calne Low and Cherhill Low, and names like Hadlow (K, 51 N.W.) may have the same origin. In the north of England and in Scotland *hlaw* has become 'law' and is used both for prehistoric burial-mounds, such as Harelaw, Fifeshire, and for natural hills, such as Hounam Law in the Cheviots.

haugr *haugr*[1] becomes *howe* in the North and East Ridings of Yorkshire and there is the usual word for a barrow. In Mortimer's *Forty Years' Researches* we find Howe Hill, Duggleby (a Neolithic round barrow); Willy Howe, near Wold Newton (p. 23); and on the Ordnance Maps the following names occur on the North Riding moors: Two Howes, Simon Howe, Brown Howe, Scarfhill Howe, Leaf Howe, Burton Howe, Flat Howe, etc. The word is of Scandinavian origin, from ON *haugr*. It occurs in the form *hougue* in the Channel Islands and in northern France. It seems never to have been used in Wessex[2].

The exact area of distribution cannot be worked out until more early forms have been collected[3]; but it would appear to extend as far south as Suffolk; according to Professor Mawer[4], it is found in Y, L, Nf and Sf. In Norfolk it occurs as a suffix in the name of the village of Stanhoe, four miles south-west of Burnham Market, as appears from the following quotation (given by Ducange from Spelmann's *Liber Shanburnensis*): *Idem Canutus dedit...unam planiciem non cultam sed vastatam...ubi idem Edwinus invenit quendam collem et hogum petrosum, et ibi incipiebat aedificare quandam villam, et vocavit illam Stanhoghiam, quae postea vocabatur Stanhowe.* This is the exact equivalent of *Stanbeorh* (common in OE bounds) and Stanlow (Ch), the reference being probably in most instances to a prehistoric burial cairn.

'tump' *tump* is still used in Gl and He and some adjacent counties to describe barrows. No distinction is made between Long and Round Barrows, one of the most celebrated of the former, near Uley (Gl), being called Hetty Pegler's Tump. The word occurs as a field-name and is a sure indication of the presence of a

---

[1] See further, Part II.

[2] A solitary but most doubtful instance may perhaps be found in the Perambulations of Savernake Forest in 1259 (P.R.O. Exch. K.K. Forest Proc. Bundle II, 25, memb. 1 *d*). The *hoga* is a round barrow in Buttermere (W, 37 S.E.), above Ball's Copse, and it is the same which is called *oswaldes berghe* in the Bounds of Ham, BCS 677. It was opened by the writer in 1908 and a burnt interment found.

[3] The question is made more difficult by the impossibility at times of distinguishing *hoh* and *haugr* (see Part II).

[4] *PN and History*, 24.

barrow, long or round. The origin of the term is obscure. It occurs frequently in Wales, but no pre-Conquest examples have been found in England.

In a ninth-century gloss *aad* is explained as meaning a funeral-pyre. Can this be an explanation of the *ealdan ad fini* of BCS 674 (Bounds of Clere, Ha)? **aad (?)**

In perambulations of the sixteenth and later centuries we frequently come across the mention of 'balls' as bound-marks: e.g. 'The Balle which divideth this mannor, Chezenburie and the said mannor of Everleigh[1].' In the same perambulations 'borrowe' also occurs, and does not seem to refer to the same object. Again 'the boundes and balles which devide as before,' and 'following the balles and boundes to the middell gate of Yarneberrie castell[2],' 'continuing the same balle southeast-warde.' A more specific instance occurs in the 'Perambulation of Everley[3],' 'to a balle without (i.e. outside) the two burrowes nere adjoinynge to Pewsey waie.' Here 'balle' is clearly distinguished from 'burrowe'; but a few lines lower down in the same bounds we come across the phrase 'to the balle or burrowe'! In a perambulation of Westbury, 1575[4], mention is made of 'two balls, one of which is on each side of the way,' and later on of 'five several balls' and 'a ball newly set up by the place where an ancient meer oak had stood.' These last 'balls' must certainly be mounds thrown up for the deliberate purpose of marking the boundary. One is reminded of the phrases *per quendam puteum ibidem de novo factum, prout de novo per puteos bundat...ut per novos puteos bundat*, which occur sometimes in forest perambulations[5]. The digging of pits to mark bounds involves the piling up of mounds by the side of them. **'ball'**

This word is first found in ME and means a mound. It came to be reserved for one of the commonest forms of mounds, namely, archery butts. In England it is sometimes used of natural hills, e.g. Robin Hood's Butts, near Weobley (He); and sometimes of tumuli, e.g. Robin Hood's Butts, Otterford (So, 86 N.E.). In France it is used of rifle-butts, e.g. the Butte de Tir, near Arras; and also of mediaeval castle mounds, such as the Butte de Warlencourt, near Bapaume, which was fiercely contested and finally demolished by gun-fire during the last stages of the Battle of the Somme. **'butts'**

[1] 'Peramb. of Upavon, 1591,' *Wilts. Arch. Mag.* VI, 1860, 190-1.
[2] 'Peramb. of Berwick St James,' *ib.* 195-6.
[3] *Id. ib.* 193-4.
[4] Colt Hoare, *Modern Wilts*, Hundred of Westbury, 54-7.
[5] The ones quoted are from those of Savernake, P.R.O. Misc. Chancery, Bundle 12, No. 12 (2); another reference to the same document is Forest Proceedings Ancient 83; date 1331.

'*moot*'   A great deal has been written about 'moot-hills.' But when we come to examine the facts they seem to reveal something like this. The meetings of the Shire and Hundred Courts took place in the open air and generally at some well-known spot where the boundaries of several parishes converged. Now parish bounds often converged towards some prominent landmark, such as a tumulus. At such a spot the Hundred Courts met and the Hundred was often called after the meeting-place. Thus the Hundred of Swanborough (W) is called after a barrow which still stands at the point where the Parishes of Manningford Bruce, Manningford Abbots and Wilcot meet (W, 41 N.E.). It was called *swanabeorh* in 907[1] and is said to have still been known as Swanborough Tump in 1884; an old man who died a little before that date remembered courts being held there. The site has been identified with the *Swinbeorgum* mentioned in Alfred's Will, where Alfred met the lords of Wessex[2], but in view of the divergence of form this identification seems impossible. Now this and other 'moot-hills' were not deliberately thrown up to form meeting-places. They were merely the rendezvous of those who attended the court. It seems unlikely that, with rare exceptions[3], any earthworks were specially made for these open-air gatherings. Why should they be?

Confusion has arisen from another source. The word 'moot' in ME means, amongst other things, a ditch, especially a ditch round a castle or 'moated' homestead. It is indeed the same word as our 'moat,' but had a slightly wider meaning. Thus not only was the wet moat round a mediaeval homestead so called, but also the dry ditches round castle mounds, and even prehistoric camps[4]. The name 'moot' occurring as a field-name is a sure guide to earthworks of some kind. The word has nothing whatever to do with 'meeting' and has an entirely different pedigree. When therefore we find a castle mound associated with the word 'moot,' it is by the second and not the first meaning that we must explain it.

[1] *Liber de Hyda*, 232.

[2] The Rev. H. G. Tomkins (*ex auct.* R. Nicholson), *The Academy*, May 24th, 1884 (xxv, 308–9). The mound has recently been added to the Ordnance Maps.

[3] *The Aveland* in S. Lincs, where the Court of Aveland Wapentake was held, and a similar work near Oxton Grange (Nt), where Thurgarton Wapentake is known to have met, are among such.

[4] The ramparts and ditch of Chisbury Camp, Little Bedwyn (W, 37 N.W.), are called 'The Moat' on the Tithe Map of 1846.

III. Miscellaneous.

Every field archaeologist knows that sites assigned by popular imagination to the Devil are sure to be of interest to him. The Devil's Den, near Marlborough (W), is a megalithic burial-chamber; two Kentish sites are so called, one being a deserted moated homestead. The same name occurs as a field name in Thatcham (Berks) and as a name of a part of the New Forest[1]. Parts of Wansdyke are called in ancient documents and maps, the 'Devil's Ditch,' and the same name is used to describe many other ancient entrenchments. In this we can see the origin of the term. Wansdyke was originally Woden's Dyke (*Wodnesdic*), a name given to it by the awestruck Saxons who thought such a mighty work must be of supernatural origin.

'The property of devils and giants'

A close parallel occurs in Bavaria, where a part of the Roman *limes*—a fortified frontier-wall like that in north Britain—is called *Teufels Mauer* (Devil's Wall)[2].

There were other patrons of ancient sites besides the Devil. It is always worth while visiting spots associated with giants, old wives, fairies, King Arthur, Puck, Robin Hood or Michael Scott. The particular patron differs in different localities according to the local folk-lore, but there is generally some solid 'archaeological' fact behind the name. Sometimes the fact is a freak of nature or some striking natural object—a remarkable rock, or a precipitous gorge; more often it is the work of man. *Scucca* (also spelt *sceucca*, *sceocca*, *scocca*) means in the singular 'the Devil,' and occurs in *scuccanhlau* (BCS 264)[3].

The attribution of remains to giants may be considered under this heading. So universal is the association of the word 'giant' with ancient and generally prehistoric remains, that it would be worth while visiting every site where it occurs. In the Cotswolds, for instance, the field name 'Giant's ground' occurs (in Bisley), where a chambered Long Barrow once stood, and indeed the existence of this name was a valuable link in determining the exact site of the barrow. Giants' Graves occur in the Scilly Isles, and the same kind of megalithic burial-mounds in Sardinia are called Tombe dei Giganti, and in Denmark, Jættestuer. We may compare the *ænta dic* (KCD 743, Bounds of Worthy (Ha))[4], and *thyrspytt* (*ib.* III, 396, Bounds of 'Poddenho').

[1] See *Proc. Hampshire Field Club*, IX, pt 2, 292.

[2] The exact spot is on the west bank of the Danube, eight kilometres south-west of Kelheim, in the Hienheimer Forest. See map opp. p. 48 of *Der Bäyerische Vorgeschichtsfreund*, Heft III, 1923.

[3] Identified by Mr Gurney of Eggington with Shecklow Warren (Bk).

[4] A field in Wonston, not far to the north of the Worthy valley, is called 'Devil's Ditch' on the Tithe Map; it is an analogous formation.

A definite reference to *chesters* as the work of giants occurs in Gnomic Verses (Cott. Tib. B I, ll. 1–2): *ceastra beoð feorran gesyne orðanc enta geweorc* ('chesters are to be seen from afar, cunning giants' works'). The fact that they are to be seen 'from afar' suggests that here *ceaster* means hill-top camps. However this may be, the description shows (as indeed do other instances) that 'giants' work' was a stereotyped description of ancient monuments. It probably had the same vague meaning as 'Roman' has to-day amongst country-folk, who describe ancient sites indiscriminately by this term.

The chambered Long Barrow, called Wayland's Smithy (par. of Ashbury, Berks, 19 N.W.), was called *welandes smidðan* in a charter of 955 (BCS 908). It belongs, like the Giant's Stone at Bisley, to the Neolithic period. According to the legend current locally, any traveller whose horse had cast a shoe on the adjacent ridgeway had only to leave a groat on the capstone and return to find his horse shod and the money taken. A remarkable light was thrown on this legend by the discovery there of two iron currency bars buried, apparently of set purpose, at the foot of one of the upright stones. These currency bars go back to pre-Roman times, when they were used as a substitute for money, and their presence here suggests that Wayland Smith was preceded in his tenancy by some Celtic blacksmith[1].

Instances such as these prove the antiquity of traditional names in England. Local researches and folklore will add to our knowledge of their character.

'*harbours*' A great deal has been written about the name Cold Harbour, but most of it is speculative and valueless. I do not propose to suggest any fresh explanation, but to quote a few parallel instances. From these it would seem that both 'cold' and 'harbour' must be explained in terms of their literal meaning at the date when the name was first applied to the sites which bear it.

Dark Harbour (So, 75 S.E.), farm in Horsington between South Cheriton and Charlton Horethorne, three miles south-west of Wincanton.

King's Arbour (Mx, 19 N.W.), in Harlington (Faden, 1796)[2].

Low Harbour (Y, 139 S.W.), farm in Linton, between Ouseburn and Tollerton.

[1] See *Ant. Journ.* July, 1921 (Peers and Smith.)

[2] The name is marked on the present edition of the 6-inch O.S. map, where it is added that it is the site of the 'west end of General Roy's Base.'' It is due south of a cross-roads called (after a public house) 'The Magpies.' In the south-west angle is what looks on the map like the remains of a moat, and half a mile to the south-east are the remains of a 'square' camp.

Oram's Arbour (Ha, 41 S.W.), immediately outside the Westgate of Winchester.

Queen's Arbour (Berks, 30 S.E.), in and 1400 yards south-east of Twyford.

Queen's Arbour (O, 49 S.E.), in Ipsden. 'The name of a field, on the west side of the Thames, overlooked in former times by Wallingford Castle.' (O.S. name-books.)

Robin Hood's Arbour (Berks, 24 S.W.), in Maidenhead; a square earthwork near Maidenhead Thicket. (See VCH Berks, I, 204. *Berks, Bucks and Oxon Journ.* Oct. 1901, 95.)

Windy Arbour or Harbour (Ch, 56 S.W.), in Worleston; (La, 25 S.W.), farm in Nether Kellet, 4½ miles north-north-east of Lancaster; (La, 59 S.E.), farm in Kirkham; (La, 70 S.W.), farm in Wheelton; (Wa, 26 S.W.), near Kenilworth.

The prefix 'cold' is applied to other names, and seems sometimes to mean 'deserted.' Thus Cold Kitchen Hill in the parish of Kingston Deverill, Wilts, is a prolific prehistoric and Romano-British site, whose black, burnt soil sufficiently explains the name 'kitchen.' The sites to which the prefix 'cold' is attached are extremely numerous and a list is quite unnecessary.

Archaeology can assist in the interpretation of obsolete *Conclusion* topographic words by explaining the true nature of the objects to which they refer. This can only be done (1) when these objects still exist for inspection, and (2) when they can be accurately located. The second condition can be fulfilled by a study of OE land charters and perambulations of later date. The study of the charters is now recognised as of great value; but mediaeval perambulations are still neglected. Their paramount advantages lie in the fact that, when a chain of points is given, it is always possible to identify some of the points; and when there is exact knowledge of the course of the line which is being followed—such as river or parish boundary— most of the points can be identified with existing features. This involves field-work; even the use of the large scale Ordnance Maps cannot alone suffice.

Apart from obvious philological uses, what is the unifying aim underlying all this research? We are gradually collecting facts in order to construct a series of maps of England, or of parts of England, as it appeared in past ages. To construct maps of prehistoric and Roman England, we need the evidence of the OE charters and of OE spellings. Prehistoric hill-top camps and barrows now ploughed flat are revealed by the charters[1]; Roman roads are discovered or confirmed; and sometimes the early spelling may be decisive in the identifica-

---

[1] And will often, I expect, be confirmed by air-photographs when ground observation shows nothing.

tion of a Roman name. No map of Saxon England could be constructed without using the charters.

In order to identify the bound-marks of the charters, we must consult perambulations, old maps, and field-names of later date. Thus the identification of the exact site of *stræt gate* (misspelt *stæt gate* in the charter) was made possible by finding the name Street Gate on an estate map of 1825[1]. (The name was 'wanted' also because it occurs in a Perambulation of Savernake Forest.) So too the sixteenth century perambulations gave us the later names of now nameless sites mentioned in the charters: Shuger Waie (*Scocera weg*), Carrell's Pit (*Ceolbrihtes seath*) and Comesdean Well (*Igean seath*); and fieldwork confirms these identifications. The charters are thus central; they are essential to those who wish to complete the maps of earlier times, and for whom no relevant facts are of merely local interest; but a study of them is barren without the commentary provided by later documents. The interest is reflected ever backwards, as by a series of mirrors illuminating successive epochs of the past.

[1] See *Wilts. Arch. Mag.* XLI, 284.

NOTE TO PAGE 148

Dr Ritter (ES 62, 109) has an interesting note on the element *cistel*, *ce(a)stel*, *cæstel* in OE charters. *stan cestil* in BCS 282 is given as the name of *uno acerbo lapidum*, and he suggests that this should be connected with ON *kǫstr*, 'heap,' rather than with Lat. *castellum*, such an etymology agreeing closely with its actual usage in the one passage which is in any way helpful as to its meaning.

CHAPTER IX

PERSONAL NAMES IN PLACE-NAMES

by *F. M. Stenton*

I

FROM the earliest times, personal names have played a great part in the creation of English place-names. Most of the enigmatical place-names, characteristic of southern and eastern England, which end with the particle *-ing*, are derived from some personal name. These names seem to go back to the very time of the migration to Britain. In the local nomenclature of the northern midlands, later in origin, and generally more intelligible, the personal element lies on the surface. Few mediaeval spellings are needed to show that the place-names Darlaston (St), Ednaston (Db) and Wolston (Wa) contain respectively the personal names *Dēorlaf*, *Ēadnōþ* and *Wulfric*. Within the Danelaw most of the village-names created by the Scandinavian settlement of the ninth century have for their first element a personal name of Scandinavian origin. In the far north-west, continental personal names, which cannot have been used in the formation of English village-names before the late eleventh century, diversify a local nomenclature, already sufficiently complex. In dealing with the place-names of every part of England, the student is confronted by the problems presented by the origin and structure of personal names[1].

---

[1] In 1897 W. G. Searle published his *Onomasticon Anglo-Saxonicum*, 'A list of Anglo-Saxon proper names from the time of Beda to that of king John.' The promise given by this title is not altogether fulfilled, for Searle made no serious attempt to collect the personal names recorded in documents later than Domesday Book. Nevertheless, this book must still form the foundation of any study of Old English personal names. Its defects have been indicated by Professor Sedgefield in an earlier essay in this volume. Some of them result from an unfortunate attempt to complete imperfect series of OE personal names by examples found only on the Continent. Others are due to the insertion of personal names inferred from OE boundary and place-names. When Searle wrote, the material provided by pre-Conquest charters had not been sufficiently studied for personal names safely to be extracted from it, and some of his most serious errors occur in this connection. But whatever criticism may be passed upon the *Onomasticon*, it retains the distinction that belongs to all systematic pioneer investigation. It has lightened the labours of all subsequent students of place-names, and

These problems are not peculiar to England. English personal names form part of the general stock of Germanic personal nomenclature. They are composed of similar elements, and have developed in a similar manner. Recent investigation has shown that many Germanic name-stems which are never recorded in England in historic times were still used by the Angles, Saxons and Jutes of the fifth and sixth centuries[1]. The Lincolnshire place-name Minting, for example, cannot be explained by reference to any personal name known to have been employed in England, but it can easily be derived from an unrecorded personal name, Menta, corresponding to the OHG *Mantio*[2]. On the other hand, the geographical isolation of the Germanic peoples who had migrated to Britain inevitably reacted upon their personal nomenclature. Many names which long continued in common use upon the Continent are only represented by sporadic English examples. Long before the end of the eighth century, English personal nomenclature had already assumed a distinctive character. Its later history was profoundly affected by the Scandinavian settlement of Alfred's time. In the south and west there was little adoption of Scandinavian names before the conquest of England by Cnut and the establishment of his followers in southern and western estates[3]. But within the Danelaw an Anglo-Scandinavian personal nomenclature developed immediately after the settlement of the ninth century, and it was destined to survive until in the thirteenth century it disappeared before the French names brought into England as a result of the Norman Conquest[4].

Types of personal name   It is usual to divide Germanic personal names into two great classes, compound names, composed of two elements, and simple names composed of one. To the first class belong such names as OE *Ealhmund, Tīdhelm, Cynewulf*; to the second, names like *Cubba, Ecga, Dealla*. That compound names form a well-defined class is evident; but a class which includes all simple names is too comprehensive[5]. It is better to recognise

made possible much of the work which has been done since its publication on Old English personal nomenclature and English place-names generally.

[1] The existence of this element in the oldest English local nomenclature is abundantly illustrated by Professor Ekwall in his recent book on *PN in* -ing (Lund, 1923)   [2] Ekwall, *op. cit.* 85.

[3] The Hampshire place-name Thruxton, representing an earlier *Þorkylles tūn*, and containing the ON personal name *Þorketill*, can hardly be earlier than the eleventh century

[4] This, of course, refers to Christian names and not to surnames.

[5] These names are discussed in detail by Redin in his *Studies on Uncompounded Personal Names in Old English* (Uppsala, 1919). Redin's work covers all the uncompounded names recorded in independent use

two distinct types of simple name. To one type belong short forms of compound names, like *Wulfa, Leofeca, Betti,* derived respectively from longer names compounded with *Wulf, Lēof* and *Beorht.* To the other type belong names which originally had a descriptive sense. Many of them are adjectives, like *Brēme,* 'the famous,' *Frōda,* 'the wise,' many others are names of animals, like *Hengest,* 'stallion,' *Eofor,* 'boar[1].' There is a small group of rare names which must once have denoted their bearers' national origin[2]. Nicknames, common in Scandinavia from a remote time, are curiously rare, though not unknown, in the oldest English personal nomenclature. The advance of place-name study will probably show that many local names are derived from personal names of the descriptive type which are never found in independent use. There is at present no evidence that the Old English words *hamor,* 'hammer,' and *hān,* 'stone,' were used as personal names, but it is difficult to avoid assuming such a usage in order to explain the place-names Hameringham (L) and Honing (Nf). The distinction between short forms and descriptive names cannot be applied rigorously to all the uncompounded names which are recorded in writing or implied in local names[3]. Many Old English personal names do not at present admit of any explanation[4]. In other cases it is uncertain what significance a given name had in the minds of those who conferred it on its bearer. The name *Dēor(a),* for example, may have been regarded either as

in Old English sources and in DB. It does not deal with names which are only known through their occurrence in place-names, nor with the material supplied by documents of later date than DB.

[1] Mawer, 'Animal and Personal Names in OE Place-Names' (*Modern Language Review,* XIV, 233–44).

[2] The personal name *Swǣf,* from which the Cambridgeshire name Swavesey is derived, must originally have meant a man belonging to the race of the *Swǣfe.* On the connection of the personal name *Gēat* with the *Gēatas* see Sigurd Holm, *Studier öfver Uppsala Universitets Anglosaxiska Myntsamling,* 7.

[3] The distinction turns on the question whether the word which forms the name is ever used as an element in OE compound names. If so, the name is best regarded as a short form of such a compound. If not, it may be considered to have originally carried a descriptive sense, though it does not follow that it was always used with definite reference to its meaning. The descriptive names which occur in OE have received less than their due of attention.

[4] No explanation, for instance, can be given of the name *Passa,* borne by a witness to an early eighth century charter of doubtful authenticity (BCS 91). Even if the charter is spurious the name is genuine. It forms the first element of the place-names Passenham (Nth) and Pasfield (Ess). It also occurs in the field name *Passedene* in an early thirteenth century charter relating to Dullingham (C) (Augmentation Office, Misc. Books, 52, No. 105).

a short form of a compound name like *Dēorwulf* or *Dēorsige*, or as the OE adjective *dēore*, 'the beloved[1].' No attempt to introduce classification into a subject so intimately connected with human life as personal nomenclature can be other than arbitrary.

Signifi-
cance of
compound
names

To speak of the significance of Old English personal names is, however, to beg an important question. Most compound names can be translated, but the translation often makes nonsense. The men who coined the names *Friþuwulf*, 'peace-wolf,' and *Wīgfriþ*, 'war-peace,' were not concerned about their meaning. These are ancient names, and they prove that at an early time the sense which a compound name bore was a matter of little importance. The same conclusion is suggested by the language used by early writers when they wish to explain a compound name. They sometimes mistranslate it and sometimes betray a consciousness that its meaning was not generally known. In the middle of the eighth century, Felix, St Guthlac's biographer, observes that his hero was named *ex appellatione illius tribus quam dicunt Guthlacingas*, and goes on to remark that 'the learned of that nation know that in the speech of the English this name is composed of two elements, *Guth* and *lac*, and represents in the splendour of the Roman speech *Belli Munus*[2].' It would be unwise to infer from this that only the learned knew that Guthlac was a name composed of two complete words, but it is evident that Guthlac was simply named after the Guthlacingas, whoever they may have been, without regard to the meaning of the name in itself. Long after Guthlac's time, people who were not learned could play upon personal names in a way which shows that their meaning was understood. Those who added the epithet *unrǣd*, 'no counsel,' to the name of King Æthelred II, undoubtedly knew that the name *Æþelrǣd* meant 'noble counsel[3].' But here the meaning of the name was obvious, and the circumstances were exceptional. In most cases, personal or family reasons determined the choice of a name, and speculation as to its meaning, if it came at all, came as an afterthought.

The appearance of meaningless compound names was, in fact, an inevitable consequence of Germanic habits of nomenclature. In royal, and doubtless in many noble, families, it

---

[1] This name, borne by the author of the early lyrical poem 'Deor's Lament,' occurs in the place-names Desford (Lei), Desborough (Nth) and Darsham (Sf). In the ninth century several examples of the name appear in the Kentish form *Diar*.

[2] Felix, *Vita Guthlaci*, ed. Birch, *Memorials of St Guthlac*, 11.

[3] This epithet is discussed by Bradley, EHR, xxxii, 399.

was customary for a son to receive a name which would alliterate with that of his father, so that the names of father and son might be handed down together in commemorative verse. The intrinsic meaning of names given under these conditions was obviously a secondary consideration. Another custom, of which there is good evidence both in the earliest and the latest phases of Early English history, must have worked more effectively towards the same result. According to this custom, parents who bore compound names themselves would give to their child a name consisting of one element derived from the father's name and one from that of the mother. Early in the seventh century, for example, *Hereríc*, nephew of king Edwin of Northumbria and his wife Bregu*swíþ*, gave to a daughter the name *Hereswíþ*. In the eleventh century a more famous person of less exalted rank, bore a name compounded in the same way. St Wulfstan, bishop of Worcester, was the son of a man named Aethel*stān* and a woman named *Wulf*gifu. This was not due to chance. St Wulfstan's biographer records expressly *Puer Wlstanus vocabulum datum ex anteriore materni et posteriori paterni nominis parte compositum*[1]. The name *Wulfstān*, 'wolf stone,' makes sense, though not much sense, but it was obviously a matter of accident whether a name framed like this happened to be intelligible, or an absurdity like *Friþuwulf* or *Wīgfriþ*. In any case, the meaning of the name did not matter to those who gave it.

Compound names were long, and shortened forms of them inevitably arose spontaneously as time went on. They had certainly arisen in great variety among the Angles and Saxons before the migration to Britain. A large number of them occur in records earlier than the ninth century, many others survive compounded in ancient place-names. Their interpretation is a difficult task. It is possible to indicate certain tendencies by which those who created shortened names were governed unconsciously. It is also possible to express these tendencies in the form of definite laws, but only with the reservation that any given law is quite likely to be broken by the next name which comes up for discussion. In the seventh century, for example, *Tuma* was used as a short form of *Trumwine*; in the early tenth century, *Aelle* was used as a short form of *Aelfwine*. In the Anglo-Scandinavian nomenclature of the twelfth century Danelaw, the same person is called indifferently *Askell* and

Shortened forms

[1] William of Malmesbury, *Vita Wulfstani*, ed. Wharton, *Anglia Sacra*, II, 244. This passage is probably derived from the lost Old English life of Wulfstan by Coleman, to which William of Malmesbury refers in his prefatory letter to the prior and monks of Worcester.

Acca[1]. It is difficult to bring any of these short forms under any express rule of general validity. All that can be attempted here is to indicate the lines on which the shortening of compound names normally proceeded, without prejudging the large number of eccentric short names which will certainly be brought to light in the advance of place-name study.

(1) Single element used   In the simplest, though not the commonest, case, one of the two elements of a compound name was used by itself without modification. The recorded names *Wine* and *Cæn*, for example, may safely be interpreted as short forms of compound names like *Winefriþ* and *Cænwulf*[2]. More often, some suffix is added to the first element of the compound name. In Old English a long series of short names is formed by the addition of the suffix *-a*[3] to the first element of the original compound, as in the names *Tīda* and *Tila*, derived respectively from longer names beginning with the stems *Tīd-* and *Til-*. In early times a suffix-*i*, which had generally developed into *-e* by the end of the eighth century, was often added to the first element of a compound. The short names *Tīdi* and *Tili* correspond to the short names *Tīda* and *Tila*, which have just been quoted. In most cases the suffix *-i* has caused mutation of the preceding stem vowel. An original *ŭ*, for example, normally becomes *ў* under these conditions, as in the name *Brȳni*, a short form of a compound beginning with *Brūn*[4]. Short names ending in *-i* are rarer than those which end in *-a*, but they provide a convincing explanation of many place-names which would otherwise be unintelligible.

(2) Hypocoristic forms (a) Suffixes   Equally important to the student of place-names are the numerous short names which consist of the first or second element of a compound, followed by some diminutive suffix. The number of these suffixes is considerable. As the suffix bore a weak stress, its vowel often became blurred, so that it

---

[1] In an original charter of the late twelfth century a certain *Aschel Mudding* grants land at Saltfleetby in Lincolnshire to Odo Galle (*Ancient Deeds*, L 2792). A confirmation of this gift by Geoffrey of Keddington (*Danelaw Charters*, 541) refers to the grantor as *Accha Muding*.

[2] The phrase *Signum manus Coen* occurs in the authentic attestation clause of an early eighth century charter (BCS 108). It is certainly this short form *Cæn*, and not a personal name formed directly from the adjective *cēne*, 'brave,' which occurs in Kensworth (Herts). Similarly, Blisworth (Nth) is probably derived from *Blīþ*, a short form of such a name as *Blīþweald*, rather than from the adjective *blīþe*, used as a descriptive name.

[3] The common termination of weak nouns in Old English.

[4] Short names, such as *Brȳni*, in which an *i*-suffix has caused mutation of the stem vowel, must have arisen before, at latest, the end of the eighth century. They remained in use after this period, but there is always a presumption that place-names in which they occur are early.

is sometimes impossible to say whether a given name ended in
-ica or -eca, in -el, -il or -ol. The names of this type which are
actually recorded in early texts are far outnumbered by those
whose existence is only known through their occurrence in
place-names. To this class belong such names as ME Leuca
(OE Lēofeca), used in the Brut (A-text) for Leouenaþ (OE
Lēofnōþ), the name of Layamon's father in the B-text,
OE Dyddel, a mutated diminutive formed from the widely-
spread but obscure stem, Dud-, and Blǣdla, formed from the
rare but adequately recorded stem blǣd, 'glory.' Names of this
kind gave rise to some of the most ancient place-names in
England. The place-name Rendlæsham, for instance, now
Rendlesham in Suffolk, is interpreted by Bede as mansio
Rendili[1]. The personal name Rendil can only be a diminutive
of some compound of the stem rand, 'shield.' This stem,
originally common to the whole Germanic world, must have
become obsolete in England within a few generations of the
settlement. It survived among the Franks, passed from them
to the Normans, and was introduced into England in the compound name Randulf at the time of the Norman Conquest[2].
The Rendlesham example proves that the stem was used in
England for at least a short time after the migration. The
absence of other examples proves its early obsolescence, and
therefore the high antiquity of diminutive names of the type
Rendil. And no type of personal name is more common in
local nomenclature.

The oldest English local nomenclature contains traces of
other suffixes, which are rarely found in the personal names of
a later period. A suffix n, of uncertain origin, occurs in the
rare name Cymen, borne, according to tradition, by a son of
Ælle, the first invader of Sussex. This suffix explains a considerable number of difficult personal names which are only
found as elements in place-names[3]. The Oxfordshire place-
name Cuddesdon, which appears in 956 in the form æt Cuþenes
dune[4], must be derived from a personal name formed from the
stem Cūð- by the addition of an n suffix[5]. Other obscure place-

---

[1] Bede, Historia Ecclesiastica, III, 22.
[2] The history of the Norman name Randulf is traced by W. H.
Stevenson in a note inserted in Round's paper on 'The Trafford Legend'
in the Ancestor, XII, 52–3.
[3] More than twenty pre-Conquest field and place-names containing
personal names ending with this suffix are enumerated by Ritter,
Vermischte Beiträge zur Englischen Sprachgeschichte, 193, n. 2.
[4] BCS 945 (contemporary).
[5] This name is generally derived from OE Cūþwine, but apart from
the difficulty presented by the unaccented e, the initial w of -wine
cannot have been lost by 956. It is normally preserved in the DB

names contain personal names created by the addition of a suffix -*isa* to a stem. It is, for example, certain that the place-name Bensington (O) is derived from a personal name, although no corresponding name is recorded in Old English sources. The early spellings of the name Bensington point to derivation from a personal name, *Banisa, and such a name could well have been formed by the addition of the suffix -*isa* to the stem *bana*, 'slayer[1].' These suffixes must have become obsolete at an early time, and their occurrence in personal names compounded in place-names materially strengthens the argument for the existence of an archaic element in the body of English local nomenclature.

(b) *Assimilation* The study of short names is complicated by the fact that their formation was often accompanied by changes in the first element of the original compound. Examples have been given of a mutation of the stem vowel produced by the suffixes -*i* or *il*, but the consonants as well as the vowels of the stem might be affected by the process of shortening. In particular, when the stem contained an *r* or *l* followed by another consonant, it was common for the *r* or *l* to be assimilated to the following consonant, so that *rþ* or *lþ* would become *þþ*[2]. Such a name as *Eorþwine* might be shortened in either of two ways. The suffix -*a* might be added to the stem, producing a name, *Eorþa*, of the simple type which has already been described. Erpingham (Nf) is probably derived from this form. It was equally possible for a short form to be created from the stem *Eorþ* by the assimilation of *rþ* to *þþ* and the addition of the suffix -*a*. The name *Eoþþa*, thus produced, is known to have been used in the seventh and eighth centuries; it forms the first element in Epwell (O), and, followed by the particle -*ing*, it has become

spellings of place-names derived from personal names containing this element, and its absence is an argument for assuming derivation from a name ending in an *n*-suffix rather than from a name compounded with -*wine*. Edwinstow (Nt), for instance, is usually derived from the name *Ēadwine*, and the derivation is supported by the existence of a chapel of St Edwin in the immediate neighbourhood. As Edwinstow, from 1086 onwards, always appears in the form *Edenestou*, an immediate derivation from *Ēadwine* is almost impossible. It is more than probable that Edwinstow is derived from an early foundation dedicated to St Edwin, but the immediate source of the name must be a short form, consisting of the stem *Ēad-*, followed by an *n*-suffix, and not the full compound *Ēadwine*.

[1] The word *bana* bore an honourable sense in heroic poetry. See Chambers, *Introduction to Beowulf*, 270–1.

[2] It should be remembered that the *þþ* would in OE be still pronounced as a double, and not as in Mod. Eng. a single consonant, as the *þþ* in hip-pocket, not as the *þþ* in slipper.

Epping (Ess). There is no evidence that short forms of the type *Eoppa* are later than, or derived from, short forms of the type *Eorpa*. Apparently it was immaterial whether a name like *Eorpwine* was shortened into *Eorpa* or into *Eoppa*. Names of the *Eoppa*-type can be traced back, in England, to the very age of the migration. Bede states that king Redwald of the East Angles was son of Tytil, son of *Uuffa*, from whom the kings of the East Angles are called *Uuffingas*[1]. This unique name *Wuffa* must be derived from the common stem *Wulf* by a process similar to that which created the name *Eoppa* from the stem *Eorp*. Similar names are well recorded in the eighth and ninth centuries, and they enter in considerable numbers into local nomenclature.

Behind many difficult place-names there lies another type of shortened name which contains not only the first element of the original compound, but also the initial consonant of the second element. In such a short form as *Wilma, derived from a compound like *Wilmund* or *Wilmǣr*, the initial of the second element is retained after the first element, and is followed by the termination -*a*[2]. Names of the simplicity of *Wilma* are rarely found. In many cases, the final consonant of the first element has become assimilated to the initial consonant of the second. It seems certain, for instance, that the name *Tubba*[3], which is quite meaningless in itself, is really a short form of such a compound as *Tūnbeorht* or *Tūnbeald*, in which assimilation has taken place between the medial consonants *nb*. Such names are very common. Rarer, but hardly less important for place-name study, are the short names in which the final *r* or *l* of a first element has been lost and the initial consonant of a second element has been doubled. The place-names Messingham (L), Massingham (Nf) and Marsworth (Bk) are each derived from a personal name *Mǣssa*. Regarded by itself this name is as meaningless as *Wilma* or *Tubba*, but it becomes intelligible when it is regarded as a short form of such a compound as *Mǣrsige*, 'glorious victory,' in which the *s* of *sige* has been doubled in compensation for the loss of the final *r* of *Mǣr-*. Names of this type were still being coined in the twelfth century. In an Assize Roll of 1208 the same man appears in the same case as Ralf *filius Normanni* and Ralf *filius Nomme*[4].

(c) Blend of two elements

---

[1] *Historia Ecclesiastica*, II, 15.

[2] The name *Wilma* is not found in independent use, but it occurs in Wormleighton (Wa) (BCS 946, *æt Wilmanlehttune*, from a twelfth century copy of a charter of 956).

[3] Compounded, for example, in Tubney (Berks).

[4] Assize Roll, no. 558.

In the latter form, the final *e* represents the suffix -*a* of earlier times, the *r* of *Norman* has been lost and the *m* doubled. The Old English habits of name-formation were not broken by the events of 1066.

(d) Gemination The doubling of medial consonants in short names is only due in part to assimilation and compensation. In many, perhaps in most, cases there is no apparent reason for its occurrence. It is possible that in some names the medial consonant has been doubled in subconscious imitation of other names in which there was a reason for the doubling. This explanation does not account for all the great mass of names which display this feature. The discussion which has arisen about the doubling of consonants has shown that no single explanation will cover all the facts. It seems probable that in most cases the force which produced the doubling was a feeling that it gave to a name a more intimate character. In a sense, short names with a double medial consonant may be regarded as diminutive formations. Unlike the diminutives created by the addition of a definite suffix to a stem, these names seem to have arisen without any deliberate intention on the part of those who first used them. It has even been suggested by various scholars that some of the more elementary of these names, such as *Lilla, Bubba* and *Nunna*, have their origin in the speech of children[1]. If all other explanations fail, this one may perhaps be adopted. Among the exceptions which may be taken to it, perhaps the chief is that it implies the contemporaneous existence of two sharply contrasted conceptions of nomenclature. The state of mind which produced the compound names with their far-fetched significance is hardly compatible with one which allowed infantile attempts at expressing a name to pass into permanent use. However uncouth may be the forms which resulted from the shortening of compound names, they were, at least, the result of an intelligible process. It is, perhaps, not too much to hope that as the materials for the study of personal names increase, it may be possible to bring forms which now admit of no explanation into relation with others of which the development can be understood.

---

[1] The editors of the *Crawford Charters*, 51, suggest that some of these names, which enter into local nomenclature in considerable numbers, may be due to 'regressive assimilation.' The name *Lilla*, if this view is correct, may be regarded as a short form of some compound of the stem *Bil-*, such as *Bilheard* or *Bilnōth*. This theory has the great merit of proposing an intelligible connection between these meaningless names and compounds of the normal Germanic type. Its chief weakness is the remoteness of the sound-association between the original compound name and the suggested simple derivative.

II

The material for the study of Old English personal names *Sources* is abundant, and drawn from varied sources. It also becomes copious at a singularly early date. Much of it comes from the ancient time before the continuity of Early English history was broken by the Danish wars. The nomenclature of the independent Northumbrian kingdom is displayed in great detail by the *Liber Vitæ* of Lindisfarne[1], of which the oldest portion was written before the year 825. The long series of diplomas by which Old English kings granted land to their followers or to churches begins in the seventh century. It is a meagre series at first. Less than a dozen charters issued before the year 750 have been preserved in contemporary writing, and the authenticity of the texts only known through later copies is often uncertain. On the other hand, the types of personal name current among the higher ranks of society in Wessex and Mercia between the accession of Offa in 757 and that of Alfred in 871 are illustrated by a considerable number of original charters. The very important series of moneyers' names recorded on coins begins in Mercia, East Anglia and Northumbria, in the second half of the eighth century, in Wessex at the beginning of the ninth. Of Bede's *Historia Ecclesiastica*, a fertile source of personal names, at least three eighth-century manuscripts are still extant. The oldest hand in the Parker Manuscript of the Anglo-Saxon Chronicle can only be a little later than the year 900. There is no lack of evidence for the personal nomenclature of the time before the reign of Alfred.

For the next phase of Early English history the material is hardly of so high a quality. No original charters have descended to the present day from the kings who bore the chief stress of the Danish wars, Alfred and Edward the Elder. Between the reigns of Æthelstan and Edward the Confessor there is an intermittent succession of original texts, but the great mass of charters which fall between these limits are only known through twelfth or thirteenth century copies. They are also very unevenly distributed over England. Most of them relate to Wessex or southern Mercia, less than a score to the Danelaw. Among sources of another kind the eleventh-century *Liber Vitæ* of Hyde is a meagre record compared with the early *Liber Vitæ* of Lindisfarne. The tenth and eleventh century sections of the *Chronicle*, and the biographies which belong to this period, add little to the knowledge of personal names.

---

[1] Commonly called *Liber Vitæ Dunelmensis*, although it is clear that the early entries in this necrology must have been written at Lindisfarne

On the other hand, the coins of this time record not only the name of the moneyer but also that of the town in which he worked. It is therefore possible to trace the local distribution of the numerous Frankish and Scandinavian names borne by English moneyers during these centuries. Even more important information is supplied by a small but invaluable set of documents drawn up by private persons or by religious houses and relating to the acquisition and management of their estates. These documents include records of the acquisition of land in Northamptonshire for Peterborough abbey[1] and of land in Yorkshire by the northern archbishop[2]. They also include a list of unfree tenants at Hatfield somewhere near the year 1000[3], and a considerable series of manumissions from the south-west of England. Wills, rare in the earlier period, become fairly common in the tenth and eleventh centuries and often contain the names of unfree dependants of the testator. Finally, for the greater part of England, Domesday Book supplies the names of those who had held manors 'on the day when king Edward was alive and dead.' This material may not be all that a student could desire, but it is at least sufficient to justify some tentative conclusions about the history of personal nomenclature in England.

History of OE personal names

That history falls naturally into two periods, separated by the Danish wars of the ninth century. It has already been observed that many stems which were still productive in the age of the migration became obsolete in the generations which immediately followed. With this reservation, it may be said that the character of English personal nomenclature underwent little change before the year 900. Most of the stems from which the names of the Lindisfarne *Liber Vitæ* are derived can be traced in Midland and southern records until the time of Alfred. A Kentish charter of 863, for example, is attested by the ealdorman Dryhtweald, by the *ministri* Mucel, Garulf, Eastmund, Wulfred, Wigstan, Ecgferth, Ealdred, Sigenoth, Elfstan, Wighelm and Wiahtred, by the reeves Heahmund and Heremod, and by thirty-two priests and laymen, among whose names occur the compounds Noðheard, Diarweald and Beagmund, and the short forms Oba, Dudda, Lulla, Diara and Tida[4]. What makes this variety of nomenclature remarkable is the narrowness of the social sphere from which the names which happen to be recorded in this earliest period are drawn. The West Saxon and Mercian evidence is supplied by documents which, with rare exceptions, give only the names of

---

[1] BCS 1130.
[2] EHR, xxvii, 12, 13.
[3] Thorpe, *Diplomatarium*, 649–51.
[4] BCS 507 (original).

kings' followers and important ecclesiastical persons. Little is known of the principles which governed nomenclature in families of humbler rank. If, as is probable, the clerks, monks and nuns of the *Liber Vitæ* and of southern ecclesiastical records were generally people of humble condition, it would follow that different social orders had not yet adopted different forms of personal name. In either case, it is certain that by the end of Alfred's reign few of the name-elements used in the seventh and early eighth centuries had yet fallen out of use.

In the course of the tenth century a large number of these elements ceased to be employed in families of rank. The change must have been working in the first decades of the century. When, in the reigns of Æthelstan and Eadmund, authentic documents become common with the establishment of temporary security after the Danish wars, the names which occur in them have already lost the variety of an earlier age. In 944, for example, king Eadmund held a court attended by two archbishops, nine bishops, seven ealdormen and fourteen *ministri*. Of this company Oda, archbishop of Canterbury, alone bore a name composed of one element. He was a Dane by birth and his name is an English form of the ON *Auði*. The archbishop of York bore the name Wulfstan, and the names of the bishops follow in the order Theodred, Ælfheah, Cenwald, Ælfric, Ælfred, Æthelgar, Burgric, Wulfhelm and Wulfsige. The ealdormen were called Æthelstan, Æthelwold, Æthelstan, Ealhhelm, Æthelmund, Eadric and Uhtred, and the names of the *ministri* run Wulfgar, Eadmund, Wulfric, Ælfsige, Wulfric, Ælfstan, Ælfsige, Ælfheah, Beorhtwald, Ælfgar, Æthered, Æthelgard, Wihtgar and Ælfred[1]. In other words, twenty-two out of this succession of thirty-three names are compounds beginning with one of the three stems *Wulf-*, *Ælf-* and *Æðel-*. An even duller monotony overhangs the attestation clauses of the innumerable charters issued by Eadwig and Eadgar. By the end of the century the class from which ealdormen and king's thegns were drawn was showing an overwhelming preference for at most a dozen out of the countless stems of an earlier time. Names of Scandinavian origin occur from time to time, and there is an occasional reversion to some stem which had long been obsolete. But these exceptions do little more than diversify the succession of names in *Ælf-*, *Æðel-*, *Wulf-*, *Ēad-*, *Sige-* and *Lēof-*. Among the higher social classes personal nomenclature was becoming stereotyped before the Norman Conquest.

---

[1] BCS 791 (original).

It is more than probable that ancient names and ancient habits of name-formation persisted throughout this time among people of lower rank. The native nomenclature which survived the Conquest points to this conclusion. The few texts which record the names of humble people in the generations preceding the Conquest show the persistence of names which, to say the least, were rare among persons of higher station. An eleventh century list of *geburas* at Hatfield contains the feminine short names Tate, Dudde, Lulle and Dunne, and the masculine short names Dudda, Brada and Wine[1]. The compound names in use among the Hatfield *geburas* were remarkably varied. In addition to the common Ælfstan, Wulfsige and Wullaf, they include the masculine Tilewine, Dryhtlaf, Cenwald, Hehstan, Ceolmund and Cenwald, and the feminine Cyneburh, Waerthryth, Herethryth and Wynburh.

Dryhtlaf is a unique name, the stems *Cēol-* and *Til-*, once common, are scarcely found in compound names after the end of the ninth century, the only other example of the name Herethryth comes from the seventh century. The names which occur in this record, when compared with the signatures to a contemporary royal charter, prove that the peasants of the eleventh century were still adhering to habits of nomenclature which their lords had lost. The contrast between this peasant nomenclature and the perpetual repetition of a few stems in the names of men and women of higher rank explains much that would otherwise be unintelligible. In particular it explains the form actually taken by the inevitable change in personal nomenclature which followed the Norman Conquest. Apart from the Danelaw, where special conditions prevailed, the stereotyped nomenclature of the higher classes of society succumbed in a generation to the new elements introduced by the new aristocracy and its followers. The peasant nomenclature had far greater resisting power. Even in the manorialised south it only gave way gradually before the new names which came in from the Continent. Forty years after the Conquest the tenants of Shaftesbury abbey, almost to a man, bore names of English origin[2]. In the Danelaw the victory of alien forms was much slower. Peasant conservatism gave way at last, but not before it had preserved into an age when records became abundant many fragments of ancient nomenclature which otherwise would have disappeared irrecoverably.

---

[1] Thorpe, *Diplomatarium*, 649.

[2] Harl. MS. 61, ff. 37 *et seqq.* The early date of the Shaftesbury surveys, which are among the most important unpublished materials for English manorial history, is not generally recognised, though it was indicated long ago by Palgrave. It is fixed by internal evidence.

This conservatism is a fact of considerable importance in *Its* social history, but it complicates the study of place-names less *bearing* than might be imagined. Apart from the Danelaw, it is prob- *on p.n.* able that most of the villages which are described in Domesday Book were already known by their present names before personal nomenclature had become stereotyped among the higher social classes. Few of the villages which arose in the tenth and eleventh centuries can have been called after the names of peasants. The age which followed the Danish wars was a time of depression for the peasantry, a time of increasing seignorial control. In any case, a very high proportion of the personal names compounded in place-names seems to have become obsolete among men of position by the beginning of the tenth century. Even in the west and the midlands, where local nomenclature has a later character than in the east and south, many place-names are derived from personal names which are not recorded in England after this time. The personal name *Forþhelm*, for example, from which the name of Forthampton (Gl) is derived, has not been noted after the eighth century. When all allowance has been made for the imperfection of the record of Old English personal names, it can safely be inferred that the name Forthampton arose in an early period of English history. Even more suggestive òf antiquity than compound names like *Forþhelm* are the numerous short forms and descriptive names which enter into local nomenclature everywhere in the country. Brinklow (Wa) and Brinkworth (W) each contain a diminutive name, *Brynca*, which is only recorded in the earliest portion of the *Liber Vitæ* of Lindisfarne. Few names of this type were used after the year 900 in the class of society whose members were likely to leave their names attached to places. Apart from the archaic names distinctive of the south-east on the one hand, and the Anglo-Scandinavian personal nomenclature of the Danelaw on the other, the personal names which enter into local nomenclature suggest the age of Offa rather than that of Eadgar. That the men who bore these names often lived in a much remoter time is more than probable, but the probability turns on the evidence of history and archaeology rather than on that supplied by place-name study.

If the great body of personal names compounded in English *Distribu-* place-names are really of this high antiquity, it is probable *tion of* that many of them go back to a time before the Anglian, Saxon, *personal* and Jutish cultures had become confused. It may therefore *in p.n.* be possible to discover names and types of name peculiar to one or other of these races. Little work has hitherto been done upon the local distribution of the personal names which enter into place-names, and only the most tentative of suggestions can at present be offered in reference to this subject. As an example of the results which may one day be obtained, the suggestive local distribution of the rare names *Cǣg* and *Cǣga* may be set out here. If these names are of English origin, they are probably derived from the OE *cǣg*, 'key,' used originally, it would seem, as a nickname, or a distinctive appellation added to some personal name in common use. The name *Cǣg* forms the first element of the name Keysoe (Beds) and of *Cassio*, the name of an ancient hundred in south-west Hertfordshire, which still survives in the modern name Cassiobury. The place-names Cainhoe (Beds), Cainham (Sa), Keyham (Lei) and Keyworth (Nt), are all derived from the weak form *Cǣga*. Keyingham in the East Riding may come either from *Cǣg* or from *Cǣga*. The interest of this distribution lies in the fact that six of the seven places which have been named are situated within Anglian territory, and the sixth, Cassiobury, is in a region which became annexed to the Anglian kingdom of the Mercians at an early time. No example of the names *Cǣg* or *Cǣga* has yet been found within Saxon or Jutish territory[1]. If it cannot be said that these names were never used by Saxons—and such a negative can never be proved—the use of them was certainly an Anglian characteristic.

Under the conditions which prevailed in Early English society, personal names might easily pass from one region to another. There were no insuperable obstacles to movement over the country. There was frequent intermarriage, and in the earliest times it was common for a chief with his followers to live for a while as an exile among people of another race. It is therefore remarkable that personal names which written materials show to have been widely distributed are often confined in local nomenclature to a curiously limited region. In particular, it is difficult to explain the limited distribution in local names of stems which must have been common to Angles, Saxons and Jutes. At present, for example, the important stem *Ēan-* seems only to occur in place-names situated within Anglian territory. The name *Ēanbeald* is contained in Ambaston

---

[1] The Somerset place-name Keynsham, which occurs in Æthelward's Chronicle in the form *Cægineshamme* (MHB 513 E), probably contains a personal name formed from *Cǣg* by the addition of an *n*-suffix. Keynsham lies immediately to the south of the Avon. the boundary between the West Saxons and the Hwicce, in a region which for a long time was debatable land between the West Saxon and Mercian kingdoms. The name cannot have arisen before the last quarter of the sixth century, and is probably much later.

(Db) and Amaston (Sa), $\bar{E}anbeorht$ occurs in Amerton (St), Emberton on the Ouse in north Buckinghamshire, the feminine $\bar{E}answīþ$ in Anslow (St). Compound names formed from the stem $Tīd$- are characteristic of the western Midlands. Gloucestershire, Worcestershire and Shropshire each contain a place-name, Tibberton, derived from the compound $Tīdbeorht$. Tidmington (Wo) is derived from $Tīdhelm$, Tytherington (Gl) from $Tīdhere$[1]. Tilstone (Ch) contains the name $Tīdwulf$, of which an isolated example occurs in Saxon country in the name Elstree (Mx). How far facts like these are really significant will only appear when all the personal names which occur in English place-names have been collected and studied. Even then, conclusions founded on the place-names which have survived to the present day will need revision in the light of evidence drawn from field names, the boundary-marks of Early English estates, and the names of extinct villages[2]. Nevertheless, it still remains probable that some of the features which distinguish the place-names of one region from those of another go back in the last resort to preferences in personal nomenclature, maintained during the two or three centuries which followed the settlement.

None of the personal names employed in local nomenclature are of greater historical importance than those which are of Celtic origin. The existence of a Celtic element in the body of Early English personal names is certain, but its extent cannot be determined[3]. It is difficult to find criteria which conclusively prove the Celtic origin of a given name, and the historical issues at stake are so serious that it is long before a suggested example finds general acceptance. The Celtic element in Old English nomenclature is thrown into inevitable prominence through the problems raised by the names used in the West

Celtic personal names

---

[1] Tytherington, near Heytesbury, in south Wiltshire, contains a West Saxon example of this name.

[2] A field-name, $Tidboldeston$, derived from the personal name $Tīdbeald$, and probably representing a lost farm or hamlet, occurs in a final concord of 1198 relating to Stewkley (Bk) (*Pedes Finium*, Pipe Roll Society, XVII, 123).

[3] The question of this Celtic element has been brought to the front by Max Förster's essay, 'Keltisches Wortgut im Englischen,' in the *Festschrift Liebermann* (Halle, 1921). There has not yet been time for criticism to do its work upon the mass of material brought together by Förster in the section of his essay which deals with personal names. If, as is probable, Förster's conclusions find general acceptance, it will be necessary to recognise a more considerable Celtic element in the body of English personal nomenclature than most scholars have hitherto been prepared to admit. This, in turn, will compel a revision of the general opinion as to the relations between English and Celts in the two centuries after the migration.

Saxon royal house. The last word on the difficult *Cerdic* has perhaps not yet been said. It is an anomalous formation, whatever its origin, but at the present time opinion seems to be tending definitely in favour of its Celtic origin[1]. Among the large number of obscure Old English names, there are cases in which a Celtic derivation removes all ambiguity. The name *Tūda*, for example, of which three early examples are known, is intelligible if it can be derived ultimately from the Old Welsh stem *tūd*, 'people,' but it is meaningless if it is regarded as a Germanic formation[2]. To the student of the earliest English history, no result of place-name study would be more welcome than the definition of this Celtic strain among Old English personal names.

III

Anglo-Scandinavian personal names

The Scandinavian personal nomenclature which was introduced into England by the settlements of the ninth century is inadequately represented by the names which happen to be recorded in Old English sources. It reached its full development in the northern and eastern shires which comprised the Danelaw, and the internal history of this region between the settlement and the Confessor's death is utterly obscure. On rare occasions during this period magnates from the Danelaw visited the king's court[3], where their names are very conspicuous among the monotonous attestations of southern earls and thegns. Their appearance does little to break the normal isolation of the Danelaw, which is an important historical fact, but has the inconvenient result that the names of the leading men of this region during a period of nearly two centuries are irretrievably lost. The only continuous record of the nomenclature of the Danelaw during this time is supplied by the names of moneyers working in the Danelaw boroughs, and this evidence tells nothing as to the types of name used among the men of the country side. At the end of the period Domesday Book contains the names of those who had held manors on the eve of the Conquest, but except in East Anglia it ignores the names of peasants. Under these conditions it becomes necessary to have recourse to material derived from later sources, such as the private charters of the twelfth century, and the Assize Rolls of the early thirteenth. This material does not cover the whole ground in equal detail. Some parts of the Danelaw,

---

[1] Arguments in favour of the English origin of *Cerdic* are stated by Stevenson, EHR, XXIII, 335.
[2] The place-name Toddington (Beds) is derived from OE *Tūda*.
[3] Especially in the reign of Æthelstan. See *Crawford Charters*, 75.

such as Lincolnshire, Norfolk and Yorkshire, are illustrated by a large number of texts, from which a great store of personal names can be derived. Other parts of this region, Leicestershire in particular, remain in little less than their pre-Conquest obscurity until the end of the twelfth century. Nevertheless, the extent and variety of the Scandinavian element in English nomenclature can only be appreciated when material drawn from the two centuries after the Conquest has been brought under review. At present this material is difficult to handle. The documents from which it is derived are all written in Latin, and it is sometimes impossible to be certain of the true nominative form of short names which occur in an oblique case. This uncertainty is fortunately lessened by the tendency of twelfth and thirteenth century clerks to treat short names as indeclinable. A far more serious difficulty is raised by the fact that the native personal names which survived the Conquest are at present very imperfectly known. Most of the records which contain them are still unprinted. Some have been published by editors who were not concerned with the exact transcription of personal names, others are only represented in print by summaries in English. Little has yet been done towards collecting native personal names from manuscript sources. The pioneer work of Björkman on Scandinavian personal names in England, invaluable as it is, covers only a small portion of even the printed material, and personal names of Old English, as distinct from Scandinavian, origin lay outside the scope of Björkman's study. The time has therefore not yet come for any general estimate of the character of Anglo-Scandinavian personal nomenclature in the phases which preceded its final disappearance. All that can be done here is to indicate a few of the conclusions which are suggested by a manuscript collection of native personal names, comprising some five thousand examples derived from unprinted records of the twelfth and thirteenth centuries.

Of the two strains in this nomenclature, the Scandinavian alone showed real vitality. The number of the Scandinavian names current in twelfth century England is very remarkable. They were not confined to the Danelaw, even if the Danelaw is understood as stretching southwards to the Thames and westwards to the Oxfordshire border. They included many diminutive formations, then, as always, proof that a system of personal nomenclature is really alive[1]. Above all, they were

(1) The Scandi-navian element

---

[1] In addition to well-known diminutive names, such as *Stainke*, this Anglo-Scandinavian nomenclature includes many similar formations

singularly varied. A large number of the stems recorded in ancient Scandinavian sources remained in living use in England for a century after the Norman Conquest. Moreover, in contrast to the English nomenclature of an earlier time, the Scandinavian names as a whole must have been intelligible to those who used them. Compound names, it is true, were preserved by conservatism when their original meaning was forgotten, but the Scandinavian nomenclature of England in the Angevin period was distinguished by the number of its descriptive names. In this respect it agrees closely with the nomenclature of ancient Scandinavia. The variety of this element proves conclusively the strength of the Scandinavian influences to which England had been subjected in an earlier time. It even raises the question whether they did not continue longer than is generally believed. It is at least suggestive that the Scandinavian element reaches its fullest development in precisely the region where friendly intercourse with Scandinavian lands could most easily be maintained—along the coasts of Norfolk and Lincolnshire, and in the country immediately behind them[1]. When an analysis of this Scandinavian element becomes possible, it may well appear that at least in part it belongs to the eleventh and twelfth centuries rather than to the time of king Alfred.

It may also be expected that the character of this Scandinavian nomenclature varied in different parts of the wide region where it prevailed. It can already be seen that many names which are common in one district are curiously rare in another. The common east Scandinavian name *Bonde*, which was very common in Angevin Norfolk, is rarely to be found in contemporary Lincolnshire. The name *Orm*, widely used in Db, Y, and further north, was not generally adopted in either L or Nf. Conversely, *Siwat*, *Ouke*, and the late formation *Rumfari*, three of the commonest Lincolnshire names, are comparatively infrequent elsewhere, and *Acca*, a favourite Lincolnshire short form of *Askell*, seems to have been almost confined to this county and to Yorkshire. It would be altogether premature at present to lay great stress on facts like these. They will certainly need reconsideration in the light of fuller

which are rarely found elsewhere. A name *Anke, Anca*, for example, which must be a short form of some name beginning with *Arn-*, was very common in twelfth century Lincolnshire. On this name see Rygh, *Gamle Personnavne i Norske Stedsnavne*, 7.

[1] That such intercourse actually occurred in the twelfth century is proved by a writ of Henry II addressed to the Norwegians who visit Grimsby and the other ports of Lincolnshire (Birch, *Royal Charters of the City of Lincoln*).

evidence, and they are only given here as illustrations of the results which are likely to follow from the study of late Anglo-Scandinavian personal nomenclature. But they prove, at the least, that in the twelfth century the men of different regions had marked preferences in personal nomenclature, and it is improbable that these preferences were less definite at an earlier time, when intercommunication was less frequent, and the particularism of individual shires was more pronounced.

There are many points of contact between the personal nomenclature of the twelfth century and that which is preserved in the place-names of the Danelaw. Any collection of twelfth century charters from the Danelaw is certain to contain examples of names like Aslac, Grim, Agmund, Swein, Thurgar, Thurketill and Hacon. Earlier bearers of these names are recorded in the place-names Aslackby, Grimsby and Hacconby (L), Thurgarton (Nt), Thurcaston (Lei), Amounderness (La) and Swainsthorpe (Nf). More interesting, because more suggestive of persistent Scandinavian influence, is the survival of the rarer names which enter into local nomenclature. The Lincolnshire place-names Careby, Beesby, Hagnaby and Manby, for example, are respectively derived from the personal names *Kari*, *Besi*, *Hǫgni* and *Manne*. None of these names are common, and one of them, *Besi*, is never recorded in Scandinavian sources, but all of them were being used in the twelfth century Danelaw[1]. In Yorkshire Uncleby contains a personal name, *Unketell*, to which no parallel has yet been found. The name reappears in the reign of Henry II at Kirby Bellars (Lei), where a certain Godric *filius Unketeli* held an oxgang of land. The name *Clac*, compounded in the numerous Claxbys of the Danelaw, occurs many times in Lincolnshire in the twelfth century, although it is rarely found in England before the Norman Conquest. The name *Sandi*, from which Saundby (Nt) is derived, is found, together with its assimilated form *Sanni*, in twelfth century Lincolnshire charters. These examples, to which many more might be added, are enough to show the general continuity of personal nomenclature in the Danelaw from the early period in which the place-names of this region arose until the twelfth century. That many personal names in use among the ninth century settlers of the Danelaw died out in a few generations may be regarded as certain. It is equally certain that when the personal nomenclature of the twelfth and thirteenth centuries is better known, parallels will appear

[1] The typically Scandinavian compound *Mannessune* occurs as a personal name in Norfolk in the early thirteenth century (Feet of Fines, Nf).

to a number of personal names, imbedded in place-names, but not yet found in independent use in England.

(2) English names The English element in the nomenclature of these regions is far less varied than the Scandinavian, but deserves more detailed study than it has hitherto received. Its real interest lies in the occasional appearance of survivals from the nomenclature of an earlier period. Old English names which had long been abandoned by the higher classes of society emerge from time to time among the peasants of the twelfth century. The nomenclature of the early Middle Ages includes many names which are otherwise unknown, and occasionally reveals the current use of names which occur in local nomenclature but are never found in pre-Conquest records. The Essex place-name Dagenham, for instance, is recorded in 692 in the form *Dæccanham*[1]. It is doubtless right to assume derivation from a personal name, *Dæcca*, but the only evidence that such a name really existed comes from a Lincolnshire charter of the twelfth century, which refers to the land of Hugh *filius Decche*[2]. Similar evidence occasionally makes additions to the various series of Old English compound names. The stem *Dēor-*, for example, was used to form many compound names in Old English, but it is only an Assize Roll of the year 1202 which proves the existence of the feminine compound *Dēorflǣd*[3]. One of the chief difficulties of place-name study is caused by the frequent necessity of seeking the derivation of difficult place-names in personal names which are not yet recorded. Derivations of this kind give a hypothetical air to the study which is discouraging. It is only through the investigation of post-Conquest personal nomenclature that any new material is likely to be found. Such investigation, in increasing the store of names known to have been in actual employment, will help to define the limits within which the hypothetical reconstruction of personal names is permissible. The study of personal nomenclature, even in the late phases which are illustrated by medieval records, is an integral part of place-name study.

Survival of Heroic names It is generally difficult to explain the survival of archaic personal names. Many of them have no intrinsic significance, and can only have been preserved as a matter of family tradition. In other cases, the preservation of an ancient name

---

[1] BCS 81. This charter, which if genuine is the second English diploma extant in contemporary writing, presents unusual diplomatic and linguistic features, but criticism has not seriously affected its authenticity.
[2] Lincoln Cathedral D ii 86/2 No. 28 *b*.
[3] Assize Roll 478, m. 9. The context relates to land at Leake in Holland, *quam...Bricius filius Walteri et Derflet uxor eius tenent*.

can be explained by its association with one of the stories which the men of the twelfth century inherited from the Heroic Age. It is, for example, highly probable that the appearance in the twelfth century of the feminine name *Swanild* is due to remembrance of the famous story in which Swanhild, wife of Eormanric, king of the Goths, played a leading part. The masculine name *Widiga*, current in Norfolk at the end of the previous century, and in Lincolnshire a generation later, probably expresses some memory of Wudga, the pattern of heroic exiles, who, like Swanhild, enters into the saga of king Eormanric. The still later survival of the rare and early name *Hengest* is even more remarkable. A certain Hengest, 'mercator,' attests a Norfolk charter of the reign of Richard I[1], and in an Assize Roll of 1198 another man of the same name, Engist, son of Langhiue, is accused of stealing corn[2]. It may be uncertain whether these men were named after the Hengest who had played a great part in the fight at Finnesburh, or the Hengest who had commanded Vortigern's mercenaries. But in either case, these names attest a memory of heroic tradition, and are good evidence that stories dating from the time of the migration had passed into currency in eastern England.

It is the isolation of names like Swanhild, Widiga and Hengest which suggests that their employment after the Norman Conquest was due to some special cause. Names equally famous in ancient stories are often compounded in place-names, and their appearance is often regarded as evidence that the stories in which they occur were familiar at the time when the place-names arose. The argument may easily be pressed too far. Many heroic names were compounded of elements widely used in Early English nomenclature, and may have been used at any period without any thought of their legendary interest. It would be highly unsafe to assume that the story of Gunter of Worms, the Guthhere of the earliest English poetry, was in the minds of those who named the Guthhere after whom Gooderstone in Norfolk was called. Other heroic names were short formations, like Becca and Witta, and may well have been derived from compound names of no particular significance. Wittenham in Berkshire contains the personal name Witta. It is a heroic name, but it is also a possible diminutive of names like *Wihtgils* and *Wihthere*, to which no especial interest

---

[1] Harleian Charters, 57 A 12.
[2] Assize Roll 559, membrane 1. Mrs Stenton has proved that this membrane, which, like the whole roll, is assigned in the Record Office List of Plea Rolls to the reign of John, belongs to the eyre of 1198.

belongs. Direct reference to a heroic story can only be proved when two or more names which figure in the same tale occur in close local association, and this condition is rarely satisfied.

Less conclusive, but nevertheless highly suggestive, is the occurrence in the place-names of a definite region of a considerable number of names familiar from heroic stories. It does not prove a definite connection between any particular story and any given name, but it certainly suggests that heroic tradition was in the air when the names arose. It is, for example, difficult to believe that the numerous heroic names which occur in the place-names of the country round Oxford are all fortuitous. Hinksey contains the personal name Hengest, about which something has already been said. The personal name Witta, compounded in Witney and Wittenham, was borne by a king of the Suevi famous enough to be included in that compendium of Germanic saga, *Widsith*. The same archaic poem records that Becca ruled the Baningas and Hagena, the Holmryge. Each of these men is known from other sources to have been a saga figure, and the name of each occurs in the nomenclature of the Oxford region. Beckley and Begbroke are derived from the name Becca, and Handborough is derived from Hagena. The name Elsa, which occurs in Elsfield, is prominent in the saga of Theodric of Verona. Seacourt, the name of a lost village west of Oxford, contains a name, Seofeca, borne in one of the most famous of ancient stories by a sinister counsellor of king Eormanric. It cannot be a mere coincidence that Frithela, the name of a man associated in the story with Seofeca, occurs in the compound *Friþelabyrig* in the tenth century boundaries of Seacourt, and in the place-name Frilford, a few miles away. The local association of Seofeca and Frithela goes far to prove direct reference to the story in which these men played a part. In regard to the other names which have been quoted, it may at least be said that the people who conferred them knew that they were famous in story. And as archaeological evidence proves the early Saxon settlement of the region in which these heroic names occur, it becomes distinctly probable that they attest a definite knowledge of the stories which made the names familiar.

Conclusion At the present time it is difficult to say anything in general terms about the history of English personal nomenclature. It is a history with an obscure beginning and a fragmentary end. Its middle phase—the period between the seventh and the eleventh centuries—is well understood, and the significance of its principal feature, the introduction of an overwhelming Scandinavian element into northern and eastern England, has always been appreciated. The beginning and the end of the history are no less important. The study of the oldest English personal names will establish new points of contact between the nomenclatures of England and continental Germany, and may be expected to produce fresh evidence as to the distribution of heroic legend. It is only by the investigation of place-names that new material can be provided for this study. At the other end of the history the documents of the twelfth and thirteenth centuries supply a unique illustration of the disappearance of a native nomenclature before the pressure of alien elements. The strange survival of archaic names into the thirteenth century emphasises the continuity of the history. It also shows that in the study of personal names, as in many related investigations, light can be thrown upon the obscure centuries which followed the migration by evidence derived from the familiar records of the early Middle Ages.

INDEX

INDEX

(a) SUBJECTS

archaeology and p.n.'s, 143 ff.
avenam, 89

ball, 159
bank, 59
barrow, v. beorg
Bat's Castle, 150
Bea-, Beau-, Bel-, Bew-names, 92,
114
beck, 59, 71
Bedfordshire p.n.'s, Danish, 77
beggar-names, 149
beorg, 156 ff.
bierlows, 86–7
bog, 33
booth, 58, 60, 71, 78, 89
breck, 59, 60, 78–9
briga, 155
British element, 15 ff.; sound-
changes, 16; population, survival of, 17; words as p.n. elements, 19 ff.; pers. names in
English p.n.'s, 20; territorial
names, 20–2; names, proportion
of, 27 ff.; reasons for disappearance, 31–2
brocc, 19
Buckinghamshire p.n.'s, Danish, 77
burg-steall, 153
burh (*bury*, etc.), 154 ff.
bury, v. burh
butts, 159
by-names, 57, 75, 78, 81–6, 91

car, 59, 71
Carlton-names, 42, 63, 76, 77, 84
carr, 19
Castle-names, 148–50
Castleton-names, 119
ceaster, v. chester
Celtic element, 15 ff.; *v.* further
s.v. British
ceorla-tun, 41
Charlton-names, 42
Cheshire p.n.'s, Scandinavian, 78

chester (*ceaster*), 20, 145–8
Cold Harbour, 162
combe, coomb, 19
crag, 33
crook, 59
Cumberland p.n.'s, Celtic, 30–1;
Danish, 76

Danes in England, 55 ff., 75 ff.
deil, 89
Derbyshire p.n.'s, Scandinavian, 86
devil in p.n.'s, 161
Devon p.n.'s, Celtic, 28
Dorset p.n.'s, Celtic, 28
dreng, 88
Durham p.n.'s, Danish, 75

eng, 58, 89
English element, 36 ff.
ergh, 34, 60, 78, 89
Essex p.n.'s, Danish, 76

feld-names, 37–8
fell, 59, 77
feudal element, 115 ff.; DB tenant
as first part of name, 116–17;
later tenants, 117–18; tenant's
name suffixed, 120 ff.; names of
nickname origin, 121; of territorial origin, 121; distribution,
126 ff.
flat, 58, 89
folk-names, 50 ff.
force, 59
forest-names, 26
foss, 20
French element, 93 ff.; hybrids,
94; Norman substitutions, 94;
suffixes, 94–5; influence on pronunciation, 96 ff.; distribution,
97 ff.; in DB, 99
funta, 19

garth, 58
gate, 59

(*b*) PLACE-NAMES

Only those place-names of which the etymology is given
in the text have been included in this index.

o

THE CHIEF ELEMENTS USED
IN ENGLISH PLACE-NAMES

ENGLISH PLACE-NAME SOCIETY

The English Place-Name Society was founded in 1924 to carry out the survey of English place-names and to issue annual volumes to members who subscribe to the work of the Society. The Society has issued the following volumes:

The volumes for the following counties are in an advanced state of preparation: *Berkshire, Cheshire, the City of London.*

All communications with regard to the Society and membership should be addressed to:

THE HON. SECRETARY, English Place-Name Society, University College, Gower Street, London, W.C.1.

THE CHIEF ELEMENTS USED IN ENGLISH PLACE-NAMES

BEING THE SECOND PART OF THE INTRODUCTION TO THE SURVEY *of* ENGLISH PLACE-NAMES

Edited by

ALLEN MAWER

CAMBRIDGE
AT THE UNIVERSITY PRESS
1969

PREFACE

THE main purpose of this volume is to provide a useful companion to the successive county volumes of the English Place-name Survey, by presenting in concise and summary form a good deal of the matter which, as it is in the nature of 'common form,' would otherwise have to be repeated in each successive volume.

The list of elements handled lays no claim to being exhaustive but an attempt has been made to deal with all those elements, English and Scandinavian, which are of anything like common occurrence. No attempt has been made to deal with the Celtic or the French elements, chiefly because they are of comparatively rare occurrence and can be satisfactorily dealt with as they occur in the different counties.

In the interpretation of the English elements the utmost possible use has been made of the material to be found in the Anglo-Saxon charters as printed by Kemble and Birch. In handling that material the work of Professor Toller in his revision and completion of Bosworth's *Anglo-Saxon Dictionary* has been invaluable. The present volume could indeed never have been written were it not for the existence of that dictionary, of the *Oxford English Dictionary*, and Wright's *English Dialect Dictionary*. Other books and articles to which the author must express himself as specially indebted are: Ekwall, *Place-names of Lancashire*, especially pp. 7–21 on 'Elements found in Lancashire Place-names'; Grundy, 'On the meanings of certain terms in the Anglo-Saxon Charters' (*Essays and Studies by members of the English Association*, 8. 36–69); Lindkvist, *Middle English Place-names of Scandinavian origin*; Middendorff, *Altenglisches Flurnamenbuch*; Liebermann, *Die Gesetze der Angelsächsen*.

In addition to the interpretation of the chief elements, an attempt has been made to deal with their distribution, at least in those cases in which a study of their distribution may ultimately throw light on problems of racial settlement and the like.

In the matter of interpretation, and still more in that of distribution, the volume suffers from a heavy but unavoidable handicap. It has had to be written at the beginning of the Survey instead of at the end, as would have been more fitting. Many of the problems with which it deals can never be handled with any hope of success until we have the full evidence at our command, but on the other hand none of the ensuing volumes could have been written without some such preliminary statements as those given here, setting forth the present condition of our knowledge. Many of these statements are clearly in the nature of suggestions rather than assertions and the whole attitude of the author towards them is tentative and exploratory rather than dogmatic or final.

For the study of the distribution of the various elements and illustration of their use, the sources of information have been threefold:

(1) The various books on place-name study already published.

(2) The author's own collections, made for the most part before the Survey was undertaken.

(3) Material placed at his disposal by various helpers and friends of the Survey. Among these he would wish especially to thank the Rev. A. Goodall for his very generous gift to the Survey of his East Riding of Yorkshire collections and interpretations, the late Mr Philip Sturge of Winscombe for extensive gazetteers of Devon and Somerset names with early forms attached, Mr J. E. B. Gover for access to his collection of Cornish material and similar facilities afforded by Mr Schram for Norfolk and Mr P. H. Reaney for Essex.

The use of each element has been illustrated by examples. The purpose of those examples is (1) to illustrate, as far as may be, the various forms under which that suffix may appear disguised in present-day place nomenclature, (2) to arouse interest in the etymology and history of particular names and types of names. No name has been included except on the authority of good early forms, but considerations of space forbade the actual quotation of such.

In using the illustrations given under each element it should be noted that:

(1) Where a p.n. is composed of two elements an attempt has been made to include both its elements. Where a name is entered only under one element it may be inferred either (i) that the first element is a personal name and therefore does not fall within the

scope of this volume, or (ii) that it is of obscure and uncertain origin, or (iii) that it is what it appears to be in the present-day form[1].

(2) No conclusion should be drawn that because a p.n. in any given example has a particular meaning that it therefore has the same meaning elsewhere (cf. Worton s.v. **ofer** and **wyrt**). Even where *passim* is given after a name it only means that that name is found in the sense given in several counties, not that it invariably has that meaning (cf. Broughton s.v. **broc** and **beorg**).

(3) None of the illustrations are exhaustive. An illustration of a name may be given from one county and other examples of the name, of the same form and history, may possibly be found in that county or in other unmentioned counties. It is in the very nature of things that, quite apart from considerations of space, no exhaustive references for the occurrence of any particular name can be given in the present state of our knowledge.

The author's special thanks are due to Professors Ekwall and Tait and to his co-editor for their kindness in reading Part II in proof. It owes much to their watchful care.

A. M.

March, 1924.

---

[1] This necessarily involves a certain measure of ambiguity but to do otherwise would involve the printing of an impossibly large number of illustrations. It should be noted further that cases of (*h*)*all* for *hale* and *borough* for *beorg* in modern p.n. forms have had to be left unnoticed for the same reason.

BIBLIOGRAPHY OF THE CHIEF BOOKS DEALING WITH THE HISTORY OF ENGLISH PLACE-NAMES

ALEXANDER, H. *Place-names of Oxfordshire*, Oxford, 1912.
BADDELEY, W. ST C. *Place-names of Gloucestershire*, Gloucester, 1913.
—— *Place-names of Herefordshire*, Bristol, 1913[1].
BANNISTER, A. T. *Place-names of Herefordshire*, Cambridge, 1913.
BOWCOCK, *Place-names of Shropshire*, Shrewsbury, 1923.
DUIGNAN, W. H. *Notes on Staffordshire Place-names*, Oxford, 1912.
—— *Warwickshire Place-names*, Oxford, 1912.
—— *Worcestershire Place-names*, Oxford, 1905.
EKBLOM, E. *Place-names of Wiltshire*, Uppsala, 1917.
EKWALL, E. *Contributions to the History of OE dialects*, Lund, 1917.
—— *Scandinavians and Celts in the North-West of England*, Lund, 1918.
—— *Place-names of Lancashire*, Manchester, 1922.
—— *English Place-names in -ing*, Lund, 1923.
GOODALL, A. *Place-names of South-West Yorkshire*, Cambridge, 1914.
GOVER, J. E. B. *The Place-names of Middlesex*, London, 1922.
JOHNSTON, J. B. *The Place-names of England and Wales*, London, 1914.
LINDKVIST, H. *Middle English Place-names of Scandinavian Origin*, Uppsala, 1912.
MAWER, A. *Place-names of Northumberland and Durham*, Cambridge, 1920.
McCLURE, E. *British Place-names in their Historical Setting*, London, 1910.
MIDDENDORFF, H. *Altenglisches Flurnamenbuch*, 1902.
MOORMAN, F. W. *Place-names of the West Riding of Yorkshire*, Leeds, 1910.
MUTSCHMANN, H. *Place-names of Nottinghamshire*, Cambridge, 1913.
ROBERTS, R. G. *Place-names of Sussex*, Cambridge, 1914.
SEDGEFIELD, W. J. *Place-names of Cumberland and Westmorland*, Manchester, 1915.
SKEAT, W. W. *Place-names of Bedfordshire*, Cambridge 1906.
—— *Place-names of Berkshire*, Oxford, 1911.
—— *Place-names of Cambridgeshire*, Cambridge, 1911.
—— *Place-names of Hertfordshire*, Hertford, 1904.
—— *Place-names of Huntingdonshire*, Cambridge, 1904[1].
—— *Place-names of Suffolk*, Cambridge, 1913.
STENTON, F. M. *Place-names of Berkshire*, Reading, 1911.
WALKER, B. *Place-names of Derbyshire*, Derby, 1914–5[1].
WYLD, H. C. and HIRST, T. O. *Place-names of Lancashire*, London, 1911.
ZACHRISSON, R. E. *Anglo-Norman Influence on English Place-names*, Lund, 1909[2].

[1] Not published in book form but found respectively in *Transactions of the Bristol and Gloucestershire Archaeological Society*, vol. XXXIX, 87–200, *Proceedings of the Cambridge Antiquarian Society*, vol. X, 317–360, *Derbyshire Archaeological and Natural History Society's Journal*, vol. XXXVI.

[2] Two other books, which do not deal primarily or entirely with p.n. material, call for special mention:

FÖRSTER, M. *Keltisches Wortgut im Englischen*, Halle, 1921.
RITTER, O. *Vermischte Beiträge zur Englischen Sprachgeschichte*, Halle, 1922.

ABBREVIATIONS

al.	*alias*	Nb	Northumberland
ASC	Anglo-Saxon Chronicle	NCy	North Country
BCS	Birch, *Cartularium Sax-*	Nf	Norfolk
	onicum	NGN	*Nomina Geographica*
Beds	Bedfordshire		*Neerlandica*
Berks	Berkshire	NoB	*Namn och Bygd*
Bk	Buckinghamshire	nom.	nominative
BT	Bosworth-Toller, *Anglo-*	Norw.	Norwegian
	Saxon Dictionary	Nt	Nottinghamshire
C	Cambridgeshire	Nth	Northamptonshire
Ch	Cheshire	O	Oxfordshire
Co	Cornwall	ODan.	Old Danish
Cu	Cumberland	OE	Old English
D	Devonshire	OFris.	Old Frisian
Dan.	Danish	OHG	Old High German
dat.	dative	OLG	Old Low German
Db	Derbyshire	ON	Old Norse[1]
dial.	dialect(al)	OSwed.	Old Swedish
Do	Dorset	pers. name	personal name
Du	Durham	pl.	plural
E and S	*Essays and Studies*	p.n.	place-name
EDD	*English Dialect Dictionary*	PNLa	Ekwall, *Place-names of*
ES	*Englische Studien*		*Lancashire*
Ess	Essex	R	Rutland
Fr.	French	s.a.	sub anno
gen.	genitive	Sa	Shropshire
Germ.	German	Scand.	Scandinavian
Gl	Gloucestershire	Sc.	Scotland, Scottish
Ha	Hampshire	SCy	South Country
He	Herefordshire	Sf	Suffolk
Herts	Hertfordshire	sg.	singular
Hu	Huntingdonshire	So	Somerset
Hund	Hundred	Sr	Surrey
K	Kent	St	Staffordshire
KCD	Kemble, *Codex Diploma-*	St. Eng.	Standard English
	ticus	Swed.	Swedish
L	Lincolnshire	Sx	Sussex
La	Lancashire	TRE	Tempore Regis Edwardi
Lat.	Latin	TRW	Tempore Regis Willelmi
Lei	Leicestershire	W	Wiltshire
LGerm.	Low German	Wa	Warwickshire
ME	Middle English	WCy	West Country
Mod. Eng.	Modern English	We	Westmoreland
ModHG	Modern High German	Wo	Worcestershire
Mon	Monmouthshire	Wt	Isle of Wight
Mx	Middlesex	Y	Yorkshire

[1] i.e. Old Scand. generally.

P

PHONETIC SYMBOLS USED IN TRANSCRIPTION
OF PRONUNCIATION OF PLACE-NAMES

p	*p*ay	z	*z*one	r	*r*un	e	*r*ed
b	*b*ay	ʃ	*sh*one	l	*l*and	ei	fl*ay*
t	*t*ea	ʒ	a*z*ure	tʃ	*ch*urch	ɛː	th*ere*
d	*d*ay	θ	*th*in	dʒ	*j*udge	i	p*i*t
k	*k*ey	ð	*th*en	ɑː	f*a*ther	iː	f*ee*l
g	*g*o	j	*y*ou	ɑu	c*ow*	ou	l*ow*
ʍ	*wh*en	χ	lo*ch*	ai	fl*y*	u	g*oo*d
w	*w*in	h	*h*is	æ	c*a*b	uː	r*u*le
f	*f*oe	m	*m*an	ɔ	p*o*t	ʌ	m*u*ch
v	*v*ote	n	*n*o	ɔː	s*aw*	ə	ov*er*
s	*s*ay	ŋ	si*ng*	oi	*oi*l	əː	b*ir*d

Examples:

Harwich (hæridʒ), Shrewsbury (ʃrouzbəri, ʃruːzbəri),
Beaulieu (bjuːli).

THE CHIEF ELEMENTS USED
IN ENGLISH PLACE-NAMES

IN using this list it should be noted that in giving the interpretation of any element, if that element has a direct descendant in Modern English speech, that descendant is printed in italics, e.g. **cweorn**, '*quern*, hand-mill.' Further, that where two or more p.n. are mentioned in succession and the county abbreviation is given only after one of them it is intended to apply to all the names alike. Where a p.n. occurs more than once in a county the number of times that it has been noted as occurring is expressed by the use of the necessary numeral before the county abbreviation, e.g. 2La denotes that the p.n. in question is found twice in La.

á, ON, 'river.' Greta (Cu), Rothay (We), Aby (L), E. and W. Ayton (Y). Gen. sg. *ar* in Ayresome (Y).

ác, OE, '*oak*.' Dat. pl. *æt þæm acum*, 'at the oaks,' gives Acomb (Nb, Y), Oaken (St). ME *at then oke(s)* becomes *at the noke(s)* and gives Noakes (He), Noke (O), Knockholt (K). Acton (*passim*), Aughton (Y), Aggborough, Harrock (Wo), Oxted (Sr), Occold (Sf), Othorpe (Lei), Hodsock (Nt). In Scand. districts it freely interchanges with **eik**.

ácen, OE, 'covered with *oaks*.' Akenside (Nb), Oakenrod (La). '*oaken*,' Noke Bridge (Ha).

æcer, OE, **akr**, ON, 'cultivated piece of land,' used only of arable land in OE. In Scand. districts it is impossible to distinguish the two forms. Gatacre (Sa), Linacre (La), Bessacar (Y), Alsager (Ch), Ackers (La), Uzzicar (Cu), Halnaker (Sx);

ǽl, OE, '*eel*.' Ely (C).

ǽmette, OE, '*ant*.' Ampthill (Beds).

æppel, OE, '*apple*.' Appleton (Berks), Eppleby (Y), Apperknowle (Db), Napleton (Wo). *æppeltun* is the OE term for an orchard, and must be so used in Appleton Gate in Newark (Nt) for there was never a village of Appleton. In other cases it may simply denote 'farm by (or with) an apple tree.'

ærn, OE, 'house.' Grundy has shown that this word is used to form compounds denoting a house for storing or making things. Thus we have Brewerne (Gl), Bruern (O), Cowarne (He), Colerne (= charcoal-house), Potterne (W) = pot-shed, Mixerne (Gl) = dung-house, Seasalter (K) = seasalt-house, Hordern, Hardhorn (La), Hordron (Y) = hoard-house, store-house. In Stanion (Nth) = stone-house, Askern (Y), Waldron (Sx) = forest-house, the compounds have a different sense. Vasterne (Berks, W) seems to be OE *fæstern*, 'stronghold.' The word is not actually found, but it seems to lie behind the forms *fæstergeat, festergeweorc* quoted in BT.

æsc, OE, '*ash*tree.' Ashton (*passim*), Aston in Kingsland (He), Aisholt (So), Avenage (Gl), Hamnish (He). Nash (Gl, He, So) shows a similar development to that given under **ac**. Esh (Du), Eshott (Nb), Eshton (Y) show another dial. development.

æspe, æps, OE, '*aspen*.' Apsley (Wa), Aspley (Beds), Apps (Sr), Asps (Wa). Dial. *esp* is found in Espley (Nb). ME *at ther apse* > *at the rapse* and gives Rapps (So).

æspen, OE, 'grown over with *aspens*.' Aspinwall (La).

æt, OE, '*at*.' The commonest of all prepositions to be used with p.n. As a result there arose the OE idiom of calling a place 'at X' instead of 'X,' thus Salisbury is called *æt Searobyrg* (ASC 552), and the stereotyped phrase of the West-Saxon royal clerks is that a grant of land is made at the place which is called 'at X.' Hence the numerous cases in which this preposition either as a whole or in some shortened form, has been prefixed to a p.n. Attercliffe (Y) is probably for *Atteclif* from *at the clif*, Thurleigh (Beds) [θəlai'] is *La Lege, Relye, Therlye* in ME documents and its varied forms are due to misdivision of *at there lye* into *at the relye* and *at therlye* with subsequent loss of *at*. Rivar in Ham (W) is from *at ther yver* (v. **yfre**) and Bradley showed that the common river-name *Rea* or *Ree* arose from similar misunderstanding of OE *æt þære ea*, ME *at ther ee*, it being taken as *at the ree* (v. **ea**). Similarly Tipton (Co) from *uptun*.

The reverse process has taken place in p.n. like Elstree (Herts), Ickenham and Oakington (Mx), Elmsworthy (Co), all of which once began with a *t*, which has now been absorbed by the final *t* of the *at* which was so·often found before them.

The common use of *at* with p.n. in the dat. case accounts for the large number of survivals of dat. forms in p.n. See, for examples of the sg., **burh, læs, mæd**, and of the pl., **cot, hus**.

ǣwiell, OE, 'river-spring.' Ewell (Ess, K, Sr), Alton (Do, Ha), Carshalton (Sr).

ǣwielm, OE, *idem*. Ewelme (O), Ewen (W).

alor, OE, '*alder*.' Aller (So), Lightollers (La), Aldreth (C), Bicknoller, Padnoller (So), Longner (Sa), Longnor (St). Gen. pl. in Ollerton (Ch, Nt), Orleton (He, Wo), Owlerton (Y).

ān(a), OE, '*one*, lonely.' Onehouse (Sf), Onecote (St), Anston (Y), Wanlip (Lei).

*anger, OE. The existence of this word in OE may be inferred from Ongar (Ess), Angram (4La, Y) and, possibly, Angerton (La, Nb). It is cognate with OHG *angar*, ModHG *anger*, 'grass-land,' especially as opposed to forest and to arable land, but also as opposed to swampy or heath-land. *Angram* is from dat. pl. and is identical with the common Dutch p.n. *Angeren*.

änstig, OE, lit. '*one*-path,' i.e. 'narrow path, defile' and perhaps 'stronghold,' a place which can only be approached in single file, glossed as *termofilae* and used as an alternative to **fæsten**. Fairly common as Ansty, Anstey, Anstie in the South and Midlands. The Scand. equivalent is Ainsty (Y).

apulder, apuldre, OE, '*apple*-tree.' Appledore (D, K), Apperfield (K), Appledram (Sx), Appuldercombe (Wt), Appleford (Wt).

askr, ON, 'ash-tree.' Aske (Y), Aspatria (Cu). Dat. pl. in Askam (We), Askham (La).

austr, ON, 'east.' Is fairly common in p.n. in Y and L in medieval times, but, as in Eastburn (Y), has now usually been replaced by the Eng. adj. It survives in such cases as Owston, Austwick, Owstwick (Y).

bæc, bece, OE, 'stream, brook,' ME *beche, bache*. It is specially common in Ch, Db, Sa, He, Gl, where it is used of a small valley. In *Piers Plowman* 'valeyes and hulles' of the A-text becomes 'beches and hilles' in the C-text. The word is still common in WCy dial. as *bache, bage* and *batch* and is so found in many p.n., simple and compound. The same element, with different dial. development is probably to be found in Landbeach, Waterbeach, Wisbech (C), Hackbeach (Nf), Holbeach (L), Debach (Sf). It is difficult to distinguish it from the palatalised form of the next suffix. Bache (He, Sa).

bæc, OE, **bak**, ON, '*back*,' is rare as a p.n. element. Bacup (La) shows the normal development with velar *k*. Burbage (Lei, W), earlier *Bur(h)bece*, might, so far as their form is concerned, go back to the suffix just discussed, but as both are away from valleys and streams, standing on high ground, they should probably be connected with the form *bacch* found in Orm, and explained as containing a palatalised form of *bæc*, possibly from a locative form. Such a palatalised form would explain the use of *batch* in So of the 'sandbanks or small hills lying near a river, the first rising ground above the level of the marshes.' To this also may perhaps be referred the Derbyshire *bage* used of a tract of moorland (EDD). Merbach (He) is definitely on a hill.

bær(e), OE, 'pasture,' especially in wooded districts, where it denoted feeding-ground for pigs. Specially common in the compounds *denbær* and *wealdbære* (v. **denn, weald**) for which the charters give the Latin alternatives *pascua* or *pastus porcorum*. As *Bere, Beer, Bear* it is common in p.n., simple and compound, in D, Do, So, Ha, Berks, but a considerable amount of confusion with **bearu** and **beorg** has taken place.

bærnet(t), OE, '*burn*ing,' and then applied to a place cleared by burning. Barnet (Mx, Herts), Burnett (So).

banke, ME, a common dial. word of Scand. origin denoting a ridge or shelf of ground, the slope of a hill.

bār, OE, '*boar*.' Borley (Ess), Boreham, Boarzell (Sx).

bēam, OE, 'tree' and then '*beam*.' Bempton (Y), Bampton (O), Benfleet (Ess), Holbeam (D). In p.n. it generally refers to a tree but in some, as in Bamford (La), it may refer to a 'beam.'

bēan, OE, '*bean*,' used as a first element to denote places where beans grow. Bamfurlong (La), Banstead (Sr), Binsted (Sx), Beynhurst (Berks).

bearu, OE, 'grove, wood.' The source of several places called *Barrow*. It is often difficult to distinguish them from those in which *barrow* is derived from **beorg**. Still in dial. use in Du and Ch to denote 'copse, thicket, dingle.' Sedgeberrow (Wo).

bēce, OE, '*beech*.' Beech (Sr), Cowbeech (Sx).

bedd, OE, '*bed*, place where plants grow.' Nettlebed (O).

bēger, OE, 'berry.' Barmoor (Nb), Byermoor (Du), Bairstow (Y).

bekkr, ON, 'stream, *beck*.' Common throughout the North of England (with the exception of Nb) and the Danelaw generally. As the word is in common dial. use in these districts, it is no definite proof of Scand. settlement. Thus in Du it has often taken the place of *burn*, the only form found in early documents. Gen. sg. *bekkjar* in Beckermet (Cu), Beckermonds (Y). *Beck-* at the beginning of names is usually from a pers. name *Becca*.

bēo, OE, '*bee*.' Beoley (Wo), Beal (Nb), Beauworth (Ha).

beofor, OE, '*beaver*.' Bevere, Barbourne (Wo).

bēonet, OE, found only in p.n. such as *beonetleah*. Late ME *bent* is used of long coarse grass or rushes, especially on moorland and near the sea, and a similar use is found in dial. That is its sense in Bentley (*passim*), Bentham (Gl, Y). The word is also used derivatively of open grassland as opposed to woodland, and of sandy hillocks covered with 'bents.' So in Chowbent (La), Totley Bents (Db).

beorc, OE, 'birch-tree.' Barkham (Berks), Berkeley (Gl), Barford (Beds). Whether spelt *Berk-* or *Bark-*, it is to be pronounced as [ba·k].

beorg, OE, 'hill,' whether natural or artificial. The former sense survives in dial. *barf*, 'low ridge or hill' (Y, L) and *barrow* used of a long low hill in Cu, La. In the South and South-west *barrow* is, and probably always has been, more generally used to denote an artificial hill, a 'barrow' in the archaeological sense of the term. In p.n. in Scand. England it is very difficult to distinguish it from ON *berg* but it should be noted that the latter term was not used of a barrow in the technical sense. It assumes a wide variety of forms in p.n., partly because the nom. and dat. sg. *beorg* and *beorge* become *berg(h)* and *berwe* respectively, while these again may show the common change of *er* to *ar*, giving *barg(h)* and *barwe*. Thus we get *Berrow* and *Barrow*. Further the suffix had in later times been completely confused with **burh** and *byrig* (dat. sg.) so that all over the South and Midlands it appears again and again as *-borough* and *-burgh* and even as *-bury*. Barham (C), Burford (O), Burghfield (Berks), Broughton (L), Berkhamstead (Herts), Whinburgh (Nf), Sharperton (Nb).

beorht, OE, 'shining, clear, *bright*.' Brightwell (O), Birtley (Du). In BCS 830 *beorhtan wille* is translated *declaratam fontem*.

bere, OE, 'barley, *bere* (dial.)' as in Baracre (K) and **beretun** and **berewic**.

bere-tūn, OE, literally 'barley-farm' (v. **tun**), but used in the Middle Ages in a special sense to denote a 'grange situated in an outlying part of a manor, where the lord's crop was stored.' The term is found in place-names all over England but only remains in living use in the South and South-West, where it denotes either (1) a farm- or rick-yard, or (2) a grange of the type just described. In Devonshire it is commonly added to a parish name to denote the manor-farm of the parish, e.g. Sampford Barton. The early forms of some of the *Bartons* compel us to postulate an OE *bær-tun* side by side with *bere-tun*, containing an alternative form of the word for barley. Cf. OE *bærlic*, 'barley.'

bere-wīc, OE, lit. 'barley-wick' (v. **wic**), but used already in the tenth century to denote an outlying portion of an estate. In this sense it forms the 'berewick' of Domesday, a tenement or group of tenements in the hands of the lord, but lying apart from the manorial centre. It usually appears as Berwick but it is also found as Barwick (Y) and Borwick (La).

berg, ON, 'hill.' The source of many p.n. in *-ber(gh)* and *-barrow* in Cu, We, La, Y and also in *-borough* as noted under **beorg**, e.g. Breckenborough (Y). The modern form *-ber* as in Hoober (Y), Kaber (We) seems often to go back to the Scand. word. In all other cases it is difficult to decide whether we have the Eng. or the Scand. word, unless the first element is also distinctively Scand. as in Aigburth (La).

berige, OE, '*berry*.' Bericote (Wa).

bern, OE, '*barn*,' often found in the pl. Berne (Do), Barnes (Sr), Whitburn (Du).

bierce, OE, '*birch*,' *birk* in NCy, when it is very difficult to distinguish from ON **birki**. Burcher (He).

biercen, 'overgrown with *birches*.' Birkenside (Nb).

bī(g), OE, '*by*.' Found in a good many p.n., the settlement having taken its name from its nearness to some prominent object. Biford (Gl), Bygrave (Herts), Byfield (Nth), Byfleet (Sr), Bythorne (Hu), Byker, Bywell (Nb), Beeleigh (Ess).

bigging, ME, 'building, dwelling-place, *biggin*.' A word in common dial. use formed from a Scand. vb. and no definite criterion of Scand. settlement.

bi(o)nnan, OE, 'within.' Is found as the first element in certain p.n. but it is not always easy to distinguish it from the pers. name *Bynna* or *Bynni*. St Mary Bynnewerk in Stamford (L), Binney in Canterbury (K), from *binnan ea*, rendered *inter duos rivos gremiales fluminis* (BCS 344), Benwell (Nb), where *well* is for *wall*.

birki, ON, 'place grown over with birch, birch-copse.' Birkland (Nt), Birthwaite (Y), Burthwaite (We), Briscoe (Cu, Y), Busco (Y).

biscop, OE, '*bishop*,' common in names of places which were once in episcopal possession. Found in Bishton (Sa, St), Bispham (La), Biscathorpe (L) and, with the dial. development which gave the fairly common early Mod. Eng. *bushoppe*, in Bushwood (Wa), Bushbury (St), Bushton (W).

blāc, OE, 'pale, white' and

blæc, OE, '*black*,' are often very difficult to distinguish owing to the shortening of vowel which the former may undergo in a compound before a consonant-group. The latter is found in Blaxton (Y), Blagdon (Nb, So), Blagrove (Berks).

blár, ON, 'dark, blue, livid,' surviving in NCy *bloa, blae,* 'livid, leaden, cheerless, cold, exposed.' Blaby (L), Blea Tarn (We), Blowick (La). Cognate with

*blā(w), OE, which we find in Blofield (Nf).

bleikr, ON, 'pale, livid,' dial. *blake* is used similarly. It is difficult in NCy to distinguish it from its Eng. cognate *blake* from **blac** and from the nickname *Bleik, Blake* to which it gave rise. Blaithwaite (Cu).

bōc, OE, 'beech,' found as the first element in p.n., generally with shortened vowel, as *Bock-* or, more usually, as *Buck-*. Buckhurst (*passim*), Bockhampton (Do). It is often very difficult to distinguish it from the pers. name *Bucca* and the common animal names **bucc** and **bucca.** Boughton (K).

*bōcen, OE, 'beechen, overgrown with beeches.' Bockenfield (Nb) and probably Bochidene (Wa). Almost impossible in ME to distinguish from *bukken*, gen. sg. of **bucca.** Probably found in a few such names as Bucknell (O), Buckenhill (He). *bōcen* is not found in OE, the form there being *bēcen*, but we may assume a double form as in **acen** and **ǣcen.**

bōcland, OE, lit. '*book*-land,' but used in the technical sense of land granted by *boc* or charter, or, more strictly, 'land over which certain rights and privileges were granted by charter.' In Latin versions of the OE laws it is variously rendered as *terra testamentalis, libera terra, terra hereditatis, feudum*. It is the source of the numerous Bucklands in England but the furthest north of these is in Mid. Lincolnshire. It is just possible that *boc* in this sense may enter into some other p.n. compounds (cf. OE *bocæceras*, meaning apparently 'fields granted by *boc*'), but it is impossible from the form alone to distinguish these compounds from those formed with *boc*, 'beech-tree.'

bóndi, ON. In Iceland this term denoted a peasant proprietor and it was an honourable one. In Norway and Denmark it came to have a less honourable sense and denoted the common people. At the time that the term was introduced into England it was still used in the earlier sense and was the equivalent of OE **ceorl**. In later times it was used of unfree tenants but the p.n. compounds in which it is found were probably of early formation and one may therefore assume the earlier sense. Thus it is the first element in Bonby (L), which was held TRE by six *taini*, the tenure probably giving rise to the name. Burstwick (Y), earlier *Bondburstwick*, took its name from the *bonde* who, as late as 1297, still held certain lands in the village from the king. Bomby (We), Bonbusk (Nt).

borg, ON, 'fort, fortified hill.' Borrowdale (Cu, We).

bóþ, ODan., **búð**, ON, '*booth*, temporary shelter.' Still in dial. use, meaning 'cowhouse' (La, Y), 'herdsman's hut' (La), 'outlying hamlet' (L). In England, as in Scandinavia, the term is usually found in the pl. The nom. pl. is found in Butterilket, the gen. sg. in Bowderdale (Cu), the dat. pl. in Bootham (Y). The two forms give respectively *bothe* and *bouthe* in ME. In Mod. Eng. the Dan. form has usually ousted the Norse but Ekwall notes Bouth (2) and Rulbuth (La). Boothby (L), Scorbrough (Y).

* bóðl, bold, bótl, OE, 'building,' but used both of an ordinary house and also of monastic buildings and of a manor-house. After the Conquest the phrase *capitale mesuagium* corresponds to OE *heafod-botl* and means 'manor-house.' Ekwall has a full discussion of these forms and their distribution in *Anglia Beiblatt*, 28, 82 ff. From them we get several names in -*bottle* in Nb and Du, one in Nth (Nobottle Grove), Bootle (Cu, La) and several p.n. in -*bo(u)ld*, both simple and compound, in the Central and West Midlands. Not found in Wessex, Southern and South-Eastern England or in East Anglia.

* bóðltun, OE, compound of **bóðl** and **tun** lies behind the numerous Boltons in Nb, Du, Cu, We, La, Y and seems to be confined to these counties and South Scotland. Ekwall suggests very plausibly (PNLa) that the term had some special technical sense and compares OSwed. *bolbyr*, a compound whose first element is cognate with *boðl*, and which is used of the 'village proper' in contrast to the surrounding outlying land.

botm, OE, **botn**, ON, '*bottom*,' used in p.n. of the lowest part of a valley or of an alluvial hollow. Starbottom (Y), Wythburn (Cu), Botton (La).

box, OE, '*box*-tree.' Boxford (Berks).

brād, OE, '*broad*.' Very common in p.n. and usually found with shortened vowel before a following consonant-group, as in the numerous Bradfields, Bradleys, Bradfords and Bradwells. Forms with *Broad*- are modern, or modern re-spellings due to the influence of the independent word. Bredgar (K). The weak dat. sg. *bradan* has given rise to Bradiford (D), Bradenham (Bk).

bræc, **brec**, OE, dial. *brack*, *breck*, 'strip of uncultivated land,' 'strip of land taken in from a forest by royal licence, for temporary cultivation.' Difficult in Scand. England to distinguish from **brekka**. Braxted (Ess).

brǣr, OE, 'thorn-bush, *briar*,' of wider application than the modern word. Its normal development is to ME *brere*, which survives in common dial. [bri·ə] and in such p.n. as Brereton (Ch), Brearton (Du). In others it has been replaced, at least in spelling, by the form *brier* which arose in the 16th cent., e.g. Brierley (St). Brierden (Nb) has the new spelling but the old pronunciation. Briestwistle (Y).

braken, ME, '*bracken*,' is allied to Dan. *bregne*, Swed. *bräken*, 'fern,' and its distribution in p.n. confirms its Scand. origin. Bracondale, Bracon Ash (Nf), Breckenborough (Y).

brame, ME, 'brier, bramble,' still used in dialect. Bramham (Y), Brampton (Hu). The wide use of the term in p.n. suggests that this word, not recorded in OE, goes back far earlier than the earliest dictionary record in 1425. Brampton (Hu) is *Bramtun* in 1121 (ASC *s.a.*).

brant, **bront**, OE, 'steep,' ME *brant*, *brent*. In many cases we may have the cognate ON *brattr*, earlier *brant*, cf. Swed. *brant*. Brantbeck (La), Brincliffe (Y), Bransty (Cu).

breiðr, ON, 'broad.' Braithwell, Braworth, Brayton (Y), Bratoft (L), Brathay (We).

brekka, ON, 'slope, hill.' Distinctively West Scand. Breck, Sunbrick, Larbrick (La), Haverbrack (We). It is often difficult to distinguish it from **bræc**.

brēmel, **brǣmel**, **bræmbel**, **brembel**, OE, '*bramble*.' Used by itself, as in Bremhill (W), or compounded, as in Bramshott (Ha), Bremilham (W).

brende, **brente**, ME, 'burnt,' as in Brandwood (La), Brentwood (Ess), Brent Pelham (Herts). In compounds with wood its meaning is clear. In other cases it probably refers to some fire in the past history of these places. It is not always easy to distinguish this element from *brant*.

bridd, OE, 'young *bird*.' Birdham (Sx).

brinke, brenke, ME, '*brink*, edge of a steep place, edge of land bordering on water.' It is the East Scand. equivalent (cf. Dan. *brink*) of the Norse *brekka*. As the first element in p.n. it cannot be assumed, except possibly in names of demonstrably late origin, in parts of England not subject to Scand. influence. In all cases when it is used as the first element in a p.n. it is difficult to distinguish it from the OE pers. name *Brynca*. Micklebring (Y).

brōc, OE, '*brook*,' but used also in K and Sx of a water-meadow or low marshy ground (EDD), a sense which is found also in the cognate Germ. *bruch*, LGerm. *brok*. Not found in p.n. in Nb or Du, little used in the North and East Ridings of Y and very rare in East Anglia. It is often compounded with **tun** giving rise to numerous Broughtons, Brocktons, Broctons and to Bratton (Sa), Brotton (Y). Here and elsewhere it is often difficult to know if we have this word, with shortening of the long vowel in the compound, or

brocc, OE, *brock*, 'badger.' Further possibility of confusion with *brocc* used as a pers. name has been suggested but, at least so far as p.n. of English origin are concerned, there is little likelihood of this. Broxbourne (Herts), Browston (Sf), Broxted (Ess).

brocc-hol, 'badger-hole.' Brockhale, Brocklehurst (La), Brockhill (Wo), Brockle (Co), Brockholds (Ess), Brockhall (Nth).

brōm, OE, '*broom*.' Common by itself and in compounds. The forms in ME often show confusion with **brame**. Brimfield (He), Brimrod (La).

brōmig, 'covered with *broom*.' Broomy Holm (Du), Brimmicroft (La).

brūn, OE, '*brown*.' Burnmoor (Y).

brunnr, ON, 'spring,' is very difficult to distinguish from its English cognate **burna**, for each may undergo metathesis of the *r* and then the Norse word resembles the English and *vice-versa*. Barbon (We).

brycg, OE, '*bridge*,' commonly found either in that form or in the NCy *brig(g)* but in the majority of p.n. the latter form has been ousted by the St. Eng. one. The form *brugge* is common in the South and South-West in ME but has usually been replaced by the St. Eng. one in present-day nomenclature. It survives in Brushford (D). Doveridge (Db).

bucc, OE, '*buck*' and **bucca**, 'he-goat,' but it is practically impossible to distinguish these animal-names from the pers. name *Bucca*.

bufan, OE, '*above.*' This preposition is sometimes compounded with the noun which it once governed but it is difficult to distinguish it from the pers. name *Bofa*. Boveridge, Bucknowl (Do), Bowlhead (Sr) may contain it.

*bula, OE, '*bull,*' is not found in OE but it is so common in OE p.n. that we must assume its use and can hardly think of it as a Scand. loan-word. At times it may be a pers. name. Bulmer (Ess, Nb), Bolney (Sx), Bulstrode (Bk), Bowforth (Y).

būr, OE, '*bower.*' In OE it is chiefly used in poetry. In glossaries it is found as the equivalent of *camera* and *cubiculum*. At times it seems to be used for a house or room, e.g. the Bishop's house at Worcester (KCD 2, 100) or a room in an Ealdorman's (ASC 1015). In p.n. it is almost invariably used in an uncompounded form and then often in the plural. Bower (D), Bure (Ha), Bures (Sf), Bowers Gifford (Ess).

burh, OE, dat. sg. **byrig**, is very common in p.n. When used by itself or as a suffix it takes various forms. If the nom. form survives we may have *borough, burgh, brough, burrough, borrow*, while the dat. appears as *bury* or *berry*. As the first element in a p.n. it is naturally the nom. form alone which is found, as in Burwell (C), Burbage (Lei, W), Burradon (Nb), Borley (Wo), Bearley (Wa) and the various descendants of **burhtun**.

The primary sense of *burh* is 'fortified place' and the term was applied by our forefathers to Roman or pre-historic defensive works, earthworks and the like, as well as to their own forts. This is certainly its sense in the great majority of those p.n. in which it forms the first element and probably in the great majority of the others as well. The former class should for the most part be interpreted as denoting places near some old *burh*, rather than as places which were themselves actually fortified, thus Burwell is the 'spring by the *burh*' rather than the 'fortified spring.'

From this primary sense various other uses developed. The word is used of a fortified house. It was also used of such towns and other places as were fortified as part of a national scheme of defence. Without a knowledge of the past history of a place, such as we do not usually possess, it is impossible to say how far one or other of these meanings may lie behind the element *burh* when found in its name. Occasionally we have the historical evidence which will settle the question. Hertingfordbury (Herts) is one of the two forts built by Edward the Elder at Hertford in 913 as part of his scheme of defence against the Danes (ASC *s.a.*). Burpham (Sx) is a *burh* in the Burghal Hidage and goes back to the same reign. In Bury St Edmunds and Peterborough we know that the element is of comparatively late origin, the earlier names of these places having been respectively, *Beadoricesuuyrthe* and *Medeshamstede*. It was only when these settlements had become towns of some importance that they came to be known as the 'burhs' of St Edmund and St Peter, and *burh* would seem to denote 'town' in contrast to the original small village or hamlet. Newbrough (Nb) on the other hand is of quite different and still later origin. It is the *novus burgus* in the manor of Thornton-in-Tynedale which took its rise from the grant of a market in 1221 (Hodgson, *History of Nb*, 2. 3. 391). Similarly Newbury (Berks) first appears in the early 12th century and was undoubtedly a new market-town created by Ernulf de Hesdinc for the benefit of his tenants.

There is one further type of name formed with this element. From the old use of *burh* to denote a fortified house, there arose the use of *bury* for a 'court or manor-house, the centre of a *soke* or other jurisdiction.' Such names are all of post-Conquest origin and first become common in the 13th century. They are almost entirely confined to Mx, Herts, Ess, Bk. They are most familiar in the London Bloomsbury, Lothbury and the like, but other examples are Flamstead Bury (Herts), Bassettsbury (Bk).

In modern p.n. much confusion with **beorg** has taken place, as in Burghfield (Berks), and it is only in the North and North Midlands that names which now end in *-burgh*, *-borough* go back at all commonly to *burh*.

In the Southern Danelaw, more especially in Nth and Lei, this suffix in Domesday often alternates with **by** and there can be little doubt that many of the p.n. which now end in *-by* once had the suffix *byrig*. A good early example is Badby (Nth) which in the same charter (BCS 792), an original document dated 944, is called both *Baddanby* and *Baddanbyrig*.

burhsteall = burh + steall, OE, i.e. site of a *burh*, as in Birstal (Lei), Birstall (Y), Burstall (Sf), Boarstall (Bk). In Borstal (2K) we may have a different word. Borstal in Rochester is *borhsteall* in the 10th century endorsement of a charter (BCS 339) while from Sx we have the form *Gealtborgsteal*. These forms would seem to go with the K and Sx dial. use of *borstal* to denote 'pathway up a steep hill.' Form and meaning alike suggest association with *borg*, 'surety' or **beorg** rather than *burh*, though *borg* cannot have come directly from *beorg*. Perhaps it is simply a case of confusion of two words, for *burhsteal* is found in an OE vocabulary glossed as *clivus* or *discensus*, and is thus given the sense of *borgsteall*. *Burhsteall* has its parallel in Germ. *borstel*, fairly common as a p.n. in Hanover and Holstein.

burhstede = burh + stede, OE, apparently the same as **burhsteall**. Burstead (Ess).

burhtun, OE, a very common compound of **burh** and **tun**, not found in OE, apart from p.n., except in the *Wife's Complaint*, where it is used in the pl., and the wife, speaking of her place of exile, says that 'the *burgtunas* are overgrown with briers, the dwellings (wic) are joyless.' This would seem to refer to the *tun* or enclosure round a *burh* or fortified house and that is probably the sense of the term in most p.n., viz. that it describes an enclosed settlement with a *burh* as its nucleus. If the name is in any case of definitely later origin it might simply mean 'settlement or farm near a *burh*,' whether earthwork or fortified house. It commonly takes the form *Burton* in later times but we also have it as Bourton (Berks), Broughton (Nth), Boreton (Sa).

burna, OE, 'stream, *burn*,' is in common use for a stream throughout England. Occasionally it undergoes metathesis of the *r* as in Brunton (Nb). Still in common dial. use in Nb and Du.

buskr, ON, 'bush.' Bonbusk (Nt), Busby (Y).

butere, OE, '*butter*,' is often compounded with *worth, wick, ley* and other suffixes and is descriptive of a settlement with good pasture. Butterleigh (D), Birley (He), Bitterley (Sa).

Late OE **by** from ON *býr, bær*, Swed., Dan. *by*. The word in Icelandic denoted a 'farm' or 'landed estate,' but in Norse, Swedish, and Danish it has come to be used of a town or village. The suffix is so common in p.n. in Scand. England, and is applied to so many places that can never have been more than a farm-stead or at most a hamlet, that it would be unsafe to render it always by 'town' or 'village.' Further evidence of this is found in the gloss in the Lindisfarne Gospels (c. 950) where the unclean spirit dwells in *hus* vel *lytelo by*. The term was in independent use in Northern dialect in ME so that it is not always safe to assume that a place whose name ends in *-by* was actually settled by Scandinavians and there are cases of p.n. in *by* containing Norman pers. names, e.g. Aglionby (Cu). There are a good many cases in Domesday of this suffix alternating with *birie* from *byrig* (cf. **burh**). The gen. sg. was *byjar* and is found in Birstwith (Y) and (Birstath) Bryning (La) where it is compounded with **staðr** and also in

*býjarlǫg, ON, 'law(s) of a *by* or township' and also 'district over which the *by*-laws held good.' The term is not actually found in ON but has its parallel in Swed. *byalag*, 'village community,' and must lie behind the common *birlag, birlawe* of medieval times and the Bierlow of several Yorkshire p.n., such as Ecclesall Bierlow.

bygg, ON, 'barley, *bigg* (dial.).' Bigland (La).

byht, OE, '*bight*, bend, curve.' Sidebeet (La), Bight in street-names in Lincoln.

bȳre, OE, '*byre*, shed, hovel.' In independent use, often in the pl., as in Byers Green (Du) and in compounds such as Burton

Joyce (Nt), Burton-on-Trent (St), Burland, Burstall Lane (Y), Edmundbyers (Du). Dat. pl. in Byram (Y).

*bysc, OE, 'bush, thicket,' assumed by Skeat to explain the various ME forms *bisshe, busshe, bysshe* found in p.n. These could not all go back to an anglicised version of ON *buskr,* hitherto taken to be the source of English *bush.* Bushey (Herts), Bushley (Wo), Bysshe Court (Sr).

*byxe, OE, 'box-tree' or perhaps rather 'box-thicket.' Such a derivative of *box* may be assumed on the analogy of þorn, þyrne and is needed to explain the forms of such names as Bix (O), Bexhill (Sx) and Bexley (K).

cærse, cerse, cresse, OE, '*cress,*' is very common in compounds with **wielle.** It develops a wide variety of forms in later times as in Kerswell (D), Carswell (Gl), Caswell (O, So), Craswall (He), Cresswell (St), Carshalton (Sr). A similar compound with **kelda** is found in Kirskill *alias* Creskeld (Y).

calc, cealc, OE, 'chalk.' The relation of these forms is the same as that of **cald, ceald,** *infra,* and is reflected in the difference between such p.n. as Chalk (K, W), Chalton (Beds, Ha), Chalford (Gl), on the one hand, and Cawkwell (L), on the other.

cald, ceald, OE, '*cold.*' The first form belongs to Anglian, the second to Kentish and Saxon England. The former gives *cald,* later *cold,* in ME but in p.n. the vowel has usually undergone shortening, so that we get initial *Cald-* in p.n. while association with the independent adj. *cold* has often led to the substitution of that form for the more correct *Cald-,* as in Coldwell (Nb). The latter form gives *Chald-,* as in Chaldwell (Do), Chadwell (Ess), Chalfield (W). There has however been a good deal of replacing of the Southern *Chald-* under the influence of Midland (i.e. St Eng.) forms in *Cald-,* especially in p.n. in which the sense association with the common adj. was readily apparent. Thus *Caldecote,* with its variants *Calcott, Caulcott,* has entirely replaced forms with initial *ch.* In So, D, Co we get, as in Chold Ash (D), a curious form which seems to result from *ceald* > *chāld* > *chōld.* (See Ekwall, *Contrib. to the Hist. of OE Dialects,* 1–39.) Challacombe (D), Cholwell (So), Goldicote (Wo).

calf, cealf, celf, OE, '*calf.*' This shows the same dial. history as **cald.** Many p.n. show the gen. pl. *cealfra* or *cealfa* rather than the nom. sg. Chaldon (Do, Sr), Chalvey (Bk), Challock (K), Cholswell (Berks), Cawston (Wa), Cawton (Y), Kelloe (Du), Chelvey (So), Kellah (Nb). Gen. pl. in Callerton (Nb), Calverton (Bk, Nt).

calu, OE, 'bald, bare.' Callaughton (Sa), Cow Honeyburn (Gl), Callaly (Nb), Calverley (D).

camb, OE, '*comb,*' then used of a crest and so of a crest or ridge of land. No example of this last sense-development is found in

OE but it is clearly evidenced in ME and has given rise to NCy and Sc *kame, kaim*, 'long narrow ridge or hill.' Combs (Sf), Cam (Y).

camp, comp, OE, as a p.n. term is only found in charter material. It is an old Teutonic loan-word from the Latin *campus*. That it could denote an enclosed area in OE seems to be clear from the expression *campæs geat* (BCS 758). For further light on its meaning we may perhaps turn to its Continental cognates. In OLG and in OFris., *kamp* denotes an enclosed piece of land. In West Hanover it denotes 'a large area of arable land in the neighbourhood of the farm-house' (Middendorff). Jellinghaus (*Die Westfälischen Ortsnamen*, 83–4) says that the term is almost entirely Saxon and Frisian and is used of enclosed land whether arable or pasture or wood-land. See also NGN iii, 342. The term is not in living use in English, and in p.n. it has as a rule been confused with some other suffix, generally *combe*, as in Swanscombe (K), Sacombe (Herts), Ruscombe (Berks), Barcombe (Sx), Bossingham (K), Bulcamp (Sf), Shudy and Castle Camps (C), Chipping Campden (Gl), though in this last name we may have *camp* in its other sense of 'battle, war, contest.' The examples illustrate the somewhat narrow distribution of this suffix.

carr, OE, 'rock,' only found in Northumbrian OE. Carham (Nb) is from the dat. pl.

catt, catte, OE, doubtless occurs in p.n. but it is impossible to distinguish it from pers. names of similar form.

cēap, OE, 'market.' Chepstow (Mon), Chipstead (K, Sr).

ceart, cert, OE, is only found in charter material but it may be assumed to have had the same meaning as dial. *chart* (K, Sr), viz. 'a rough common, overgrown with gorse, broom, bracken' (EDD). Each settlement will have had its 'chart' in certain parts of those counties and it will originally have been forest-land which was later absorbed as the settlers spread themselves. Thus we hear of Kemsing's *ceart* (BCS 370) and to this day we have names like Seal Chart and Chart Sutton. These 'charts' are found in the greensand and Weald clay districts. Other examples are Chartham (K) and Churt (Sr). It is doubtful if the term is found outside these counties.

ceaster, cæster, OE. A loan-word from the Lat. *castra*, 'camp' and used independently in OE to denote a large city or town. It may have this sense in the names of some of the towns and cities famous in Roman times, as in Gloucester, Chester, Bath (earlier *Baþanceaster*), but its wide use in p.n. and the size and character of many of the places, indeed the great proportion of them, show that there it is used of any site whatever on which fortifications of any kind, or the remains of such, were to be found. There is no doubt also that the term is applied to sites in which the defensive works were of pre-Roman origin. Our forefathers were not archaeologists.

By itself, and as prefix and suffix, this element takes three definite forms. The commonest is *chester*, the other two are *cester* and *caster*, with variants Castor (Nth) and Caistor (L, 2Nf). The form *cester* slightly disguised in Craster (Nb), Mancetter (Wa), Exeter (D), Wroxeter (Sa), is due to Anglo-Norman influence upon English spelling and pronunciation, and its distribution need not be discussed. *chester* is found in Nb, Du, La (S. of the Ribble), Ch, St, Db, Wa, He, Gl, O, So, D, Do, Ha, Sx, K, Ess, Herts, C, Hu and one example in South Nth. *caster* is found in Y, La (N. of the Ribble), Cu (in the form *castle*), We, L, Nf, R, Nth (one in the North). Two explanations of this distribution have been offered. The first is that the *caster* forms are due to Scand. influence and it cannot be denied that the *caster* forms are found in just the right places to fit this theory but there are grave difficulties in accepting it. If *caster* forms are due to the well recognised substitution of Scand. *k* for English *ch*, as in Yorkshire *Skyrack* for *scirac*, 'shire-oak,' then we should expect two things, viz. (i) that the form in ME would be *kester* rather than *caster*, (ii) that at least a few stray *chester* forms would have survived unchanged, but such is not the case. The difference is rather to be sought, as Ekwall (*Anglia Beiblatt*, 30, 224-5) has shown, in differences between Northern and Eastern and Southern and Western dialects, the palatalisation and assibilation of initial *c* never having been completely carried through in the former. Nb and Du in this word and others with initial *c* hold a peculiar position which has yet fully to be explained. Bewcastle (Cu), Castleford (Y), Cheshunt (Herts), Cester Over (Wa).

celde, OE, 'spring,' only found in charter material, the Eng. equivalent of ON **kelda**. Honeychild, Bapchild (K), Absoll Park (Ess).

ceorl, OE, 'peasant, rustic,' contrasted with the *eorl* on the one hand, who was of noble birth, and with the *þeow*, who was a slave, on the other. In place-names it is commonest in the Charltons and Chorltons found throughout the country, as also in Charaton (Co), which go back to OE *ceorla tun*, 'farm of the *ceorls*.' It is difficult to determine the precise sense of this compound. Is it simply, where the churls live, or has it some more technical sense? Found also in Chorley (La), Cherubeer (Co), Chalgrave (O), Churlwell (Y). It is noteworthy that this element *ceorla* (gen. pl.) is not found in compounds with **ham** and **burh**—Charlbury (O) is misleading—and probably not with **worþ**. In Chelsworth (Sf), Cholstrey (He) we probably have the singular *Ceorl*, used as a pers. name.

Q

ceosol, cisel, OE, 'gravel, shingle.' Cf. Chesil Bank. Chesilborne (Do), Chiselhurst (K), Chillesford (Sf).

cieping, OE, 'market,' found in a good many p.n. of the type Chipping Ongar (Ess) and denoting a place with a market.

ciese, OE, '*cheese*,' used like **butere** to denote a good cheese-making farm. Chiswick (Ess), Cheswick (Nb), Cheswardine (Sa). It is often difficult to distinguish it from **cis** and from the pers. name *Cissa*. In Scand. Eng. it is Scandinavianised to *Kes-* in Keswick (Cu, Nf, Y).

cietel, OE, 'kettle' is found in OE in the compounds *cytelwylle* (BCS 610) and *cytelflod* (ib. 682), where it must describe a 'bubbling' spring or stream. The former has survived in Chitterwell (So). In such p.n. as Chattlehope (Nb) it seems to describe the shape of a valley. The Scand. cognate is probably found in Kettlewell (Y) but it is difficult to be sure in many of these names whether we may not have the pers. names which have given us later *Chettle* and *Kettle*.

cild, OE. This word, the ancestor of *child*, enters into a good many p.n. as the first element. Found as a rule in the gen. pl. form *cilda* or *cildra*, as in *cilda stan* (BCS 667), *cylda tun* (ib. 565) and Childerley (C). It is found in most of the Chiltons and Chilcotes and in Child Hanley (St). Its exact sense is uncertain. The sg. is used as a title of honour in late OE times and this is found also throughout the Middle Ages, as in '*Childe* Roland.' Of the social status of the 'children' who gave their name to certain places we know nothing definite. They were not children in the modern sense of the term and possibly a ray of light may be thrown on their status by the fact that Childerley, TRE, was held by 4 *Sochemanni*.

cirice, OE, **kirkja,** ON, '*church*.' In Northern England it is often impossible to tell whether we have a Northern form *kirk* of the OE word or the Scand. loan-word. In p.n. too one has to distinguish this element very carefully from that found in Kirkley (Nb), Crich (Db), Crick (Nth), Crichel (Do), Creech (So), Croichlow (La), Crickley (Gl) and numerous other p.n. such as Woodcray (Berks). The clue to these names is to be found in an OE charter (BCS 62) in which a grant is made on the Tone (OE *Tan*) near the hill *qui dicitur brittanica lingua Cructan apud nos Crycbeorh.* This is the modern Creech St Michael (So) and in another charter (BCS 550) the same place is apparently called *cyricestun*, i.e. farm of the *cyric*. This British *cruc*, OE *cryc*, (?) *cyric*, is the same as the Irish *cruach*, Welsh *crug*, Cornish, Breton *cruc*, 'hill, barrow.' It is noteworthy that the English in taking it over frequently added their own word to the name, thus **beorh** in *crycbeorh*, **hlaw** in Kirkley (Nb), Croichlow (La), **hyll** in Crichel. Further topographical investigation is needed but we may note that there are such 'hills, motehills' or 'barrows' at Crich, Crick, Kirkley, Woodcray, Crickley and probably at all the others as well. Barrows, unluckily, may have disappeared. If *Pennocrucium* in the Antonine Itinerary is to be identified with Penkridge (St), *Pencric* in BCS 1317, we have a Latin transcription of this British word. The change of vowel from *u* to OE *y*, *i* is explained by the fact that already in the 7th century *u* in British approached an *i*-sound. (Cf. Strachan, *Introd. to Early Welsh*, p. 1.)

*cis, OE, 'gravel,' is not actually recorded in OE but seems to be found in the p.n. *cisburna* (BCS 356) and in certain other names surviving in later forms, such as Chesham, Cheesden (La), Chishall (Ess), while the deriv. adj. *cisen* would account for Chisnall (La). It is the stem from which ceosol is derived.

clǣfer, OE, '*clover*.' Claverley (Sa), Clarborough (Nt), Clarewood (Nb).

clǣg, OE, '*clay*.' Clayhanger (Ess), Clehonger (He), Clinger (Gl), Cley (Nf), Clare (O).

clǣgig, '*clayey*.' Claydon (O, Sf).

clǣne, OE, '*clean*, clear of weeds or other hurtful growth.' In the OE trans. of the *Cura Pastoralis* the Lat. *terra quae nullas spinas habuit* is rendered by *clæne land*. Clanfield (Ha, O), Clennell (Nb), Glendon (Nth), Glenfield (Lei), Glanville (D).

clāte, OE, '*clote*, burdock.' Clatworthy (So), Clatford (W).

clif, OE, '*cliff*,' but in OE, as in modern local usage, it was not confined to a 'steep face of rock, a precipitous declivity.' In D the form *cleve* (v. *infra*) is used of the steep side of a hill, any steep sloping ground, while in L the 'Cliff' is the name now given to the sloping and cultivated escarpment of the oolite which runs down the county from the Humber to Lincoln. The topography of many places whose name ends in *clif* shows that it cannot there be used in the modern St. Eng. sense.

Final *f* is often lost (cf. Fr. *joli* from *jolif*) and the suffix is then assimilated to *ley*, as in Hockley (Beds). OE *clif* had a pl. *clifu* or *cleofu* and from the latter, or from the fresh singular *cleof* made to fit it, come the forms *cle(e)ve* found in dial. and in p.n. Cleveland (Y), Cleadon (Du), Clevedon (So), Clewer (So), Clee (He), Cleobury (Sa), Clibburn (We).

clōh, OE, '*clough*, ravine,' is still in common dial. use in the North and N.W. Midlands. The common dial. pron. is [kluf] or [klau]. Catcleugh (Nb), Cowclough (La), Haltcliff (Cu).

cnæpp, OE, 'top, summit of a hill, short sharp ascent.' In p.n. in Scand. England it is difficult to distinguish from ON *knappr*. Knapp (So), Knepp (Sx).

cniht, OE, 'boy, youth, servant' and then 'servant of some

military superior such as the king.' It is our *knight* but in OE usage and in p.n. had not got beyond the stages just given. Common in various Knightons, Knightcotes and Knightleys. Its exact sense in such names, where it represents OE *cnihta* (gen. pl.), is uncertain, but we may note that Knighton (Berks) was held by 5 *liberi homines*, (Do) by 2 *taini*, (Ha) by 8 *liberi homines*, all TRE.

cnoll, OE, '*knoll*,' but used in earlier times of the rounded top of a larger hill and not confined as now to a hillock or mound. Knole (K), Knowle (So), Chipnall (Sa).

cocc, OE, '*cock*.' Doubtless found in a good many names but difficult to distinguish from the OE pers. name *Cocc(a)*.

cofa, OE, '*cove*.' Its sense in p.n. is indicated by its use in OE to gloss Lat. *spelunca* and its dial. use of a 'cave, cavern, den, deep pit.'

col, OE, '*coal*, char*coal*.' Colerne (W).

cōl, OE, '*cool*.' Colwall (He), Colwell (Nb).

copp, OE, 'top, summit.' Warcop (We), Coppull, Pickup (La).

coppede, OE, 'having the *copp* or summit cut off,' hence 'pollarded,' but also 'rising to a *copp*,' hence 'peaked' and the like. We have the former in Copdock (Sf), Copthorne (Sr), Cowbeech (Sx), Copster (La), the latter in Copt Hall (Ess, Mx).

corn, OE, '*corn*,' is seldom used in OE of the growing crop, as we now employ it, and it is probable that it but seldom lies behind *Corn-* in p.n. Ritter and Ekwall have suggested that in a good many names it may be a metathesised form of OE **cron, cran*, 'crane,' a bird once very common in England. This metathesised form is made probable by the actual use in OE of *cornoc* for *cranoc*, 'crane,' and it will explain names like Cornbrook (La, Wo) and Cornwell (O) which certainly do not contain *corn* = corn. It is doubtful if this explanation can be carried as far as Ekwall would suggest, for no independent form *cron* or *corn* has been found in OE, neither is there any example of a *Corn-* name in which there are any signs of alternation between *Corn-* and *Cran-*, such as we should expect if they were really 'crane' names.

cot(e), OE, '*cot*, cottage.' The possibility of a more dignified sense is suggested by the use of OE *cotlif*, apparently as the equivalent of manor (BT *s.v.*). The pl. form is the commonest in p.n., the nom. in the numerous *Co(a)tes*, the dat. pl. in Coatham (L), Coton (C, Nth), Cotton (Nth), Cotham, Cottam (Nt). Forms which now have no sign of the pl. may well go back to OE pl. *cotu* or *cotan*. It is very often corrupted to *court* in modern times as in Maidencourt (Berks). It is very common in the compound *Caldecot(e)*, lit. 'cold cottages.' This may be simply a name descriptive of cheerless hovels or, as its frequency might suggest, may have some technical sense such as 'place of shelter from the weather for wayfarers.' It should be added that, apart from p.n. evidence, we have no knowledge of the existence of such. Froggatt (Db).

cran, OE, '*crane*.' Cranleigh (Sr). See also **corn**.

cranoc, cornoc, OE, 'crane.' Cranshaw, Cronkshaw (La).

crāwe, OE, '*crow*.' There is an OE pers. name *Crawe* (fem.) and one cannot therefore always be sure about this element, but it may be assumed in most cases. Crawley (Ha, Nb), Craycombe (Wo), Croydon (C), Croham (Sx), Cranoe (Lei).

cristelmǣl, OE, 'cross,' lit. *Christ*-sign. Kismeldon Bridge (D), Christian Malford (W).

croft, OE, '*croft*,' is used dial. of a small enclosed field or pasture, with the difference between Northern and Southern England that in the former adjacency to a house is generally understood though such is not the case in La and Ch.

croh, OE, 'saffron.' Crookham (Berks), Crowle (Wo), Croughton (Ch).

cros, late OE, '*cross*,' a Norse loan-word. Buckrose (Y).

crouche, ME, 'cross,' a French loan-word. Crouch End (Mx), Crutch (Wo).

crumb, OE, 'crooked.' Cromford (Db), Cromwell (Nt), Cronkley (Nb), Crunkley (Y). The correct pron. in all these names was once [krʌm] but a spelling one [krɔm] now usually prevails.

crundel, OE = *crundle* in the dial. of Sx and Ha. There it is said to be a 'living term' and to describe a 'ravine, a strip of covert dividing open country, always in a dip, usually with running water in the middle' (EDD). It is probably only 'living' in the sense that it is fairly common in modern place and field names and for its exact sense we must certainly take into account Grundy's statements, based upon the Charter material (*E and S*, 47–9), that it seems as a rule to be used of 'quarries or chalk-pits, especially diggings which are elongated and irregular in outline because they have had to follow the narrow lines and twists and turns of a balk or some other form of boundary.' See also Baring in EHR 24, 300. The form *crumdel*, once found, suggests that the first element in the compound is **crumb**, an etymology which would accord with the facts just recorded. Crondall (Ha), Crundel End (Wo).

cū, OE, '*cow*.' Quy (C), Quickbury (Ess), Cuffell (Ha), Cowpe (La). *cȳ* in Keyhaven (Ha), Kyo (Nb).

culfre, OE, 'pigeon, dove.' Culverden (K), Cullercoats (Nb).

cumb, OE, '*coomb*, valley,' is still in living use in SCy of a 'hollow or valley on the flank of a hill, especially one closed in at the head, on the sides of or under the chalk downs.' In OE it was of wider application. In p.n. it is specially common in D, Do, So, while it is unknown in East Anglia, Nb, Du (with one apparent exception) and very rare in Y. In Cu we have several p.n. in *Cum-* which apparently show this element but only in Cumdivock is there any evidence that the form was *cumb* rather than *cum*. As a suffix this element is very rare in La, Cu and We. See further Ekwall, *Scand. and Celts*, 109 ff. The distribution of this element at first sight favours the view that it is a Celtic loan-word, but there are difficulties. The greatest is that while the element is very common indeed in D, it is rare in Co and does not seem ever to be used with a Celtic first element. Further it is not found in Breton names. As a first element it is very common in the p.n. *Compton*, to be pronounced [kʌm(p)tən] rather than [kɔm(p)tən] which is a spelling-form. Comden (K).

cweorn, OE, '*quern*, hand-mill,' in p.n. is usually compounded with **dun** and the compound denotes a hill from which mill-stones were quarried, the full form perhaps being *cweornstandun*, with common loss of the middle element. Quarndon (Db), Quarrendon (Bk), Quorndon (Lei), Quarrington (Du), Quarlton (La), Whernside (Y).

cyln, OE, '*kiln*.' Dat. pl. in Kilham (Nb), [kil] being a common dial. form.

dæl, OE, **dalr**, ON, 'valley, *dale*,' is still in living use in the North and North Midlands, and the counties in which it is at all common in p.n. are Nb, Cu, We, La, Y, L, Nt, Lei, Db, Nf, Sf. Isolated examples have been noted in St, Wo, So, Sx and four examples in K. In Scand. England one cannot be sure whether one has the English or Scand. word, except where the first element is a Scand. pers. name, when it is presumably the latter. Further, owing to the common use of *dale* in Northern dialect, there has been some replacement of earlier *dene*, from **denu**, by *dale* as in Oxendale (La), Arkendale (Y), Harsondale (Nb), Tursdale (Du), all of which were originally *dene*-names.

The distribution is curious. It would seem to be distinctively Anglian, and indeed North and East Anglian, except possibly for Doverdale (Wo) and the little group in K and Sx. The charter material is of interest on this point. It gives us *doferdæl* (BCS 360) for Doverdale, *imbesdæl*, with dat. *imbesdælle* (unidentified) in Ha (BCS 707) and *ruge dæl* in Ha (BCS 629), with *deopan delle* in the same charter. This points to early confusion with the allied **dell** and it may be that the Southern *dales* are really *dells*. Unluckily we have only 13th and 14th century forms for these, viz. Crundale, Dodingdale, Luckingdale, Rundal (K), Woodsdale (Sx) and Stavordale (So). These all show *dale*.

dāl, OE, 'portion or share of land, especially of a common field.' It survives in dial. *dale* and *dole* used in this sense and is more common in field-names than in p.n. Dole Hundred (W), earlier *Doleffeld*.

deill, ON, is the Scand. equivalent of dal and like that word is almost confined to field-names. It is very common in Y and L and in the form *dayle* was in common dial. use in ME. Howdales (L). The term seems to have been coined, or at least revived, on English soil in order to describe English agricultural conditions. See an excellent discussion of the term in Lindkvist, *P.N. Scand. Origin*, 130 ff.

(ge)delf, OE, 'digging,' hence 'quarry.' King's Delph (C), Standhill (O).

dell, dæll, OE, 'deep natural hollow or vale of no great extent.' This seems to be a distinctively Southern form and in OE charters is only found in Ha and possibly once in Berks. Dell Quay, Arundel (Sx), Fardle (D), Dell Farm (Bk). See further under dæl.

denn, OE, in independent use in OE to denote (i) the lair of a wild beast, (ii) a woodland pasture for swine, the two words being probably of different origin. The latter is its sense in p.n. It is found specially frequently, both as an independent word and as a suffix, in charters from the old Weald area and it was doubtless similarly used in other parts of England also. In p.n. for which we have to rely on ME evidence alone it is often impossible to determine whether we have this suffix or denu. The former may be suspected in forest areas. Austin (K).

denu, OE, 'valley,' used in p.n. all over England, except in those districts which have been Scandinavianised and there it is doubtless concealed behind many a present-day *dæl*. As *dene* or *dean* it is still in living use in Nb and Du, where it is applied to the narrow deep-cut valleys which are so common in those counties. As a suffix it is difficult to distinguish from denn; as a prefix, especially in the common name Denton it is difficult to be sure whether we have this element or *Dena* (g. pl.) from *Dene*, 'Danes,' at least in certain parts of the country. The suffix very often appears as *don* in Mod. Eng., natural confusion of unstressed suffixes being assisted by liability to topographical ambiguity, since every valley must have its corresponding hill. When this *don* follows an unvoiced consonant such as *k*, the *d* often becomes *t* and further confusion arises. Hunden (Sf), Compton (Db), Nookton (Du), Timberdine (Wo).

dēop, OE, '*deep*.' Specially common with ford and denu. Debden (Ess), Dipton (Du, Nb), Dibden (Ha), Debach, Depden (Sf), Deptford (K, W), Defford (Wo), Deopham (Nf), Dippenhall (Sr), Dibble Bridge (Y).

dēor, OE, 'animal.' Darley (Db), Dordon (Wo), Durley (Ha), Darvell (Sx), Dyrham, Deerhurst (Gl), Dereham (Nf).

dīc, OE, 'ditch, dike.' In p.n. the term has the *ditch*-meaning of *dyke* as well as that of 'earthwork' and, except in certain obvious cases, it is very difficult to say now in what sense it is used in any particular name. Not all the Dittons are so clearly 'earthwork farms' as is Fen Ditton (C), on the line of Fleam Dyke, nor is the earthwork often so clearly visible as it is in Wrekin Dike (Du). Deighton (Y), Flendish Hundred (C), Detchant (Nb).

dierne, derne, dyrne, OE, 'secret, hidden,' used doubtless of that which one comes upon unexpectedly. Dernford (C), Darnbrook (Y), Darnhall (Ch), Durnford (St, W), Dearnley (La), Durnaford (Co), Dunford (Sr).

dor, OE, 'door, gate,' and then topographically, 'narrow pass.' Dore (Db), Mickledore, Lodore (Cu), Dorton (O).

dræg, OE, is found in several p.n. in OE charters. It is found in Drayton (Berks, Ha, Nth) in BCS 1032, 102 and KCD 736, probably in Dundry (So), *ib.* 816, in *drægstan* (BCS 699) and possibly also in Old Drax (Y) in the dat. form *Ealdedrege* (BCS 1052). It is found also in 30 or more Draytons and Draycot(t)s in the Midlands and South and in two Drayfords (D), for which we have no OE evidence. Its meaning is still a matter of discussion. It is worthy of note that the element is, in the vast majority of cases, used as the first element of a p.n. This would point to the meaning not being purely topographic in character for if it were there would be no reason, or so it would seem, why it should not be freely used as a final element. Rather it would seem to denote some material object commonly found in or about a *tun* or *cote*. Skeat advanced the suggestion that it is the common dial. *dray*, 'squirrel's nest,' but the ultimate history of that word is not known and it seems unlikely that such a word would appear in this large group of names. Ritter (*Vermischte Beiträge*, 78–80) suggests that it is OE *dræge*, 'dray' or 'drag-net,' but examination of the topography of the places in question shows that many of them are right away from water, on the slopes of downs, etc. The suggestion has also been made that we should compare ON *drag*. Ekwall (*Angl. Beibl.* 1923, 28) has suggested that Scand. *drag* and OE *dræg* might have been used to denote a place where timber is dragged or where a boat is dragged overland to cut off a river-bend. Cf. the sites of Drayton (Nf), Draycot (Db), Drayton (Berks), Drayton near Dorchester (O).

drag, ON, used in various topographical senses, but chiefly of a small hollow or glen. Dundraw (Cu), Draughton (Nth, Y).

dreng, late OE, **drengr**, ON, 'young man, lad, servant' with no special technical sense. On English soil the word came to denote a man holding by a particular form of free tenure, combining services and money payments with a certain measure of military duty. The word was already in use in OE at the end of the 10th century and long survived the Conquest. In Norse it was also used as a nickname and that may be its use in Drinkstone (Sf), Dringhoe (Y), while in Dringhouses (Y) and Drointon (St) we probably have the common noun.

drȳge, OE, '*dry*.' Driffield (Gl) and numerous Drybecks and Dryburns.

dūn, OE, '*down*, hill,' often used of a very slight slope. Farringdon (Berks), Dowland (Co). When the vowel is shortened as in Dunclent (Wo), Donhead (W), Dutton (Ch), it is not always easy to distinguish it from the pers. name *Dunn(a)*. As a suffix it is often confused with **denn** and **tun**. Quarrington (Du), Quarlton (La).

dweorg, OE, '*dwarf*.' Dwariden (Y), Dwerryhouse (La).

ēa, ēu, OE (Anglian), 'island,' must be inferred from several p.n. in Bede, e.g. *heoroteu = insula cervi* and such a form as *Lindisfarna ea* in the Mercian OE Martyrology. The more common form is **eg, ieg**.

ēa, OE, 'river, stream.' Eaton (Db), Eton (Bk). Found also in the river-name Ree, Rea (v. **æt**).

ēaland v. **ēgland**.

eald, OE, ald, Angl., '*old*.' In some such names as Oldland (Gl) it may have a specialised sense like the dial. *old-land* and denote land that has long remained untilled. Very difficult to distinguish from the pers. name *Eald(a)*. Aldglose, Yaldham (K).

ēamōt, OE, 'river-meet,' used of the confluence of two streams. Emmott (La), Eamont Bridge (We).

earn, OE, 'eagle,' but it is almost impossible to distinguish it from the pers. name *Earn(a)*.

ēast, OE, '*east*,' found in the numerous Astons, Eastons, Astleys, etc. The compar. form is found in Asterley (Sa). E(a)sedike (Y), Astol (Sa), Astrop (Beds).

ecg, OE, '*edge*.' Badenage (So), Hathersage, Heage (Db).

edisc, OE, 'enclosed pasture, park.' Cf. the OE glosses '*edisc, deortuun*, broel,' '*broel, hortus cervorum* deortuun *vel* edisc' (BT). The word must be identical with *eddish*, which first appears in the 15th cent. meaning 'aftermath of grass,' possibly also 'brushwood.' In the OE charters it is the equivalent of *agellus* (BCS 225). In p.n. it probably has the OE meaning rather than that which developed later. Standish from **stan** (Gl, La), Bendish (Ess) from **bean**, Thornage (Nf), Greatness (K).

efes, OE, '*eaves*, border,' especially of the edge of a wood, also of the brow of a hill. Habergham Eaves (La).

ēg, īeg, OE, ey, ON, 'island,' as we now understand it, and also 'land in the midst of marshes and the like.' In many cases the evidence of the island character is not so clear now as it once was. Eye (Sf), Sandy (Beds), Eyton (Sa), Arlesey (Beds). In East Anglia it has undergone a corruption found also elsewhere at times. In p.n. like Mersey, Osey (Ess), Horningsey, Whittlesey (C) where the *ey* follows a genitival *s*, the influence of the common word *sea* has led to a re-spelling with final -*sea* as in Mersea, Osea. This *ea* has spread even to names in which there was no preceding *s* as in Manea and Stonea (C). Stiffkey (Nf), Bolney (Sx), Battersea (Sr), Hornsea (Y), Long Eaton (Db), Iford (W), Billinghay (L), Bevere (Wo). Eyam (Db) shows the dat. pl.

ēgland, īegland, '*island*,' with the same topographical extension as for **eg**. Confused in later times with ealand, used of the same kind of ground. It is very difficult now to distinguish them. Ponteland (Nb), Elland (Y), Ealand (L) and Nayland (Sf). v. æt.

eik, ON, 'oak,' freely confused with ME *ake* from **ac** in NCy p.n. Aike (Y), Aigburth (La), Eyke (Sf), Ayscough, Ackton, Oakdale (Y), Akehead (Cu).

einn, ON, 'one, alone.' Ainsty (Y), Aintree (La), Anthorn (Cu).

elle(r)n, OE, '*elder*-tree.' Elsted (Sx), Elstob (Du).

elm, OE, '*elm*-tree.' Elmstead (Ess). It is very difficult to distinguish from a pers. name found in Elmington (Nth), Elmham (Nf).

elri, ON, 'place overgrown with alders.' Ellerker (Y).

ende, OE, '*end*,' but also 'quarter or division of a town, village or district.' Brook End (Beds), Mile End in Colchester (Ess).

ened, OE, 'duck.' Enford (W), Enborne (Berks).

eng, ON, 'pasture, grassland,' the source of NCy dial. *ing*, 'meadow-land,' more especially in marshy places, found also occasionally elsewhere. It is much more common in field-names than in p.n. and it has been assumed in explanation of p.n. in -*ing* far too frequently. Ekwall (*English PN in -ing*, 28–9) shows that it must not be assumed unless the early forms show *eng* rather than *ing*. Halling (Y), Mickering (La).

eofor, OE, 'boar,' is doubtless found in a large number of p.n. in *Ever*- but it is almost impossible to distinguish it from the pers. name *Eofor*.

eorþ, OE, '*earth*,' found only in p.n. from *eorþburh*, used in OE charters. Ekwall demonstrates this for Arbury (La) and suggests it for Arbury (C, Herts), which have old camps. He notes also that Burrow-on-the-Hill (Lei) was *Erdborough* in 1316.

ēowestre, OE, 'sheepfold.' Austerfield (Y), Ousterley (Du), Osterley (Mx).

erg, ON. In *Orkneyingasaga* when Earl Rögnvald was trying to find Thorbjörn in Caithness, he went up a dale at night and found lodging in a certain *erg*, 'which we (i.e. the Norsemen) call **setr,** i.e. mountain-pasture.' In the same saga some 'deserted shealings' are called *Asgrimeserg.* These two passages show its primary sense and agree with the meaning of Gael. *airidh* from which the Norsemen in Ireland or Scotland borrowed the word. That is defined as 'a shealing, hill-pasture, summer residence for herdsmen and cattle, a level green among hills.' (See further Battersby's excellent note in Moorman, *PN of the West Riding,* 216–8.) The term must have gained a wider significance in England for it is often used of places which certainly were never mountain or hill-pastures. Feizor, Golcar (Y), Docker, Mansergh, Sharrow (We), Anglezark (La), Arrow (Ch). Nom. pl. in Battrix, Arras (Y), dat. pl. in Arram, Argam, Airy Holme, Eryholme (Y), Arkholme (La).

ersc, ærsc, OE, is only found in charter material but its meaning may be assumed to be the same as dial. *earsh, arrish,* used of a stubble field and also of the aftermath in SCy. Owing to its comparative rarity it has often been confused with other suffixes in p.n. Ryarsh (K), Pebmarsh (Ess), Beynhurst (Berks), Burwash (Sx), Lagness (Sx), Langrish (Ha), Irish (Co), Wonersh (Sr).

erþ, ierþ, OE, 'ploughed land, arable land.' Cornard (Sf), Bridzor (W), Brightside (Y), Hengarth (La).

eski, ON, 'place grown over with ashes.' Escowbeck (La), Eastoft in Adlingfleet (L).

eyrr, ON, 'sandbank.' Ayre (La), Ravenserod (Y) (now under the sea).

fæger, OE, **fagr,** ON, '*fair,* beautiful.' Fairley (Nb).

fælging, OE, 'fallow-land,' a derivative of **fealh.** Falling, Falinge (La).

fær, OE, 'passage, track.' Hollinfare (La), Laver, Walkfare (Ess).

fæsten, OE, 'stronghold.' Holdfast (Wo), Brinfast (Sx).

fāg, OE, 'stained, variegated.' Fawside (Du), Fawcett (We), Facit (La), Fawler (O), Foolow (Db). From the weak dat. sg. *fagan* come Fownhope (He), Faintree (Sa). Frome Vauchurch (Do), Vowchurch (He) show WCy voicing of *f* to *v* and are the English equivalents of Sc. Fa(l)kirk. It is sometimes difficult, at least in NCy, to distinguish this from **fealg.** In compounds with *church* it may refer to the colour-effect of the stonework or it may describe a half-timbered building. In most other cases it probably refers to the colour of the soil. Voaden (D).

fal(o)d, OE, '*fold,*' but not confined as it usually now is to 'sheepfold.' In OE it glosses *ovile, stabulum, bovile.* Vaulde (He), Cuffell (Ha), Darvell (Sx).

fall, ON, 'place where trees have been felled.' Threlfall (La). Ekwall cites examples of its use to denote enclosures from woodlands.

fealcen, fealca, OE, '*falcon.*' Falkbourne (Ess), gen. pl. in Fawkham (K).

fealh, fealg, OE, 'ploughed land,' later 'ploughed land left uncropped for a whole year or more,' '*fallow* land.' The nom. gives ME *falegh, fal(u)gh,* dial. *faugh* (Nb) and *fauch* (Sc), pronounced [faf], while the dat. case gives *falwe, falou* in ME and *fallow* in Mod. Eng. It is often very difficult to distinguish this element from **fealo.** Fallodon (Nb), Falthwaite (Y), Fallowfield (La), Felpham (Sx).

fealo, OE, 'pale yellow or red-coloured, like withered grass or leaves.' Without the OE forms it is very difficult to distinguish it from **fealh.**

fearn, OE, '*fern.*' Faringdon (Berks), Farleigh (Ha, K, So), Farley (Sr), Farnborough (Berks, K), Farmborough (So), Vernham's Dean (Ha), Fairley (Sa).

fearnig, '*ferny.*' Fernilee (Nb).

fearr, OE, 'bull.' Farcett (Ha), Fazeley (St).

feld, OE, Mod. Eng. *field.* These though etymologically identical differ widely in meaning. Stevenson puts the case clearly (*Phil. Soc. Trans.* 1895–8, p. 531) when he points out that OE *feld* was just the opposite of our *field,* for it meant a great stretch of unenclosed land, and the Dutch use of *veldt* brings this home to us. Arthur Young uses *field land* as a term opposed to *woodland* and we may note that in BCS 464 a grant is made to the abbey of Peterborough of land with *feld* and *wudu* and *fenn* thereto pertaining, the three apparently covering all possible types of land. This must be its sense in the great majority of p.n. in which it is found. It could only have the modern sense in those of quite recent origin. It is corrupted to *ville,* especially in the WCy, as in Glanville (D), Cheney Longville (Sa), Enville (St). Note also Cavil (Y).

fell, fiall, ON, 'mountain, hill, *fell.*' Common in NCy dial. and therefore no definite criterion of Scand. settlement. Hampsfield (La).

fenn, fænn, OE, 'dirt, mud, *fen.*' Fenacre (D), Venn (He), Venn Ottery (D), Ratfin (W), Gorvin, Hawson (D). There are definite traces of a ME form *fann* in such names as Bulphan, Fanton (Ess), Vanne (K), Fambridge (Ess).

fennig, '*fenny,* muddy.' Sutton Veny (W).

feorðung, OE, 'fourth part.' Allfarthing (Sr).

ferja, ON, 'ferry.' *ferry* in p.n. of any age seems to be confined to the Danelaw and must be assumed to be of Scand. origin. Ferrybridge (Y), Ferriby (L, Y).

filiþe, OE, 'hay.' Filleigh (D), Feltham (So).

fin, OE, 'heap of wood' and fina, 'woodpecker,' must be found in some p.n. such as Findon (Sx), but they are almost impossible to distinguish from the pers. name *Finn*.

flasshe, flosshe, ME, 'pool, marshy place, *flash, flosh*,' still used in NCy, Ch, Sa. Cf. ME *flask* used in the same sense and Damflask (Y). These must go back to Dan. *flask(e)* used in p.n. of a 'creek with shallow water, swampy or low-lying stretches of grass-land,' senses closely paralleled by the illustrations for *flash* in NED. The distribution of the term and its close semantic relation to the Danish word suggests that it is a Scand. loan-word, with common substitution of English *sh* for Scand. *sk*, assisted in this case by the better onomatopoeic effect, as of plashing through water, produced by the new English form. Flass (Du).

flat, ME, a loan-word from ON *flǫt*, denoting a level piece of ground, is specially common in field-names where it is used of one of the larger portions into which the common field was divided. Flatworth (Nb), Tarn Flat (La).

fleax, flex, OE, '*flax*.' Flaxley (Gl), Flexborough (Sx).

flēot, OE, fljót, ON, 'creek, inlet, estuary.' Fleet (Ha), Benfleet (Ess), Fleetham (Nb), Hunslet (Y). In Scand. England it is impossible to keep the two words apart.

flōde, OE, 'channel of water,' used as a gloss for *cloaca, lacunar*. Found in p.n. in Ha and Berks. Grundy (*E and S*, 54–5) shows that it is specially applied to intermittent springs, notably those which burst out in the chalk downs at intervals of several years. Fulflood (Ha), Inglewood (Berks).

flōr, OE, '*floor*.' Its exact sense in p.n. is uncertain. It may refer to a threshing floor or some other such floor or it may have developed something of the sense of its German cognate *flur*, the common term for a field. In Fawler (O), in which it is compounded with fag it may refer to a tesselated pavement. The hall of Heorot had a *fagne flor* (*Beowulf* 725).

fola, OE, '*foal*.' Foulridge (La).

folcland, OE, or *folk-land*, i.e. land descending according to folkright or common law. Faulkland (So).

ford, OE, '*ford*,' is very common in the form *forth* in p.n. forms from 1300 onwards. This is not due, as has been suggested, to association with ON *fjǫrðr*, '*firth*,' which was never loaned into English but is due to a regular phonetic development of final *rd* in an unstressed syllable. Ford (Nb), Spofforth (Y), Baxterwood (Du), Flatworth (Nb), Clanver End (Ess), Broadward (Sa), Harvington (Wo).

fors, ON, 'waterfall, *force*.' Hall Foss (Cu).

forsc, OE, pl. **froxas**, 'frog.' Froxfield (Ha, W), Frostenden (Sf).

fox, OE, '*fox*.' Foscote (W), Fewston (Y).

fox-hole, ME. Foxhall (Sf).

fugol, OE, 'bird, *fowl*.' Foulness (Ess), Foulmire (C), Fulmer (Bk). One cannot be always sure that one has not the OE pers. name *Fugol* (rare).

fūl, OE, '*foul*, dirty,' is very common in such p.n. as Fulford, Fulwell. Fulford (So) is *sordidum vadum* in BCS 476. Some of these names may contain the adj. *full* but that element is exceedingly rare in p.n. to judge by the unambiguous charter material. Foulford (Ha), Fooden (Y), Philip (Nb), Fulready (Wa).

funta, OE, 'spring,' and possibly also 'stream,' is only found in charter material. Ekwall (ES, 54, 103–8) has shown it to be a loan-word from Latin through Celtic. Havant (Ha), Bedfont (Mx), Chalfont (Bk), Fovant (W).

furlang, OE, 'an area of land a *furrow-long*.' Very common in field-names. Bamfurlong (La).

fyrhþ(e), OE, 'wood, wooded country.' In ME often contrasted with *fell* and *field* in alliterative phrases. NED *s.v.* Pirbright (Sr), Firber (La), Chapel-en-le-Frith (Db). Cf. Kent dial. *frightwood*.

fyrs, OE, '*furze*.' Furze (Co, D).

gærs, græs, OE, '*grass*.' Gresham (Nf).

gærs-tūn, 'grassy enclosure.' Cf. BCS 699 '*pratumquoque quod juxta civitatem habetur, quod Saxonice Garstone appellatur*.' Garston (Gl, Ha, Herts). Still used in Sr and Sx dial. *Not* present in Garston (La) and East Garston (Berks).

gagel, gagolle, OE, '*gale*, bog-myrtle.' Gailey (St), Gomer (Ha).

gāra, OE, 'triangular piece of land,' but used later, especially in field names, of a wedge-shaped strip of land on the side of a field which results from dividing a field whose sides are not parallel into 'lands' or 'leys.' Gore Hundred (Mx), Langar (Nt), Bredgar (K), Garland (D), Overgrass (Nb).

garðr, ON, '*garth*, enclosure.' Lingart (La), Hawsker (Y), Plungar (Lei).

gāt, OE, '*goat*.' Gatton, Gatwick (Sr), Goathurst (So), Gotham (Nt), Gay(t)hurst (Bk), Gappah (D).

gata, ON, 'road, *gate*,' still in living use in NCy. It is as a rule very difficult to distinguish this from the ordinary word *gate*, 'opening,' from OE *gatu*, pl. of **geat**. One of the least ambiguous cases is the common use of *gate* in street-names in the large Northern towns.

gealga, OE, **galgi**, ON, '*gallows*.' Galliber (We), Gawber (Y), Gallow Hundred (Nf).

gear, OE, only found in charter material, but used in the same sense as dial. *yair, yare,* 'enclosure for catching fish.' Kepier (Du). Dat. pl. in Yarm (Y).

geard, OE, 'enclosure, *yard.*' Bruisyard (Sf), Lizard (Sa).

geat, OE, '*gate,*' must refer in the majority of p.n. in which it is found to some permanent 'gate' in a fence or hedge, but as has been noted by Stevenson and Grundy it can also be used of a hollow or gap which gives the effect of a 'gate' on the sky-line. Similarly it is used of a narrow passage in *Symond's Yat* on the Wye, in the *Win(d)gates* up and down England, in Whinyates (Y) and in the well-known Winnats Pass (Db) where it describes a passage through which the wind sweeps. The nom. sg. gives dial. *yat* or *yet*. The OE pl. *gatu* becomes *gate* and then in Scand. England it is difficult to distinguish it from *gate* 'road,' from **gata**. Yate (Gl), Burnyate, Pickett (Do), Bozeat (Nth), Leziate (Nf), Ditcheat, Donyatt (So), Bagshott (W). v. **hlidgeat, hlypgeat.**

geil, ON, 'ravine, cleft.' Scalegill, Galefield (Cu), Hugill (We).

geiri, ON, cognate with **gara**. Fairly common in NCy field-names and in dial. *gair* (Nb, L, Y), used of (i) a triangular piece of land in the corner of a field, (ii) an isolated spot of tender grass. Found as a first element in Garstang (La), Gargrave, Garforth (Y), Gartree Wapentake (L), but it is difficult to distinguish it from the Norse pers. name *Geir.*

geit, ON, 'goat.' Gatesgill (Cu), Gayton (La).

gil, ON, 'ravine, *gill.*'

gnípa, ON, 'hill, peak.' Knipe (We), Knipton (Lei).

gor, OE, 'dung, dirt, filth.' Gorhuish, Gorvin (D), Gorewell (Do), Gorwell (Ess).

gorst, OE, '*gorse.*' Gorse Hill (Wo).

gorstig adj. Goscote (St).

gōs, OE, '*goose,*' is specially frequent in numerous Gosfords and Gosforths, meaning 'fords haunted by geese,' a common country sight, not 'fords used by geese.' Goswick (Nb).

græf, OE, 'pit, trench, *grave,*' but in p.n. it is almost impossible to keep this element separate from

grāf(a), '*grove,* copse,' and the allied

græfe, used in the same sense, which became Early Mod. Eng. *greave,* used of a thicket and of brushwood.

Seldom are the forms so unambiguous as they are in Temple Grafton and Griff (Wa), which are certainly respectively from **græf** and **græfe.**

grǣg, OE, **grá**, ON, '*grey.*' Greystead (Nb), Grayrigg (Cu).

grēat, OE, '*great.*' Grateley (Ha), Gratwich (St), Greatham (Sx). Not always easy to distinguish from **greot.**

grein, ON, 'division, branch, fork, *grain,*' used in NCy of a small valley opening from another. Haslingden Grane (La), Greenah Hall (Cu).

grēne, OE, **grœnn,** ON, '*green,*' adj. Very common with shortened vowel and also with further raising of *e* to *i* before the following nasal. Greenhead (Nb), Grendon (Wa), Grinstead (Sx), Grindlow (Db), Grandborough (Bk, Wa), Little Gringley (Nt). The substantival use of this word to denote a 'grassy spot,' still more the sense of a village 'green' are of late origin. Hollins Green (La).

grēot, OE, **grjót,** ON, 'gravel,' dial. *greet.* In Scand. England the two cannot be kept separate. Greta (Cu), Greet (Sa, Wo), Greetland (Y), Girton (C), Girtford (Beds).

gríss, ON, 'pig,' NCy *grice,* is found in a good many Grisedales and Grisebecks and the like, but cannot be kept definitely apart from the same word used as a pers. name.

grund, OE, ON, 'bottom, *ground.*' It is impossible to say which of the numerous sense-developments of this word is to be postulated for a p.n. such as Stanground (Hu). Ekwall refers its use in North La p.n. to the ON word and suggests that it has the dial. sense of 'farm, especially an outlying one.'

gryfja, ON, 'hole, pit,' NCy *griff,* 'deep narrow glen,' etc. Griff (Db, Y), Grief, Skinningrove, Mulgrave, Stonegrave (Y).

há(r), ON, 'high,' possibly, like **heah,** used to denote 'chief' also. Habrough (L).

hæcc, hec, OE, dial. *hatch, hack, heck. hatch* is used of a gate or wicket, a floodgate or sluice, a grating to catch fish at a weir, *heck* is used in the last of these senses, while *hack* has a slightly different sense-development which hardly enters into p.n. Topographical knowledge can alone settle its exact meaning in each case. In Colney Hatch (Mx) it refers to a gate of Enfield Chase, in Heckdike (L) it is clearly associated with water. Hatch (So), Heck (Y), Maidenhatch (Berks).

There is the possibility of another word **hæcce,** 'fence of rails,' entering into some of these names. Toller postulates this word on the strength of the charter material (BT *s.v.*).

(ge)hæg, OE, 'hedge' and then 'enclosure.' Bromhey (K). This is the probable source of the common ME *hay,* 'part of a forest fenced off for hunting.' It is very difficult to keep this word distinct from **heg** and **hege.** Licky (Wo), Oxney (K), Littley Ess).

hæfen, OE, **hǫfn,** ON, '*haven,* harbour.' Keyhaven (Ha), Whitehaven (Cu).

hǣme, OE, pl., is not used by itself in OE but might be added to the first element in any p.n. and then used to denote the inhabitants of that place, thus *dræghæme* (KCD 736) denotes the inhabitants of Drayton (Nth). It is actually incorporated in the p.n. Ditchampton, Sevenhampton (W), Poolhampton (Ha). It is a derivative of **ham**.

hæsel, OE, '*hazel.*' In p.n. we often have the dial. [hezl] and then in Scand. England it is very difficult to distinguish it from ON **hesli**. Heazills (D), Hasbury (Wo), Monk Hesleden (Du), Hazelwood (Sx), Helshaw (Sa), Batsaddle Lodge (Nth). Halse (D, So) preserves dial. *halse.*

hæþ, OE, '*heath,*' used in p.n. of 'wild uncultivated country.' Hatton (Sa), Hatfield (Ess), Hadley (Mx), Hedley (Nb), Haydon (K), Headley Heath (Wo), Hethel (Nf).

hafri, ON, 'oats, *haver.*' Haverthwaite, Haverigg (La), Haverbrack (We).

haga, OE, **hagi**, ON, '*haw*, hedge,' then 'enclosure' and then 'messuage.' See Grundy (*E and S* 57–8) as to possible further limitations of meaning in OE charters. It usually denotes 'enclosure' in p.n. The Scand. and the Eng. term cannot be kept apart. Haw (Gl, Lei), Haigh, Turnagh (La), Briary, Becca (Y), Wellow, Thorney, Belaugh, Bylaugh (Nf), Bilhagh (Nt), Haugh (L), Locko (Db), Little Haugh (Sf).

haining, ME, 'the preserving of grass for cattle, protected grass, any fenced field or enclosure,' still used in NCy dial. A loan-word from Dan. *hegning*, used of enclosed as opposed to common land. Haining (Du, Nb), Heyning (L), Hyning (La).

hālig, OE, '*holy*,' becomes North. ME *hāly* and South. *hōly* which, with the usual shortening of a long vowel in a trisyllable, should give Mod. Eng. *Halli-* and *Holli-* in p.n. but these have often been replaced by forms due to the independent word *holy* in St. Eng. Hallatrow (So), Halliford (Mx), Hallikeld (Y), Holystone (Nb) and numerous Halliwells, Holliwells, Holywells, and Halwills. Halstock (D).

hals, ON, 'neck,' NCy and Sc. *hause*, used for a 'connecting ridge, a *col.*' Esk Hause (Cu), Wrynose (La).

hām, OE, is used in the first instance of a farm or estate (Lat. *praedium, praediolum*) and then in the more technical sense of a vill or a manor. Thus we have *biscopham* used of an episcopal (cf. Bispham, La) and *cyneham* of a royal manor. A passage in the OE trans. of Bede suggests that it was thought of as denoting something larger than a **tun** for the Latin *inter civitates sive villas* is rendered *betwih his hamum oþþe tunum*. For *ingaham*-names v. **ing**.

Its precise significance as a p.n. element is difficult to determine. Its distribution would suggest that it was passing out of use as the English conquest advanced westwards. The counties in which it is most frequent are Nf, Sf, Ess, C, Sr, Sx, while it is comparatively very rare in Db, Ch, Sa, He, Gl, Wa, Wo, St. There is no evidence that it continued in use as a living suffix as late as the Norman Conquest. At present we are hardly in a position to translate it by other terms than those used for tun, viz. 'farm' or 'manor.' Consideration of the distribution, meaning and use of this term is rendered more difficult by its liability to confusion with

hamm, OE. This confusion is already fairly common even in OE documents themselves and it is even more likely to arise if we have only ME forms. ME *ham* in unstressed syllables remains as *ham* in spelling, though the vowel is shortened, while *hamm* appears as *ham* or *hom*. Unless therefore we have an OE form preserved or a tell-tale form in ME with double *m* or with *o*, it is very difficult to know which suffix we have.

hamm denotes 'enclosed possession, fold,' the word being allied to the vb. *hem*, 'shut in.' It is the source of dial. *ham*, confined to the South and South Midlands, and denoting 'flat low-lying pasture, land near a river,' but it is not clear whether the association with water was already developed in OE. It may have been in such compounds as *flodhamm*, *wæterhamm* and possibly in *mylenhamm* but this was certainly not always the case. Its common use to denote land in the bend of a river may have been influenced by the word *hamm*, 'bend of the knee.' It is very doubtful if we are justified in finding this suffix in NCy p.n. at all.

Both *ham* and *hamm* are often confused with holmr, the former in Barholm, Bloxholm (L), Hestholm (Y), the latter in Kingsholm (Gl). *ham* is present in Appledram (Sx).

hāmsteall = hām + steall, OE, is used in OE as an alternative gloss to tun for Lat. *praediolum*, used of the 'garden' of Gethsemane. Dial. *homestall* is used of a 'farm-house and adjacent buildings, farmyard and appurtenances, place of a mansion-house, enclosure of ground immediately connected therewith.' It is clear that in this compound ham has developed that further sense of 'dwelling, abode' which it had in OE, beside those given above. Hempstalls (Ess), Hamstalls (Gl).

hāmstede = hām + stede, OE. In this compound, as in hamsteall, we must have reference to the actual site of the chief house of the farm or manor. It is often found by itself and in compounds in Nf, Ess, Herts, Mx, Beds, Berks, Bk, Gl, Sx, Wt, D. Sometimes it takes the form *Hempstead* as well as the more common *Hampstead*. In some p.n., such as Berstead (K), Tisted (Ha), the *ham* element is found in the OE form of the names. Further in OE we find some p.n. in -*ham* with alternative forms in -*hamstede* as in the case of Sidlesham, Bracklesham (Sx) (BCS 132).

hāmtun = ham + tun, OE, though some, such as Hampton
Lovet (Wo), are from hamm + tun. A good many ME *hamton*
forms go back also to OE *hean-tun* (v. heah), to judge by such forms
as *Henton*, *Hanton*, though even here the *n* is not absolutely
conclusive evidence. The precise sense of *ham + tun* is difficult
to determine. It would seem to refer to the presence of a
(?) defensive tun around a *ham* but the compound came early to
mean something very like the modern 'home farm' and denoted
the centre of an estate in contrast to its outlying farms or other
properties. The compound is fairly common by itself and, when in
combination with another element, that seems to be some descriptive word rather than a pers. name, e.g. broc in Brockhampton
passim, ceosol in Chiselhampton (O), brycg in Bridgehampton (So),
stræt in Strettington (Sx), norð in Norrington (Ha). Many modern
-*hamptons* do not contain this element at all.

*hamel, OE, must be assumed on the basis of the charter material
and of numerous p.n. in *Hamble-* and *Humble-* in Modern English.
It is an adj. related to OE *hamela*, 'mutilated person,' and MHG
hamel, 'steep abrupt cliff,' *hamel-stat*, 'shelving terrain.' Its exact
sense in English remains to be determined by careful topographic
investigation. Hambledon (Ha, Do), Hambleton (R, Y), Humble-
don (Du), Humbleton (Du, Nb), Hambleden (Bk), all of which
really end in dun, and, possibly, Hamble R. (Ha).

hangra, OE, 'wood on a slope, *hanger*.' In unstressed positions
it is liable to various corruptions. In the WCy where it is often
found as *honger* in ME, it is specially liable to confusion with the
word *hunger* and is often so spelt. Oakhanger (Ch), Clehonger (He),
Clinger (Gl), Shelfanger (Nf), Songar (Wa), Binegar (So), Barnacle
(Wa), Rishangles (Sf).

hār, OE, 'grey, *hoar*,' is often applied to stones and trees, especially when they are lichen-covered. OE *har-stan*, lit. grey or old
stone, survives as *hoarstone* (Sc. *hairstane*), 'boundary-stone,' and
is present in disguised form in Harsondale (Nb), Harsenden,
Hastingley (La). *har* is very common in other compounds also,
even if we take into account the possibility that in some cases we
have OE *hara*, 'hare,' and it is noteworthy that in a large number
of cases the places are on the bounds of a county or parish. This
led Duignan to advance the view that from its use in har-*stan*
the element *har* may be descriptive of a 'boundary' in other
compounds also. The examples which he adduces and observations
on the site of other places seem to prove his theory.

Hoarwithy (He), Whorridge (D), Horewell (Wa), Harrock (Wo),
are all certain cases of *har* rather than *hara* and in Whorridge,
Horewell it is difficult to see how *har* can have any of its ordinary
meanings.

hassuc, OE, 'coarse grass, *hassock*.' Haske (D), Haxmore Farm (W).

haugr, ON, 'hill, barrow, *how*,' used in ON and probably also in English of a hill whether natural or artificial. In its ME form *howe* it is very difficult in Scand. England to distinguish it from *howe* from the dat. sg. of **hoh**. Where the first element is a Scand. pers. name we may assume that we have the Norse rather than the English word. Carlinghow (Y), Ulpha (Cu, We), Gallow Hund. (Nf), Greenah Hall (Cu), Becconsall (La), dat. pl. in Holme-on-the-Wolds (Y), Hoone (Db) and possibly Haume (La).

heafoc, OE, '*hawk*,' is present in many p.n. but it is difficult to distinguish it from ON *haukr*, used as a pers. name = *Hawk(e)*.

hēafod, OE, '*head*,' and used in various senses in p.n., the chief being that of ground which by its outline suggested a head. Where it is used after an animal's name it may refer in some cases, as Bradley suggested, to a custom of setting up the head of an animal, or a representation of it, on a pole, to mark the meeting-place of a hundred. In boundary marks it is used to denote the *headland* where the plough turned after ploughing the parallel strips of the corn-land. Manshead (Beds), Swineshead (L), Fineshade (Nth), Farcett (Hu), Shepshed (Lei), Hartside (Nb), Lindeth (La), Broxted (Ess), Macknade (K).

hēah, OE, '*high*,' and possibly in some p.n. 'chief,' as in 'high street' and similar expressions. In dial. the word is variously pronounced with the vowels [ai], [ei], [i·] and these forms are found in p.n. also. Further a great many of these show forms going back to the weak dat. sg. *hean*, e.g. Henley from (*æt þæm*) *hean leage*, and these again give rise to fresh forms in *Hen-*, *Han-*, and *Hean-*. Highworth (W), Heage (Db), Heaton, Healey *passim*, Heeley (Y), Henley *passim*, Heanton (D), Henbury (Gl, W), Hinton (Ha), Hampton-in-Arden (Wa), Handley (Db), Hanbury (Wo).

heald, OE, 'sloping, inclined.' Hawstead (Sf), Halstead (Ess).

healh, OE, 'corner, angle, secret place, recess.' Such are some of the meanings of this term in ordinary OE usage. Bede equates it with Latin *sinus*, 'bay.' In BCS 225 we have in a list of boundaries '*in quoddam petrosum clivum et ex eo baldwines healh appellatur*,' suggesting association with a rocky slope, but one should probably not lay too much stress on the 'rocky.' Grundy on the evidence of the charter material says that it means a 'small hollow in a hillside or slope.' All these senses can be reconciled if we take the primary idea behind *healh* to be something 'hidden,' the word being ultimately allied to **holh**. The nom. sg. form survives in NCy *haugh*, pronounced [ha·f] in Nb and [ha·χ] in Sc., where it is used of the flat alluvial land by the side of a river, formed in its bends.

The dat. sg. gives *hale*, similarly used in dial. and also applied to a triangular corner of land. It is one of the commonest of all p.n. elements. The nom. sg. *haugh, halgh* is confined to Northern England. The form *hale* from the dat. sg. is often confused with **hyll** and **heall**. Hale (Ch), nom. pl. in Hales (St), dat. pl. in Halam (Nt). Willenhall (St), Beard Hall (Db), Stancill (Y), Lobsell (W), Northolt (Mx), Taxal (Ch), Hepple (Nb), Renhold (Beds), Roall (Y), Haulgh (La), Kirkhaugh (Nb), Earnshaw (L). *healhtun* gives Halloughton (Nt), Hallaton (Lei), Holton (O, So), Halton (Nb, Sa), Haighton (La).

heall, OE, '*hall*,' hence 'manor-house' is not common in p.n., where it seems to be of post-Conquest origin, except possibly where it is compounded with **stede** and gives such names as Halstead (La, L). Most modern p.n. in -*hall* go back to ME *hale* (v. healh).

hēap, OE, '*heap*,' hence 'hill.' This is suggested by Ekwall for Heap, Heapey, Hapton (La) and more doubtfully for Shap (We). Not found in OE charter material.

hearg, OE, 'sacred grove, heathen temple.' Harrow (Mx), Peper Harrow (Sr), Harrowden (Nt).

hēg, hieg, OE, '*hay*,' is difficult to distinguish from **hege**, **(ge)hæg**. It is probably found in most of the English Haydons. Hayley (Ha).

hege, OE, 'hedge,' is very difficult to differentiate from **(ge)hæg**. Haylot (Sa).

heim, ON, 'homestead,' often interchanges with its English cognate **ham**.

helm, OE, **hjalmr**, ON, primarily 'helmet,' but used in p.n. of something which resembled or fulfilled the functions of a helmet. Thus the Norse word and dial. *helm* are used of a cattle-shed. Possibly this is its sense in p.n. Its distribution suggests Norse rather than English origin for this element. Helm (Nb, Y), Helme Park (Du), Helmshore (La).

henge, OE, 'hanging,' 'precipitous.' Hinchwick (Gl), Inchfield, Hengarth (La), Hinchcliffe (Y).

hengest, OE, 'horse, stallion.' Henceford, Henscott, Hexdown, Hiscott (D), Hingston Down (Co), but it is difficult to distinguish it from the pers. name of the same form.

henn, OE, '*hen*,' but it is difficult to distinguish this from *hean* (v. heah). Henley (W), Hendale (L).

hēope, OE, 'dog-rose, *hip*.' Hipbridge (L), Hepple, Hepden (Nb), Hebden Bridge (Y), Hetton-le-Hole (Du). Difficult to distinguish from a closely similar pers. name.

heordewic, OE, the source of many *Hardwicks*, is derived from *heord*, 'flock,' rather than from *hierde*, 'shepherd,' as suggested in NED. Vinogradoff (*Growth of the Manor*, 224), says that it refers to a pastoral settlement, but usually signifies the grange and stable in a small manorial settlement, as opposed to the berewic.

heorot, OE, 'stag, *hart*,' in names in *Hart-* (*passim*). Hurtmore (Sr).

here, OE, 'army,' especially 'raiding army.' Hereford (He), Harvington near Evesham (Wo), Harefield (Mx), Harwich (Ess).

herebeorg, OE, used once in the sense 'army-quarters.' ME *herberwe*, reinforced by ON *herbergi*, has given rise to such names as Harbour House (Du) and the numerous *Cold Harbours* throughout the country, meaning 'place of shelter from the weather for wayfarers.'

herepæþ, OE, lit. 'army-path,' used, says Grundy, of 'any through road of any age, Saxon or pre-Saxon,' but usually of the former. Harepath (D), Harpford (So), Harford, near Crediton (D).

hēse, hæse, hȳse, OE, only found in charter material but used of 'woodland country, land with bushes and brushwood' (BT). The cognate Germ. *hees* (OHG *he(i)si*) is applied to similar country, and Low Latin *heisia* = silva sepibus septa. Hayes, Heston (Mx), Heysham (La), Tapners (K).

hestr, ON, 'horse.' Hesket (Cu), Hesketh (2La, 2Y), Hestholm (Y).

hīd, hīgid, OE, '*hide*,' denoted in the oldest times a holding which supported an ordinary free household. It came to denote a measure of land of which the size must have varied between one region and another. Common as Hyde (*passim*) and disguised in Hullasey (Gl) and Tilshead (W). Groups of five, of ten, and of other multiples of ten hides were common and have given rise to *Fyfields* and *Fiveheads* in various parts of England, to Tinhead (W) and Combe-in-Teignhead (D) and Piddle Trenthide (Do).

hielde, helde, OE, 'slope, declivity.' Tyler Hill (K), Merrils Bridge (Nt), Murrells End (Wo), Stockeld (Y).

hīgna, OE, gen. pl. of *hīwan*, 'members of a family,' and specially of a monastic community. Hinton Martell (Do), Hinstock (Sa), Henwood (Wa), Hainault (Ess).

hind, OE, '*hind*, female of the hart.' Hindlip (Wo), Heindley (Y).

hīwisc, OE, 'family, house,' and then 'measure of land on which a household is settled.' Closely allied to **hid**, the first part of the word being the same, and often used interchangeably with it in early documents. Common in S.W. England as *Huish, Hewish*. Buckish, Langage (D).

hlaða, ON, 'barn, *lathe* (NCy).' Aldoth (Cu). Nom. pl. in Laithes (Cu), dat. pl. in Lathom (La), Laytham (Y).

hlāw, hlǣw, OE, 'hill, *law, low* (dial.),' is used of a hill, especially a rounded one, either natural or artificial. Grundy says that in the charters it always denotes a tumulus and the Db *lows* are all said to be burial mounds. It is certain, however, that in NCy the term is of wider application and it may also be so elsewhere. In the South, and still more in the South-West, it is rare in p.n. *law* is specially common in Nb and Du, *low* in Db, Ch, Sa, St, He. As a suffix it is very often confused with *-ley* from **leah**. Harlow (Ess), Spellow (La), Heatherslaw, Crawley, Kirkley, Kellah (Nb), Kelloe (Du), Rudloe (W). **hlæw** gives Lew (O).

hlēo, OE, 'shelter, *lee*.' Libbery (Wo).

hlidgeat, OE, 'swing-*gate*,' especially of one set up between meadow or pasture and ploughed land, or across the highway to prevent cattle straying. Dial. *lidgitt*, Lydiate (La), Lidgett (Y), show the normal development. Lidgate (Sf), Leadgate (Du), show the same change of form as is noted under **geat**.

hlinc, OE, 'bank, rising ground, *lynch, link* (dial.),' used in various technical senses as of a 'ledge of ploughland in a hillside formed gradually by ploughing in such a way as to turn the clod down hill,' 'an unploughed strip serving as a boundary between fields.' NCy *link* is used of undulating sandy ground. In p.n. one should probably take it in its more general senses. Standlynch (W), Stallenge (D). Ekwall has recently pointed out that some names in *-ling*, e.g. Swarling (K), Sydling (Do), really contain this suffix. Liscombe (Bk).

hliþ, OE, **hlið**, ON, 'slope.' Ainstable (Cu), Adgarley (La), Kelleth (We), Bowlhead (Sr), Lydd (K), Litton (Db). Gen. sg. in Litherland (La), dat. pl. in Lytham (La), Upleatham (Y).

hlōse, OE, 'pigsty, *looze* (dial.).' Loose (K, Sf), Loosebeare (D), Luzzley (La), Aldglose (K).

hlynn, OE, 'torrent, waterfall, pool.' Lowlynn, Linshields (Nb).

hlȳp(e), OE, '*leap*ing-place, place to be jumped over' and possibly also 'steep-place' generally. Lipe (W), Hindlip (Wo), Birdlip (Gl), Pophlet Park (D).

hnutu, OE, '*nut*.' Nuthurst (Wa), Notley (Ess), Nursling (Ha).

hōc, OE, '*hook*,' may be descriptive of a place at a sharp bend in a stream or it may have the sense of its Dutch and Frisian cognates, viz. 'projecting corner, point or spit of land.' Hook (Ha, Y), Liphook (Ha).

hǫfuð, ON, 'head.' Used in Norse p.n. of any projecting peak, of something which resembles a head in shape and also of a source. Holleth, Hawkshead in Bolton-le-Sands (La), Howden (Y), Whitehaven (Cu). Cf. *Howth* Head, near Dublin.

hǫgg, ON, 'cutting, right of cutting trees,' hence dial. *hagg* and *hagwood* used in much the same senses. Hagg Wood (Nb), Barns Hagwood (L).

hōh, OE, 'projecting ridge of land, promontory,' probably identical with *hoh*, 'heel,' used in p.n. of any piece of land projecting into more level ground. Sc. and NCy *heugh*, pron. [hiuχ, hjuf], is used of a 'craggy or rugged steep, glen, deep cleft in the rocks.' In p.n. it takes the forms *hough*, *heugh*, but there are alternative forms *hoo* and *hoe* from OE *hō*, as in Luton Hoo (Beds), Wivenhoe (Ess). This element, together with tun, gives many names such as *Ho(u)ghton*, *Ho(o)ton*, *Hutton*, and occasionally *Haughton*. Dat. sg. *hoge*, ME *howe* has given *-how* in p.n., and in Scand. England it is difficult to distinguish it from haugr. This suffix is specially common in Beds and Nth, fairly so in Sf, Ess, Herts, Bk, and is very common in Nb, Du. In SCy it is of much milder significance than in the North. It is subject to many corruptions as a suffix, as in Salpho, Budna (Beds), Belsay, Kyo (Nb), Wixoe (Sf), Trunnah (La). We seem to have the nom. pl. in Hose (Lei). Hoyland (Y), Holton-le-Moor (L).

holegn, OE, '*holly*-tree, *hollin*, *holm* (dial.).' Hollinfare (La), Hulne (Nb), Holne (D), Holmside (Du), Hollington (Db), Holdfast (Wo).

holh, hol, OE, hol, holr, ON, noun and adj., '*hole, hollow*.' Staynah, Greenhalgh (La), Hollym (Y), dat. pl. in Hulam (Du). The adj. is specially common with burna, broc and weg as in Holborn, Holbrook, Holloway *passim*. Holbeach (L), Holbeam (D), Hoborough (K), Howgill (Y). See also brocchol, foxhole.

holmr, holmi, ON, 'islet, *holm*,' but used also of any piece of ground isolated from its surroundings. Thus it was used in Iceland of a 'meadow on the shore, with ditches behind' (Cleasby-Vigfusson). In England we have the same twofold use, the former surviving in p.n. only, the latter in dial. *holm*, 'piece of low-lying ground by a river or stream.' For the form *hulme*, from ODan. *hulm*, see Ekwall, *PNLa*. Grassoms (Cu).

holt, OE, 'wood, *holt*.' Not found in NCy. Occold (Sf), Poulshott (W), Hainault (Ess).

hop, OE, 'piece of enclosed land in the midst of fens or marshes or of waste land generally.' In ME and in p.n. we have a word *hope* used of a small enclosed valley, especially 'a smaller opening branching out from the main dale, a blind valley,' which is commonly assumed to be the same word. There is little doubt that the 'valley' sense is more common in p.n. than the 'enclosure' one but the whole question needs study. It certainly bears the former sense in the p.n. in Nb and Du, where it is most frequent, and probably also in He and Sa, the other counties in which it is most common. It seems to be unknown in England South of the Thames. Cleatop (Y), Ritherope, Bacup, Cowpe (La), Philip, Snope (Nb), Gater Top (He), Alsop (Db).

hord, OE, '*hoard*, treasure.' Hordron (Y), Hardhorn (La), Hurdlow (Db), Hordle (Ha).

horh, horu, OE, 'filth,' common in *Horton*. Harpole (Nth, Sf).

horn, OE, '*horn*,' used in p.n. of something which suggests a horn. Woodhorn (Nb).

hræfn, OE, '*raven*,' appears in p.n. as *Raven-*, *Ram-*, *Ran-*, *Ren-*, *Rem-*, but it is seldom possible, at least in Scand. England, to be sure that we have not the same word used as a pers. name. Further confusion with *ramm*, 'ram,' is also possible.

hrēod, OE, '*reed*,' should give *Reed-*, *Red-* or *Rod-* in p.n. as in Redbridge (Ha), Rodborne (W). Forms in *Rad-* however are also common as in Radbourne (Wa), Radham (Gl). It is often difficult to distinguish from read and from the pers. name *Rǣda*.

hreysi, ON, 'cairn, heap of stones.' Dunmail Raise (We), Roseacre (La).

hring, OE, ON, '*ring*,' hence 'circular.' Ringstead (Nf, Nth), Ringmer (Ess, Sx), Eakring (Nt).

hrīs, OE, hris, ON, 'shrubs, brushwood.' Risbridge (K), Ruston (Nf), Riston (L), Ryston (Nf). Dat. pl. in Riseholme (L), Rysome Garth (Y), Hamble-le-Rice (Ha).

hrōc, OE, '*rook*,' is very difficult to distinguish from a similar pers. name.

hrycg, OE, hryggr, ON, '*ridge, rigg*.' Different dial. developments are reflected in the common *Ridge* by the side of Rudge (Gl), Rodge (Wo), Rudgwick (Sx) and Reach (K). Courage (Berks), Elmbridge (Wo).

hryding, OE, 'clearing, cleared or *rid*ded land.' Riddings (Db), Riding Mill (Nb), Woodridden (Ess). Very common in field-names.

hrȳðer, OE, 'ox, cattle.' Rotherfield (Ha, O), Ritherope (La), Rotherhithe (Sr).

hungor, OE, '*hunger*,' is fairly common, especially in field-names, to denote places with poor pasturage or crops. It is often very difficult to distinguish it from hangra.

hunig, OE, 'honey,' common in compounds with some word denoting water and probably referring to its pleasantness. Honeychild (K), Honeybourne (Wo), Honiley (Wa).

hunte, ME, '*hunt*' and then 'district hunted.' This development is, according to the dictionaries, quite modern, but it would seem that we must postulate its use much earlier to explain such p.n. as Chadshunt (Wa), Bonhunt, Tolleshunt (Ess), Cheshunt (Herts), Boarhunt (Ha).

huntena, OE, gen. pl. of *hunta*, 'huntsman.' Huntingford (Gl), Huntington (He, Sa).

hūs, OE, hús, ON, '*house*,' is rarely found in the South, as in

Stonehouse (D, Gl), Onehouse (Sf), but is common in Scand. England, and there, as in Scandinavia, is very common in the pl. Woodhouse *passim*, Lofthouse, Loftus (Y). Dat. pl. in Newsome, News(h)am, Newsholme *passim*, Howsham (L, Y), Gildersome, Loftsome, Wothersome, Ayresome (Y). Uzzicar (Cu).

hwǣte, OE, '*wheat*.' Whatcombe, Whitcombe (Do), Watcombe (O), Waddon (So, Wo), Whaddon (W), Whiteacre (K).

hwamm, hwomm, OE, **hvammr**, ON. The OE word is glossed *angulus*, the ON word is used of a 'short valley or depression surrounded by high ground, but with an opening on one of the sides.' One or other of these words lies behind NCy *wham*, 'marshy hollow, hollow in a hill or mountain,' and such p.n. as Wham, Whitwham (Nb).

hwēol, OE, '*wheel*, circle,' suggested by Ekwall for Wheelton (La), Wheldale (Y). Welbatch (Sa).

hwetstān, OE, '*whetstone*.' Westernhope (Du), Whetstone (Lei).

hwīt, OE, '*white*, shining.' Dialectically the term *white* is sometimes applied to dry open pasture ground in opposition to woodland and black-land growing heath. At times it is difficult to distinguish it from the pers. name *Hwita*. Wheatfield (O), Whetenham (Ess).

hwyrfel, OE, **hwirfill**, ON, are cognate terms allied to OE *hweorfan*, 'to turn.' *hwyrfel* is only found in p.n. material in OE and is there applied to a **mere**, a **dic** and a **dun** and seems to mean 'circular,' or perhaps in the first case, 'eddying.' The Norse word is used of a 'circle' and of a 'hill with rounded top.' Whorwelsdown (W), Whorlton (Y), at the foot of the *Whorl*, a well-rounded hill, Quarles (Nf).

hyll, OE, '*hill*,' appears in ME as *hill* and *hull* but in p.n. the *hull* forms have for the most part been levelled out in favour of St. Eng. *hill*. Monyhull (Wa), Coppull (La), Crichel (Do), Hill, Hull (Sa), Hulton (St), Bucknell (Nth), Hordle (Ha), Shottle, Smerril (Db), Apsell (W), Odell (Beds), Caswell (Co), Royle (La), Beal (Nb), Shelfield (Wa), Wardle, Caughall (Ch), Hethel (Nf). Dat. pl. in Hillam (Y).

hylr, ON, 'pool, deep place in a river.' Lickle, Troutal (La), Dibble Bridge (Y).

hyrne, OE, 'corner.' Different dial. forms are found in Guyhirne (C), Hurne (Ha), Hurley (Berks, Wa), Herne (K).

hȳrness, OE, lit. *hearing*, then 'subjection, service, jurisdiction.' The exact extent and nature of the jurisdiction is uncertain. At times it seems to denote 'parish.' Berkeley Harness (Gl), Lugharness (He).

hyrst, OE, 'hillock, knoll, bank' and 'copse, wood,' a twofold sense which still survives in dial. *hurst* and is found also in the cognate *horst* of the Low Germ. dialects. Probably the original meaning was one combining the two, viz. 'wooded height.' The normal forms in Mod. Eng. are *hirst* in the North and the East Midlands, *hurst* elsewhere. Hartest (Sf), Titness (Berks), Staplers (Wt), Copster (La), Horsebridge (Sx).

hȳð, OE, 'port, haven,' and then 'landing place on a river.' ME *hithe, huthe, hethe* in different dialects, but there is always a tendency to level out in favour of the first and St. Eng. form. Rotherhithe, Lambeth, Stepney, and Chelsea on the Thames, Maidenhead (Berks), Old Heath in Colchester (Ess), Earith (Hu), Aldreth (C), Stockwith (L), Hive (Y).

ifig, OE, '*ivy.*' Ivychurch (W).

īggoð, OE, 'islet, *eyot.*' The Aits (Sr).

ikorni, ON, 'squirrel.' Icornhurst, Ickenthwaite (La), Ickornshaw (Y).

ing[1] is found in many English p.n. and in dealing with it we may first dismiss those in which it is not original. Examples of final -*ing* from ON eng, OE (hl)inc are dealt with under those elements. Medial -*ing*- often represents the gen. sg. in -*an* of an OE weak form of a pers. name, as in Abingdon (Berks) from *Abbandun*. Such are not however to be expected in NCy where the *n* of *an* was early lost. These false *ing*-types are general and widespread but often difficult to detect in the absence of conclusive OE evidence. In addition to these types, so frequent are the legitimate *ing*-names, with *ing* medial or final, that, under their influence, *ing* may be found intruding in haphazard fashion into a large number of other names, especially medially.

Final ing, so far as it goes back to OE, is found in

(i) a number of common nouns such as cieping, fælging, feorðing, hryding;

(ii) a limited number of names, often of obscure and difficult origin, in which the suffix -*ing* has been added, as a rule, though not always, to a pers. name. Lawling (Ess) is an example of a pers. name while Clavering (Ess) seems to go back to clæfre;

(iii) a large number of names in which the pl. *ingas* has been added usually to a pers. name, but sometimes to a river-name or some other element. Billing (Nth), Barling (L) are -*ingas* names from pers. names while Avening (2Gl) and Blything (Sf) are from river-names and Hertingfordbury (Herts) from *Hertford.*

---

[1] In dealing with this element one can for the most part, at least so far as one is dealing with -*ing* and -*ingham* names, do little more than summarise the conclusions of Ekwall's book on *English P.N. in -ing*, though there is serious danger that in so doing one may understate the difficulties of the problem by failing, for lack of space, to reproduce all the qualifying statements and critical discussions in his most scholarly book.

In distribution, types ii and iii are common in the East and South-East, rare in the West and South-West.

The interpretation of type ii is difficult but Ekwall argues on good grounds that at least in the case of those p.n. formed from pers. names we must interpret them as 'X's place, stream' or whatever else it may be applied to.

Type iii when formed from a pers. name must not be interpreted as a patronymic pure and simple, 'sons of X,' but 'people of X,' 'people who have to do with X,' 'family, followers, slaves of X,' the meaning probably being almost as wide and general as in those names of this type which are derived from river-names, where it must simply denote 'dwellers by.'

Beside these, we have names with medial -inga- and -ing-. -inga, the gen. pl. of ingas, is found in such compounds as -ingatun, -ingafeld, -ingaleah, -ingaworþ, -ingahamm, but is most common in -ingaham which must denote the ham of X's people, or something of that kind (v. supra), ham having the sense of 'settlement, estate' or the like, and denoting a collection of dwellings rather than a single homestead. They are, like the -ingas names, without doubt among the oldest English names in the country. -ingatun is a good deal less common and the relation of these names to the -ingaham ones needs careful study.

These -inga- names are very frequent on the Continent and specially so in the coastal districts of North-East France. In England their distribution is much the same as that of the -ing(as) names (v. supra). Unless we have OE evidence it is very difficult to distinguish -ingatun (-ingafeld, -ingaleah, etc.) p.n. from those in -ingtun (-ingfeld, -ingleah). The clue to the interpretation of such forms is to be found in such a case as that of Wilmington near Lyminge, in Kent, which in an original 7th cent. charter (BCS 97) is called wieghelmestun, and in an early 11th cent. endorsement is called wigelmignctun (sic). Bradley suggested the right interpretation of this change when he argued that the farm which was once called 'W's farm' later came to be known as 'W-ing farm,' in which the -ing indicated the past association with W, in the same general way that the suffix is used in types ii and iii above.

iw, eōw, OE, 'yew.' Uley (Gl).

ka, North. ME, 'jackdaw,' is commonly supposed to go back to ON *ká, cf. Norw. dial. kaa, but it is possible that there may have been a North. OE cā, parallel to Mid. ME co, a native word. Cawood and Cavil (Y) which began with Ca- in the 10th cent. have an English second element. The first element is either this English word or is a late OE loan-word from the Scand. Cabourne (L), Kaber (We).

karl, ON, 'freeman, son of the common folk,' as opposed to the noble-born *jarl*, the two words standing in the same relation as OE **ceorl** and *eorl*. Except in the compounds *butse-* and *hus-carl* this word is not found in English till about 1300. It is however extraordinarily frequent in the p.n. *Carl(e)ton* found all over Scand. England and extending into neighbouring counties, such as Beds and C, which were never really Scandinavianised. This must go back to

karla-tun, ON, 'carls' farm,' though such a form is not actually found in Norse. In some cases forms such as *Carlentun, Karlintone* in DB show that *karl* must have been Anglicised and given a pseudo-English gen. pl. in *-ena*. Some may also contain the pers. n. *Karli*.

kaupa-land, ON, 'purchased land' as opposed to 'inherited land.' Coupland (Nb), Copeland (Cu, Du).

kaupmaðr, ON, 'merchant,' gen. pl. *kaupmanna*, though in p.n. it may be a pers. name, ultimately a nickname, rather than denote the actual carrying on of trade. Copmanthorpe (Y), Capernwray (La), Coppingford (Hu).

kelda, ON, 'spring, deep water-hole, smooth-flowing stream.' NCy *keld*, 'marshy place.' Keld, Hallikeld, Kirskill (Y), Ranskill (Nt), Kelleth (We).

kiarr, ON, 'copsewood, brushwood,' Norw. *kjerr*, 'pool, hollow place, marsh, low-lying ground.' The latter is the sense of dial. *car* and the sense which we may assume in p.n. generally. Byker (Nb), Carbrook (Y). Not a definite criterion of Scand. settlement.

kirkja, ON, 'church,' especially common in the numerous *Kir(k)bys*. Curthwaite (Cu).

kleif, ON, 'steep hillside.' Claife (La), Raincliff (Y).

klettr, ON, 'cliff, rock.' Dan. **klint** (in which assimilation of *n* and *t* has not taken place). The first form is found in Cleatham (L), Cleator (Cu), Cleatop (Y), Cleatlam (Du) and the second in Clints (Nb, Y). *clint* is still used in NCy to denote a 'hard rock projecting on the side of a hill or river.'

knappr, ON, cognate with OE **cnæpp** and very difficult to distinguish from it in Scand. England.

knǫtt, ON, Late OE *cnotta*, '*knot*,' used in p.n. of a 'rocky hill or summit.' Only found in the North. Hardknott (Cu).

konungr, ON, 'king.' Coniston (La), Conington (Hu), Cunswick (We), Congerstone (Lei), Coney Weston (Sf), Coney St in York (Y), Conesby (L).

kráka, ON, 'crow,' but very difficult to distinguish from the pers. name *Kraki*. Possibly in Cracoe, Cragdale (Y), Cracroft (L).

kringla, ON, 'circle.' Cringleford (Nf), Crindledyke (Cu).

krókr, ON, '*crook*, bend,' is often used in Norw. p.n. to describe position in a bend of a river, but is also used of a piece of land which is hidden away or cut off from the rest. In the sense 'odd corner, nook of land' it is very common in field-names. Crookes (Y), dat. pl. in Crookham (Nb). As a common dial. word it is not a definite test of Scand. settlement.

lā, ODan., 'water along the sea, creek.' Goxhill (L, Y), Sixhill (L).

lache, leche, ME, 'slow sluggish stream, dial. *lache, letch,*' also 'muddy hole, bog.' Shocklach (Ch), Lashbrook (D, O), East Leach (Gl), Fulledge (La).

lacu, OE, 'stream, watercourse,' and still so used in the dial. of D, So, Co, Ha. Lake (W), Standlake (O), Medlock (La).

(ge)lād, OE, 'track, watercourse, dial. *lode.*' Abload (Gl), Bottisham Lode (C), Linslade (Bk), Shiplate (So).

læfer, lefer, OE, dial. *lavers, levers,* 'wild yellow iris.' Laverton (Gl), Larford (Wo), Livermere (Sf).

læge, OE, 'fallow, unploughed,' not found independently but inferred from OE *læghrycg* later *lea-rig,* and *lea-land.* Leyland (La), Layriggs (Cu).

læs, OE, 'pasture, meadow-land, dial. *leaze.*' Summerlease (Co), Summerley (Db), Leziate (Nf). From the dat. sg. *læswe* comes dial. *leasowe* and Leasowe (Ch).

(ge)læte, OE, 'junction of roads, etc.' Longleat (W), Haylot (Sa).

lágr, ON, '*low.*' Laskill Pastures (Y), Lodore (Cu).

lām, OE, '*loam,*' which may be found in Lomer (Ha), is almost impossible to distinguish from

lamb, OE, '*lamb,*' in Lambley (Nt), Lambeth (Sr), Lambourne (Berks). Lamberhurst (K) is from the gen. pl. *lambra.*

land, OE, land, ON. The OE term is used to denote 'earth, soil, landed property, estate,' 'one of the strips into which a cornfield or a pasture field that has been ploughed is divided.' In the charter material it is very rarely compounded with a pers. name. The first element describes the tenure (e.g. folcland, bocland, sundorland), or the state of cultivation, e.g. *irþland, wuduland,* or the crop, e.g. *linland* from lin. Candlet, Swillen *al.* Swilland (Sf).

lane, lanu, OE, '*lane.*' Markland (La). Dat. pl. in Laneham (Nt).

lang, OE, '*long,* tall.' Landford (W), Lamport (Nth), Launton (O), Lagness (Sx), Longner (Sa).

launde, ME, from OFr. *launde,* 'open space in woodland, glade, pasture.' Laund (Lei).

lāwerce, OE, '*lark.*' Larkfield Hund. (K), Lavertye (Sx).

lēactun, OE, 'kitchen-garden.' Leighton (Beds, Hu, La), Laughton (Sx, Y).

lēah, OE, dat. sg. lēage. lēa is only found in charter material in OE but there it is very common, both by itself and in compounds. In BCS 322 it is the equivalent of Lat. *campus* and in BCS 792 it is contrasted with **hamm**, the contrast apparently being that of open and enclosed land. Etymologically it is allied to Lat. *lucus*, 'grove,' and OHG *lôh*, 'low brushwood, clearing overgrown with small shrubs.' Its history would seem to be that in the first instance it denoted woodland and then a 'clearing' in such. The great forest of the Weald is called alternatively *Andredesweald* and *Andredesleage* (ASC) and the transition stage is illustrated in BCS 669 where we have a grant *cum silva campisque ad eam jacenti-bus, quae Earneleia dicitur*. The association with woodland is further illustrated by the high percentage of names in *-ley* to be found in counties like Ha, Wo, St, Ch, Db which were once thickly wooded, and by the numerous compounds of *leah* with tree-names found in OE charters. Other compounds such as those with **beonet, brom, fearn, hæþ, hreod, risc, þorn** point to rough and un-cultivated clearings but we have the suggestion of pasturage in compounds with **hriþer, falod, hors, sceap** and of cultivation in numerous compounds with such elements as **bere, ryge, hwæte**. It is clear from these instances that the term came to be of wide application and that one would not be justified in assuming that every *ley* was really one-time forest-land. It had probably come in course of time to mean little more than 'open country,' whether heathland, pasture or cultivated. It is very common in p.n. by itself, as in *Lea, Lee, Leigh*, but still more so as a suffix, where it is sometimes confused with **hlaw** as in Barlow (Db, Du). The suffix is rare in Y and extremely so in Cu, We, L. Crowle (Wo), Marcle, Ocle (He), Ashill (Nf), dat. pl. in Leam (Db), Lyham (Nb).

leger, OE, 'lying-place, *lair*,' but only used in OE of a grave or burial-place. The association with animals is quite late. Layer (Ess).

leikr, ON, 'play, sport,' and then place for such. Ullock (2Cu).

leirr, ON, 'clay,' leira, 'clayey place.' Larbrick (La), Larpool (Y).

leoht, OE, 'bright, *light*,' common with tree-names. Lighthorne (Wa), Lightollers (La), Lightbirks (Nb).

leysingi, ON, 'freedman.' Lazenby (Y), Lazonby (Cu).

līc, OE, 'body.' Lickberrow (Cu), Lickpit (Ha).

līn, OE, lín, ON, 'flax.' Linacre, Lingart (La), Linton *passim*, Lylands (Y).

lind, OE, 'lime-tree.' Lindeth (La), Linford, Linwood (Ha), Lingwood (Ess), Limber (L).

loc(a), OE, '*lock*ed place, enclosure.' Challock (K), Parlick (La).

lœkr, ON, 'brook.' Leek (La), Leake (2Nt, L).

lopthús, ON, lit. *loft*-house, but used of a room found in or forming the second floor of a building, to which access could be had by an outside staircase (Fritzner *s.v.*). It is probably descriptive of a house whose lower part is used as stables or as a barn. Loftus (Y). Dat. pl. in Loftsome (Y).

lundr, ON, 'grove, small wood.' Lowne (Db), Lound (L, Nt), Lount (Lei), Lunt (La), Lumby (Y). As a suffix often confused with land as in Rockland (Nf), Birkland (Nt). Gen. sg. in Londonthorpe (L).

lyng, ON, '*ling*, heather.' Ling (Nf).

lytel, OE, '*little*.' Litchurch (Db).

mæd, OE, dat. sg. mædwe, whence *mead* and *meadow*, both denoting grassland. Medbourne (Lei), Metfield (Sf).

mæl, OE, 'cross, sign.' Maldon (Ess), Maulden (Beds).

(ge)mære, OE, 'boundary,' still used in dial. *meare* of a 'strip of grassland forming a boundary,' and also of a 'boundary road.' In the charters it is prefixed to various elements such as ac, broc, cnoll, dic, hege, lacu, pol, pytt, stan, þorn, weg to denote that these objects were on the bounds of an estate. It is very difficult to distinguish it from mere unless we have the OE form or the topography is decisive for the latter. Probably found in Marten (W), Mearley (La), Merbach (He).

mapel, OE, only found in *mapel-treow*, '*maple*-tree.' Maplestead (Ess), Mappleton (Y).

mapuldor, OE, 'maple-tree.' Mappowder (Do), Mapledurham (Ha, O), Malacombe (W).

mearc, OE, 'march, boundary.' Mark (So), Marcle (He), Marden (W).

melr, ON, 'sandbank, sandhill,' dial. *meal, meol*. Meols (Ch), Rathmell (Y), Ingoldmells (L).

meol(u)c, OE, '*milk*,' indicates good pasturage as in Melkridge, Milkhope (Nb) or turbidity as in Milkwell (Du).

mēos, OE, 'moss.' Meesden (Herts), Miswell (Sx), Muswell Hill (Mx), Maizley Coppice (W).

mere, OE, '*mere*, pool,' is very difficult, except on topographical grounds, to distinguish from mære. Often confused with mor as in Tedsmore (Sa), Peasmore (Berks). Martin (La), Foulmire (C).

mersc, OE, '*marsh*.' Common by itself and in the compound *Marston*. Merston (Y), Maresfield (Sx). In NCy it sometimes appears with final *sk* as in Marske (Y).

meðal, ON, 'middle.' Melton (Lei, Sf, Y), Melton Ross, Medlam (L), Middleton in Ilkley (Y).

micel, OE, mikill, ON, 'great, large, *mickle*,' assumes many different forms in p.n., partly owing to dial. differences. Mickle-field (Herts), Michelmarsh (Ha), Michel Grove (Sx), Muchelney (So), Mistlebury (W), Middleton *sic* (He).

middel, OE, '*middle*,' as in *Middleton* and *Milton* (*passim*), so far as the latter is not derived from myln. Medland (D), Mealrigg (Cu). It is often difficult to distinguish it from ON meðal with which there has been a good deal of interchange.

minte, OE, '*mint*.' Minstead (Sx), Minety (W).

mixen, OE, '*mixen*, dunghill.' Mixen (St), Mixenden (Y).

monig, OE, '*many*.' Monyash (Db), Moneyhull (Wo), Money-laws (Nb). At times folk-etymology may have been at work as in Moneyfarthing Hill (He) in which the first element is Welsh *mynydd*, 'hill.'

mōr, OE, 'waste land, barren land.' It is our word *moor* but, at least in the South and South Midlands, it is used in p.n. of 'swampy ground' rather than in the modern sense in which high ground is usually implied. Found in numerous *Mor(e)tons*, *Murtons*, *Morcotes*, *Murcotts*, etc. Murrells End (Wo).

mos, OE, '*moss*, peatbog.' Common in NCy. Moze (Ess), Moseley (Wo).

(ge)mōt, OE, 'meeting-place,' especially of two streams. Emmott (La), Eamont (We).

mūs, OE, '*mouse*.' Musbury (La).

mūþa, OE, '*mouth*, estuary.'

myln, OE, '*mill*.' Numerous *Miltons*. Milnrow (La), Mells (So), Millow (Beds). Dat. pl. in Millom (Cu).

myncen, OE, 'nun.' Minchinhampton (Gl), Mincing Lane (Mx).

mynni, ON, 'junction of two streams,' the etymological equiva-lent of (ge)myð. Airmyn (Y), Stalmine (La).

mynster, OE, 'monastery,' used also in the 12th cent. of a church generally. These are what we must look for in p.n. in *minster*, rather than for a large church as in York *Minster*. Misterton (Lei, Sa).

myrig, OE, 'pleasant.' Merrifield (Co), Merevale (Wa), Marden (Sr).

mýrr, ON, '*mire*,' used of swampy moorland. Mirfield (Y), Myerscough (La).

(ge)mýðe, OE, a derivative of muða. Its primary sense is 'opening,' but it is used in p.n. of the opening of one stream into another. The Mythe (Gl), Mitton, Myton *passim*, Mytholmroyd (Y).

næss, OE, nes, ON, 'headland, cape.' Totnes (D), The Naze (Ess), Crossens (La).

nēat, OE, 'cattle, dial. *neat*.' Neatham (Ha), Neatmarsh (Y), Netton (W).

s

neoðera, OE, '*nether*, lower.' Neithrop (O).

nese, ME, 'nose,' and then applied to a 'ness' or headland. Nesbit (Nb), Neasden (Mx), Neasham (Du).

netel(e), OE, 'nettle.' Nettlebed (O).

nīwe, OE, '*new*.' The weak dat. sg. *niwan* has given rise to a large variety of forms such as *Naunton, Newnton, Neenton, Ninham, Newington*. Nobury (Wo), Nowton (Sf), Nobottle Grove (Nth), Ninfield (Sx), Nyetimber (Sx).

norð, OE, '*north*.' Norton *passim*, Nordley (Sa), Norham (Nb), Narborough (Lei).

oddr, ON, 'point, spit of land,' the Norse cognate of ord. Greenodd (La), Ravenserod (Y).

ōfer, OE, 'shore, bank.' Noverton, Nurton (Wo), Haselor (Wa), Oreton (St), Orton (La, We), Nether and Over Worton (O), Over (Ch), Burcher (He). Dat. pl. in Owram (Y).

ōra, OE, 'border, margin, bank.' Oare, Boxford (Berks), Ore (Sx), Wardour (W), Clare (O), Rowner (Ha). Unless we have early forms it is often difficult to distinguish it from ofer.

orceard, OE, '*orchard*,' but of wider application, not being restricted to an enclosure where fruit is grown. Norchard (Wo), Orcheton (D).

ord, OE, 'point, corner, spit of land.' Ord (Nb).

oter, OE, '*otter*.' Otterburn (Nb), Atterburn (Wo).

pæð, OE, '*path*.' In the Lindisfarne glosses it is given as an alternative to **dene** and from this arose Sc. and NCy *peth*, 'hollow or deep cutting in a road, steep road.' Gappa (D), Roppa (Y), Morpeth (Nb).

parke, ME, from OFr. *parc*, ultimately identical with

pearroc, OE, 'small enclosure, *paddock*,' the diminutive of a lost OE *pearr*, dial. *par*, 'enclosure for beasts.' Parr (La), Paddock (K), Parrock (Sx).

penn, OE, 'enclosure, *pen*.' Penn (Bk).

pīc, OE, 'sharp pointed instrument,' not found in the charter material in a topographic sense. ME *pike*, 'pointed hill,' is confined to NCy and has probably been reinforced by Norw. *pik*, 'pointed mountain.' Pickup (La), Pigdon (Nb).

pigh(t)el, ME, 'small field, enclosure.' Found chiefly in fieldnames. Colepike Hall (Du), Pickledean (W).

pīpe, OE, '*pipe*, channel of a small stream.' Dial. 'small ravine, dingle.' Pipe (St).

pirige, pyrige, OE, '*pear*-tree.' Perry (Wo), Puriton (So), Purton (W), Potterspury (Nth), Buttsbury (Ess), Perham (W), Pirbright, Pyrford (Sr).

pise, OE, '*pease*.' Peasfurlong (La), Peasemore (Berks), Pested (Herts).

plæsc, OE, 'shallow pool, dial. *plash*,' only found in charter material. Plaish (Sa, So), Plesh (Do).

plega, OE, '*play*,' but used in p.n. to denote the place where animals disport themselves. Deerplay (La), Oterplay (K).

plegstōw, OE, '*play*-place,' glossed by *amphitheatrum*, *palaestra*, *gymnasium*, referring in p.n. to the place where village sports and the like were held. Plaistow (Db, D, Ess, Sx), Plestins (Wa).

plūme, OE, '*plum*, *plum*-tree.' Plumpton *passim*. Plungar (Lei).

pōl, OE, '*pool*, deep place in a river, tidal stream.' Poole *passim*, Polstead (Sf), Lappal (Wo), Cople (Beds), Poulton *passim*. Dat. pl. in Poolham (L).

port, OE, 'town,' used specially of one possessing market-rights and rights of minting, possibly also with some reference to its having defensive works, if we may judge by its frequent use as an alternative gloss to **burg** and to render the Lat. *castellum*. The numerous *Newports* were probably first so called when they were given market-rights.

prēost, OE, 'priest.' Found in numerous *Prestons*, *Prescot(t)s*, *Prestwicks*, where the first element is usually the OE gen. pl. *preosta*. It is difficult to determine whether these places were owned by priests, used for their endowment, or occupied by them. Purston (Y), Prustacott (Co), Prenton (Ch).

pūca, OE, 'goblin, *puck*, dial. *pook*.' Poughill, Pophlet Park (D), Pownall (Ch).

pull, OE, used with the same sense as **pol** and often difficult to distinguish from it. Pull Court (Wo), Overpool (Ch).

pyll, OE, 'tidal creek on the coast, pool in a creek at the confluence of a tributary stream, dial. *pill*,' still used in Co and He, a Celtic loan-word. Huntspill, Pylle (So).

pytt, OE, ME *pitte*, *putte*, *pette*, '*pit*, grave.' Only St. Eng. *pit*, as in Woolpit (Sf) and *pet*, as in Pett (K, Sx) seem to have survived.

rā, OE, '*roe*-buck.' Rogate (Sx), Rocombe (D), Raydale (Y).

rá, ON, 'landmark.' More than one *Raby* and Roby (La).

rǣge, OE, 'wild she-goat.' Rayleigh (Ess).

ramm, OE, '*ram*.' Ramshorn Down (D). Very difficult to separate from **hræfn**.

rand, OE, 'border, edge, dial. *rand*, *rond*.' The dial. word is used in Eastern England of a strip or border of ground in various technical senses. Only noted in ECy p.n. Rand (L), Raunds (Nth).

rauðr, ON, 'red,' cognate with **read**. Rawcliffe (2La, 3Y),

Roecliffe, Roppa (Y), Rockliffe (Cu), Rothay (We), Rathmell (Y).
Not always easily distinguished from the pers. name *Rauði* or
Routh.

rāw, rǣw, OE, '*row*.' The first form gives St. Eng. *row* and NCy
raw, the latter dial. *rue*, 'row,' in various senses. Milnrow (La),
Rattenraw (Nb), and probably Rew (Wt), Rewe (D).

rēad, OE, '*red*.' Radwell (Beds), Radford (D), Ratcliffe (Mx).
Not always easy to distinguish from **hreod**.

refr, ON, 'fox.' Reagill (We).

ridde, ME, 'cleared, p.p. of *rid*, to clear,' commonly derived from
ON *hryðja*, but as there was an OE noun *hryding* we are probably
right in assuming a corresponding OE verb which would better
explain this widespread element than if we assume it to be a
Scand. loan-word. Ridley (specially in Nb, Du), Redland (Gl),
Rudloe (W).

riþ, riþig, OE, 'small stream, brooklet, dial. *rithe* (Sr, Sx, Wt).'
The expanded form is found in Fulready (Wa), Cropredy (O) and
seems to be confined to the South Midlands; the shorter one
belongs to the South generally as in Hendred, Childrey (Berks),
Meldreth (C), Shottery (Wa).

rod, OE, 'clearing, assart,' only found in charter material.
Roade (Nth), Road (So), Odd Rode (Ch), Royd (Y). Nom. pl.
in Rhodes *al.* Royds (Y). See more fully *PN Nb and Du*, 167–8.
royd is the common dial. development in La, Y.

rūh, OE, '*rough*.' This adj. takes various forms in p.n., some
going back to the nom., others to dat. case forms, especially the
weak dat. sg. *rugan*, ME *rowe(n)*. Rowley *passim*, Rufford (Nt),
Rusper, Roffey (Sx), Rowner (Ha), Roall (Y).

rūm, OE, 'roomy, spacious.' Romford (Ess), Romiley (Ch),
Rumworth (La), Roomwood (Nt).

rúm, ON, 'forest-clearing.' Dendron, Dertren (La). See further
PN La, 16.

ryge, OE, '*rye*.' Found often in *Ryton, Ryley, Ryhill* and the
like. Reydon (Sf), Royton (La), Ryle (Nb), Roydon (Nf).

rygen, adj. from **ryge**. Renacres (La).

rysc, OE, '*rush*.' ME *risshe, resshe, russhe* and 16th cent.
rossh, roche. Hence many places in *Rush-, Rish-*. Roseden (Nb),
Ruislip (Mx). Dat. pl. in Rusholme (La).

(ge)ryðre, OE, 'clearing,' allied to **hryding**, only found in p.n.
Ryther (Y).

sæppe, OE, 'spruce-fir.' Sapley (Hu), Sabden (La).

sǣte, OE, 'house, *seat*,' is rare but is found in charter
material. It may be confused with

sǣte, pl. 'dwellers, inhabitants' is common. It is found in names
of districts such as Somerset and can be added to the first element

of any p.n. to denote the inhabitants of that place, e.g. *Ombersete* (BCS 361) for the inhabitants of Ombersley (Wo).

Both alike appear in later English as *-set(t)* and in each case careful consideration is needed as to which is the most likely source. The suffix, from whichever source it may come, is specially common in Nf, Sf. In Nb, Du it often appears as *side*. Simonside (Nb).

sǣtr, ON, 'summer-pasture farm, shieling.' See more fully *PN La*, 16–7. It is almost always corrupted to *-side* or *-shead* in present-day forms, as in Ambleside (We), Cadishead (La). Blennerhasset (Cu), Satterthwaite (La). Very difficult sometimes to distinguish from **sǣte**.

sand, OE, '*sand.*' Sambourne (Wa), Saunton, Sampford (D), Sound (Ch).

saurr, ON, 'mud, dirt,' is common in the p.n. *Sowerby*. Lindkvist aptly quotes from *Landnamabók* where Steinulfr built a farm on his new settlement in Iceland and called it *Saurbœ*, i.e. Sowerby, 'because the ground there was very swampy' (*PN Scand. Origin*, 162). Still surviving as dial. *saur.*

sceaga, OE, 'small wood, copse, thicket, *shaw.*' Dial. *shaw* is used of (i) a shady wood in a valley (Y), (ii) a broad belt of underwood around a field. It is significant that the only compound with a tree in OE charters is with **alor** (BCS 1331) and no compounds with *oak*, *ash*, and *elm* have been noted. In BCS 227 we have mention of *mariscem, vocabulo scaga*. This hardly means that *scaga* is to be interpreted 'marsh' but points to the fact that it could be aptly used of the low underwood which one gets on marshy ground. Wilshers (La), Shaugh Prior (D).

sceald, OE, 'shallow,' only known in charter material. Shadwell (Sf), Shalfleet (Wt), Shadforth (Nb).

scēap, scīp, OE, '*sheep.*' Sheffield (Sx), Shapwick (D), Shibden (Y), Shifford (O), Shiplate (So), Shopwyke (Sx).

sceard, OE, 'notch, gap, dial. *shard,*' still used of a gap in a hedge or bank. Shardlow (Db), Sharperton (Nb). Cognate with **skarð**.

scearn, OE, 'dung, filth, dial. *sharn.*' Sharnbrook (Beds), Sherrington (W), Sharrington (Nf), Sherwoods (Ess), Shernden (K). For *-ing* forms cf. **cweorn**.

scearp, OE, '*sharp*, pointed, precipitous.' Sharpness (Gl), Sharpway (Wo).

scēat, OE, 'nook, corner, point.' Bagshot (Sr), Bramshott (Ha). It is very common in field-names.

*scelde, ME, 'shallow,' allied to **sceald**. Shelford (Nt), Shilford (Nb).

sceolh, OE, 'oblique, awry.' Showley (La).

schele, ME, the English cognate of ON skáli, used first of a shepherd's summer-hut and then of a small house, cottage or hovel. Confined to Nb, Du and South Sc. *shealing* is a derivative form. Shiels *passim*, North and South Shields (Nb, Du).

scīd, OE, '*shide*, shingle, piece of thin wood.' Shidfield (Ha).

scīene, OE, 'beautiful.' Sheinton (Sa), Shenington (O), Shelland (Sf), Shenfield (Ess). Cf. *scenfeld* used in OE of the Elysian fields and of the vale of Tempe. (BT *s.v.*)

scipen, OE, = '*shippen*, cattle-shed.' Shippen (Y), Shippon (Berks).

scīr, OE, 'jurisdiction, district, *shire*.' Its exact significance depends upon the history of the place. Found as a prefix in Shiremoor (Nb) to denote 'moor in Tynemouth*shire*' and in Shireoaks (Nt, Y) to denote oaks on the border of two shires.

scīr, adj. 'clear, shining,' as in the numerous p.n. (spelt either *Shir-* or *Sher-*) like Shirb(o)urn(e), Shirford, Shirbrook, also in Shurnock (Wo). In some cases we may have the noun scir used adjectivally to describe something which is on a boundary. Sheerness (K). Scandinavianised in Skyrack (Y).

scīr-gerēfa, OE, 'sheriff.' Shrewton (W).

scucca, OE, 'demon, goblin, dial. *shuck*.' Schuckton (Db), Shugborough (St), Shecklow (Bk).

scylf, OE, 'rock, pinnacle, crag,' to judge from the glosses in which it is found, but there can be little doubt that it had already developed the meaning 'shelving terrain, *shelf*' at an early date, possibly through association with the very rare and rather doubtful *scilfe* = shelf, ledge. Such must be its sense in a good deal of charter material. Shelf (Y), Shelfield (Wa), Shelley (Sf, Sx), Gomshall (Sr), Shareshill (St), Shilton (Wa), Shell (Wo), Oxhill (Wa), Minshull (Ch), Sufton (He), Bashall Down (Y).

scyttels, OE, 'bar, bolt, dial. *shuttle*.' Still used of 'the horizontal bar of a gate, a flood-gate.' Shuttleworth (3La).

sealh, salig, OE, 'willow, dial. *salley*.' The large variety of forms taken by this element in p.n. is due in part to different development of nom. *sealh* which gives dial. *saugh* (NCy) and dat. *seal(h)e* but also to the second form *salig* found in OE. Saul (Gl), Sale Green (Wo), Sawley (Y), Salford (La), Salpho (Beds), Salehurst (Sx), Saighton, Saughall (Ch).

sealt, OE, '*salt*.' Salcombe (D), Salford (O, Wa). A *salt*-ford must have been a ford on one of the old *salt*-roads.

sēaδ, OE, 'pit.' Roxeth (Mx).

secg, OE, '*sedge*,' is very difficult to distinguish from *Secg*, a pers. name.

sef, ON, 'sedge, dial. *seave* (NCy).' Sefton (La).

sele, OE, 'hall, building.' Newsells (Herts), Seal (K), Zeals (W).

selja, ON, 'willow,' cognate with **sealh**. Selker, Sillyrea, Sile-croft (Cu).

setberg, ON, 'seat-hill,' i.e. one with a flat top. Sedbergh (Y), Sadberge (Du).

shingle, ME, has two meanings, (i) 'thin piece of wood used as a house-tile,' (ii) 'small pebbles.' The etymology of these words is obscure and in both cases we get forms with initial *s* as well as *sh*. It is the former which we usually get in p.n. We probably have (i) in Singleton (La), and (ii) in Chingford (Ess), Singlewell (K), Singleborough (Bk). See *PN La* 154.

sīc, OE, **sík**, ON, dial. *sitch*, *sike*, 'small stream in marshy ground, gully, stretch of meadow.' Gorsuch (La).

sīd, OE, 'broad, wide.' Sidebeet, Siddal (La), Sidestrand (Nf), Sydling (Do).

sīde, OE, '*side*,' is used in p.n. of the 'slope of a hill or bank, especially one extending for a considerable distance,' possibly also of the bank or shore of a stream. Confined to NCy. Langsett (Y), Fawcett (We).

skáli, ON, cognate with **schele** and used in the same sense. Very common in the pl. See more fully *PN Scand. Origin* 190. Seascale, Gatesgill, Horsegills (Cu), Scholes (La, Y), Scarrow (Cu), Scowcroft (La), Laskill Pastures (Y).

skarð, ON, 'notch, cleft, mountain-pass.' Gatesgarth (Cu), Scarcliff (Db). It is often difficult to distinguish it from the pers. name *Skarði*, really a nickname meaning 'harelip.'

skeið, ON. Found in Norse p.n. in more than one sense but all going back to the primary idea of 'separation,' the word being allied to *shed* in water*shed*. Its exact sense in English p.n. needs investigation. Wickham Skeith (Sf), Brunstock (Cu). In Hesket (Cu), Hesketh (2La, 2Y) it is compounded with **hestr** and denotes 'track marked off for or suitable for horse-racing.'

skírr, ON, 'pure, clear, bright.' Skirwith (Y).

skógr, ON, 'wood,' cognate with **sceaga**. Briscoe, Busco (Y), Skewkirk, Ayscough (Y), Myerscough (La). Gen. sg. *skógar* in Scorbrough (Y).

slá(h), OE, '*sloe*.' Sloley (Nf, Wa), Slaugham (Sx), Slaithwaite (Y).

slæd, OE, 'low flat valley.' Dial. *slade* is used of a 'breadth of green sward in ploughed land (NCy), a dried watercourse (Ess), a strip of greensward between woods (Nth), low flat marshy ground.' See more fully EDD. Castlett, The Slad (Gl), Bagslate (La), Weetslade (Nb).

slæp, OE, 'slippery place, dial. *slape*.' Slepe (Hu), Slape (Do, Sa), Sleap (Sa), Hanslope, Slapton (Bk).

slāhtrēo, OE, '*sloe-tree.*' Slaughter (Gl), Slaughters (Sx), but probably not in Slaughterford (Gl).

slakki, ON, dial. *slack*, 'shallow valley, depression in a hill-side or between two hills.' Distinctively West Scandinavian.

slétta, ON, 'plain, level field, dial. *sleet* (NCy).' Slates (L), Sleights (Y), Misslet (We).

*slinu, OE, 'gentle slope,' postulated by Ekwall to explain Slyne (La), Slinfold, Slindon (St, Sx). See *PN La* 185.

smæl, OE, '*small*, narrow.'

smár, ON, 'small.' Smeathwaite (Cu).

smeoru, OE, smjǫr, ON, 'fat, grease.' The Norse word was certainly used as a first element in p.n. to describe rich pasturage and the English word was probably similarly so used. Smerden (Wt), Smardale (We), Smerril (Db).

smēðe, OE, 'smooth.' Smedmore (Do), Smeeton (Lei), Smeaton (Y), Smithfield (L, Mx), Smithdown (La). Weak dat. sg. in Smithencote (D).

snād, snǣd, OE, only found in charter material, denotes something which is 'cut off,' e.g. an isolated wood or a clearing in a wood. From *snad* we have Snodhurst (K), Snodhill (He), Whipsnade (Beds), Kingsnorth, Oxenheath (K). From *snæd* come Snead (Wo), Sneyd, Pensnett (St), Snedham (Gl).

sneið, ON, cognate with **snad** and with similar meaning. Snaith (Y).

sōcn, OE, 'right of jurisdiction,' and then the area over which it is exercised. Soke (Ha), Soke of Peterborough (Nth), Walsoken (Nf).

sol, OE, 'muddy or miry pool, dial. *sole* (K).' Barnsole, Runsell (K), Rodsell (Sr).

spær, OE, found only in charter material and then in association with forest areas. It is allied to ME *sparre*, 'balk, pole,' and probably denotes some form of enclosure. Rusper (Sx), Holtspur (Bk), Sparham, Sporle (Nf).

spánn, ON, 'chip, shaving, shingle for tiling.' Spaunton (Y).

speld, OE, 'chip, splinter of wood,' found in forest areas. Speldhurst, Spilsill (K).

spell, OE, 'speech, story, *spell*,' used probably in p.n. to describe some old place of public assembly. Spelthorne Hund. (Mx), Spellow (La).

spōn, OE, 'chip, shaving,' used also of a 'shingle.' In Spoonley (Sa) it probably refers, as in *sponleoge* (BCS 343), to a forest area. Spondon (Db).

spring, spryng, OE, '*spring.*' Some names must show the dial. *spring* = copse. Hazelspring (O), Oxspring (Y), Ospringe (K).

stæf, OE, 'rod, *staff*,' is not found in the charter material but it is difficult not to think that we have it in Staveley (Db, La), Stalybridge (Ch), which perhaps come from *stæfa-leah*, i.e. *ley* of the staves, or *ley* marked out by such.

*stæfer, OE, 'stake, pillar,' or the like, is postulated by Ritter (*Vermischte Beiträge* 125–6) to explain Staverton (Gl, Sf, W), Starton (Wa), Stears (Gl), all with ME *stavre*. He takes it to be the English cognate of Dan. *staver*, 'stake,' and quotes several continental parallels. The names thus formed are parallel to those in **stapol**. Starbottom (Y) may contain the Dan. word itself.

stæþ, OE, 'bank, shore, landing-place.' Stafford (St). In Scand. England it is very difficult to distinguish from ON stǫþ.

stān, OE, '*stone*, rock,' may have various meanings in p.n. It may denote the presence of a rock as in Dunstanborough (Nb), of some quarry, as in Whetstone (Lei), or of boundary stones, as in Fourstones (Nb), or that something is made of stone, as in Stanbridge (Beds) and probably in the great majority of the very numerous *Stantons* and *Stauntons*. Staine (C), Staines (Mx), Stondon (Ess), Stoford, Stowell (So), Stowford (D, W), Staward (Nb), Standlynch (W), Stallenge (D), Standlake (O), Steane (Nth). There has been much confusion between p.n. in *stan* and those in **tun** preceded by the gen. sg. in *-es* of a pers. name or common noun, for both alike in Mod. Eng. naturally end in *ston*. Kingstone (He) is really 'King's *tun*,' while Wroxton (O) is 'Wrocc's *stan*.' Blaxton (Y).

stapol, OE, 'post, pillar, *staple*.' Stapleton (D), Staplers (Wt), Stalbridge (Do), Dunstable (Beds), Stapleford *passim*. Sometimes confused with **stiepel** in later documents.

staðr, ON, pl. **staðir**, is the cognate of OE **stede** and in the sg. is used to denote 'site, position,' and is not compounded with a pers. name. In the pl. it is very common and there is frequently compounded with such. Frequent confusion with **stede** has occurred and it is also very difficult to distinguish it from stǫþ. Birstwith (Y), Bickerstaffe (La).

steall, OE, 'position, site, place, cattle-*stall*.' Possibly in Stalisfield (K). See further **hamsteall**, **tunsteall**.

stede, styde, OE, 'place, position, site.' It is only very rarely indeed that this element is compounded with a pers. name. The usual types of compound are those in which we have (i) a descriptive adj. as in Greenstead, Fairstead (Ess), reference (ii) to its trees as in Alderstead (Sr), Buxted (Sx) from **boc**, (iii) to the character of the land, as in Felstead (Ess) from **feld**, Medstead and Morestead (Ha) from **mæd** and **mor**, Densted (K), Fenstead (Sf), (iv) to its crops, as in Pested (Herts), Banstead (Sr) from **bean**, Plumste(a)d (Nf, K, Sx), Whetsted (K), (v) to some premises upon it as in Worstead (Nf) from **worþ**, Tunsted (Nf), Kirkstead (L),

Burstead (Ess), Halstead *passim,* Cowsted (K) from **cot** and **hamstede,** (vi) to animals kept there as in Swinstead (L), Horsted (Sx), Oxted (Sr), or (vii) to its use for some specific purpose, as in Chipsted (Sr) and Flamstead (Herts) respectively from **ceap** and *fleam,* 'flight,' hence 'place of refuge.' The counties in which this suffix is chiefly found are Ess, Herts, Sf, Nf, K, Sr, Sx, Ha, Wt. It is very rare in NCy except in a few names of comparatively modern origin, in which it may have the sense 'property, estate' (NED *stead,* sb. 7) and is almost equally rare in the West and South-West. The Stude (Wa), Stidd (La).

steinn, ON, 'stone, rock,' cognate with OE **stan.** It is very common in p.n. in numerous *Staintons* and *Stainforths* but is not always easily distinguished from the pers. name *Steinn.* It is often replaced in the present-day form by English *stan* or *stone.* Stenwith (L), Stanwix (Cu), Stonegrave (Y).

steort, OE, 'tail,' hence applied to a piece of land which by its shape or situation suggests such. Stert (W), Steart (Co), Gastard (W), Start Pt. (D). .

sticol, OE, 'steep, dial. *stickle.'* Sticklepath (D), Stickledon (Mx) *lost.*

stiepel, OE, 'steeple.' Steeple Bumpstead (Ess). In p.n. such as Steepleton (Do) and Stapleton (He) reference must be made to a neighbouring church steeple or other such high tower.

stīg, OE, **stíg,** ON, 'path.' Ansty (v. **anstig**), Stifford (Ess), Styford (Nb), Bransty (Cu).

stīgel, OE, '*stile,*' of whatever shape or form. Henstill (D), Steel (Sa), Steelhill (Co). Dial. *steel* is still used.

stigu, OE, '*sty.*' Housty, Houxty (Nb).

stirc, styric, OE, 'young bullock, heifer, *stirk.'* Stirchley (Sa), Strickland (We), Storthwaite (Y).

stoc, OE, 'place,' is very rare in OE apart from p.n. material. It is found once as an alternative to **stow.** It is used in the compounds *stoclif, stocweard, stocwic,* the first two of which are glossed as *oppidum* and *oppidanus* respectively, and the third of which is used to describe the monastery on Monte Cassino. In later times it appears as *Stoke* passim, which must be from the dat. sg. *stoce,* and as *stock,* e.g. Culmstock (D). It is not always easy to distinguish it from

stocc, OE, 'stump, trunk, *stock.'* Stockland (Do), Stockleigh (D), numerous Stocktons as well as Staughton (Beds), Stoughton (Lei, Sr, Sx) in which we probably have reference to a **tun** actually made of 'stocks.'

stoccen, OE, adj., 'made of *stocks,* logs or trunks.' Middendorff quotes BCS 458, where we have reference to *lignea capella...quae anglice Stocckin appellata* (est) side by side with *lapidea capella...*

anglice stonin appellata. Stokenchurch (Bk), Stocking Pelham (Herts).

stocking, ME, 'clearing of *stocks,*' and later 'piece cleared of *stocks.*' Ekwall (*PN in -ing* 26) finds this in Stocking (St) and in many field-names.

stōd, OE, '*stud,* herd of horses.' Studley (Y), Stodmarsh (K), Stoodleigh (D).

stōdfald, OE, '*stud*-enclosure.' Stuffle (Co). It is often difficult to distinguish this from compounds with **stott.**

stofn, OE, ON, 'stump of a tree, dial. *stoven.*' Stoven (Sf), Stewnor (La).

stǫng, ON, 'pole, stake, dial. *stang.*' Stanger (Cu), Mallerstang (We).

storð, ON, 'brushwood, young plantation.' Storrs (La), Storiths (Y).

stǫþ, ON, 'landing-place,' cognate with **stæþ,** from which it is often difficult to distinguish it, as also from ON **staðr,** pl. *staþir.* Toxteth (La). Pl. in Burton and Flixborough Stather (L).

stott, OE, 'horse, bullock.' Stotfold (Beds), Statfold (D, St), Staddon (D).

stōw, OE, denotes primarily a place or site and forms in OE a series of compounds with **cot, ceap, plega, wic** and other common nouns which have left their trace in such p.n. as Costow (W), Chepstow (Mon), Plaistow (Ess), Wistow (Y). The main source however of names in *stow* in English is the use of this word to denote land dedicated to some saint or used for some religious purpose. That is its meaning in the large majority of p.n. which contain this element, whether standing by itself or used as a suffix. The first element is usually a saint's name as in Instow (D), from *Johannestou,* Wistow (Lei) from St Wigstan, while Stow-on-the-Wold (Gl) was once Stow St Edward. The parish church is as a rule dedicated to the saint in question. Sometimes we have other compounds, such as Godstow (O) and Halstow (D), from **halig.** It is the equivalent of Welsh *llan,* Bridstow (He) being known as *Lann san Bregit.* Bristol (So).

strǣt, OE, a loan-word from Latin *via strata* and primarily applied to roads of Roman construction but in course of time applied by our forefathers to any made-up road. Names like Street, Stretton, Stratton, Stratford, Stretford, Stre(a)tley, Streetley, Streatham, almost without exception contain this element. Stradbrooke (Sf), Sturton (Nb, Nt), Stirton (Y), Strelley (Nt), Strete (D), Startforth (Y), Strat(h)fieldsaye (Ha), Stretting-ton (Sx).

strand, OE, 'shore, bank, *strand.*' Overstrand (Nf), Stranton (Du).

strōd, strōð, OE, 'marshy land overgrown with brushwood,' only known from charter material. Strode (Do), Stroud (Gl), Strood (K), Bulstrode (Bk), Langstrothdale (Y), Strudwick (Nth).

strother, ME, 'marsh,' a derivative of **strod** and confined to NCy. Strother, Broadstruthers (Nb).

stubb, OE, 'stump of a tree, *stub*.' Elstub (W). Common in the pl. Nom. in Stubbs House (Du), dat. pl. in Stubham (Y).

***styfic**, OE, 'stump,' is made probable by the OE vb. *styfician*, 'to root up,' and *styficung*, 'clearing.' Stukeley (Hu), Stewkley (Bk), Stiffkey (Nf).

sundorland, OE, lit. *sunder*-land, land set apart for some particular purpose. In the OE Bede it is used to translate *territorium* in reference to the lands of the monastery of Wearmouth and Jarrow.

sūð, OE, '*south*,' as in numerous Suttons, Sudburys and the like. Songar (Wa), Sowdley (Sa), Sidnal (He), Suffield (Y). Comparative *suðerra* in So(u)therton (Sf).

swān, OE, 'herd,' more especially 'swine-herd.' Swanage (Do), Swannacott (Co), Swanton (Nf), Santon (Beds). Only found in SCy p.n.

swēora, OE, 'neck, col.' Swyre Head (Do), Sourton (D).

swīn, OE, 'pig, boar, *swine*.' Swinford *passim*, Sunbrick (La), Swingfield (K), Swilland (Sf).

syle, OE, 'miry place,' derivative of **sol**. Selham (Sx), Sulhampstead (Berks), Sulgrave (Nth).

taile, ME, '*tail*,' used in Sc. of a slip of land irregularly bounded, jutting out from a larger piece, and so found in NCy p.n. Bartle (La), Croxdale (Du).

***tang, twang**, OE, alike meaning primarily 'tongs' and then 'tongue of land' at the tong-like junction of two streams are postulated for p.n. by Ekwall (*PN La* 18), to explain the early forms of Tong (K, Sa), Tonge (Lei, Y), Tangley, Tongham (Sr).

tēag, OE, only found in charter material but there used as the equivalent of Latin *clausula*. As *tigh* or *tye* it is in dial. use in Sf, Ess, K, and in p.n. it is found in Teigh (R), Minety (W), Marks Tey, Tilty (Ess), Bramblety, Lavertye (Sx).

þel, OE, 'plank.' Thele (Herts), Theale (Berks, So), Thelwall (Ch).

þelbrycg, 'plank or wooden bridge.' Thelbridge (D), Elbridge (Co, K, Sx), Elmbridge (Gl).

þēod, OE, 'nation, people,' hence OE *þeodweg*, 'highway,' corrupted to the Ede Way (Bk). Thetford (Nf), Tetford (L).

þing, OE, ON, 'meeting, assembly, court.' Thinghill (He), Tingley (Y), from *Thinglaw*, Finedon (Nth), Fingest (Bk). It is significant that in each case it is compounded with a word denoting a hill.

þing-vǫllr, ON, 'place of assembly,' a p.n. used in Iceland of the place of meeting of the Allthing or parliament. Thingwall (La, Ch).

þorn, OE, ON, 'thorn-bush.' Places whose name begins with Thorn- must for the most part have been so called owing to the presence of some thorn-bush close at hand, but some Thorntons and the like may denote enclosures actually made from thorn-bushes. Bythorne (Hu), Shuckton (Db).

þorp, OE, or, much more commonly, þrop, ON þorp, ODan. thorp, in one form and another, are fairly common in England but their distribution is unequal. The suffix is fairly common in Gl, O, W, Ha, Berks, Bk and found occasionally in Do, So, St, Wo, Wa, Sr, while it is apparently unknown in D, Wt, K, Mx, He, Sa, Ch. Then it is very common in Y (much more so in the East than in the North and West Ridings), L, Lei, Nt, Nth, R, Nf and slightly less common in Db, Hu, Sf, We, while it is occasionally found in Ess, Beds, Herts, Du, La and is unknown in Nb, Cu, C. This grouping suggests (i) that there were two centres of distribution of the suffix, so to speak, one in the South Midlands, the other in Scand. England, and (ii) that, with the exception of a few examples in We, the suffix in Scand. England must be of Danish rather than Norse origin. The twofold origin of this suffix is confirmed by its form. In the first group of counties it is very rarely found in the form thorp at all. We find such forms as Thrupp (Berks), Throope (W), Souldrop (Beds), Astrop (O), Williamstrip, Hatherop, Pin-drup (Gl), Huntingtrap (Wo), all going back to ME thrope and OE þrop(þ). In the other group it is very rare to get anything except a thorp-form and this must go back to the Scand. form.

þorp, OE, is found in very early glosses as an alternative to tun and as the equivalent of Lat. competum, 'cross-roads,' fundus, 'estate,' villa, 'farm,' and also as an alternative to þingstow, 'place of assembly.' It is as difficult to be precise about its meaning as about that of tun. It is perhaps best rendered 'village' or 'hamlet,' though medieval usage suggests that in names of late origin it was generally used of some smaller form of settlement.

þorp, ON, denotes a group of homesteads, perhaps also a farm or croft, but as the word in England seems to be of Danish origin rather than Norse we should perhaps look rather to the meaning of ODan. thorp, 'smaller village due to colonisation from a larger one.' That is certainly its significance in the numerous cases like Welwick Thorpe (Y) in which we have Thorpe added to a village name.

þræll, ON, 'thrall, serf.' Threlkeld (Cu), Trailholme (La).

þveit, ON, lit. 'piece cut out or off,' hence 'parcel of land, clearing, paddock.' In NCy it is still used, and describes 'a forest clearing, a low meadow, the shelving part of a mountain side, a single house or hamlet.' In p.n. it is very common in Cu, We, North La, West Y, and a great deal less common in the rest of Scand. England. See Ekwall, *PN La* 19, and also a full discussion in Lindkvist, *PN Scand. Origin* 96 ff. Lindkvist shows that most of the names containing this element are probably of comparatively recent origin, representing new land taken into cultivation, at first often only a field. Its commonness in the North-West and its comparative rarity elsewhere may perhaps be due not so much to difference of race, as between Norse and Danes, as to the fact that the Midland districts were already more fully cultivated when the Viking settlers came. It is usually written in the full form *thwaite* in the suffixes of p.n. in the North-West, but pronounced [θət]. In districts where it is less common it is subject to alteration and corruption as in Swathwick (Db), Crostwick, Guestwick (Nf), Eastwood (Nt), Brackenfield (Db), Stainfield in Kesteven (L), Braworth (Y).

*þwīt, OE, or *þvít, ON, is postulated by Ekwall to explain names like Inglewhite (La), Trewhitt (Nb), Crostwight (Nf). It would be allied to þveit and have something of the same sense.

þȳrel, OE, 'pierced, hollow.' Thurlestone (D), Thirlwall (Nb).

þyrne, OE, 'thorn-bush.' Thurne (Nf), Thearne (Y). Dat. pl. in Thurnham (La), Farnham (Nb). Caistron (Nb), Casterne (St), Chawston (Beds), Winster (Db), Baythorne End (Ess). In Scand. England it is impossible to distinguish it from ON *þyrnir*.

þyrs, OE, þurs, ON, 'giant.' Thirsden, Thursclough, Thrushgill (La).

ticcen, OE, 'kid.' Titchwell (Nf), Ticehurst (Sx), Tisted (Ha).

tigel, OE, '*tile.*' Tyley Bottom (Gl), Tilehurst (Berks).

timber, OE, ON, '*timber.*' Timberland (L), Nyetimber (Sx), Timberdine (Wo).

tiǫrn, ON, '*tarn.*'

topt, ON, 'piece of ground, messuage, homestead.' Such are also the senses of its descendant *toft.* Cf. 'with toft and croft,' in which *toft* refers to the homestead, **croft** to the land attached. The term came also to be used of a field or piece of land generally, not necessarily the site of a house. The root-idea of the word is that of a 'clearing,' more especially on high or exposed ground. Cf. dial. *toft*, used of a knoll or hillock. See more fully *PN Scand. Origin* 208 ff. As the word was in common use in ME it is not a definite test of Scand. settlement. It is Danish rather than Norwegian and is commonest in L, Nf, Y.

torr, OE, 'high rock, pile of rocks, rocky peak, hill, dial. *tor* (D, Co, Db).' Ekwall (ES 54, 108–110) shows it to be a Celtic loanword. Dunster (So), Notter (Co), Hay Tor (D).

trani, ON, 'crane.' Tranmere (Ch), Trenholme (Y), Tarnacre

(La). See more fully Ekwall in NoB 8, 94. In some cases it may be a nickname.

trēo(w), OE, '*tree.*' Oswestry (Sa), Austrey (Wa), Holmstrow (Sx), Cator, Trewe (D). It is not always easy to distinguish it from **trog.**

trog, OE, '*trough,* conduit,' but used also in a topographical sense as in the '*Trough* of Bowland' (Y). Not always easy to distinguish from **treo.** Trafford (Ch), Trawden (La), Trowes (Nb).

trynde, OE, 'round lump,' allied to which there must have been an adj. form which in p.n. could describe something which is 'circular' as in Trindhurst (K), Tryndehayes (Ess), Trindle Down (Berks), Trundle Mere (C), Trundlebeer, Trendwell (D). Some of these p.n. may contain OE *trindæl*, which Grundy takes to be a compound of *trinde* and **dæl.**

tūn, OE, is the commonest of all p.n. suffixes and it is clear from its OE usage generally that it must have a wide range of meaning in p.n. Its primary sense is 'enclosed piece of ground' and that is its meaning in such compounds as **æppeltun, leactun, gærstun.** From that it came to mean 'enclosed land with dwellings on it, estate, manor, vill, village.' These are probably its meanings in the vast majority of p.n. The idea of some lord's authority over the *tun* is implied in such phrases as *mannes tun, eorles tun* and *cyninges tun* (= villa regia), whence numerous *Kingstons,* and the fact that in 859 you could make a grant of a *healf tun* (BCS 497) suggests that by this time the enclosure-idea may have been weakened. As early as the 7th century, in the Laws of the Kentish Hlothere and Eadric we find *tun* implying a community of persons, for the thief is to be cleared by the oaths of persons from the *tun* to which he belongs. Similarly in the Laws of Aethelstan a certain fine is to be divided among the poor who are in the *tun.* In another passage in the Laws (ed. Liebermann, p. 453) we hear how the reeve should have cognisance of what happens both in *tun* and *dun,* in which the contrast seems to be between the dwellings of men as found in the *tun* and the open uninhabited country on the *dun* or hill. So similarly *toune* is used in ME of the dwellings of men generally. As noted under **ham** there is at least one passage in OE in which it seems to be definitely contrasted with that word and to be used of a smaller unit, at least so far as population is concerned. There is no reason for thinking that in p.n. it was ever in early times used with the sense 'town,' which it undoubtedly has in some OE passages, more especially in translations from Latin. Its most common Latin equivalent is *villa* and the best general rendering would seem to be 'farm' or even 'manor.' Traces of the older senses of *tun* are still to be found in dial. *town,* 'farmstead and its buildings' (Sc.) and 'cluster of houses,' especially those round the church, very common in various parts of the country and in America.

tūnsteall, OE, = **tun + steall,** would seem to have been used in much the same sense as *hamsteall,* viz. farm and its buildings, farmstead. Tunstal(l) *passim,* Dunstall (L), Tounstal (D).

tūnstede, OE, = **tun + stede,** is used in the same sense as tunsteall. Tunste(a)d *passim.*

twī-, OE, 'double.' Twyford *passim,* from OE *twi-fyrde,* lit. 'with a double ford,' found also in Twerton (So), Tiverton (D). Twywell (Nth).

twisla, OE, 'fork.' Used in p.n. of the fork where two streams meet. Twizel (Nb), Twiston, Bastwell (La), Haltwhistle (Nb), Briestwistle (Y).

ufera, OE, 'upper.' West Overton (W), Overpool (Ch).

ūle, OE, '*owl.*' Ulcombe (K), Oldcoats (Nt), Outchester (Nb).

úlfr, ON, 'wolf.' Ulpha (Cu, We). Difficult to distinguish from the pers. name *Ulfr.*

upp(e), OE, '*up,* above.' Upavon (W), Tipton (Co). (See under æt.)

vangr, ON, '*campus.*' The Swed. cognate is used of a cultivated field. Wetwang (Y).

varða, varði, ON, 'cairn, heap of stones.' Warcopp (We), Warbreck (La).

vað, ON, 'ford,' cognate with **wæd.** Langwith (Db, Nt, Y), Langworth, Waithe (L), Solway, Langwathby (Cu).

veggr, ON, 'wall.' Stanwix (Cu) and possibly in Stanwick (Nth, Y).

veiðr, ON, 'fishing, hunting, place for such.' Wedholme (Cu), Waitham (La).

vík, ON, 'bay, creek,' NCy *wick,* used of a creek or inlet and often applied in the form *wyke* to the small bays on Lakes Windermere, Esthwaite and Coniston[1]. One may get it inland on the shores of a mere or on land which was once a mere, as in Blowick (La)[1]. Careful topographical study is needed in Scand. England to distinguish it from *wick* from **wic.** It may possibly also be used of a 'nook or corner in the hills.' Rygh (*Indledning* s.v.) notes the possibility of such in Norway and this would agree with the further NCy use of *wick* to denote a 'corner, angle, hollow.'

viðr, ON, 'wood.' Skirwith (Y). A good many names in *with* really go back to **vað.**

(v)rá, ON, 'nook, corner,' dial. *wray* (We), used of a remote or secluded spot. Wreay, Sillyrea, Stanger (Cu), Haverah (H), Bramery (Cu), Wray (La), Dockray (Cu), Scarrow (Cu).

---

[1] From information kindly given by Mr F. H. Cheetham, F.S.A.

wād, OE, '*woad*.' Wadborough (Wo), Woodhill Whaddon (W), Odell (Beds).

wæd, OE, 'ford,' cognate with **vað**. Landwade (C), Wadebridge (Co).

(ge)wæsc, OE, 'ground washed over by water, ford,' and, in the compound *sceap-wæsc*, 'place for washing sheep.' Sheepwash (Nb), Shipston-on-Stour (Wo), Strangeways (La). Formerly thought to be found also in Alrewas, Hopwas (St), Rotherwas (He) and other similar names, but Ritter (*op. cit.* 71–2) raises certain difficulties which have not yet been solved and there is the further possibility in the unstressed suffix that we may have to do with OE *wāse*, 'mud, *ooze*.'

wǣt, OE, '*wet*.' Weetwood (Nb), Wheatshaw (La).

ware, OE, 'inhabitants,' not used independently. Canterbury (K), Clewer (Berks, So), Burmarsh (K).

wēala, OE, gen. pl. of *wealh*, 'foreigner, Welshman, serf,' often applied by the English to the Britons. Very common in numerous Waltons, Walworths, Walcotes. Wherever we find them we probably have traces either of a distinctive survival of the old Celtic population for a short time at least after the English Conquest or of settlements of British servants belonging to some large estate. Wawcott (Berks).

weald, wald, OE, is certainly used in OE of forest-land and more especially of high forest-land. In ME it developes forms *we(e)ld* and *wold* in different dialects and the meaning is by no means so clear. *we(e)ld* seems for the most part to have kept its old sense but *wold* came frequently to be used of waste ground, wide open country, still, as in the *Cotswolds* and the Yorkshire and Lincolnshire *Wolds*, on high ground. The change from wooded to open country has its parallel in the development of **leah**, the term having been transferred from the forest to the ground which has been cleared of forest. In names of comparatively recent origin we should hardly be right in assuming that the ground must necessarily ever have been wooded at all. Hammill, Ringwould (K), Wield (Ha), Weald (Ess), Old, Walgrave (Nth), Oldridge (D), Old Hurst, Old Weston (Hu), Horninghold (Lei). For the dial. development v. Ekwall, *Contrib. to Hist. of OE Dial.* 5 ff.

weall, OE, '*wall*.' Wall (Nb, St).

weard, OE, 'watch, *ward*.' Wardlow (Db), Wardle (Ch).

weg, OE, '*way*, path, road.' Holloway (Mx), Wickey (Beds).

welig, wylig, OE, '*willow*.' Willey Hund., Willington (Beds), Willitoft (Y). Dat. pl. in Welwyn (Herts), Willen (Bk).

(ge)weorc, OE, 'fort, defensive work.' Aldwark (Y), Newark (Nt, Sr), Foremark (Db).

wer, OE, '*weir*.' Weare (So), Edgware (Mx), Wear Gifford (D), Wareham (Do).

west, OE, '*west.*' Comparative form in Westerfield (Sf), superl. in Westmeston (Sx).

whin, ME, 'gorse, *whin.*' Probably a Scand. loan-word. See Ekwall, *PN La* 20. Whinfell (Cu), Whinburgh (Nf).

wic, OE, denotes primarily 'dwelling-place, abode, quarters,' and is very commonly used in the plural. It is clear from such glosses as *wic* vel *lytel port* (v. **port**), *castellum, vicus* that it also developed the meaning 'village.' From its use in the compound *wic-gerefa*, the name of some kind of king's officer in Saxon times, it is evident also that the word must have acquired a more or less definite technical sense. In Domesday, especially in Essex, it often has the meaning 'dairy-farm,' a sense in which it survived locally until the 16th cent. In p.n. in OE we find it in the compounds **berewic** and **heordwic** where the 'farm' sense of *wic* must be prominent as also in *gatawic* (from **gat**), *oxenawic* and *sceapwic*, from which we have the p.n. Gatwick (Sr), Oxwick (Nf), Shapwick (So).

In BCS 129 we have mention of a grant *in Wico emptorio quem nos Saltwich vocamus* (14th cent. copy) and this passage has been used to support the view that OE *wic* might also denote a brinespring, but the passage does not necessarily imply that. It is a well-known fact that in the Worcestershire Droitwich and in the Cheshire Nantwich, Northwich, and Middlewich we have p.n. in *-wich* for places in which, at least in the present day, there are salt-workings, while in dial. glossaries the term *wich* is sometimes equated with 'salt-works.' The association with salt is however purely a chance one and the *wic* only refers to the buildings which sprang up around the salt-workings[1].

Grundy has noted that this element is comparatively rarely compounded with a pers. name and this fact points to its denoting as a rule something which belongs to a community rather than to an individual. The *wick* was often the dairy farm of the community.

It is a loan-word from the Lat. *vicus* and its normal phonological development should be to Mod. Eng. *wich*, from OE *wic*, which was pronounced with a palatal *c*. Forms in *wick* are however much more common in Mod. Eng. than those in *wich*. Apart from the general confusion of palatalised and non-palatalised forms of such words in present-day speech, there is a special reason for confusion in p.n. in *wic*. The word was much more common in the pl. than in the sg. in OE, and such forms as *wican, wicum* (dat. pl.) would keep the *c* unpalatalised, whence it would be extended

---

[1] The statements given above have since been more than confirmed by very full and precise evidence as to *wick* and *wich* in Wo, kindly placed at my disposal by Mr F. T. S. Houghton, F.S.A.

to other forms of the same word. It would be unsafe therefore to draw any conclusions as to palatalisation of OE *c* from the distribution of *wich* and *wick* forms. The normal development is to *wich* or *wick* but sometimes, especially when the word is used independently as a p.n. we have the form *wyke* and, in the South-West, *week*. Forms like Wyken (Wa), Wicken (C) are from the dat. pl. In Scand. England it is often difficult to distinguish it from **vik**. Quickbury (Ess).

The suggestion has sometimes been made that there was another OE *wic*, denoting 'bay, creek,' the English counterpart of **vik** and that this lies behind such p.n. as Sandwich, Greenwich, Woolwich (K), Harwich (Ess), but apart from names of places like this, which are on estuaries or creeks or bays, there is no evidence for the existence of such a word in OE and as these names are all capable of explanation with the ordinary *wic*, we should probably rest content with that. Guttridge (Ess), Cowage (W), Wix (Ess), Swanage (Do).

wice, OE, '*wych*-elm,' is very difficult to distinguish from **wic**.

wicham and **wichamm**, OE, for both forms are found in OE, are the source of several *Wickhams*. Their exact significance is obscure. Do they denote 'farms' or 'enclosures' by a *wic*, and is it possible, in some cases at least, that the *wic* is really a Roman *vicus*, for there are a good many cases in which Wickhams are by Roman remains?

wicing, OE, 'pirate, viking,' probably, as suggested by Craigie, one who takes up his *wic* or quarters in some other land. The word was in use in England long before the actual coming of the Vikings, though that term is its Norse equivalent. The OE word or the ON *viking* or the same word used as a pers. name is found in Wigston Magna (Lei), Wickenby (L), Whissonsett (Nf).

wīd, OE, '*wide*,' is often very difficult to distinguish from **wiðig**.

wielle, **wiella**, OE, **wælle**, **wælla**, Angl., 'spring, *well*.' These should develop respectively in later English to *well* and *wall* but the *wall* forms have survived but rarely, as in Craswall (He). Usually they have been replaced by St. Eng. forms, as in Bradwell (St). Nom. pl. in Wells (Nf, So), dat. pl. in Welham (Nt). See more fully Ekwall, *Contrib. Hist. OE Dial.* 4 ff. Colwall (He), Satchfield, Halwill (D), Dewsall, Cobhall (He), Astol (Sa), Sneachill (Wo), Hassal, Thelwall (Ch), Rusthall (K), Bexfield (Ess).

wilde, OE, '*wild*.' Eyton-on-the-Weald-Moors (Sa), Willand (D).

wincel, OE, 'nook, corner, angle,' only found in p.n. Winchcomb (Gl, K), Aldwinkle (Nth).

winter, OE, '*winter*,' used in Wintercote (Ha) of that which is 'used in winter' and in the numerous Winterbournes in South-

West England of a stream which is only worthy of the name in that season.

wisc, OE, 'damp meadow, marsh, *wish* (dial.).' Only found in charter material. Cranwich (Nf), Dulwich (Sr), Wissington (Sf), Whistley (Berks), Sledwick (Du).

wiðig, OE, '*withy.*' Hoarwithy (He), Weethley (Wa), Weeton (La, Y), Widford (Gl), Widdecombe (D), Woodbatch (Sa), Wissington (Sf). Often difficult to distinguish from **wid**.

wōh, OE, 'crooked, twisting.' Woburn (Beds), Wooburn (Bk), Oborne (Do). Wonersh (Sr) shows the weak dat. sg. *wo(h)an*.

worþ, weorþ, wyrþ, OE, is only found in p.n. material in OE and in a few Biblical glosses. In the former we have grants of land at various places bearing names with this suffix and the estate is variously rendered in the Latin as *villula, villa, viculus, aliquantulum terrae, aliquam telluris partem*. In the latter it is used to render the Lat. *atrium* and *platea*. From the frequent mention of a **hege** in connexion with a *worþ*, it would seem that the latter, like its derivative **worðig** denoted an enclosed area and this is confirmed by the similar use of the LGerm. *word, wurd*. The Latin renderings, in contrast to those of **tun** and **ham** suggest that it was used of a relatively small enclosure. The fact that it is not found in independent use in OE tends to show that it was obsolescent soon after the Saxon Conquest and there is no evidence that it was in living use at the time of the Norman Conquest. It is fairly evenly distributed throughout the country, except that it is not found in Cu, We, and is very rare in the North and East Riding of Y. In D it often gives place to the allied **worðig** and in the West Midlands to **worðign**. In the unstressed suffix position it is often liable to corruption as in Clarewood (Nb), Pertwood (W), Duxford (C), Barkwith (L), Ember (Sr). See further Ekwall *PN La* 20-1.

worðig, OE, an expanded form of **worþ**, with which it often interchanges in p.n. There is an excellent discussion of it in BT s.v. It is clear from the statements in the Laws about the necessity for a ceorl's putting a *tun* or hedge round his *worðig* that the primary idea is that of an enclosure. It is used as a gloss for Lat. *agellus, fundus, praedium*. The chief home of this suffix is D and So and it must have continued in living use a good deal later than **worþ**, to judge by the large number of p.n. in the Exeter Domesday in which this element is compounded with the name of the actual holder of the estate TRE or TRW. It is found in King's and Martyr Worthy (Ha), has been replaced by *worth* in Tamworth (St) and was once found in *Norþworþig* Db, the old name of Derby itself. A good many of the *worthys* in D, on the other hand, were originally *worths*.

worðigr., OE, an expanded form of **worðig** and used with the same meaning. It survives in dial. *worthine* (He), 'a division of land.' See further Schlutter in Anglia, 43, 99–100. It usually appears as *wardine* in p.n. but is found in other forms in Marden (He), Ruardean (Gl), Northenden (Ch), Ellerdine (Sa). In a good many names it was once found but has now been replaced by the more common *worth* or some development of it, as in Minsterworth (Gl), Chickward, Strongwood (He). The suffix is confined to Ch, Sa, He, Gl, Wa except for a few cases in D, where some of the p.n. which now end in *worthy* once haᵥ this suffix, e.g. Badgeworthy, Bradworthy. It is just possible that it is found in Worthing (Nf).

wrang, Late OE, 'twisted, crooked,' a Scand. loan-word. Wrangdyke Hund. (R).

wrīd, wrīþ, OE, 'thicket, *ride* (dial.),' only in charter material. Easwrith Hund. (Sx), Wordwell (Sf).

wudu, OE, 'wood.' Very common in *wudu-tun*, later *Wo(o)tton* and *Woodhouse*. Manhood (Sx), Wothersome (Y).

wulf, OE, '*wolf*,' is very difficult to distinguish from pers. names formed with the same element, but we certainly have the gen. pl. *wulfa* in Woolpit (Sf) and a good many *Woolleys*.

wyrt, OE, 'vegetable, *wort*.' Worton (Mx, O).

yfre, OE, is only found in charter material in OE. Etymologically it would seem to be identical with Goth. *ubizwa*, itself closely related to OE *efes*, 'eaves.' If this is correct its meaning may well be that of 'edge' or (as Grundy on other grounds suggests) 'escarpment.' It survives in two or three p.n. in the form River (Sx) and Rivar (W). v. æt.